LIARS FOR JESUS

Volume I

LIARS FOR JESUS

The Religious Right's Alternate Version of American History

Volume I

CHRIS RODDA

Published by the author
somewhere in the Garden State
2006

Liars for Jesus:
The Religious Right's Alternate Version of American History

ISBN: 1-4196-4438-6

The Liars For Jesus website, www.liarsforjesus.com, contains a footnote archive, allowing those reading this book to view images of the documents cited in its footnotes, as well as links to the many books cited that, thanks to a number of recent digitization projects, are now freely accessible online.

This book is dedicated to
everyone working in any way
to combat the religious right's
revisionism of American history.

Table of Contents

Acknowledgements

First and foremost, I'd like to thank my parents, Jim and Anne, for all their support and encouragement, and, most importantly, for paying my rent so I wouldn't have to finish writing this book on a laptop plugged into my car lighter. I'd also like to thank everyone else – particularly Debbie, Michele, Ricky (a.k.a. Tito from the Bronx), Ron, and Al – who helped me pay my bills, bought the books and other stuff I needed, got my electricity turned back on so I could keep writing, and bought food for me and Mac. I'm guessing that my thanks alone probably aren't enough reward, and that they'll all be expecting me to pay them back now.

I'd also like to thank Bill (who wrote the foreword) and everyone else who, for some reason, thought I could write a book. Apparently, they were right.

Also indispensible in getting this book written were all my friends and neighbors who proofread, made suggestions, and gave me ideas – particularly my friends (as well as a few of my adversaries) from the message boards.

And, last but not least, I'd like to thank Mac for all the times he patiently waited to go outside while I finished just one more paragraph or looked up just one more thing.

Foreword

The work that you hold in your hands has been a labor of love and of will. It has taken almost three years to come to print. Along the way there were many preliminary working deadlines. Many of us closest to Chris Rodda's work yearned for those deadlines to be met and the promise of her work to be fulfilled. This was for very selfish reasons. We wanted a credible and thorough way of addressing the numerous lies and misrepresentations being spread by some Christians and their leaders concerning the faith and religion of our Founding Fathers.

The deadlines we pressured Chris to meet were more often temptations because of the political climate than realistic expectations. The Newdow Case concerning the Pledge of Allegiance coming before the Supreme Court of the United States of America, the emergence of Faith-based Initiatives, the battle over Roy Moore's rock and the posting of the Ten Commandments in "his" courtroom in Alabama, and the election campaigns of 2004 with the increased mixing of religion and politics in public policy: these were all used for political gain and/or turning out the vote of well-intentioned and often misled Christians. With those temptations resisted, the book you have in your hands is far better and far more thorough than the original concept, plus there are now more volumes to follow.

Chris was impassioned by the cause of confronting those who distort and reconstruct history to the shape of their own political and religious goals. As Daniel Patrick Moynihan said, "Everyone is entitled to his own opinion, but not his own facts." Chris heard arguments over and over again from radical, conservative Christians about the lives and intentions of the Founders – arguments that contradicted her recollections of their work.

Chris Rodda loves primary source research. She loves reading old and difficult script manuscripts and finding bits and pieces of a puzzle long forgotten by others. On numerous occasions she would Instant Messenger me asking if we could talk about some new and exciting piece of information that drew a clearer and clearer picture of just how strong the wall of separation conceived by Jefferson and Madison was meant to be. How much I came to love and appreciate her digital signature clause, "What Would Jefferson Do?" whenever I saw it. Most often, Chris was responding to someone who had bought in to the polemic she, generally, referred to as the "Liars for Jesus," regurgitating via cut and paste something from David Barton's WallBuilders or some similar website. Chris and I disagreed about and debated her use of the term "Liars for Jesus." I felt using the term in the title might alienate some of the very people who most needed to read her work, but she has stood by her convictions.

Whatever our opinions about religion and political causes, the Founding Fathers had their own, forged in the midst of a mixture of faiths and philosophies much like our own. The religious mix of their world included Christians: many of whom considered other Christian denominations nothing less than heretics. There were the New England Congregationalists, the Baptists, and the Anglicans of Virginia. There were Lutherans, Reformed, and Moravians among the German immigrants. There were Roman Catholics and Quakers. There were Jews and the Musselman or Mohametan (as the Islamic faith was known in their time). And there were the philosophical deists and Unitarians, the secret Masonic societies, and even rationalistic atheists.

As the Founding Fathers lived in the midst of this diverse world experience, they reflected on the knowledge of the political and religious conflicts lived out on the European continent in the preceding centuries. They read and debated the philosophies of Thomas Hobbes, John Locke, David Hume and other rationalists and empiricists. Then, personally religious or not, they made a choice to create a separation between the public life of law and politics and the private realm of personal religious life and practice. They separated the process of governing under the Constitution into three branches of government and secured to the people the protection of personal life under the Bill of Rights. Religion was never to be used as a test for fitness to serve in public office, nor was government ever to make law suppressing religious activity of any particular faith. What was good for one was to be good for all.

So why would any Christian pastor write a foreword to a book entitled "Liars for Jesus?" As I said above, I debated the title with Chris and argued against it. Nonetheless, I understand and support her efforts to establish strong arguments from the historical record and primary source documents concerning the political and religious truths about the Founding Fathers. That some people have tried to obscure and manipulate these events and writings to their own end will I believe become clear as you read her work. Besides the obvious implications of the eight or ninth commandment, depending on the enumeration of one's particular faith community, and with a belief that nothing good or permanent can be built on deception or misrepresentation in good Trinitarian tradition, I will give you three answers;

1) A conviction that religion is a deeply personal issue and one that falls to each person to practice for themselves, privately or corporately, with or without favor, support, or restraint of the government.

2) A deep respect for the Constitution of the United States of America, the Bill of Rights, and the work of the framers;

3) A equally deep belief that the strength of religious life in this country is the direct result of that freedom of religion so carefully constructed by the framers and recognized for two centuries by the Supreme Court.

The American experience has been marked by a deep and abiding religious content. From the landing of the pilgrims and my ancestors with them at Plymouth to the religious right political wars of today, religion has been a consistent catalyst for judgment and division. The pilgrims had no interest in philosophical concepts of religious freedom. Their pursuit was for a religious freedom for themselves and they were quite prepared to enforce their concepts of right behavior on all other members of the community. Absence from worship could result in severe punishments including fines, imprisonment and whipping. Similarly, harsh punishments, including capital punishment, existed for all sorts of violations of religious and civil law as they were merged in the life of the colony. The Law of God, not the grace of Jesus Christ, was the hallmark of Puritan religion and all had to comply.

The intolerable conditions of the Puritan way were so great that they resulted in the first expression of religious freedom in the New World when in 1636 Roger Williams fled controversy and trial in the Massachusetts Bay Colony over his teaching of a complete separation of church and state. Settling in Providence, he founded Rhode Island as the first colony based on religious freedom. In all issues religious, Williams believed in the freedom of the conscience and so created a relationship between government and religion that was unprecedented. It was Williams who became the first promoter in the colonies of the term "wall of separation."

Today, we are once again under great pressure to prop up the practice of religion in this country by finding increasing ways of involving government in affairs of faith and conscience. We are having passionate and bitter debates of the role of religion in public life. We struggle over whether the words "under God" belong in the Pledge of Allegiance despite the fact that Francis Bellamy, a Baptist pastor, who first wrote the Pledge, intentionally, left them out. We argue over the appropriateness of judges posting the Ten Commandments in courthouses, as if justice exists no where in the world without them being posted. We have used the words "In God We Trust" on our currency beginning in 1957 more to prove we are not mid-50s communists than as an act of confession by true believers. In all these things and more, some American Christians have behaved as if the absence of government sanction and support of religion means they cannot believe or hold sacred in themselves what they believe is received as a gift from God in the work of his Holy Spirit. Some Christians have behaved as if the Lord of creation is of such a fragile ego that he must be placated by mindless, rote acts of civil religion or else he will cause another plague, another Katrina, or some other form of eschatological judgment.

If the faith of Americans is already so weak that these things above are necessary to sustain our faith, then we are in far greater trouble, spiritually, than we may be willing to admit. Where have gone the people, especially Protestants, who believed that an act of conscience was so inviolable that it led Martin Luther to stand before the state and church at the Diet of Worms proclaiming, "… it cannot be right for a Christian to speak against his conscience. Here I stand, I can do no other. May God help me! Amen!" If our conscience is clear and our faith is true, government can neither sustain nor deny us that faith as it comes from God. That belief does not, however, give us the right to distort the beliefs of the Founding Fathers or compel others to be subject to our religion, denying them the same freedom we would seek. If the Founders, as individuals, were Christians so let them be, and if they were not, then let that be, too. Let each of us be bold in our confessions and, also, defend the right of our neighbor to his own as well.

What the Founders and framers of the Constitution and Bill of Rights did accomplish was to minimize to the point of elimination the interrelation, if not the interaction, of state and church.

While Jefferson was not present for the negotiations and writing of the Constitution and Bill of Rights, his close friend and communicant James Madison was. Madison, skillfully and ably with others, represented the cause of separation.

One cannot overestimate the desire of the fledgling nation to avoid the religious conflicts of the previous centuries in Europe and some American colonies. They also understood that they had no extensive resources of finances or energy to waste on such issues if the nation was to survive.

The Congregationalists, the Anglicans, and the Roman Catholic Church all had colonies in which they were the dominant state faith by fact or de facto and in which they were heavily invested; and all were still wary of each other and power sharing. There were populations of Lutherans, Baptists, Presbyterians, Methodists and others within the various colonies raising minority concerns, as well. Adding deists and rationalists to the mix and trying to create a national policy addressing religious issues would be a nightmare.

In the end, the solution was simple. Create at national government that treated all men (yes, women weren't really a concern) as equals before the government without regard to their sectarian religious preferences. Religion and the state were to be so separated that the religious tests used by some of the states as a qualification for office would not apply, such as membership in the Anglican Church in Virginia had once been required. In one brilliant stroke, they resolved a roadblock that might have resulted in years of quarreling about how this law or that ordinance was favoring one religious party or the next. Building a "wall of separation," as Baptist preacher Roger Williams had once erected in Rhode Island, the framers secured to each person free exercise of religion and right of peaceful assembly. Jefferson would later refer to this "wall of separation" in correspondence with another Baptist group in Connecticut, defining the issue as one of conscience not to be interfered with through governmental power:

> "Believing with you that religion is a matter which lies solely between Man & his God, that he owes account to none other for his faith or his worship, that the legitimate powers of government reach actions only, & not opinions, I contemplate with sovereign reverence that act of the whole American people which declared that their legislature should 'make no law respecting an establishment of religion, or prohibiting the free exercise thereof,' thus building a wall of separation between Church & State. Adhering to this expression of the supreme will of the nation *in behalf of the rights of conscience,* I shall see with sincere satisfaction the progress of those sentiments which tend to restore to man all his natural rights, convinced he has no natural right in opposition to his social duties."

By the time that Alexis de Tocqueville arrived in America in 1831, the separation of church and state created under the U.S Constitution and Bill of Rights had played itself out for over a generation. Although his initial task was to study and make a report on the U.S. penal system, which he published in 1833 under the title *Du systeme penitentiaire aux Etats-Unis et de son application en France,* Tocqueville became enamored of the vibrant faith and religious spirit he found.

During his visit, Tocqueville became interested in the growth and expression of democracy and religion in America. By the end of 1835 he had published the first volume of *Of the Democracy in America.* It was primarily a political and social study of the country. It was, also, based on his experiences of 1831 while in America. This was at the height of the second Great Awakening and he had been taken with the religious fervor of the nation. He saw that fervor as a direct result of the separation of church and state in America in contrast to the state churches of Europe. He wrote:

> "On my arrival in the United States the religious aspect of the country was the first thing that struck my attention; and the longer I stayed there, the more I perceived the great political consequences resulting from this new state of things. In France I had almost always seen the spirit of religion and the spirit of freedom marching in opposite directions. But in America I found they were intimately united and that they reigned in common over the same country. My desire to discover the causes of this phenomenon increased from day to day. In order to satisfy it I questioned the members of all the different sects; I sought especially the society of the clergy, who are the depositaries of the different creeds and are especially interested in their duration. As a member of the Roman Catholic Church, I was more particularly brought into contact with several of its priests, with whom I became intimately acquainted. To each of these men I expressed my astonishment and explained my doubts. *I found that they differed upon matters of detail alone, and that they all attributed the peaceful dominion of religion in their country mainly to the separation of church and state.* I do not hesitate to affirm that during my stay in America I did not meet a single individual, of the clergy or the laity, who was not of the same opinion on this point."

And, also;

> *"Care (is) taken by the Americans to separate the church from the state*—The laws, public opinion, and even the exertions of the clergy concur to promote this end—Influence of religion upon the mind in the United States attributable to this

> cause—Reason for this—What is the natural state of men with regard to religion at the present time—What are the peculiar and incidental causes which prevent men, in certain countries, from arriving at this state."

> "The philosophers of the eighteenth century explained in a very simple manner the gradual decay of religious faith. Religious zeal, said they, must necessarily fail the more generally liberty is established and knowledge diffused. Unfortunately, the facts by no means accord with their theory. There are certain populations in Europe whose unbelief is only equaled by their ignorance and debasement; while in America, one of the freest and most enlightened nations in the world, the people fulfill with fervor all the outward duties of religion."

Tocqueville's observation of the state of religious life in America was that it was vibrant, passionate, and filled with zeal. There was an enthusiasm and practicality to religion in the American experiment in democracy.

> "Not only do the Americans follow their religion from interest, but they often place in this world the interest that makes them follow it. In the Middle Ages the clergy spoke of nothing but a future state; they hardly cared to prove that a sincere Christian may be a happy man here below. But the American preachers are constantly referring to the earth, and it is only with great difficulty that they can divert their attention from it."

Religion and government both seemed to be thriving in their separation and the result was a form of practical religion that sought to address the many needs of the communities outside the rule of government.

These passages from *Of the Democracy in America* should caution us concerning the present struggles to institutionalize civil religion. In what appear to be social niceties, there may be a danger in supplying people with mindless public rituals in contrast to personal accountability for the practice one's faith.

Tocqueville had experienced first hand the state churches of

Europe as a Roman Catholic layman and met little passion in the laity there. Nothing in the European churches depended on them and the exercise of their faith in the world. They were passive recipients of the work of the priest and the church. Such religious acts emptied of active faith seemed to inoculate the public to the real power of personal faith that Tocqueville witnessed in America. Faith where each person was responsible for their own faith and not labeled Catholic, Lutheran or Reformed simply because of where they lived or the religion of their monarch. In contrast to religion in Europe, American religion freed from the burden of the government led Tocqueville to write, "The Americans combine the notions of religion and liberty so intimately in their minds that it is impossible to make them conceive of one without the other."

So in the United States of America, even to this day, it is a natural right of a person in liberty to exercise faith according to their conscience and to worship God as they may or may not be moved. This right was protected from the tyranny of government by the Founding Fathers as they attempted to prevent age-old conflicts between religions from consuming the limited resources of their young country. To the surprise of many, maybe almost everyone, the result was a passion for religion that exceeded anything found in the old homelands of Europe. This passion continues even to this day when the state churches in Europe record attendance figures of about 3-5% weekly in contrast to the almost 30-50% figure across religious communities in America.

So it is that we, as a nation of diverse religious sentiments, have not just survived but flourished, politically and spiritually, because of this "wall of separation" that some would tear down. The question is "To what end would the tear down this wall of separation?" Sandra Day O'Connor expressed this very concern during rulings on cases involving displays of the Ten Commandments in 2005, when she said, "Those who would renegotiate the boundaries between church and state must therefore answer a difficult question: why would we trade a system that has served us so well for one that has served others so poorly?"

Tocqueville was not entirely optimistic with everything he found here, however, and wrote of the ways in which intolerance could raise its head in the nation. "In America the majority raises formidable barriers around the liberty of opinion; within these barriers an author may write what he pleases, but woe to him if he goes beyond them." How prophetic his words are proving to be as we in America seem to have turned from a culture that valued and celebrated the right of "every" American to stand equally free before our government. Chris Rodda may push us beyond these barriers by taking us back to the origins of our government and how these courageous men built a nation with true freedom of religion and freedom of government.

Rev. William N. Esborn

Introduction

One day about three years ago, I happened to be reading a news story on AOL about the Ten Commandments monument in the Alabama courthouse. Having a little time to kill, I decided to click on the link to a message board about the story. Little did I know when I clicked on that link that I was about to discover a whole new version of American history, or that six months later I'd be writing a book about it.

Once I got to the message board, I couldn't resist the urge to respond to a few of the posts, many of which were defending the Ten Commandments monument by copying and pasting lies from what I soon found out were literally thousands of Christian American history websites. At first, my responses were short – nothing more than correcting a misquote or briefly explaining why something couldn't be true. It soon became apparent, however, that these brief rebuttals were not working. I was usually accused of being a liar, and occasionally accused of being the antichrist. So, I began taking a little time to look things up, and started posting longer, more detailed rebuttals, complete with footnotes. Before long, other people who were battling the lies began emailing me posts from the both the Ten Commandments board and other boards, asking me whether or not they were true. Apparently, they had gotten the impression from my posts that I was some sort of expert on the subject. I wasn't, but I did know enough about history to be able to answer many of these emails, or at least to tell the people where they could find the information to disprove whatever lie they were trying to disprove. Between posting my own messages on the boards and answering emails, what had begun as a click on a link to kill a few minutes soon became something I was spending several hours a day on.

From time to time over the next few months, someone would respond to one of my posts by saying that I should write a book. While I appreciated the compliment, I didn't take the idea very seriously – at least not at first. For one thing, I was was sure that there must already be plenty of books on the subject, written by people far more qualified than I was to write about it. When I tried to find such a book, however, I couldn't. I found a few books that refuted the lies to a certain degree, but none providing the amount of information I was including in my message board posts. At this point, the idea of writing a book was starting to seem a little less crazy. When I mentioned the idea to a few of my real life friends, I was surprised to find that they didn't think it was crazy at all. So, never having written anything before, and having no particular qualifications to write a history book, I started writing a history book.

My first step was to read a few of the most popular religious right history books and compile a list of all the lies. So far, all I had seen were the various versions of the lies from the internet. People on the message boards, however, much more familiar than I was with the sources of these lies, told me which books to buy. These books led me to other books and other lies, which led me to even more books and even more lies. I found so many lies, in fact, that I soon realized that they weren't all going to fit one book without omitting some of the information that I felt was necessary to thoroughly explain and disprove them. So, I decided to write not just one book, but two – the first focusing mainly on the founding era, up until around the 1830s, and the second covering the rest of the nineteenth and the early twentieth century. Because most of the lies in the religious right history books are about the founding era, however, the first volume began to get too long, and I was once again faced with the decision of leaving stuff out, or including everything and splitting it up. Since my goal from the beginning was to write a book that left no stone unturned, and provided as much information as possible, I decided to split the first volume into two volumes. This book, therefore, is the first of what will eventually be three volumes.

For those already familiar with the religious right version of American history, my choice of topics for the first volume might seem a little odd. If I had planned from the start to divide this into two volumes, I would have put a few more of the most often lied about subjects in the first volume. By the time I decided to split the volume up, however, it was too late to change the chapter order. A number of things in the later chapters rely on information provided in earlier chapters, so this would have required rewriting large sections of certain chapters. So, this volume contains the first thirteen chapters, and the second volume will contain the second thirteen. Since most of the second volume is already written, its chapter titles, which are unlikely to change, can be listed here.

1. George Washington and Gouverneur Morris
2. Were Half of the Founders Really Ministers?
3. Days of Prayer, Fasting, and Thanksgiving
4. Did James Madison Really Oppose the Bill of Rights?
5. Putting the Founders on Pedestals
6. Thomas Jefferson and the Laws of Virginia
7. Mr. Jefferson's Bible
8. Tocqueville's Democracy in America
9. Sabbath and Blasphemy Laws
10. Toleration vs. Religious Freedom
11. James Madison and the General Assessment
12. Religious Tests and Oaths
13. Thomas Jefferson and the Danbury Baptists

It is my sincere hope that this book, and the two to follow, will be useful to those already aware of and fighting the religious right's revisionism of American history, and, even more importantly, that it will inform those who are unaware, as I was three years ago, of the dangerous extent to which this revisionism has spread.

Chris Rodda

— CHAPTER ONE —

Congress and the Bible

Myths regarding the printing, financing, distribution, or recommending of Bibles by our early Congresses are among the most popular of all the religious right American history lies. Most are variations of the same three stories – two involving the Continental Congress, and one an act signed by James Madison.

The first is the story of the Continental Congress importing Bibles in 1777.

> **According to William Federer, in his book *America's God and Country Encyclopedia of Quotations*: "Continental Congress September 11, 1777, approved and recommended to the people that 20,000 copies of The Holy Bible be imported from other sources. This was in response to the shortage of Bibles in America caused by the Revolutionary War interrupting trade with England. The Chaplain of Congress, Patrick Allison, brought the matter to the attention of Congress, who assigned it to a special Congressional Committee, which reported:**
>
>> **That the use of the Bible is so universal and its importance so great that your committee refers the above to the consideration of Congress, and if Congress shall not think it**

> **expedient to order the importation of types and paper, the Committee recommends that Congress will order the Committee of Commerce to import 20,000 Bibles from Holland, Scotland, or elsewhere, into the different parts of the States in the Union.**
>
> **Whereupon it was resolved accordingly to direct said Committee of Commerce to import 20,000 copies of the Bible."**

While most versions of this story are similar to William Federer's, some authors turn it into a completely different story.

> **According to Tim LaHaye, in his book *Faith of Our Founding Fathers*: "The Bible, the greatest book ever written, is indispensable to Christianity. That fact was clear in the very first act of Congress, authorizing the printing of twenty thousand Bibles for the Indians."**

It also appears in various lists of lies circulated by email, and eventually copied onto hundreds of websites.

> **From *History Forgotten,* the most widely circulated of the internet lists: "Did you know that 52 of the 55 signers of the Declaration of Independence were orthodox, deeply committed, Christians? The other three all believed in the Bible as the divine truth, the God of Scripture, and His personal intervention. It is the same Congress that formed the American Bible Society.[1] Immediately after creating the Declaration of Independence, the Continental Congress voted to pur-**

1. The American Bible Society, which did not exist until 1816, was not formed by the Continental or any later Congress, nor did it have Thomas Jefferson as its first chairman, an addition made to the *History Forgotten* list as it was circulated. It should be noted that a handful of those copying the list have corrected one of its many inaccuracies, changing *"55 signers of the Declaration of Independence"* to the correct number, fifty-six. Apparently, there are a few Liars for Jesus out there who find it important to be accurate about the number of people they are lying about.

chase and import 20,000 copies of Scripture for the people of this nation."

William Federer's version of the 1777 Bible story is typical of those found in the majority of religious right American history books. It tells half of the real story, includes a quote from an actual committee report, but ends with a fabricated resolution. The resolution is created to change the outcome of the story from Congress dropping the matter, which is what really happened, to Congress proceeding to import the Bibles. Tim LaHaye's version, that Congress printed Bibles for the Indians, has absolutely no basis in fact. But, as drastically different as their stories are, both Federer and LaHaye cite the same pages from the *Journals of the Continental Congress* as their source.

In addition to changing the outcome of the story, none of the religious right American history books fully explain why Congress was considering importing the Bibles in the first place. Most mention that the war with England caused a shortage of Bibles, which is true, but this is only half the story. Congress's consideration of the matter had to do with the prevention of price gouging.

Not all Americans during the Revolutionary War were the virtuous, Christian citizens portrayed in the religious right version of American history. Many were taking advantage of war shortages and charging outrageous prices for just about anything they could get their hands on. No product was safe – not even Bibles. The widespread problem of price gouging prompted numerous attempts by individual states, groups of states, and Congress to regulate prices, none of which were very successful. With less than half the country in favor of the war to begin with, Congress was very concerned with minimizing hardships like high prices and shortages of items previously imported from England.

In 1777, three ministers from Philadelphia, Francis Alison, John Ewing, and William Marshall, came up with a plan to alleviate the Bible shortage. Their idea was to import the necessary type and paper, and print an edition in Philadelphia. The problem with this plan, however, was that, if the project was financed and controlled by private companies, the Bibles would most likely be bought up and resold at prices that the average American couldn't afford.

Rev. Alison wrote a memorial to Congress, explaining the dilemma and asking for help. What the ministers wanted Congress to do was finance the printing, as a loan to be repaid by the sale of the Bibles. As Rev. Alison explained in the memorial, if Congress imported the type and paper, and Congress contracted the printer, then Congress could regulate the selling price of the Bibles.

> We therefore think it our duty to our country and to the churches of Christ to lay this danger before this honourable house, humbly requesting that under your care, and by your encouragement, a copy of the holy Bible may be printed, so as to be sold nearly as cheap as the common Bibles, formerly imported from Britain and Ireland, were sold.
>
> The number of purchasers is so great, that we doubt not but a large impression would soon be sold, But unless the sale of the whole edition belong to the printer, and he be bound under sufficient penalties, that no copy be sold by him, nor by any retailer under him, at a higher price than that allowed by this honourable house, we fear that the whole impression would soon be bought up, and sold again at an exorbitant price, which would frustrate your pious endeavours and fill the country with just complaints.[2]

Rev. Alison's memorial was referred to a committee, who concluded that it would be too costly to import the type and paper, and too risky to import them into Philadelphia, a city likely to be invaded by the British. The committee proposed the less risky alternative of importing already printed Bibles into different ports from a country other than England. If Congress did this, they would still be able to regulate the selling price, and would still be reimbursed by the sales. The report of this committee is cited by every religious right American history author as their source, whatever their version of this story, including Tim LaHaye, with his tale of Congress printing the Bibles for the Indians.

The committee's report is misquoted in various ways. Usually omitted is anything indicating that importing the Bibles was proposed

2. *Papers of the Continental Congress,* National Archives Microfilm Publication M247, r53, i42, v1, p35.

as an alternative to Rev. Alison's original request that Congress import the type and paper. Always omitted is that what Congress was considering was only a loan. With these omissions, no real explanation for Congress's involvement is necessary. The committee's report appears to fit the story that the ministers simply alerted Congress to the shortage of Bibles, and Congress considered this to be such a serious problem that they immediately imported some.

> **In his book *Original Intent*, David Barton quotes only the following pieces of one sentence from the committee's report:**
>
> > **"[T]hat the use of the Bible is so universal and its importance so great...your committee recommend that Congress will order the Committee of Commerce to import 20,000 Bibles from Holland, Scotland, or elsewhere, into the different ports of the States in the Union."**

The following is the entire report, as it appears in the *Journals of the Continental Congress.*

> The committee appointed to consider the memorial of the Rev. Dr. Allison and others, report, "That they have conferred fully with the printers, &c. in this city, and are of opinion, that the proper types for printing the Bible are not to be had in this country, and that the paper cannot be procured, but with such difficulties and subject to such casualties, as render any dependence on it altogether improper: that to import types for the purpose of setting up an entire edition of the bible, and to strike off 30,000 copies, with paper, binding, &c. will cost £10,272 10, which must be advanced by Congress, to be reimbursed by the sale of the books:"
>
> "That, your committee are of opinion, considerable difficulties will attend the procuring the types and paper; that, afterwards, the risque of importing them will considerably enhance the

> cost, and that the calculations are subject to such uncertainty in the present state of affairs, that Congress cannot much rely on them: that the use of the Bible is so universal, and its importance so great, that your committee refer the above to the consideration of Congress, and if Congress shall not think it expedient to order the importation of types and paper, your committee recommend that Congress will order the Committee of Commerce to import 20,000 Bibles from Holland, Scotland, or elsewhere, into the different ports of the states in the Union."[3]

Prior to considering the alternative of importing Bibles, the committee did two things. They had several Philadelphia printers submit quotes for printing the Bibles, and drafted a list of fifteen proposed regulations for their printing. The third through the seventh of these regulations dealt with the arrangement to be made between Congress and the printer, and clearly show that Congress intended to be reimbursed, and that the goal of the plan was to regulate the selling price of the Bibles.

> 3. That as there are not Types in America to answer this Purpose, there should be a compleat Font, sufficient for setting the whole Bible at once, imported by Congress at the Public Expence, to be refunded in a stipulated Time by the Printer.
>
> 4. That in Order to prevent the Paper Makers from demanding an extravagant Price for the Paper, and retarding the Work by Breach of Contract or otherwise there should also be imported with the Types a few Reams of Paper, not exceeding a thousand, at the Beginning of the Work, to be paid for by the Printer in y[e] same Manner as y[e] Types are to be paid for.
>
> 5. That a Printer be employed, who shall undertake the Work at his own Risque & Expence, giving a Mortgage on y[e] Font

3. Worthington C. Ford, ed., *Journals of the Continental Congress, 1774-1789*, vol. 8, (Washington D.C.: Government Printing Office, 1907), 733-734.

> & Printing Materials, with sufficient Personal Securities for his Fidelity, until the first Cost of ye Font, ye Paper, & such Sums of Money as the Congress may think proper to advance to him for Dispatch of the Work, be refunded to the Public.
>
> 6. That in Order to render the Price of Binding as low as possible, the Congress order their Commissary General for Hides etc to deliver to the Printer at a moderate Price all the Sheep Skins furnished at ye Camp, to be tanned for this Purpose.
>
> 7. That the Printer be bound under sufficient Penalties to furnish Bibles to ye Public at a limited Price, not exceeding ten Shillings each, & to prevent any Retailer, under him in the United States from asking an higher price on any Pretence whatsoever.[4]

What appears in the *Journals of the Continental Congress* after the committee's report is the following motion.

> Whereupon, the Congress was moved, to order the Committee of Commerce to import twenty thousand copies of the Bible.[5]

The problem for the religious right authors who claim that the Bibles were imported is that, although this motion passed, it was not a final vote to import the Bibles. It was a merely a vote on replacing the original plan of importing the type and paper with the committee's proposal of importing already printed Bibles. In other words, they were only voting on what they were going to be voting on. The vote on the motion was close – seven states voted yes; six voted no. A second motion was then made to pass a resolution to import the Bibles, but this was postponed and never brought up again. No Bibles were imported. This little problem is solved in the religious right history

4. *Studies in Bibliography*, Vol. 3, (Charlottesville, VA: University Press of Virginia, 1950-1951), 275-276.
5. Worthington C. Ford, ed., *Journals of the Continental Congress, 1774-1789*, vol. 8, (Washington D.C.: Government Printing Office, 1907), 734.

books by either rewording the motion to turn it into a resolution, or omitting the motion altogether and ending the story with some statement implying that the Bibles were imported.

> **In William Federer's version, the motion is reworded: "Whereupon it was resolved accordingly to direct said Committee of Commerce to import 20,000 copies of the Bible."**

> **David Barton ends his version of the story with the following statement: "Congress agreed and ordered the Bibles imported."**

The *Religion and the Founding of the American Republic Exhibit* on the Library of Congress website presents this story in as misleading a manner as Federer or Barton, also giving the impression that the Bibles were imported. It is only in the companion book to the exhibit, published at the time of the physical exhibit at the Library in 1998, that James H. Hutson, Chief of the Manuscript Division at the Library of Congress, and curator of the exhibit, bothers to mention that the Bibles were never imported. Of course, far more people will visit the exhibit on the website than will ever see the book, which is no longer even available.

> **The following is all that appears on the Library of Congress website version of the exhibit: "The war with Britain cut off the supply of Bibles to the United States with the result that on Sept. 11, 1777, Congress instructed its Committee of Commerce to import 20,000 Bibles from "Scotland, Holland or elsewhere."**

> **This is what appears in the companion book: "An unfailing antidote to immorality was Bible reading. Hostilities, however, had interrupted the supply of Bibles from Great Britain, raising fears of a shortage of Scripture just when it was needed most. in the summer of 1777, three Presbyterian ministers warned Congress of this danger and urged it to arrange for a**

> **domestic printing of the Bible. Upon investigation, a committee of Congress discovered that it would be cheaper to import Bibles from continental Europe and made such a recommendation to the full Congress on September 11, 1777. Congress approved the recommendation on the same day, instructing its Committee of Commerce to import twenty thousand Bibles from 'Scotland, Holland or elsewhere' but adjourned—the British were poised to take Philadelphia—without passing implementing legislation."**

The problem with using the approach of the British as the reason that Congress never got around to the Bible resolution is that this was postponed a week before Congress knew the invasion of Philadelphia was imminent. The letters of the delegates from this week clearly show that they were cautiously optimistic. They heard that Howe's army had sustained three times the casualties of Washington's troops in the Battle of Brandywine, and that two days later the British were still at the battlefield dealing with their wounded, a delay that might allow reinforcements to arrive from New Jersey in time to prevent Howe from reaching Philadelphia.

On September 11, the day of the battle, and also the day the Bible motion was voted on, the resolution was postponed until September 13. On September 13, the Congress was still in Philadelphia, and determined to stay there. It wasn't until the evening of September 18 that they received the letter from Washington's aide, Alexander Hamilton, advising them to leave. Other than deciding on September 14 that, if it did become necessary to evacuate, they would reassemble in Lancaster, it was business as usual in Philadelphia until the receipt of Hamilton's letter.

Hutson's claim that the Bible resolution was dropped because of the British is an easy one to get away with because of the language used at the time to designate an upcoming day. When the Continental Congress, on a Thursday, postponed something until *"Saturday next,"* they meant in two days, not a week from Saturday. The Bible resolution was only postponed from Thursday, September 11 to Saturday, September 13. It was not postponed until September 20, the Saturday that would fit Hutson's story.

The British approaching excuse also makes no sense for a few other reasons. The first is that the whole point of changing the plan from printing Bibles in Philadelphia to importing Bibles into other ports was that Philadelphia was likely to be invaded. Congress didn't just permanently drop other business, even after they actually did move, so why didn't they just vote to import the Bibles into these other ports after they moved? The second is that Congress never took up the issue at any later date. The Bible shortage still existed – a year later, two years later – yet, the issue of Bibles didn't even come up again until over three years later, when James McLene, a delegate from Pennsylvania, proposed a resolution to regulate the printing of Bibles in the individual states.

> **According to James H. Hutson, in the *Religion and the Founding of the American Republic* companion book: "The issue of the Bible supply was raised again in Congress in 1780 when it was moved that the states be requested 'to procure one or more new and correct editions of the old and new testament to be published.'"**

The following was McLene's entire resolution.

> Resolved, That it be recommended to such of the States who may think it convenient for them that they take proper measures to procure one or more new and correct editions of the old and new testament to be printed and that such states regulate their printers by law so as to secure effectually the said books from being misprinted.[6]

The timing of McLene's proposal makes it next to impossible that it wasn't prompted by the fact that Philadelphia printer Robert Aitken had begun work on an edition of the Bible. But, it wouldn't have been Aitken's edition that McLene feared would be misprinted. Aitken was a reputable printer who had not only been the official printer to Congress until 1779, but had already printed several good editions of the New Testament. The potential problem was that, if Aitken's Bibles

6. Gaillard Hunt, ed., *Journals of the Continental Congress, 1774-1789,* vol. 18, (Washington D.C.: Government Printing Office, 1910), 979.

sold well, any number of not so reputable and less skilled printers would try to get a piece of the action by rushing to produce their own editions, with little regard to their accuracy. There is also a pretty good chance that McLene, along with John Hanson, who seconded McLene's motion, wanted to give their friend Robert Aitken an edge in the Bible printing business by making it more difficult for anyone else to print a competing edition.

What's interesting about McLene's resolution, however, isn't why he proposed it, but its unusual wording. This wording may actually provide the explanation for the unexplained disappearance of the 1777 Bible resolution. Resolutions of the Continental Congress were almost always addressed to *all* of the states. The only exceptions to this were resolutions that for some reason wouldn't apply to all of the states, such as a request to supply the army with a commodity that was only produced in certain states. In these cases, the states that the resolution applied to were listed by name. Resolutions were never addressed only to the states that might *"think it convenient."* This odd wording, as well as Congress dropping the plan to import Bibles three years earlier, may have resulted from a question of states' rights, specifically the freedom of the press.

When the committee on the memorial of Rev. Alison drafted their proposed regulations for printing Bibles in 1777, they included the following two regulations designed to eliminate competition and ensure that the printer would sell enough of the Bibles to reimburse Congress.

> 14. That the Printer employed in the Work devote himself to this Business alone; & that no other Printer in the united States be suffered to interfere with him in the Printing of that Form or Kind of a Bible, which he has undertaken.
>
> 15. That after the Bible is published, no more Bibles of that Kind be imported into the American States by any Person whatsoever.[7]

In 1777, when Congress was considering the Bible supply problem, they were also in the middle of writing the Articles of Confederation.

7. *Studies in Bibliography,* Vol. 3, (Charlottesville, VA: University Press of Virginia, 1950-1951), 276.

At this time, the question of how much authority Congress should have over the states would certainly have been on the minds of all the delegates. Most of them would have seen any regulation giving Congress any power over the freedom of the press in their states as setting a dangerous precedent. Regulation number fourteen, prohibiting any printer in America from printing a similar edition of the Bible, would make Congress no better than the British government, which prohibited the printing of the Bible without a government license.

Because the proposed regulations were for the printing of Bibles, but the motion was to import them, it's pretty likely that these regulations were simply disregarded until it occurred to someone that even if the Bibles were imported, the regulations to ensure their sale would still be necessary. This could easily have happened at some point in the two days following the vote on the motion. If even one of the seven states that voted in favor of the motion decided that the freedom of the press was more important than importing Bibles, and made it known that they were going to vote the other way on the resolution, there would have been little point in proceeding.

The only logical explanation for McLene limiting his 1780 resolution to the states that might *"think it convenient"* is that he already knew a resolution suggesting that any state whose constitution guaranteed freedom of the press should pass a law infringing on this right wouldn't stand a chance, and the only time that such a suggestion had been made prior to this was in the regulations proposed in 1777.

The second of the top three myths about Congress and the Bible involves the edition of the Bible begun by Robert Aitken in 1780, and completed in 1782.

> **According to William Federer, in his book *America's God and Country*: "Robert Aitken (1734-1802), on January 21, 1781, as publisher of *The Pennsylvania Magazine,* petitioned Congress for permission to print Bibles, since there was a shortage of Bibles in America due to the Revolutionary War interrupting trade with England. The Continental Congress, September 10, 1782, in response to the shortage of Bibles, approved and recommended to the people that *The Holy Bible* be printed by Robert Aitken of**

> **Philadelphia. This first American Bible was to be 'a neat edition of the Holy Scriptures for the use of schools':**
>
>> **Whereupon, Resolved, That the United States in Congress assembled...recommend this edition of the Bible to the inhabitants of the United States, and hereby authorize [Robert Aitken] to publish this recommendation in any manner he shall think proper."**

Elsewhere in the same book, Federer includes a second version of the story, in which Aitken was *"contracted"* by Congress to print his Bibles.

> **According to Federer: "Congress of the Confederation September 10, 1782, in response to the need for Bibles which again arose, granted approval to print 'a neat edition of the Holy Scriptures for the use of schools.' The printing was contracted to Robert Aitken of Philadelphia, a bookseller and publisher of *The Pennsylvania Magazine,* who had previously petitioned Congress on January 21, 1781."**

There are many versions of this story floating around, all worded to mislead that Congress either requested the printing of the Bibles, granted Aitken permission to print them, contracted him to print them, paid for the printing, or had Bibles printed for the use of schools. Congress did none of these things. All they did was grant one of several requests made by Aitken by having their chaplains examine his work, and allowing him to publish their resolution stating that, based on the chaplains' report, they were satisfied that his edition was accurate. The words *"a neat edition of the Holy Scriptures for the use of schools"* are taken from a letter written by Aitken,[8] not the resolution of Congress.

The actual resolution is edited in various ways. The purpose of

8. *Papers of the Continental Congress,* National Archives Microfilm Publication M247, r48, i41, v1, p63.

this editing is to omit that Congress also had a secular reason for recommending Aitken's Bible, and, in most cases, to turn the resolution into a recommendation of the Bible itself, rather than a recommendation of the accuracy of Aitken's work.

> **This is the typical, and often copied, version of the resolution that appears on James H. Hutson's religion exhibit on the Library of Congress website: "Congress 'highly approve the pious and laudable undertaking of Mr. Aitken, as subservient to the interest of religion...in this country, and...they recommend this edition of the Bible to the inhabitants of the United States.'"**

The following is the entire resolution.

> Whereupon, Resolved, That the United States in Congress assembled, highly approve the pious and laudable undertaking of Mr. Aitken, as subservient to the interest of religion as well as an instance of the progress of arts in this country, and being satisfied from the above report, of his care and accuracy in the execution of the work, they recommend this edition of the Bible to the inhabitants of the United States, and hereby authorise him to publish this recommendation in the manner he shall think proper.[9]

Aitken actually asked Congress for quite a bit more than they gave him. In addition to his work being examined by the chaplains, Aitken requested that his Bible *"be published under the Authority of Congress,"*[10] and that he *"be commissioned or otherwise appointed & Authorized to print and vend Editions of the Sacred Scriptures."*[11] He also asked Congress to purchase some of his Bibles and distribute them to the states. Congress did not grant any of these other requests. The only help Aitken ever got from Congress was the resolution endors-

9. Gaillard Hunt, ed., *Journals of the Continental Congress, 1774-1789,* vol. 23, (Washington D.C.: Government Printing Office, 1914), 574.

10. *Papers of the Continental Congress,* National Archives Microfilm Publication M247, r48, i41, v1, p63.

11. *ibid.*

ing the accuracy of his work.

The secular benefit of this resolution, omitted by Hutson and others, was that it acknowledged *"an instance of the progress of arts in this country."* Publicizing the accuracy of this Bible was a great way for Congress to promote the American printing industry.

Few American printers at this time were printing books. Most limited their businesses to broadsides, pamphlets, and newspapers. The books that were printed in America were not only more expensive than those imported from England, but had a reputation for being full of errors. Congress knew that as soon as the war was over and books could once again be imported, any progress that the book shortage had caused in the printing industry would end. The war had created an opportunity for American printers to prove themselves, and Robert Aitken had done that. Printing an accurate edition of a book as large as the Bible was a monumental task for any printer, and Congress wanted it known that an American printer had accomplished it. But, by omitting the part of the resolution acknowledging this *"instance of the progress of arts,"* it is easily made to appear that Congress passed this resolution for the sole purpose of promoting religion.

In 1968, the American Bible Society published a reprint of the Aitken Bible. Appearing in the center of the title page of this reprint, in very large type, are the words *"As Printed by Robert Aitken and Approved & Recommended by the Congress of the United States of America in 1782."* Although this page was added by the American Bible Society, it is quoted on many websites as the title page of the original. The first few pages of Aitken's Bible contained the resolution of Congress, the letter from the committee to the chaplains requesting that they examine the edition for accuracy, and the report of the chaplains.

The following is the committee's letter to the chaplains, as it appears in the *Journals of the Continental Congress.*

> Rev. Gentlemen, Our knowledge of your piety and public spirit leads us without apology to recommend to your particular attention the edition of the holy scriptures publishing by Mr. Aitken. He undertook this expensive work at a time, when from the circumstances of the war, an English edition of the Bible could not be imported, nor any opinion formed

> how long the obstruction might continue. On this account particularly he deserves applause and encouragement. We therefore wish you, reverend gentlemen, to examine the execution of the work, and if approved, to give it the sanction of your judgment, and the weight of your recommendation. We are with very great respect, your most obedient humble servants.[12]

The chaplains, Rev. Dr. White and Rev. Mr. Duffield, reported back to the committee:

> Gentlemen, Agreeably to your desire, we have paid attention to Mr. Robert Aitken's impression of the holy scriptures, of the old and new testament. Having selected and examined a variety of passages throughout the work, we are of opinion, that it is executed with great accuracy as to the sense, and with as few grammatical and typographical errors as could be expected in an undertaking of such magnitude. Being ourselves witnesses of the demand for this invaluable book, we rejoice in the present prospect of a supply, hoping that it will prove as advantageous as it is honorable to the gentleman, who has exerted himself to furnish it at the evident risk of private fortune. We are, gentlemen, your very respectful and humble servants.[13]

On many Christian American history websites, and in a handful of books, the Aitken Bible is called "*The Bible of the Revolution,*" implying that this was what the Bible was called at the time it was published. In reality, however, this title was invented much later, when individual Aitken Bible leaves were packaged for sale.

> **According to Mark Beliles and Stephen McDowell in their book *America's Providential History*: "In 1782, Congress acted the role of a Bible society by officially approving the printing and distribution of the 'Bible**

12. Gaillard Hunt, ed., *Journals of the Continental Congress, 1774-1789,* vol. 23, (Washington D.C.: Government Printing Office, 1914), 573.
13. *ibid.*

of the Revolution,' an American translation prepared by Robert Aitken."

The Aitken Bible was first dubbed "*The Bible of the Revolution*" by Robert Dearden and Douglas Watson in 1930. Dearden and Watson, who were trying to sell over five hundred Aitken Bible leaves, had the leaves, along with facsimilies of various documents related to the Bible, made into books. The books were sold as *An Original Leaf from the Bible of the Revolution, and an Essay Concerning It By Robert R. Dearden, Jr. and Douglas S. Watson.* The essay written by Dearden and Watson for this book is one source of the versions of the lies used by today's religious right for both their 1777 and 1782 Bible stories.

Myths about the Aitken Bible have also been perpetuated by the antique book dealers now selling these Dearden and Watson leaves, or those from another copy dismembered in 1998 to create a similar collectible item, who describe Aitken's Bible as small enough to fit in the coat pocket of the soldiers, implying that this was the reason for its size. Some of these book dealers also list the other documents printed in the Dearden and Watson book, including what is often described as "*the text of George Washington's letter commending Robert Aitken for helping to meet the American soldiers' need for Bibles.*"

Washington did write a letter regarding the Bibles, but it was not a letter to commend Robert Aitken for helping to meet the American soldiers' need for Bibles. These Bibles never even ended up in the hands of the soldiers. Washington's letter was a reply to a letter from Aitken's friend Dr. John Rodgers, a Presbyterian minister who was trying to help Aitken sell his Bibles to Congress.

By the time Aitken finished his Bible, the war was winding down. He knew that if peace was declared, and trade with England resumed, he would be stuck with thousands of Bibles that he would never be able to sell. On September 9, 1782, three days before Congress passed their resolution, Aitken wrote the following to John Hanson, the President of Congress, requesting that Congress buy some of the Bibles.

> It need not be suggested to the Wisdom of that Honourable Body that the Monarchs of Europe have hitherto deemed the Sacred Scriptures peculiarly worthy of the Royal Patronage, nor that a Work of such magnitude must nearly crush an

> individual unless assisted by exterior Aid in supporting so great a weight; nor will I presume to prescribe the Mode in which Such Aid may be afforded; but I beg leave to intimate, that as I apprehend my greatest risque arises from the Near Approach of Peace, my utmost wishes would be accomplished if Congress will purchase a proportion of the edition on Acc[t] of the United States. One Fourth of it will not Amount to 200 Bibles for each State; And as I am anxious merely to *secure the sale* of the Books, it will not be inconsistent with my views to allow a Moderate Credit.[14]

As already mentioned, this request was denied. Eight months later, despite his anticipation of a great demand for Bibles in America, the recommendation of Congress, and no competition from imports, Aitken hadn't sold many Bibles. In April 1783, Congress officially declared the end of hostilities, and the army was beginning to disband. In May 1783, Aitken tried again to get Congress to buy his Bibles – this time to give as gifts to the soldiers being discharged. Aitken knew that Congress would deny the request if he made it himself, so he had a minister friend, Dr. John Rodgers, write to George Washington suggesting not only that Congress buy the Bibles for the soldiers, but that Washington propose the idea as if it was his own. Congress, of course, would be extremely unlikely to deny a request that came from George Washington. The following is from Dr. Rodgers's letter.

> There is another Subject I beg Leave to mention to your Excellency, & that is the case of a worthy citizen of these states, Mr. Robert Aitkin, who has published an Edition of the Bible in our Language; and which was undertaken at a Time when that sacred book was very scarce & the Inhabitants of these States in great Want of it—but the peculiar difficulty & expence attending a Work of such Magnitude in the then State of our Country delayed it's Completion till the Approach of Peace; and British Bibles being imported much cheaper than he can afford to sell His, He is like to be ruined by His generous Effort in behalf of our Divine Religion—Painful

14. *Papers of the Continental Congress,* National Archives Microfilm Publication M247, r90, i78, v1, p421.

Thought, and not very honorable is this rising Empire, that the first Man who undertook to print the holy Scriptures in our language in America, Should be beggared by it.

What I would take the Liberty to suggest to your Excellency, is the presenting each Soldier, & Non Commissioned Officer in the American Army, with a Copy of this Bible, by Congress, on their being disbanded. This would serve not only to save a deserving Citizen from Ruin who highly Merits Attention; but would serve to furnish those brave Men to whom America is so greatly indebted for their Liberties, in the Hand of Heaven with a sure Guide to eternal Life, if they will but take heed to it.

Such are the Obligations that your Country, & Congress as their grand representation, are under to your Excellency, and such is just Sense they have of these obligations, that a Line from your Excellency to Congress on the Subject, and I would wish it as a *** Motion of your own, would probably have the desired Effect — I take a Liberty — to suggest the Thought, and your Excellency will make such Use of it as your Prudence shall dictate.[15]

The following was Washington's reply.

Your proposition concerning Mr. Aikin's Bibles would have been particularly noted by me, had it been suggested in season, but the late Resolution of Congress for discharging part of the Army, taking off near two thirds of our numbers, it is now too late to make the attempt. It would have pleased me well, if Congress had been pleased to make such an important present to the brave fellows, who have done so much for the security of their Country's rights and establishment.[16]

This letter was nothing more than a polite reply to Dr. Rodgers. It

15. John Rodgers to George Washington, May 30, 1783, *George Washington Papers at the Library of Congress, 1741-1799: Series 4, General Correspondence.*

16. George Washington to John Rodgers, June 11, 1783, *ibid.*

is highly unlikely that Washington would have asked Congress to buy the Bibles, even if the idea had been proposed earlier. Most of the soldiers being discharged were owed months, or even years, of back pay and Congress was deeply in debt. There was dissent among the officers who knew that Congress didn't have the money to pay their promised pensions. This problem was so bad that a group of politicians was able to instigate the Newburgh Conspiracy. With the goal of raising money to pay the country's debts, these politicians hatched a plot to scare the American people into allowing Congress to impose taxes on them, a power that it didn't have under the Articles of Confederation. A few anonymous addresses was all it took to get some of Washington's officers to go along and cook up what would look like a threat of an armed takeover of the government by the disgruntled army. Washington had just managed to put a stop to this a few months before receiving Dr. Rodgers's letter. In another incident not long after this, a mob of armed soldiers marched into Philadelphia demanding to be paid. These soldiers surrounded the State House, forcing the Congress to move to Princeton. It's a pretty safe bet that Washington would have been far more concerned with paying the soldiers than giving them Bibles.

Aitken ended up losing over £3,000 on the 10,000 Bibles he printed. Few stories about the Aitken Bible mention that it sold poorly, and those that do blame it on the competition of cheaper British Bibles. The problem with this theory is that Aitken completed his Bible seven months before the end of hostilities was declared by Congress, and over a year before the peace treaty with Great Britain was ratified. According to the treaty, American ports would not be open to British ships until all British troops were removed, which was clearly going to take a while, so the possibility of a supply of imported Bibles was still uncertain even at this point.

In 1777, Rev. Alison had written to Congress that the *"number of purchasers is so great, that we doubt not but a large impression would soon be sold."* Obviously, Rev. Alison greatly overestimated the demand for Bibles because, in 1782, after five more years without a supply, Robert Aitken couldn't sell his.

In 1790, Aitken wrote to George Washington, using his losses from printing his Bibles as one of the reasons that Washington should help him get the job of Printer and Stationer to Congress. In this letter,

Aitken not only exaggerated the involvement of Congress in his 1782 printing, but hinted that he was still looking for government help to print Bibles. Aitken claimed in this letter that *"the scarcity of that valuable book was such, as to claim the attention of Congress, and excite their solicitude for a supply"* and *"that the Book was undertaken in a great measure at the instance, and under the Patronage of Congress."* Congress never solicited a supply of Bibles, nor did Aitken undertake his printing in any way at their instance. The Papers and Journals of the Continental Congress clearly show this was all initiated by Aitken himself.

The following is from Aitken's 1790 letter to George Washington. Washington, who did not know Aitken personally, did not answer this letter personally. He had his secretary, Tobias Lear, inform Aitken that he should apply to Congress if he wanted to be the printer to Congress.

> I doubt not Your Excellency recollects, that I printed an Edition of the Bible, at a time when the scarcity of that valuable book was such, as to claim the attention of Congress, and excite their solicitude for a supply; It was done under the inspection of a Committee of that Honorable Body, though at my sole expence, and the work was highly approved and recommended to the inhabitants of the United States — "by the Act of Congress of September 12th 1782." The peace which took place soon after, removed the obstructions to importation, and so glutted the market with Bibles that I was obliged to sell mine much below prime cost; and in the End, I actually sunk above £3000 by the impression. These two circumstances render my losses exceedingly heavy, and indeed, almost unsupportable: But, Sir, I flatter myself I may hope for some compensation, in a small share of Public Favour; especially when it is considered, that the Book was undertaken in a great measure at the instance, and under the Patronage of Congress — Under this impression, together with the perfect conviction of Your Excellency's benevolence; and your sympathy with all the virtuous feelings of Human Nature; I humbly trust that you will be pleased to have me appointed Printer & Stationer to Congress; or in any other way in which I might be of Public Service, in the

> line of my business. I had it in Contemplation, to Petition your Excellency for an exclusive right, for a term of Years, to print the Bible within the United States, conceiving that my Sufferings, in consequence of my former Undertaking would entitle me to a preference: But a faithful execution of this Work would require, in Order to carry it on with propriety and good effect, such large sums of money, as I am utterly incapable of commanding; and therefore, however pleasing an employment it would be to me, while I live, I am constrained to relinquish former intentions in this respect, for want of the Means to carry them into effect.[17]

In his book *America's Christian History: The Untold Story,* Gary DeMar uses another popular approach to the 1777 and 1782 Bible stories. He manufactures a connection between the failure of Congress to import Bibles in 1777 and the printing of the Aitken Bible, making it appear that Aitken's Bible was somehow printed in place of the Bibles that weren't imported five years earlier.

In a section of his book titled *"The Congressional Bible,"* DeMar begins the 1777 story with the typical lie, claiming that *"Congress issued an official resolution instructing the Committee on Commerce to import 20,000 copies of the Bible,"* but truthfully states that the Bibles were never actually imported. He then explains the failure to import Bibles by implying that Congress, as a substitute for the Bibles that weren't imported, had something to do with the printing of Aitken's New Testaments, the first of which was published in 1777.

> **According to DeMar: "Even though the resolution passed, action was never taken to import the Bibles. Instead, Congress began to put emphasis on the printing of Bibles within the United States. In 1777 Robert Aitken of Philadelphia published a New Testament. Three additional editions were published in 1789, 1779, and 1781. The edition of 1779 was used in schools. Aitken's efforts proved so popular that he announced his desire to publish the whole Bible; he**

17. Robert Aitken to George Washington, June 9, 1790, *George Washington Papers at the Library of Congress, 1741-1799: Series 4, General Correspondence.*

> **then petitioned Congress for support. Congress adopted the following resolution in 1782..."**

Aitken did not print his 1777 edition of New Testament because Congress *"put emphasis on the printing of Bibles within the United States."* There is no connection whatsoever between Congress not importing Bibles in 1777 and any edition of the Bible printed by Aitken.

In his book *Original Intent,* David Barton also tries to connect the two stories, but since Barton claims that Congress *did* import Bibles in 1777, his version is a little different. According to Barton, Congress was having Robert Aitken print Bibles so that they wouldn't have to *continue* to import them. As already mentioned, Barton ends his version of the 1777 story with the statement *"Congress agreed and ordered the Bibles imported."* A few pages later, he begins his version of the Aitken Bible story.

> **According to Barton: "As the war prolonged, the shortage of Bibles remained a problem. Consequently, Robert Aitken, publisher of *The Pennsylvania Magazine*, petitioned Congress on January 21, 1781, for permission to print the Bibles on his presses here in America rather than import them."**

> **Barton goes on to claim: "On September 12, 1782, the full Congress approved that Bible, which soon began rolling off the presses."**

Obviously, Congress didn't do anything *"rather than"* importing Bibles, because they weren't importing any Bibles to begin with. Barton's claim that Aitken asked for permission to print his Bible is, of course, untrue because he was already printing it when he petitioned Congress in January 1781, and it was nearly completed when the September 12, 1782 resolution was passed.

> **Barton ends his story with the following quote from what he refers to as *"an early historian."***

> **"Who, in view of this fact, will call in question**

> **the assertion that this is a Bible nation? Who will charge the government with indifference to religion, when the first Congress of the States assumed all the rights and performed all the duties of a Bible Society long before such an institution had an existence in the world!"**

The quote is accurate. For this one, Barton misquotes the title of the book that the quote comes from. In his endnotes, he lists the book as *History of the American Society from its Organization to the Present Time.* The actual title is *History of the American* ***Bible*** *Society from its Organization to the Present Time*. Barton's "*early historian*" is W.P. Strickland. That would be Reverend W.P. Strickland, a nineteenth century Liar for Jesus.

The following is a longer excerpt from Rev. Strickland's book, which contains the 1849 versions of the 1777 and 1782 Bible stories.

> The Congress of 1777 answered a memorial on the subject of Bible destitution in this country by appointing a committee to advise as to the printing an edition of thirty thousand Bibles. The population of the country then was only about three millions, and all the Bibles in the entire *world* at that period did not exceed four millions. Thus it will be seen that its circulation in this and all other countries at that time was exceedingly limited.
>
> The report of the committee appointed by Congress forms one of the brightest epochs in the history of our country, and sheds a clear and steady light over every subsequent eventful period. The public recognition of God in that act was of infinitely greater importance in giving stability to the times, and securing the permanency of our institutions, than all the imposing and formidable array of legal enactments ever made for the establishment of religion.
>
> The committee, finding it difficult to procure the necessary material, such as paper and types, recommended Congress "the use of the Bible being so universal, and its importance

> so great—to direct the Committee on Commerce to import, at the *expense* of Congress, twenty thousand English Bibles from Holland, Scotland, or elsewhere, into the different ports of the States of the Union." The report was adopted, and the importation ordered.
>
> In 1781, when, from the existence of the war, an English Bible could not be imported, and no opinion could be formed how long the obstruction might continue, the subject of printing the Bible was again presented to Congress, and it was, on motion, referred to a committee of three.
>
> The committee, after giving the subject a careful investigation, recommended to Congress an edition printed by Robert Aitken, of Philadelphia; whereupon it was "*Resolved,* That the United States, in Congress assembled, highly approve the pious and laudable undertaking of Mr. Aitken, as subservient to the interests of religion; and being satisfied of the care and accuracy of the execution of the work, recommend this edition to the inhabitants of the United States."
>
> How interesting is such a history of the early circulation of the Bible in this country! What moral sublimity in the fact, as it stands imperishably recorded and filed in the national archives! Who, in view of this fact, will call in question the assertion that *this is a Bible nation?* Who will charge the government with indifference to religion, when the *first* Congress of the States assumed all the rights and performed all the duties of a *Bible Society long before such an institution had an existence in the world!* What a standing, withering rebuke this to ecclesiastico-political demagogues, who, imitating the example of a late minister of instruction for France, would expel the Bible from the schools of our land![18]

The third of the top three religious right myths about Congress and the Bible is that our early Congresses passed acts that financial-

18. W.P. Strickland, *History of the American Bible Society from its Organization to the Present Time,* (New York: Harper and Brothers, 1849), 19-21.

ly aided Bible societies. The most popular example is an act signed by James Madison in 1813.

> **According to David Barton, in his book *Original Intent*: "...in 1812 [sic], President Madison signed a federal bill which economically aided a Bible Society in its goal of the mass distribution of the Bible."**

This act, entitled *An Act for the relief of the Bible Society of Philadelphia,*[19] had absolutely nothing to do with aiding this society in its goal of distributing the Bible. It merely waived an import duty on one shipment of printing plates, determined by Congress to have been unfairly charged.

At the beginning of the War of 1812, an act was passed doubling all import duties to fund the war. The Bible Society of Philadelphia had ordered a shipment of printing plates from England in 1809. By the time their order reached England, their plates were manufactured, and the shipment arrived in America, it was 1812 and the new tariff schedule had gone into effect. Because this particular shipment was ordered three years before the war began, Congress granted the society's request that it be taxed according to the pre-war tariff schedule. The following is the description of the Bible Society's request from the Senate Journal.

> Mr. Leib presented the memorial of the managers of the Bible Society of Philadelphia, stating that, to enable them to promote the object of the institution, the gratuitous distribution of the sacred Scriptures, they had ordered, in the year 1809, a set of stereotype plates from England, and praying that these plates may be exonerated from the additional duties since imposed on British manufactures; and the memorial was read.[20]

Some versions of this story claim that three Bible Societies were

19. Richard Peters, ed., *The Public Statutes at Large of the United States of America*, vol. 6, (Boston: Charles C. Little and James Brown, 1846), 116.

20. *Journal of the Senate of the United States of America,* vol. 5, (Washington D.C.: Gales & Seaton, 1821), 231.

aided financially by acts signed by James Madison. The other two were the Bible Societies of Baltimore and Massachusetts.

An Act for the relief of the Baltimore and Massachusetts Bible Societies, signed on April 20, 1816, was a single act granting the requests of both societies. The Massachusetts Society was granted a drawback, which is a refund of import duties paid on goods that are exported within a certain amount of time from the date they were imported. The following excerpt from the act shows that this society was subject to the same laws as any other merchant, and was required to furnish proof that the Bibles they exported had arrived in a foreign port.

> *And be it further enacted,* That the Comptroller of the Treasury be, and he is hereby, authorized to direct a debenture to be issued to the Massachusetts Bible Society, for a drawback of duties upon an invoice of Bibles exported from the port of Boston, on board the brigantine Panther, in the year one thousand eight hundred and fifteen: *Provided, however,* That the said Society shall produce satisfactory evidence to the said comptroller, as the law directs, that the invoice aforesaid has been landed in some foreign port or place.[21]

The act does not indicate the specific reason for the remission of duties on a set of printing plates to the Baltimore Society, but, like all such acts, it was for an individual incident. Each of these acts was for one invoice, and specified the boat, year, port, and goods that the act applied to. They were just like any of the many similar acts passed for all types of merchants for a variety of reasons. They were not general laws enacted to permanently aid any religious organization.

When Congress was petitioned to enact a general law exempting Bible societies from import duties, the request was denied. In April 1816, the same month that *An Act for the relief of the Baltimore and Massachusetts Bible Societies* was passed, a memorial from the Philadelphia Bible Society was rejected.[22] This memorial requested that all Bible societies be exempt from import duties on all Bibles. The

21. Richard Peters, ed., *The Public Statutes at Large of the United States of America,* vol. 6, (Boston: Charles C. Little and James Brown, 1846), 162.

22. *The Debates and Proceedings of the Congress of the United States of America,* vol. 29, 14th Cong., 1st Sess., (Washington D.C.: Gales & Seaton, 1854), 298.

Committee on Finance, to whom this memorial was referred, reported to the Senate that the request should not be granted because it would be unfair to other Bible importers, and would deter American printers from printing Bibles because they would be unable to sell them as cheaply as the Bible societies.[23]

As a "Plan B," the Philadelphia Bible Society, which apparently anticipated that the Senate would reject this petition, presented another, less extensive petition to the House of Representatives at the same time. This one made it through Congress, but the bill was not signed by Madison, as will be explained in Chapter Nine.

> **According to Chief Justice Burger, delivering the opinion of the court, Walz v. Tax Commission of the City of New York, 1970: "As early as 1813 the 12th Congress refunded import duties paid by religious societies on the importation of religious articles."**
>
> **The following was Burger's footnote for this: "See 6 Stat. 116 (1813), relating to plates for printing Bibles. See also 6 Stat. 346 (1826) relating to church vestments, furniture, and paintings; 6 Stat. 162 (1816), Bible plates; 6 Stat. 600 (1834), and 6 Stat. 675 (1836), church bells."**

The 1813 and 1816 acts in Chief Justice Burger's footnote are, of course, the acts for the Philadelphia, and Baltimore and Massachusetts Bible Societies.

The 1826 act relating to church vestments, furniture, and paintings was one of a number of acts for the relief of Bishop Benedict Joseph Flaget of Kentucky. Bishop Flaget had a big problem on his hands in the 1820s. Wealthy people in Italy and France, including the King of France, wouldn't stop sending him stuff. Flaget was founding a college and many Catholics in Europe wanted to help him. In 1824, they began sending him all sorts of expensive items. Most of these donations consisted of furniture, paintings, and equipment for the college. Some included items for Flaget's church and residence. The

23. Walter Lowrie and Walter S. Franklin, eds., *American State Papers: Finance,* vol. 3, (Washington D.C.: Gales & Seaton, 1834), 115.

problem was that Flaget couldn't afford to pay the import duties on these donations, and neither he nor Congress wanted to offend the donors, particularly the King of France, by not accepting them. In 1826, a year and a half after referring Flaget's first memorial to the Ways and Means Committee, Congress decided to waive the duties on the items that were then sitting at the New York customs house. Donations continued to arrive, so several more acts were passed over the next six years. When the objection was raised in 1832 that it was unfair to allow this only for Flaget, Congress started allowing other churches to receive similar donations from Europe duty-free. The justification for this was that the import duties on these items were protective tariffs, the purpose of which are to make imports more expensive to protect American manufacturers. Because the items received by churches as donations were not items that the churches were likely to buy for themselves if they didn't happen to receive them as donations, charging an import duty on them wasn't protecting anything.

The 1834 act regarding church bells in Justice Burger's footnote was for church bells received as a donation from Europe.

The 1836 church bell act remitted the import duties on a set of bells because the bells weren't being imported. They had been sent to England by a church in Philadelphia to be repaired and were only being returned.

— CHAPTER TWO —

The Northwest Ordinance

In his books *The Myth of Separation* and *Original Intent,* David Barton, using one sentence from the Northwest Ordinance, and a number of misquotes from early state constitutions, leads his audience to the erroneous conclusion that the founders of our country not only intended, but required, that religion be included in public education.

Barton's claim, like similar claims found in many other religious right American history books, is based on the following sentence from the ordinance's Article III.

> Religion, Morality and knowledge being necessary to good government and the happiness of mankind, Schools and the means of education shall forever be encouraged.[1]

Although mentioning in his earlier book, *The Myth of Separation,* that the Northwest Ordinance was initially passed by the Continental Congress, Barton omits this in *Original Intent,* the later book in which he refined many of the lies from *The Myth of Separation*. In *Original Intent* he attributes the ordinance entirely to the framers of the First Amendment, concluding from this that the men who wrote the First Amendment didn't consider promoting religion in public schools to be a violation of that amendment.

1. Richard Peters, ed., *The Public Statutes at Large of the United States of America,* vol. 1, (Boston: Charles C. Little and James Brown, 1845), 52.

In *Original Intent,* Barton begins his Northwest Ordinance story with the following statement: "Perhaps the most conclusive historical demonstration of the fact that the Founders never intended the federal Constitution to establish today's religion-free public arena is seen in their creation and passage of the 'Northwest Ordinance.' That Ordinance (a federal law which legal texts consider as one of the four foundational, or 'organic' laws) set forth the requirements of statehood for prospective territories. It received House approval on July 21, 1789; Senate approval on August 4, 1789 (this was the same Congress which was simultaneously framing the religion clauses of the First Amendment); and was signed into law by President George Washington on August 7, 1789.

Article III of that Ordinance is the only section to address either religion or public education, and in it, the Founders couple them, declaring:

> Religion, morality, and knowledge, being necessary to good government and the happiness of mankind, schools and the means of education shall forever be encouraged.

The Framers of the Ordinance—and thus the Framers of the First Amendment—believed that schools and educational systems were a proper means to encourage the 'religion, morality, and knowledge' which they deemed so 'necessary to good government and the happiness of mankind.'"

In *The Myth of Separation,* Barton claims: "A strong declaration that the First Amendment was never intended to separate Christianity from public affairs came in the form of legislation approved by the same Congress which created the First Amendment. That legislation, originally entitled 'An Ordinance for the

Government of the Territory of the United States, North-west of the River Ohio' and later shortened to the 'Northwest Ordinance,' provided the procedure and requirements whereby territories could attain statehood in the newly United States."

Also from *The Myth of Separation*: "Since the same Congress which prohibited the federal government from the 'establishment of religion' also required that religion be included in schools, the Framers obviously did not view a federal requirement to teach religion in schools as a violation of the First Amendment."

The 1789 dates on which the ordinance was approved by the House and the Senate and signed by George Washington are correct. In *Original Intent,* Barton just leaves out that the 1789 Congress was merely reenacting an ordinance passed over two years earlier by the Continental Congress to give it force under the new Constitution. Of the twenty-eight senators and over sixty representatives in the 1789 Congress, only six, four senators and two representatives, were present when the Continental Congress passed the ordinance in 1787. It was not framed by the same Congress that was *"simultaneously framing the religion clauses of the First Amendment."*

Before getting to the rest of Barton's lie, it's important to understand how the religious wording ended up in Article III of the ordinance in the first place, and why the Congress of 1789 would not have seen it as conflicting with the First Amendment.

Article III was the work of a Massachusetts man named Manasseh Cutler. Dr. Cutler, a minister and former army chaplain, was also one of the directors of the Ohio Company of Associates, a land speculating company comprised mainly of former army officers. In the summer of 1787, the Ohio Company was negotiating with the Continental Congress to buy a large amount of land in the Northwest Territory.

To pay off the large public debt from the Revolutionary War, Congress asked those states with sparsely populated western lands to cede these lands to the United States. The ceded lands would then be sold by Congress to reduce the debt. Most of the Northwest Territory was ceded by Virginia, but it also contained the smaller cessions of

Massachusetts and Connecticut.

In 1785, two years before the Northwest Ordinance, Congress passed the first ordinance for the disposal of land in the territory. One problem with this earlier ordinance, however, was that few people could afford the large tracts it required them to buy. Land speculating companies began negotiating with Congress to buy large tracts at a low price. These tracts could then be divided into smaller lots and resold at a profit. This was the plan of the Ohio Company when they sent Manasseh Cutler to meet with the Continental Congress in July 1787.

The Ohio Company knew they had the upper hand in these negotiations, and would not make a move towards purchasing the land until Congress adopted a new ordinance that better suited their plans. The result was the Northwest Ordinance.

Nathan Dane, a delegate from Massachusetts, has been credited with drafting the ordinance, but there is little doubt that Dr. Cutler arrived in New York with the provisions required by his company already written in some form. On his way to New York, Cutler met with two other founders of the Ohio Company, General Rufus Putnam in Boston and General Samuel Holden Parsons in Connecticut, to decide on the conditions their company would require. This, along with the fact that parts of the ordinance were borrowed from the laws of Massachusetts, explains how the committee was able to draft the ordinance literally overnight.

Cutler had his first meeting with what he referred to in his journal as *"the committee"* on the morning of Monday, July 9, 1787. This meeting was actually only with Edward Carrington and Nathan Dane, two of the five members of the committee originally appointed. The other three were not in New York when Cutler arrived. Two of them, James Madison and Rufus King, were in Philadelphia at the Constitutional Convention. It wasn't until later on that first day that Richard Henry Lee, John Kean, and Melancton Smith were appointed to replace the three absent members. By the next morning, the committee had finished drafting the ordinance and submitted a copy to Dr. Cutler for his approval. Within a matter of hours, Dr. Cutler returned it to the committee with a few additional provisions, including the education provision that became part of Article III.

Cutler knew the Ohio Company had Congress over a barrel.

Congress was so broke in 1787 that they had to choose between making the payments due on the foreign debt to France or those due to Holland. That year, they decided to default on the loan to France and use all their resources to pay Holland. Repaying Holland was a priority for two reasons. First, Holland was in a position to lend the United States more money in the near future, while France was not. Second, the Dutch were likely to start seizing American ships if they weren't paid. Cutler didn't even stick around for the ordinance to be voted on. He left New York for Philadelphia that evening, confident that his provisions would be added and the ordinance would be passed. Cutler wasn't even concerned that the ordinance needed seven votes to pass, and out the eight states present in Congress, half were southern states. He knew that the necessity of selling the land would outweigh any objections, even to the provision prohibiting slavery in the territory.

Nathan Dane, however, wasn't quite as confident as Dr. Cutler about the anti-slavery provision. When the ordinance was read for the first time on July 11, this provision was left out. Dane wanted to be sure that the rest of the ordinance would be favorably received before bringing up the slavery issue. By the next day, when the ordinance was read for the second time, this provision had been restored. The following day, Friday, July 13, only four days after Cutler's arrival in New York, the ordinance was read for the third time and enacted.

After the ordinance was passed, the Ohio Company continued to put pressure on Congress, threatening to back out of the deal if other demands were not met. The following is from a letter written by Dr. Cutler and Major Winthrop Sargent to the Board of Treasury while negotiating the contract for their land purchase.

> If these terms are admitted we shall be ready to conclude the Contract. If not we shall have to regret, for a numerous Class of our Associates, that the Certificates they received as Specie, at the risque of their lives and fortunes, in support of the Common cause, must, for a considerable time longer, wait the tedious and precarious issue of public events; (altho' they are willing to surrender their right in them on terms advantageous to the public;) and that the United States may lose an opportunity of securing in the most effectual manner, as well as improving the value of their western

> lands, whilst they establish a powerful barrier, against the irruptions of the Indians, or any attempts of the British power, to interrupt the security of the adjoining States.[2]

There was only one provision that Dr. Cutler assented to compromise on. Although the Continental Congress could not levy taxes, each state was responsible for its share of the public debt and government expenses, paid by taxes levied by the state legislatures. The Northwest Ordinance made the future states in the territory responsible for their share of the country's debts and expenses, and gave the temporary legislatures the power to levy taxes for this purpose. Dr. Cutler considered this to be taxation without representation, and proposed that no such taxes be levied in a new state until that state was represented in Congress. The compromise was that the temporary legislatures could levy taxes, but would also elect a non-voting delegate to Congress.

There is no question that the Northwest Ordinance provisions regarding religion, education, and slavery were written and insisted on by Dr. Cutler. A number of nineteenth century articles about the history of the ordinance refer to a note written in the margin of the Ohio Company's copy crediting Cutler with these provisions.

From an 1887 article in the *New Englander and Yale Review:*

> There is, indeed, at this moment, in the hands of Dr. Cutler's descendants a printed copy of the ordinance of 1787, with a memorandum in the margin, stating that Mr. Dane asked Dr. Cutler to suggest such provisions as he deemed advisable, and that at his instance was inserted what relates to religion, education, and slavery.[3]

From an 1895 article in *The New England Magazine:*

> There has been found, too, among the papers of the Ohio Company, a copy of the ordinance of 1787, with a pencil

2. Roscoe R.. Hill, ed., *Journals of the Continental Congress, 1774-1789,* vol. 33, (Washington D.C.: Government Printing Office, 1936), 428-429.

3. Rev. A. P. Peabody, D.D., "Manasseh Cutler," *New Englander and Yale Review,* Vol. 46, No. 205, April 1887, 326-327.

> note in the margin to the effect that the provisions relating to religion, education and slavery were the contribution of Manasseh Cutler; and his son remembers to have heard his father say, a year after the passage of the ordinance, that he was the author of these provisions.[4]

Although the education provision in Article III was written by Dr. Cutler, Congress made some changes to it. Cutler's provision clearly gave the government of the Northwest Territory the authority to promote religion. As much as Congress had to go along with the demands of the Ohio Company, this apparently went too far. The following was the original wording.

> Institutions for the promotion of religion and morality, schools and the means of education shall forever be encouraged...[5]

This is what appeared in the ordinance.

> Religion, Morality and knowledge being necessary to good government and the happiness of mankind, schools and the means of education shall forever be encouraged....[6]

Congress kept enough of the original wording to appease Dr. Cutler, but stripped the provision of any actual authority to promote religion or religious institutions. The final language of Article III only gave the government authority to promote education. The first part of the sentence was turned into nothing more than an ineffectual opinion of what was necessary to good government.

When the Congress of 1789 reenacted the ordinance, they knew Article III didn't give the government any power to promote religion. There was no conflict with the First Amendment. Other parts of the Northwest Ordinance, however, did raise constitutional questions for the early Congresses, leading to an opinion in 1802, and reaffirmed in

4. Elizabeth H. Tetlow, "The Part of Massachusetts Men in the Ordinance of 1787," *The New England Magazine,* Vol. 18, No. 1, March 1895, 60.

5. Roscoe R.. Hill, ed., *Journals of the Continental Congress, 1774-1789,* vol. 32, (Washington D.C.: Government Printing Office, 1936), 318.

6. Richard Peters, ed., *The Public Statutes at Large of the United States of America,* vol. 1, (Boston: Charles C. Little and James Brown, 1845), 52.

1816, 1818, and 1835, that the ordinance was nothing more than an act of Congress, with no more force or inviolability than any other act of Congress. In fact, as will be explained more fully later in this chapter, the very first time that Congress used the ordinance to admit a state, they substituted a different education provision for the one in Article III. This substituted provision was similar to that in the earlier ordinance, the 1785 *Ordinance for ascertaining the mode of disposing of lands in the Western Territory.*

The 1785 ordinance, as originally drafted by Thomas Jefferson in 1784, contained nothing regarding either religion or education. In 1785, the committee appointed to prepare this ordinance proposed that the following be added.

> There shall be reserved the central Section of every Township, for the maintenance of public Schools; and the Section immediately adjoining the same to the northward, for the support of religion. The profits arising therefrom in both instances, to be applied for ever according to the will of the majority of male residents of full age within the same.[7]

A debate on this proposal quickly removed most of it. First, a motion was made to replace the words *"for the support of religion"* with *"for religious and charitable uses,"* then another to delete from that *"religious and,"* so that it would simply read *"for charitable uses."* When the ordinance was read again three days later, the land grant for religion had been removed entirely. The following is all that was left of the proposed article.

> There shall be reserved the central section of every township, for the maintenance of public schools within the said township.[8]

James Madison couldn't believe that the original proposal had even been considered by the committee, writing the following to James Monroe.

7. John C. Fitzpatrick, ed., *Journals of the Continental Congress, 1774-1789,* vol. 28, (Washington D.C.: Government Printing Office, 1933), 293.
8. *ibid.,* 301.

> It gives me much pleasure to observe by 2 printed reports sent me by Col. Grayson that, in the latter Congress had expunged a clause contained in the first for setting apart a district of land in each Township for supporting the Religion of the majority of inhabitants. How a regulation so unjust in itself, foreign to the Authority of Congress, so hurtful to the sale of the public land, and smelling so strongly of an antiquated Bigotry, could have received the countenance of a Committee is truly matter of astonishment.[9]

Madison's letter to Monroe also clears up a bit of a mystery regarding Virginia's votes through this debate. The Virginia delegates, completely out of character, voted in favor of leaving the religious land grants in. Madison guessed that this was just a misguided move on the part of these delegates to protect the interests of their own state, albeit at the expense of another part of the country. The following was the next sentence of Madison's letter.

> In one view it might have been no disadvantage to this State, in case the General Assessment should take place, as it would give a repellent quality to the new Country in the estimation of those whom our own encroachments on Religious liberty would be calculated to banish to it.[10]

The General Assessment bill, introduced in the Virginia legislature by Patrick Henry, would have levied a tax on all Virginians for the support of the Christian religion. In April 1785, when the debate over religious land grants was going on in Congress, the fate of Henry's bill was still uncertain. The Virginia delegates in Congress knew that if the General Assessment passed, Virginians who opposed it might start moving to the Northwest Territory as a way to escape religious intolerance, and the new territory would be more attractive to immigrants who might otherwise settle in Virginia. But, if the Northwest Territory had an equally obnoxious system of government support for religion, religious freedom wouldn't be a reason for anyone to choose it over

9. James Madison to James Monroe, May 29, 1785, *Letters and Other Writings of James Madison,* vol. 1, (New York: R. Worthington, 1884), 154.
10. *ibid.*

Virginia.

Despite their 1785 vote against religious land grants, the necessity of selling land forced Congress in 1787 to give in to the Ohio Company and grant Lot No. 29 of each township in their purchase for religious purposes. This grant was made in only two contracts – that of the Ohio Company and that of John Cleeves Symmes, who was also purchasing a large amount land. Symmes required, with a few exceptions unrelated to the land grants, that his purchase be on the same terms as that of the Ohio Company.

A number of religious right websites present images of maps showing townships in Ohio with Lot No. 29 designated for religious purposes. These maps are claimed to be representative of the entire Northwest Territory. They are not representative of the territory, or even the state of Ohio. They are maps of the townships in the original Ohio Company and/or Symmes purchases, the only townships ever to receive this land grant. Technically, these maps aren't even representative of the entire Ohio Company purchase. Some of the Lot No. 29 religious grants were not made by Congress, but were actually paid for by the Ohio Company.

The original Ohio Company purchase in July 1787 was to be a million and a half acres, but a few months later the company backed out of half of this. Five years later, they petitioned Congress to purchase part of the half they had backed out of. The first section of the 1792 act of Congress authorizing this purchase confirmed the boundaries of, and land grants in, the seven hundred and fifty thousand acres already purchased. The second section described a two hundred and forty thousand acre tract being purchased in 1792. This section said nothing about land grants.[11] The Ohio Company wrongly assumed that Congress intended to make the same land grants made in 1787 for this tract, and that the failure to mention this in section two of the act was merely an oversight. As townships in this new tract were settled, the Ohio Company appropriated the usual lots for schools and religion. By the time they realized that Congress had not granted these lots, they had appropriated them in ten townships, giving away twenty lots that they had to pay for. In addition to any lots reserved or granted for other purposes, there were, in every township, three

11. Richard Peters, ed., *The Public Statutes at Large of the United States of America*, vol. 1, (Boston: Charles C. Little and James Brown, 1845), 257-258.

lots reserved for the *"future disposition of Congress."* When the Ohio Company realized their mistake, they petitioned Congress to grant them twenty of these lots to make up for the twenty they had given away. In 1806, Congress denied this request.[12]

In 1811, the inhabitants of one township in the original Ohio Company purchase petitioned Congress, requesting that a different lot in their township be designated for religious purposes. The system of dividing the Northwest Territory into square townships had left a number of fractional townships. These were the townships that, due to being along the rivers, were not square. Townships were divided into thirty-six lots, uniformly numbered according to their position, and whatever lots a fractional township happened to contain were numbered according to their position as if they were in an entire township. The township that petitioned Congress in 1811 was a fractional township that did not have a Lot No. 29. Because their township was in the original Ohio Company purchase, the petitioners felt they were entitled to a land grant for religion. Their request was that Congress grant them Lot No. 26, one of the lots reserved by Congress, in lieu of Lot No. 29. Congress did not grant this request.[13]

Religious right American history books rarely contain anything about the Northwest Ordinance other than the religious wording of Article III, and a claim that this article is proof that our founders promoted religion in public schools. One book, however, *America's Providential History* by Mark Beliles and Stephen McDowell, does include a sentence about Manasseh Cutler. The following sentence appears in a chapter listing clergymen who were politicians and statesmen: *"Manassas [sic] Cutler was the author of the Northwest Ordinance written in 1787."* In this book, which is one of the most often recommended American history books for Christian homeschooling, the Northwest Ordinance is mentioned five times – once to mention that *"Manassas"* Cutler was a clergyman, once to mention that it prohibited the sin of slavery in the new states, and three times to bring up the religious wording of Article III. Nowhere do the authors of this American history book actually bother to explain

12. Walter Lowrie, ed., *American State Papers: Public Lands,* vol. 1, (Washington D.C.: Duff Green, 1834), 236-237.

13. *ibid.,* vol. 2, 220.

what the Northwest Ordinance was. Instead, they present statements like the following.

> **From *America's Providential History*: "'Virtue... Learning...Piety.' These words are found throughout our official documents and statements of our Founders. Sometimes they are called 'Morality,' 'Knowledge,' and 'Religion,' such as are found in the Northwest Ordinance. 'Religion' meant Christianity. 'Morality' meant Christian character. 'Knowledge' meant a Biblical worldview."**

As mentioned at the beginning of this chapter, David Barton, in his books *The Myth of Separation* and *Original Intent,* uses a number of misquotes from state constitutions to support his claim that the same Congress that wrote the First Amendment also required that religion be included in schools. Barton takes the fact that Article III of the Northwest Ordinance mentions both religion and schools, combines that with the fact that the enabling acts for some states required that their state governments conform to the ordinance, and concludes from this that Congress required all new states to include religion in their schools as a condition of statehood.

Most religious right authors don't go as far as Barton's claim that the federal government *required* religion in the public schools, but use Article III to claim that religion was expected to be promoted.

> **In his book *America's Christian History: The Untold Story,* Gary DeMar quotes the following from *Religion and Politics: The Intentions of the Authors of the First Amendment* by Michael J. Malbin: "...One key clause in the Ordinance explained why Congress chose to set aside some of the federal lands in the territory for schools: 'Religion, morality, and knowledge,' the clause read, 'being necessary to good government and the happiness of mankind, schools and the means of learning shall forever be encouraged.' This clause clearly implies that schools, which were to be built on federal lands with federal assistance, were**

expected to promote religion as well as morality. In fact, most schools at this time were church-run sectarian schools."

David Barton's evidence that Congress required religion in public schools consists of language similar to that of the ordinance's Article III appearing in four state constitutions, three of which he misquotes, and the fact that the enabling acts for certain states required a conformity to the ordinance.

An enabling act, the act giving a territory permission to frame a state constitution, contained certain basic requirements for statehood, such as the state government being republican in form. Six states, in addition to the usual requirements, were required to be *"not repugnant to"* the Northwest Ordinance. These six states included four of the five Northwest Territory states – Ohio, Indiana, Illinois, and Michigan. The other two were Mississippi and Alabama.

Mississippi and Alabama were formed from land ceded by the state of Georgia. When the states ceded their land, they did so under conditions negotiated by their state legislatures and Congress. One of Georgia's conditions was that the federal government establish in the ceded territory a temporary government similar to that in the Northwest Territory, but that the Northwest Ordinance's anti-slavery provision would not apply. Because the temporary government of their territory had been established according to the ordinance, the enabling acts for Mississippi and Alabama contained the not repugnant to the ordinance requirement.

By not repugnant to the Northwest Ordinance, Congress meant not repugnant to the ordinance's provisions prohibiting things like taxing land owned by the federal government and charging tolls on the Mississippi River, and that a state government could not take away the rights guaranteed to individuals by the ordinance. David Barton, of course, makes not repugnant to the Northwest Ordinance synonymous with requiring its Article III, and, although the ordinance itself was only used for six states, implies that *all* new states were admitted on the condition of complying with this article.

From *The Myth of Separation*: "Following the passage of that legislation, Congressional enabling acts

> **which allowed territories to organize and form a state government and ratify a state constitution required that those potential states adhere to the 'Northwest Ordinance' as a requisite for admission. Consequently, the state constitutions of the newly admitted states frequently included exact wordings from portions of the 'Northwest Ordinance,' specifically Article III."**
>
> **From *Original Intent*: "Subsequent to the passage of the Ordinance, when a territory applied for admission as a state, Congress issued an 'enabling act' establishing the provisions of the Ordinance as criteria for drafting a State constitution. For example, when the Ohio territory applied for statehood in 1802, its enabling act required that Ohio form its government in a manner 'not repugnant to the Ordinance.' Consequently, the Ohio constitution declared:**
>
>> **[R]eligion, morality, and knowledge being essentially necessary to the good government and the happiness of mankind, schools and the means of instruction shall forever be encouraged by legislative provision."**

As already mentioned, three of Barton's four state constitution examples are misquotes. This is the first one. Barton cuts off the last seven words of the sentence. It actually ends *"by legislative provision, not inconsistent with the rights of conscience."* This is the last sentence of the religious freedom section from Article 8, which was the bill of rights in Ohio's 1802 constitution. The following is the entire section.

> Article 8.
> § 3. That all men have a natural and indefeasible right to worship Almighty God according to the dictates of their own conscience; that no human authority can in any case whatever, control or interfere with the rights of conscience; that no man shall be compelled to attend, erect, or support, any

> place of worship, or to maintain any ministry, against his consent; and that no preference shall ever be given by law to any religious society or mode of worship; and no religious test shall be required as a qualification to any office of trust or profit. But religion, morality, and knowledge, being essentially necessary to the good government, and the happiness of mankind, schools, and the means of instruction shall forever be encouraged by legislative provision, not inconsistent with the rights of conscience.[14]

In Ohio's 1851 constitution, the wording was further modified, clearly separating laws protecting religious worship from laws encouraging education.

> Religion, morality and knowledge, however, being essential to good government, it shall be the duty of the general assembly to pass suitable laws to protect every religious denomination in the peaceable enjoyment of its own mode of public worship, and to encourage schools and the means of instruction.[15]

Also added in Ohio's 1851 constitution was the following prohibition of religious control of state school funds.

> The general assembly shall make such provisions, by taxation, or otherwise, as, with the income arising from the school trust fund, will secure a thorough and efficient system of common schools throughout the state; but no religious or other sect, or sects, shall ever have any exclusive right to, or control of, any part of the school funds of this state.[16]

Ohio is the only Northwest Territory state among Barton's four

14. *The American's Guide: Comprising the Declaration of Independence; the Articles of Confederation; the Constitution of the United States, and the Constitutions of the Several States Composing the Union,* (Philadelphia: Towar, J. & D. M. Hogan, 1830), 307.

15. *The American's Guide: Comprising the Declaration of Independence; the Articles of Confederation; the Constitution of the United States, and the Constitutions of the Several States Composing the Union,* (Philadelphia: J.B. Lippincott & Co., 1864), 335.

16. *ibid.*, 341.

examples of states using the language of Article III. Barton includes nothing from the constitutions of Indiana, Illinois, and Michigan, the three other Northwest Territory states whose enabling acts contained the Northwest Ordinance requirement. This is because none of these states' constitutions contained anything remotely like Article III. The following are the reasons for establishing schools from the education sections of the original constitutions of Indiana and Michigan. Neither of these states included religion among their reasons. (The Illinois constitution did not contain anything at all regarding education.)

Constitution of Indiana – 1816:

> Article 9.
> § 1. Knowledge and learning generally diffused through a community, being essential to the preservation of a free government, and spreading the opportunities, and advantages of education through the various parts of the country, being highly conductive to this end, it shall be the duty of the general assembly to provide by law for the improvement of such lands as are, or hereafter may be, granted by the United States to this state, for the use of schools, and to apply any funds which may be raised from such lands, or from any other quarter, to the accomplishment of the grand object for which they are or may be intended....[17]

Constitution of Michigan – 1835:

> Article X.—*Education.*
> 2. The Legislature shall encourage, by all suitable means, the promotion of intellectual, scientifical, and agricultural improvement. The proceeds of all lands that have been or hereafter may be granted by the United States to this State, for the support of schools, which shall hereafter be sold or disposed of, shall be and remain a perpetual fund; the interest of which, together with the rents of all such unsold lands,

17. *The American's Guide: Comprising the Declaration of Independence; the Articles of Confederation; the Constitution of the United States, and the Constitutions of the Several States Composing the Union,* (Philadelphia: Towar, J. & D. M. Hogan, 1830), 324-325.

> shall be inviolably appropriated to the support of schools throughout the State.[18]

Michigan's constitution also expressly prohibited the use of public money for religious teachers and religious schools.

> Article I.
> 4. Every person has a right to worship Almighty God according to the dictates of his own conscience; and no person can of right be compelled to attend, erect, or support, against his will, any place of religious worship, or pay any tithes, taxes, or other rates, for the support of any minister of the gospel or teacher of religion.
>
> 5. No money shall be drawn from the treasury for the benefit of religious societies, or theological or religious seminaries.[19]

Since Ohio was the only Northwest Territory state to include anything close enough for Barton to misquote, he has to look elsewhere for constitutions containing the Article III language. He next moves on to the Mississippi Territory, the territory formed from Georgia's cession.

> **Barton continues: "While this requirement originally applied to all territorial holdings of the United States in 1789 (the Northwest Territory—Ohio, Indiana, Illinois, Michigan, Wisconsin, and Minnesota), as more territory was gradually ceded to the United States (the Southern Territory—Mississippi and Alabama), Congress applied the requirements of the Ordinance to that new territory.**
>
> **Therefore, when Mississippi applied for statehood in 1817, Congress required that it form its government in a manner "not repugnant to the provisions of the**

18. *The American's Own Book; or the Constitutions of the Several States in the Union; Embracing the Declaration of Independence; Constitution of the United States, and the Constitution of Each State, with the Amendments and Much Other Matter of General Interest; from Authentic Documents,* (New York: J.R. Bigelow, 1847), 444-445.
19. *ibid.,* 436.

> **Ordinance." Hence, the Mississippi constitution declared:**
>
> > **Religion, morality, and knowledge being necessary to good government, the preservation of liberty and the happiness of mankind, schools and the means of education shall be forever encouraged in this State."**

Barton's quote from the Mississippi constitution is accurate. It is the only one of his four examples that he doesn't have to misquote. But, to give the impression that this quote is representative of similar provisions found in *all* state constitutions, he mentions seven other states in the paragraph introducing it. To the four Northwest Territory states already mentioned, he adds Wisconsin and Minnesota. Minnesota shouldn't be in this list. Wisconsin was the fifth and last of the Northwest Territory states. For geographic reasons that would make governing it impractical, there was an area of Northwest Territory land in the Wisconsin Territory that did not become part of the state of Wisconsin. It made more sense to attach this area to Minnesota, so that's what Congress did. The rest of Minnesota was not part of the Northwest Territory. Other than being an example of the general inaccuracy of Barton's books, however, this doesn't really matter because neither Wisconsin's or Minnesota's enabling acts contained any mention of the Northwest Ordinance, and neither of their constitutions contained anything like the language of Article III.

Wisconsin's constitution included a lengthy education section containing no mention of religion, and none of which is relevant here. And, like Michigan, Wisconsin's Declaration of Rights expressly prohibited state funding of religious schools.

Constitution of Wisconsin – 1848:

> Article 1.
>
> *Declaration of Rights.*
>
> 18. The right of every man to worship Almighty God according to the dictates of his own conscience, shall never be

> infringed, nor shall any man be compelled to attend, erect, or support any place of worship, or to maintain any ministry, against his consent. Nor shall any control of, or interference with the rights of conscience be permitted, or any preference be given by law to any religious establishments, or modes of worship. Nor shall any money be drawn from the treasury for the benefit of religious societies, or religious or theological seminaries.[20]

Like Wisconsin and Michigan, Minnesota prohibited state funding for religious schools, and did not mention religion in its reason for establishing schools.

Constitution of Minnesota – 1857:

> Article 8.
> *School Funds, Education and Science.*
> § 1. The stability of a republican form of government depending mainly upon the intelligence of the people, it is the duty of the legislature to establish a general and uniform system of public schools.[21]

In addition to adding Minnesota to the Northwest Territory, Barton is clearly confused about which territory became Mississippi and Alabama. The source he cites for his statement about *"the Southern Territory—Mississippi and Alabama"* is the 1790 act establishing a territorial government for the land ceded by North Carolina.[22] This was the territory that became Tennessee. The land ceded by Georgia in 1802 that became the states of Mississippi and Alabama was named the Mississippi Territory in 1798 when the act was passed authorizing the president to appoint commissioners to negotiate the cession with the legislature of Georgia.[23]

20. *The American's Guide: Comprising the Declaration of Independence; the Articles of Confederation; the Constitution of the United States, and the Constitutions of the Several States Composing the Union*, (Philadelphia: J.B. Lippincott & Co., 1864), 539.
21. *ibid.*, 584.
22. Richard Peters, ed., *The Public Statutes at Large of the United States of America*, vol. 1, (Boston: Charles C. Little and James Brown, 1845), 123.
23. *ibid.*, 549-550.

Barton groups Alabama with Mississippi to give the impression that Alabama's constitution contained something similar to his quote from the Mississippi constitution. But, unlike Mississippi, Alabama did not use the language of Article III in its education provision.

Constitution of Alabama – 1819:

> Article 6. *General Provisions.*
> *Education.*
> Schools, and the means of education, shall forever be encouraged in this State; and the general assembly shall take measures to preserve, from unnecessary waste or damage, such lands as are or hereafter may be granted by the United States for the use of schools within each township in this State, and apply the funds, which may be raised from such lands, in strict conformity to the object of such grant....[24]

Barton works as many states and territories as possible into his story for two reasons. The first, of course, is to imply that *all* state constitutions contained something similar to Article III. The second is to give the impression that the Northwest Ordinance continued to be used for a long time after the Northwest Territory states were admitted. Barton is using a common tactic of the religious right American history authors – transforming something that never actually happened in the first place into a long standing practice by giving the impression that it happened many times over a period of many years. The truth is the Northwest Ordinance wasn't even used for all of the Northwest Territory states. For reasons explained later in this chapter, Congress stopped using the ordinance upon the admission of Michigan, writing a different act to establish the temporary government for Wisconsin.

To give the impression that Congress *continued* to use the ordinance for *later* territories, Barton implies that his so-called *"Southern Territory"* wasn't formed until after all of the Northwest Territory states were admitted. The Mississippi Territory, as already mentioned, was

24. *The American's Guide: Comprising the Declaration of Independence; the Articles of Confederation; the Constitution of the United States, and the Constitutions of the Several States Composing the Union,* (Philadelphia: Towar, J. & D. M. Hogan, 1830), 400.

created in 1798, four years before Ohio, the first Northwest Territory states, was admitted. The state of Mississippi was admitted in 1817, and Alabama in 1819, decades before the last of the Northwest Territory states. Michigan wasn't admitted until 1836, Wisconsin in 1848, and Barton's additional Northwest Territory state, Minnesota, in 1857.

> **Barton then continues, adding even more territories: "Congress later extended the same requirements to the Missouri Territory (Missouri and Arkansas) and then on to subsequent territories. Consequently, the provision coupling religion and schools continued to appear in State constitutions for decades. For example, the 1858 Kansas constitution required:**
>
> > **Religion, morality, and knowledge, however, being essential to good government, it shall be the duty of the legislature to make suitable provisions...to encourage schools and the means of instruction.**
>
> **Similarly, the 1875 Nebraska constitution required:**
>
> > **Religion, morality, and knowledge, however, being essential to good government, it shall be the duty of the legislature to pass suitable laws...to encourage schools and the means of instruction."**

Up until this point in his story, the only dates provided by Barton were those of the Ohio and Mississippi constitutions, 1802 and 1817 respectively. This makes these next quotes, from 1858 and 1875, appear to support his claim that Congress *later* extended the ordinance to the Missouri and other unspecified territories. But, the Missouri Territory was established in 1812[25] – prior to the admission of every state mentioned so far by Barton with the exception of Ohio. The Missouri Territory was what remained of the Louisiana Purchase

25. Richard Peters, ed., *The Public Statutes at Large of the United States of America*, vol. 2, (Boston: Charles C. Little and James Brown, 1845), 743.

when Louisiana became a state. The Louisiana Purchase had actually been divided into two territories eight years earlier, in 1804, the part that would become the state of Louisiana being called the Orleans Territory. Arkansas Territory was what was left of the Missouri Territory when the state of Missouri was split off in 1819.

Parts of the Northwest Ordinance, including the language of Article III, were copied into the 1812 act forming the Missouri Territory, but all of this was dropped in the 1819 act forming the Arkansas Territory. The enabling act for Missouri contained no mention of either the ordinance or the act of 1812, and the education provisions in neither the Missouri or Arkansas constitutions contained anything like the language of Article III.

Constitution of Missouri – 1821:

> Article 6.
> *Of Education.*
> § 1. Schools and the means of education, shall for ever be encouraged in this State; and the general assembly shall take measures to preserve from waste or damage such lands as have been, or hereafter may be granted by the United States for the use of schools within each township in this state, and shall apply the funds which may be arise from such lands in strict conformity to the object of the grant; and one school or more, shall be established in each township as soon as practicable and necessary, where the poor shall be taught gratis.[26]

Constitution of Arkansas – 1836:

> Article IX.— *General Provisions.— Education.*
> Sec. 1. Knowledge and learning, generally diffused through a community, being essential to the preservation of a free government, and diffusing the opportunities and advantages of education through the various parts of the State

26. *The American's Guide: Comprising the Declaration of Independence; the Articles of Confederation; the Constitution of the United States, and the Constitutions of the Several States Composing the Union,* (Philadelphia: Towar, J. & D. M. Hogan, 1830), 417.

> being highly conducive to this end, it shall be the duty of the General Assembly to provide by law for the improvement of such lands as are or hereafter may be granted by the United States to this State for the use of schools, and to apply any funds which may be raised from such lands, or from any other source, to the establishment of the object for which they are or may be intended. The General Assembly shall from time to time pass such laws as shall be calculated to encourage intellectual, scientific and agricultural improvement, by allowing rewards and immunities for the promotion and improvement of arts, science, commerce, manufactures and natural history; and countenance and encourage the principles of humanity, industry, and morality.[27]

Barton's quotes from the 1858 Kansas and 1875 Nebraska constitutions are both misquotes. These states used the Article III sentence as modified by Ohio in 1851, separating legislation to protect religious freedom from legislation to encourage education. Barton removes the middle of the sentence from both. He also neglects to mention that the 1858 Kansas constitution was not the Kansas constitution approved by Congress. Kansas drafted several constitutions between 1857 and 1861. It was the constitution of 1861 that was approved. Barton uses the unapproved 1858 version because the approved 1861 version didn't contain anything even close enough to the Article III language to misquote.

Constitution of Kansas – 1861:

> Article VI.
> *Education.*
> § 2. The Legislature shall encourage the promotion of intellectual, moral, scientific and agricultural improvement, by establishing a uniform system of common schools, and

27. *The American's Own Book; or the Constitutions of the Several States in the Union; Embracing the Declaration of Independence; Constitution of the United States, and the Constitution of Each State, with the Amendments and Much Other Matter of General Interest; from Authentic Documents,* (New York: J.R. Bigelow, 1847), 479.

> schools of higher grade, embracing normal, preparatory, collegiate, and university departments.[28]

The 1861 Kansas constitution also prohibited religious control of state education funds.

> § 8. No religious sect or sects shall ever control any part of the common-school or University funds of the State.[29]

In addition to misquoting the Nebraska constitution, Barton adds eight years to the length of time of his story by using the date of the state's second constitution, 1875. Nebraska's first constitution, approved by Congress in 1867, also contained the provision misquoted by Barton. The following is the entire sentence, as it appeared in both the 1867 and 1875 Nebraska constitutions.

> Religion, morality, and knowledge, however, being essential to good government, it shall be the duty of the Legislature to pass suitable laws to protect every religious denomination in the peaceable enjoyment of its own mode of public worship, and to encourage schools and the means of instruction.[30]

In its 1875 constitution, Nebraska added not only a general prohibition on religious control of state education funds like those in other state constitutions, but the following, prohibiting even privately funded religious education in public schools.

> Article VIII.—*Education.*
> Sec. 11. No sectarian instruction shall be allowed in any school or institution supported in whole or in part by the public funds set apart for educational purposes, nor shall

28. *The American's Guide: Comprising the Declaration of Independence; the Articles of Confederation; the Constitution of the United States, and the Constitutions of the Several States Composing the Union,* (Philadelphia: J.B. Lippincott & Co., 1864), 626.
29. *ibid.,* (Philadelphia: J.B. Lippincott & Co., 1864), 627.
30. M.B.C. True, *A Manual of the History and Civil Government of the State of Nebraska. Designed for the Use of the Schools of the State,* (Boston and New York: Leach, Shewell, and Sanborn, 1885), 34.

> the State accept any grant, conveyance or bequest of money, lands or other property to be used for sectarian purposes.[31]

In an 1885 state history and civil government textbook produced by the state of Nebraska for use in its public schools, each article of the Nebraska constitution was explained to the students. The following was the explanation of the constitution's religious freedom section, the section at the end of which the modified version of the Article III language is found. Just as protection of religious freedom and the promotion of education were separated in the state's constitution, they were separated in this textbook.

> No one has a right to regulate our consciences or our worship for us. The right of each one to obey his own conscience in the matter of worship cannot be defeated by any law. This applies to his right to attend such church as he chooses, or not to attend; and to helping in the erection and support of any church or religious organization. That a person belongs to any particular church, or does not belong to any, cannot be urged as a qualification or disqualification for an office, nor deny to any suitor in court the right to call him as a witness. This does not say, nor does it mean, that the state, or the law, or the court, only, shall not apply the "religious test;" it means that no one has a right to apply that test. If a voter votes for a candidate solely because of that candidate's religious belief, that voter violates the letter and spirit of this section of the bill of rights. As all the people have the right to their religious belief, it is right that the law shall not give any preference to any religious body or organization, but that it should fully protect each body in the enjoyment of its own organization and mode of worship. As education makes better citizens, the state ought to encourage it.[32]

31. M.B.C. True, *A Manual of the History and Civil Government of the State of Nebraska. Designed for the Use of the Schools of the State,* (Boston and New York: Leach, Shewell, and Sanborn, 1885), 59.

32. *ibid.,* 34-35.

In his story about the Northwest Ordinance, David Barton mentions a total of twelve states. To recap, only one of these twelve used the ordinance's Article III in its constitution without changing its meaning, two modified it so significantly that Barton had to misquote their versions, and nine omitted it entirely. Nevertheless, Congress approved the constitutions of each and every one. Clearly, Barton's claim that the Northwest Ordinance proves that Congress *"required that religion be included in the schools"* is not true.

What Congress did require of new states, however, was that their governments guarantee certain rights to their citizens. Among these rights was religious freedom. Although Congress could not impose any such requirement on the original states, it could, and did, make it a condition of admission for new states. Clearly, the early Congresses, well over a century before the Supreme Court used the Fourteenth Amendment to extend the First Amendment to the states, did not think *"Congress shall make no law respecting an establishment of religion"* meant that they couldn't require religious freedom in the states they were admitting.

In one way or another, religious freedom was a condition of statehood for all new states beginning with Ohio. For some states, it was explicitly stated in their enabling acts. It was occasionally even required that this right be irrevocable in any future constitutions without the consent of Congress. In a few cases, there was no need to specify any conditions in an enabling act because a territory had already gone ahead and written a state constitution that met the approval of Congress. For the Louisiana Territory states, religious freedom was guaranteed in the treaty by which France ceded the territory to the United States. Although there was some debate in Congress over whether or not the president had the right to guarantee that this territory would be admitted as states, there was no question that the rights guaranteed to the inhabitants of the territory by the treaty could not be taken away by a state constitution. For the six states admitted under the Northwest Ordinance, not repugnant to the ordinance was clearly understood to mean not repugnant to the following.

> Sec. 13. And, for extending the fundamental principles of civil and religious liberty, which form the basis whereon

> these republics, their laws and constitutions are erected; to fix and establish those principles as the basis of all laws, constitutions, and governments, which forever hereafter shall be formed in the said territory:
>
> Sec. 14. It is hereby ordained and declared by the authority aforesaid, that the following articles shall be considered as articles of compact between the original States and the people and States in the said territory, and forever remain unalterable, unless by common consent, to wit:
>
> Art. 1. No person, demeaning himself in a peaceable and orderly manner, shall ever be molested on account of his mode of worship or religious sentiments, in the said territory.[33]

The authority of Congress to require anything whatsoever of new states that it couldn't require of the original states was questioned in 1819, but this was not prompted by the requirement that new states guarantee their citizens religious freedom and other rights. The question was raised by those who didn't want Congress to prohibit slavery in Missouri. Their argument was that new states, once admitted, were considered to be *"on an equal footing"* with the original states, so, if Congress didn't have the authority to prohibit slavery in the original states, it didn't have the authority to prohibit it in new states. The counter argument, of course, was that Congress had imposed conditions on every new state since Ohio. It was decided in 1802 that Congress, by having the power to admit states, also had the power to dictate any reasonable conditions under which they were to be admitted. This opinion was not changed by the question raised in the debate over Missouri. Congress continued to require that new states guarantee civil and religious liberties as a condition of admission.

None of the states objected to the condition of including these civil and religious liberties in their constitutions. In fact, all but a few went far beyond the basic religious freedom required by Congress. Most, as already mentioned, explicitly prohibited state funding of religion and religious schools, and many prohibited religious tests for

33. Richard Peters, ed., *The Public Statutes at Large of the United States of America,* vol. 1, (Boston: Charles C. Little and James Brown, 1845), 52.

public offices in their state constitutions as the federal Constitution did for federal offices.

In spite of the opinion of the early Congresses that the ordinance was no more than an ordinary act of Congress, the numerous times that they disregarded its provisions, and the fact that both Congress and the inhabitants of the territories considered the governments established by it to be pretty bad, the ordinance is considered to be one of the foundational documents of the United States. The *U.S. Code Annotated* lists it as one of four *"Organic Laws of the United States."* The other three are the Constitution, the Declaration of Independence, and the Articles of Confederation. Religious right authors, of course, use this to support the notion that Article III of the ordinance was as inviolable as an article of the Constitution.

In 1802, the first time the ordinance was used to admit a state, Congress decided to alter some of its provisions, offering the prospective state of Ohio different provisions in lieu of some of those in the ordinance. One of the substitutions offered to and accepted by Ohio replaced the education provision in Article III. So, in complete contrast to David Barton's claim that Congress required Article III as a condition for admission of all new states, this article, or at least its sentence regarding education, was superceded in the enabling act for the very first Northwest Territory state. The rest of the article, regarding fair treatment of Indians, remained in effect.

Although the 1785 land ordinance was no longer in force in 1802, both ordinances were taken into consideration by the committee that drafted the substitute provisions for Ohio. Congress's goal was to get Ohio to agree to giving up the right to tax any land sold by the United States until ten years after it was purchased. This, of course, would make it easier for Congress to sell the land. The deal offered to Ohio in exchange for this included land grants for schools, as in the ordinance of 1785, in lieu of the vague statement about encouraging schools in Article III of the Northwest Ordinance. Since no legislation had been passed that conflicted with the 1785 provision for school land grants, the committee simply drafted a new education provision, similar to that of 1785, for Ohio's enabling act.

> The committee observe, in the ordinance for ascertaining the mode of disposing of lands in the Western Territory of the

20th of May, 1785, the following section, which, so far as respects the subject of schools, remains unaltered:

"There shall be reserved for the United States out of every township, the four lots, being numbered, 8, 11, 26, 29, and out of every fractional part of a township, so many lots of the same numbers as shall be found thereon. There shall be reserved the lot No. 16 of every township, for the maintenance of public schools within the said township. Also one third part of all gold, silver, lead and copper mines, to be sold, or otherwise disposed of, as Congress shall hereafter direct."

The committee also observe, in the third and fourth articles of the ordinance of the 13th of July, 1787, the following stipulations, to wit:

"Art. 3rd. Religion, morality, and knowledge, being necessary to good government and the happiness of mankind, schools, and the means of education shall forever be encouraged," &c.

"Art. 4th. The legislatures of those districts or new States, shall never interfere with the primary disposal of the soil by the United States in Congress assembled, nor with any regulations Congress may find necessary for securing the title in such soil to the bona fide purchasers. No tax shall be imposed on lands the property of the United States; and, in no case, shall nonresident proprietors be taxed higher than residents."

The committee, taking into consideration these stipulations, viewing the lands of the United States within the said Territory as an important source of revenue; deeming it also of the highest importance to the stability and permanence of the union of the eastern and western parts of the United States, that the intercourse should, as far as possible, be facilitated; and their interests be liberally and mutually con-

> sulted and promoted; are of the opinion that the provisions of the aforesaid articles may be varied for the reciprocal advantage of the United States, and the State of —— when formed, and the people thereof; they have, therefore, deemed it proper, in lieu of the said provisions, to offer the following to the Convention for the Eastern State of the said Territory, when formed, for their free acceptance or rejection, without any condition or restraint whatever; which, if accepted by the Convention, shall be obligatory upon the United States:
>
> 1st. That the section No. 16, in every township sold, or directed to be sold by the United States, shall be granted to the inhabitants of such townships, for the use of schools.[34]

When the House of Representatives debated the committee's recommendations, the education provision substituted for Article III wasn't even mentioned. The House debated several resolutions at the beginning of the report regarding things such as the state's boundaries and method of holding a constitutional convention, then skipped right to the other provisions being offered, salt springs and ten percent of the proceeds from federal land sales for road construction. Apparently, nobody cared that the new education provision didn't mention religion.

Substituting other provisions for those in the Northwest Ordinance did not violate the ordinance, as long as the prospective state consented to the changes, as was the case with Ohio in 1802. What prompted a debate over Congress's authority to deviate from the ordinance on this occasion was the committee's proposal that Congress dictate the time, place, and mode of selecting representatives for Ohio's constitutional convention. This was objected to on the grounds that by attaching conditions for a state's admission beyond those contained in the ordinance, Congress was violating the ordinance. The prevailing opinion was that the ordinance was no more than an act of Congress, so Congress did have the authority to do this.

One part of the ordinance that Congress did adhere to when writ-

34. *The Debates and Proceedings of the Congress of the United States of America*, vol. 11, 7th Cong., 1st Sess., (Washington D.C.: Gales & Seaton, 1851), 1099-1100.

ing the enabling act for Ohio was Article V, the article specifying the boundaries of the states that would be formed from the territory. When establishing the boundaries of Illinois and Indiana, however, Congress disregarded this article. But, it was the boundaries of Ohio, laid out according to the ordinance, that later caused a problem.

The dispute over Ohio's boundaries resulted from the fact that the Continental Congress, when writing the Northwest Ordinance in 1787, had used a bad map. According to the ordinance, the Northwest Territory was first to be divided from north to south into three states – and eastern state, a central state, and a western state. At the discretion of Congress, the territory could be further divided by making the northern part of it into two states, with dividing line between the northern and southern states being an east-west line even with the southern end of Lake Michigan. For some reason, although newer and more accurate maps existed, the committee drawing the dividing lines for the future states used a map from 1755 that placed the southern end of Lake Michigan much farther north than it actually was. When the line that would be the northern boundary of Ohio and southern boundary of Michigan was drawn eastward from the southern end of Lake Michigan, it appeared that most of Lake Erie would fall below the line, giving Ohio a good amount of access to the lake. In reality, a line drawn eastward from the southern end of Lake Michigan barely skimmed the southern side of Lake Erie.

During Ohio's constitutional convention, a trapper who happened to be in Chillicothe, where the convention was being held, brought it to the attention of some of the convention members that Lake Michigan extended much further south than they thought it did. The convention immediately attached a proviso to the boundaries laid out in their enabling act to ensure that, if this trapper was correct, the northern boundary of their state would be moved far enough north to give them the part of Lake Erie that met the Miami River. When the convention received no rejection of this proviso from Congress, they assumed it had been adopted. But, although Congress didn't object to it, they never formally adopted it. By the time the Michigan Territory was being established two years later, they had completely forgotten about it. The southern boundary of the Michigan Territory was drawn according to the Northwest Ordinance, causing it to overlap what Ohio thought was the northern part of its state.

Three decades later, when Michigan was preparing for statehood, Congress reaffirmed what had been decided in 1802 – that the Northwest Ordinance was nothing more than an act of Congress. To admit Michigan as a state, Congress had to confirm the boundaries of the part of the Michigan Territory that would become the state of Michigan, and establish the remainder as a new territory. The new territory being formed, which would eventually become the western state in the northern part of the Northwest Territory, was the Wisconsin Territory. According to the ordinance, the southern boundary of Wisconsin, like the southern boundary of Michigan, was to be even with the southern end of Lake Michigan. Congress, however, had already altered this boundary when admitting Illinois, the state directly to the south of Wisconsin. In order to give Illinois a fair share of the shoreline of Lake Michigan, its northern boundary had been placed farther north than the line in the ordinance.

In 1835, Congress had to settle the boundary dispute between Michigan and Ohio, and define the boundaries of the Wisconsin Territory. This resulted in the final debate over Congress's authority to disregard the Northwest Ordinance. Michigan, of course, wanted the land claimed by Ohio in 1802, which, according to Article V of the Northwest Ordinance, belonged to them. Michigan claimed that the ordinance was a compact that could not be broken by Congress, and the few members of Congress who sided with Michigan, particularly John Quincy Adams, unsuccessfully tried to use this argument. Those who sided with Ohio argued that Congress had decided three decades earlier that it did not have to adhere to the ordinance, and, in addition to that, giving in to Michigan would cause another problem. The Wisconsin Territory, when it later applied for statehood, might demand that the northern boundary of Illinois, which had been moved even farther north than the disputed Ohio boundary, also be moved back to the line specified in the ordinance.

John Reynolds, a Representative of Illinois, made the following comments regarding his state's constitution and northern boundary.

> ...This constitution has been made in pursuance of an act of Congress, passed in 1818, authorizing the people of the Territory of Illinois to form a constitution and State Government, and which State, so formed, was admitted into

> the Union with the limits as prescribed in the constitution. This course of proceeding showed the sense of Congress on the ordinance of 1787, made for the government of the people of the Northwestern Territory. Congress, as early as 1802, expressed an opinion on this ordinance in the admission of the State of Ohio into the Union. They considered the ordinance then, and they have so considered it ever since, down to a very recent date, as changeable by their legislation. It is, in fact, nothing more than an ordinary act of Congress, changeable, like other acts, for the public good.[35]

After noting that the ordinance actually said only that the northern states were to be formed *north of* the specified line, not that their southern boundaries had to be *on* that line, Reynolds continued.

> ...But we are not compelled to resort to this rigid construction of the ordinance, which was peculiarly made, not to regulate boundaries of new and future States, but for the government of the people in the Northwestern Territory. It can be demonstrated, according to the principles of our constitution and the laws of the country, that the ordinance is nothing more than an act of Congress. Its assuming to itself the high-sounding titles of "ordinance," and "compact," does not make it so. It is not contended that the Congress that passed this act in question possessed any more power or authority under the Constitution of the United States than the present or any other Congress possess. Each Congress that existed under the same constitution of Government must possess the same power, and no more. Could the present Congress make a compact between any people in this Government? It is useless to inform this House what a contract or compact is. There must be competent parties, in the first place. Who were the parties in this "compact" mentioned in the ordinance? Congress were the only party concerned in the whole transaction. It is clearly not a compact, as there were no parties to it. The people in the new Territory were not

35. *Register of Debates in Congress,* vol. 11, 23rd Cong., 2nd Sess., (Washington D.C.: Gales and Seaton, 1835), 1252.

> present, represented in the Congress that enacted this organic law of the Northwestern Territory.
>
> The Congress of the United States have no power to make constitutions for any people. They may make organic laws for the Territories of the United States, and no more. These laws are always in the control and power of Congress, to alter and change at pleasure, which they have done on various occasions. They are completely within the constitutional competency of Congress, to change and alter whenever the public good requires it. Congress have so considered the subject since this act or ordinance had existed. They admitted the State of Ohio into the Union with an alteration of the ordinance act. The same has been done with Indiana and Illinois. It has been the uniform course of legislation, when it became necessary, since the ordinance was enacted in 1787...[36]

John Quincy Adams, after reading the part of the ordinance stating that it was an unalterable compact between the original states and the people of the territory, and reading the boundaries specified in Article V of the ordinance, made the following comments.

> These are the terms of the compact—a compact as binding as any that was ever ratified by God in heaven.
>
> The further provision is for the admission of these States into the Union at the proper time. I pass that over because it has no reference to the question now at issue before the House. I pass over, also, the laws which have been enacted by Congress from that time to the present; and the question whether Congress has, by its subsequent acts, violated this provision. I appeal to it now, in order to say that it cannot be annulled; that it is as firm as the world, immutable as eternal justice; and I call upon every member of this House to defend it with his voice and vote, and to sustain the plighted faith of this nation—of the thirteen original States by which

36. *Register of Debates in Congress*, vol. 11, 23rd Cong., 2nd Sess., (Washington D.C.: Gales and Seaton, 1835), 1253-1254.

> the compact was made.
>
> In the year 1805, the Territory of Michigan was formed by law, and the Southern line of the Territory is identical with these words of the provision: "an east and west line drawn through the southerly bend or extreme of Lake Michigan." And what do these twenty-nine members ask Congress to do? They call upon you to repeal this provision; to declare that it is not binding; to say that this shall not be the line, and to establish a different one. And why? Because it suits their convenience, and the convenience of their States, that the line should be altered....[37]

Adams then asserted that the earlier Congresses had deviated from the ordinance because they didn't understand what they were doing.

> ...It is true that the boundary of Indiana and Illinois has been formed by Congress, without knowing, as I believe, what they were doing, or what principles were involved; and if this question does not come to the arbitrament of the sword, as has been intimated by the member from Illinois, who says that the people of Illinois will not suffer their boundary line to be touched—all I ask, and all the people of the two Territories ask, is, that you will not touch the line at all—that Congress will no more commit itself. There is no necessity for it. If they have committed an error in establishing a new boundary, drawn from a Territory which has no one to represent its interests, let them be satisfied with the evil they have done, and not repeat it now, when they know what is involved in the question.[38]

Thomas Hamer of Ohio responded to Adams with the following.

> ...Now sir, can Congress pass a law that cannot be repealed? Can one Congress by a law bind their successors and the

37. *Register of Debates in Congress,* vol. 11, 23rd Cong., 2nd Sess., (Washington D.C.: Gales and Seaton, 1835), 1255-56.

38. *ibid.,* 1256.

> country through all time to come? Yet such is the doctrine advanced in opposition to our claim. The ordinance is an act of Congress. It is no compact, as to the country north of the line named, whatever it may as to the rest. A compact requires two parties to its execution. Here there was but one, the Congress of the United States. Virginia had no claim; the other States gave up theirs without reserve, and there was no assent or dissent of the people residing in the Territory.
>
> He could but admire what he might be permitted to call the ingenuity of the gentleman from Massachusetts. He had remarked that Congress had no power to change the line prescribed in the ordinance, and that it was wholly unimportant what their subsequent legislation had been upon the subject. Yet he carefully passes over the laws which conflict with this line, and brings out those only which accord with it. Thus, sir, he passes by the laws of 1816 and 1818, admitting Indiana and Illinois into the Union, and fixing their boundaries north of this line; but presents the law of 1805, erecting Michigan into a Territory, to show that Congress had regarded the line as fixed, by their adoption of it on that occasion. Why not bring out all, on both sides?...[39]

As in all prior debates on the subject, the prevailing opinion in 1835 was that Congress did not have to adhere to the ordinance. Ohio kept the northern boundary it had claimed in 1802, and the boundaries of Indiana and Illinois were left where Congress placed them in 1816 and 1818. As a consolation prize, Michigan was given its upper peninsula, an area it didn't want in the first place.

In the act establishing the Territory of Wisconsin, and the later act enabling Wisconsin to become a state, the Northwest Ordinance was not even mentioned. Congress wrote a new act for the temporary government of Wisconsin. So, contrary to David Barton's claim that the ordinance was required for all new states, and was still being used decades after the Northwest Territory states were admitted, it wasn't even used for all of the Northwest Territory states.

39. *Register of Debates in Congress,* vol. 11, 23rd Cong., 2nd Sess., (Washington D.C.: Gales and Seaton, 1835), 1258.

The Northwest Ordinance has been used as historical evidence by a few Supreme Court justices in their opinions in cases regarding religion in public schools.

> **Justice Thomas, in his concurring opinion, Rosenberger v. University of Virginia, 1995: "A broader tradition can be traced at least as far back as the First Congress, which ratified the Northwest Ordinance of 1787....Article III of that famous enactment of the Confederation Congress had provided: 'Religion, morality, and knowledge...being necessary to good government and the happiness of mankind, schools and the means of learning shall forever be encouraged.'...Congress subsequently set aside federal lands in the Northwest Territory and other territories for the use of schools....Many of the schools that enjoyed the benefits of these land grants undoubtedly were church-affiliated sectarian institutions as there was no requirement that the schools be 'public.'"**

> **Justice Rehnquist, in his dissenting opinion, Wallace v. Jaffree, 1985: "The actions of the First Congress, which reenacted the Northwest Ordinance for the governance of the Northwest Territory in 1789, confirm the view that Congress did not mean that the Government should be neutral between religion and irreligion. The House of Representatives took up the Northwest Ordinance on the same day as Madison introduced his proposed amendments which became the Bill of Rights; while at that time the Federal Government was of course not bound by draft amendments to the Constitution which had not yet been proposed by Congress, say nothing of ratified by the States, it seems highly unlikely that the House of Representatives would simultaneously consider proposed amendments to the Constitution and enact an important piece of territorial legislation which conflicted with the intent of those proposals. The**

> **Northwest Ordinance, 1 Stat. 50, reenacted the Northwest Ordinance of 1787 and provided that '[r]eligion, morality, and knowledge, being necessary to good government and the happiness of mankind, schools and the means of education shall forever be encouraged.'...Land grants for schools in the Northwest Territory were not limited to public schools. It was not until 1845 that Congress limited land grants in the new States and Territories to nonsectarian schools."**

Justice Rehnquist claimed that it was not until 1845 that Congress limited school land grants in the new states and territories to non-sectarian schools. Apparently, he derived this from the fact that the act admitting Florida as a state was worded a little differently than the acts for other states and designated Lot No. 16 in each township for the use of *public* schools, rather than simply schools. This is ridiculous. Some enabling and admission acts said schools, some said public schools, and others said common schools. Obviously, they all meant public schools.

Justice Thomas, in *Rosenberger v. University of Virginia,* also used an 1833 act regarding disposal of the religious land grants in the Ohio Company and Symmes purchases.

> **According to Justice Thomas: "See, e.g. Act of Feb. 20, 1833, ch. 42, 4 Stat. 618-619 (authorizing the State of Ohio to sell 'all or any part of the lands heretofore reserved and appropriated by Congress for the support of religion within the Ohio Company's...purchases...and to invest the money arising from the sale thereof, in some productive fund; the proceeds of which shall be for ever annually applied...for the support of religion within the several townships for which said lands were originally reserved and set apart, and for no other use or purpose whatsoever')."**

When Congress gave the legislature of Ohio permission to sell the land reserved for religious purposes in the Ohio Company and Symmes purchases, they had no choice but to require that the proceeds from these sales be used for the support of religion. The reason for this was that the contracts with the Ohio and Symmes Companies specified that any proceeds from the future sale of these lands could not be used for any other purpose. Justice Thomas omits the fact that Congress could not violate these contracts, and misquotes the 1833 act to hide this fact.

The following is the section of *An Act to authorize the legislature of the state of Ohio to sell the land reserved for the support of religion in the Ohio Company's, and John Cleeves Symmes' purchases* misquoted by Justice Thomas with the omitted parts of the sentence restored.

> That the legislature of the state of Ohio shall be, and is hereby, authorized to sell and convey, in fee simple, all or any part of the lands heretofore reserved and appropriated by Congress for the support of religion within the Ohio Company's, and John Cleeves Symme's purchases, in the state of Ohio, and to invest the money arising from the sale thereof, in some productive fund; the proceeds of which shall be for ever annually applied, under the direction of said legislature, for the support of religion within the several townships for which said lands were originally reserved and set apart, and for no other use or purpose whatsoever, according to the terms and stipulations of the said contracts of the said Ohio Company's, and John Cleeves Symme's purchases within the United States....[40]

Justice Rehnquist, in *Wallace v. Jaffree,* misquoted the same 1833 act, omitting even more of the sentence than Justice Thomas. Rehnquist also threw in the 1792 Ohio Company act. As mentioned earlier in this chapter, this was the act for the second Ohio Company purchase, in which Congress confirmed the land grants made in the 1787 contract, but did not make the same grants in the new purchase.

40. Richard Peters, ed., *The Public Statutes at Large of the United States of America,* vol. 4, (Boston: Charles C. Little and James Brown, 1846), 618-619.

> **According to Justice Rehnquist: "In 1787 Congress provided land to the Ohio Company, including acreage for the support of religion. This grant was reauthorized in 1792....In 1833 Congress authorized the State of Ohio to sell the land set aside for religion and use the proceeds 'for the support of religion...and for no other use or purpose whatsoever....'"**

In the companion book to the *Religion and the Founding of the American Republic Exhibit,* James H. Hutson, Chief of the Manuscript Division at the Library of Congress, includes the Northwest Ordinance among the examples of what he describes as *"Congress's broad program to promote religion."*

> **According to Hutson: "Continuing to share the widespread concern about the corrupting influence of the frontier, Congress, in the summer of 1787 Congress revisited the issue of religion in the new territories and passed, July 13, 1787, the famous Northwest Ordinance. Article 3 of the Ordinance contained the following language: 'Religion, Morality and knowledge being necessary to good government and the happiness of mankind, Schools and the means of education shall be forever encouraged.' Scholars have been puzzled that, having declared religion and morality indispensable to good government, Congress did not, like some of the state governments that had written similar declarations into their constitutions, give financial assistance to the churches in the West. Although rhetorical encouragement for religion was all that was possible on this occasion, Congress did, in a little noticed action two weeks later, offer financial support to a church."**

The *"little noticed action two weeks later,"* a land trust put in the name of a religious society for a completely non-religious reason, is the subject of Chapter Four of this book.

— CHAPTER THREE —

Indian Treaties and Indian Schools

The religious right version of American history is full of tales about government efforts to promote Christianity to the Indians. The reason for the large number of lies on this subject is the availability of material that can be turned into lies. There were no actual instances, for example, of the early Congresses passing legislation that aided sectarian schools for children who were American citizens. There was, however, a good deal of cooperation between the government and the Indian mission schools of the 1800s. Although the government's reasons for this were always secular, the fact that this cooperation existed means there are actual acts, reports, etc., that can be misrepresented or misquoted to support claims that the government aided sectarian schools. The same is true of Indian treaties. Congress never funded the building of churches for the American people. It did, however, appropriate funds to fulfill treaty provisions, which occasionally included things such as the building of a church.

The most popular of the Indian treaty stories involves a treaty signed by Thomas Jefferson in 1803. Almost every religious right American history book and website contains some version of this story.

This is the version found in William Federer's book *America's God and Country:* "On December 3, 1803, it was recommended by President Thomas Jefferson that the Congress of the United States pass a treaty

with the Kaskaskia Indians. Included in this treaty was the annual support to a Catholic missionary priest of $100, to be paid out of the Federal treasury. Later in 1806 and 1807, two similar treaties were made with the Wyandotte and Cherokee tribes."

During his presidency, Thomas Jefferson signed over forty treaties with various Indian nations. The treaty with the Kaskaskia is the only one that contained anything having to do with religion. No other Indian treaty signed by Jefferson, including the other two listed by William Federer, contained any mention of religion.

The following is the third article from the 1803 treaty with the Kaskaskia.

> And whereas the greater part of the said tribe have been baptized and received into the Catholic Church, to which they are much attached, the United States will give annually, for seven years, one hundred dollars toward the support of a priest of that religion, who will engage to perform for said tribe the duties of his office, and also to instruct as many of their children as possible, in the rudiments of literature, and the United States will further give the sum of three hundred dollars, to assist the said tribe in the erection of a church.[1]

The Kaskaskia treaty is used by different religious right authors in different ways. For those attempting to prove that Jefferson was a devout Christian, it is evidence that he wanted to promote Christianity to the Indians. Much more often, however, it is used as evidence that he approved of using government funds to promote religion.

The problem with using this provision as evidence that Jefferson approved of using government funds to promote religion is that it was in a treaty with a sovereign nation. Unless a treaty provision threatened the rights or interests of Americans, there was no constitutional reason not to allow it, even if that same provision would be unconstitutional in a law made by Congress. This was made very clear in a lengthy 1796 debate in the House of Representatives on the treaty

1. Richard Peters, ed., *The Public Statutes at Large of the United States of America*, vol. 7, (Boston: Charles C. Little and James Brown, 1846), 79.

making power, excerpts of which appear later in this chapter.

The problem with using the provision as evidence that Jefferson was trying to promote Christianity to the Indians is that the Kaskaskia were already Catholic, and had been for some time. Article 3 of the treaty even begins by stating that *"the greater part of the said tribe have been baptized and received into the Catholic Church."* The support of a priest and help building a church were provisions that the Kaskaskia asked for, not things the government recommended or pushed on them.

The Kaskaskia Indians began converting to Catholicism over a century before this treaty. A Jesuit priest from France, Father Jacques Marquette, first encountered the tribe in 1673 while exploring the Mississippi River with Louis Jolliet. Jolliet had hoped that the Mississippi would lead them to the Pacific Ocean, but when they reached what is now Arkansas, they were told by the natives that it flowed into the Gulf of Mexico. Fearing that if they continued they might be captured by the Spanish, they turned around. On their way back up the Mississippi, they met and befriended the Kaskaskia, who told them about a short cut back to Quebec. Upon leaving, Father Marquette promised that he would come back. He kept his promise, returning in 1675 and establishing the Immaculate Conception mission.

The Kaskaskia were one of a loose confederation of tribes known as the Illinois. At the time that Father Marquette established his mission, the Illinois population is estimated to have been well over ten thousand, the Kaskaskia being one of the larger tribes. During the 1700s, their numbers dwindled due to epidemics, attacks by other tribes, and intermarriage with the French. By the time the treaty was signed in 1803, only about two hundred and fifty Illinois were left. No longer able to defend themselves against other tribes, the remaining Illinois wanted the protection of the United States. In exchange for a promise of protection and a few other provisions, the Illinois, represented by the Kaskaskia chief Jean Baptiste DuQuoin, ceded almost nine million acres to the United States.

Almost every version of the Kaskaskia story contains the second claim in William Federer's version, that Jefferson signed two other Indian treaties that contained provisions for Christian ministers – one with the Wyandots in 1806, and one with the Cherokees in 1807. This lie usually comes in the form of an implication. The statement that the Kaskaskia treaty contained a provision for a priest is immediately followed by a phrase such as *"two similar treaties were enacted during Jefferson's administration,"* implying, of course, that the similarity was a provision for a priest.

These other two treaties first became part of the Kaskaskia story in Robert L. Cord's 1982 book *Separation of Church and State: Historical Fact and Current Fiction.* Cord, however, did not lie about these treaties. This is a case of the Liars for Jesus misquoting one of their own to create a better lie. While Cord's book does contain its share of lies, this isn't one of them. Cord in no way implies that these other two treaties contained religious provisions. In fact, he mentions them specifically because they *did not* contain religious provisions. What they did contain were provisions for money that wasn't designated for a particular purpose. Cord uses these provisions to argue that Jefferson, if he had wanted to avoid provisions for religious purposes in the Kaskaskia treaty, could have done so with a similar provision that did not specify what the money was for.

> **The following is Cord's argument: "Lest it be argued to the contrary, if Jefferson had thought the 'Kaskaskia Priest-Church Treaty Provision' was unconstitutional, he could have followed other alternatives. An unspecified lump sum of money could have been put into the Kaskaskia treaty together with another provision for an annual unspecified stipend with which the Indians could have built their church and paid their priest. Such unspecified sums and annual stipends were not uncommon and were provided for in at least two other Indian treaties made during the Jefferson Administration – one with the Wyandots and other tribes, proclaimed April 24, 1806, and another with the Cherokee nation, proclaimed May 23, 1807."**

Cord's words were first twisted by John Eidsmoe in his 1987 book *Christianity and the Constitution.*

> **According to Eidsmoe: "In 1803 President Jefferson recommended that Congress pass a treaty with the**

> **Kaskaskia Indians which provided, among other things, a stipend of $100 annually for seven years from the Federal Treasury for the support of a Catholic priest to minister to the Kaskaskia Indians. This and two similar treaties were enacted during Jefferson's administration – one with the Wyandotte Indians and other tribes in 1806, and one with the Cherokees in 1807."**

Eidsmoe gives the impression that this is what appears in Cord's book by summing up the paragraph containing his altered version of the story with this sentence: *"Citing these and other facts, Professor Robert Cord concludes, 'These historical facts indicate that Jefferson ...did not see the First Amendment and the Establishment Clause requiring 'complete independence of religion and government'.'"*

David Barton, in his 1991 book *The Myth of Separation,* copies Eidsmoe's version of the story word for word, presenting it as a quote. He does not, however, cite Eidsmoe as the source of this quote. Barton cites Daniel Dreisbach's 1987 book *Real Threat and Mere Shadow: Religious Liberty and the First Amendment.* But, Dreisbach's book contains nothing even close to Eidsmoe's lie. Dreisbach, like Cord, does not in any way imply that these other two treaties contained religious provisions. Dreisbach doesn't even mention these treaties in the text of his book. He uses Cord's argument that the Kaskaskia could have been given money for an unspecified purpose, but names the other two treaties only in a footnote.

This story is a good example of how the religious right lies evolve, and, by being copied from book to book, and then to the internet, eventually lose any connection to their original sources. Robert Cord, whose book was published in 1982, mentions the other two treaties, but does not imply that they contained religious provisions. Daniel Dreisbach, whose book was published in 1987, uses these treaties for the same reason as Cord. John Eidsmoe, whose book was also published in 1987, twists Cord's words and creates the lie. David Barton, in 1991, copies Eidsmoe's lie, but cites Dreisbach as his source. In 2000, William Federer, whose version of the lie appears at the beginning of this chapter, cites both Dreisbach and Barton. In 2003, the lie appears in D. James Kennedy's book *What If America Were A*

Christian Nation Again?, with no source except William Federer's book. Various forms of the lie are now found on Christian American history websites, many of which, like the following, change the one Catholic priest into plural Christian missionaries.

> **This is one popular internet version: "As President of the United States, Jefferson negotiated treaties with the Kaskaskia, Cherokee, and Wyandot tribes, wherein he provided – at the government's expense – Christian missionaries to the Indians."**

The following are the articles from the Wyandot and Cherokee treaties, which, although containing no mention of religion whatsoever, are cited by both Barton and Federer among the sources for their claims.

Article IV of the 1806 Treaty with the Wyandots, etc.:

> The United States, to reserve harmony, manifest their liberality, and in consideration of the cession made in the preceding article, will, every year forever hereafter, at Detroit, or some other convenient place, pay and deliver to the Wyandot, Munsee, and Delaware nations, and those of the Shawanee and Seneca nations who reside with the Wyandots, the sum of eight hundred and twenty five dollars, current money of the United States, and the further sum of one hundred and seventy five dollars, making in the whole an annuity of one thousand dollars; which last sum of one hundred and seventy five dollars, has been secured to the President, in trust for said nations, by the Connecticut land company, and by the company incorporated by the name of "the proprietors of the half million acres of land lying south of lake Erie, called Sufferer's Land," payable annually as aforesaid, and to be divided between said nations, from time to time, in such proportions as said nations, with the approbation of the President, shall agree.[2]

2. Richard Peters, ed., *The Public Statutes at Large of the United States of America*, vol. 7, (Boston: Charles C. Little and James Brown, 1846), 88.

Article II of the 1807 Treaty with the Cherokees:

> The said Henry Dearborn on the part of the United States hereby stipulates and agrees that in consideration of the relinquishment of title by the Cherokees, as stated in the preceding article, the United States will pay to the Cherokee nation two thousand dollars in money as soon as this convention shall be duly ratified by the government of the United States; and two thousand dollars in each of the four succeeding years, amounting in the whole to ten thousand dollars; and that a grist mill shall within one year from the date hereof, be built in the Cherokee country, for the use of the nation, at such place as shall be considered most convenient; that the said Cherokees shall be furnished with a machine for cleaning cotton; and also, that the old Cherokee chief, called the Black Fox, shall be paid annually one hundred dollars by the United States during his life.[3]

As already mentioned, neither Robert Cord nor Daniel Dreisbach lie about the Wyandot or Cherokee treaties. These two authors take a different approach. In addition to their speculation that the specifically religious provisions in the Kaskaskia treaty could have been avoided with an unspecific provision, they do a little blurring of the government's separation of powers. Because the First Amendment specifies that ***"Congress** shall make no law respecting an establishment of religion...,"* Cord and Dreisbach imply that *Congress* had the power to reject the Kaskaskia treaty. The point they attempt to make is that if Congress didn't approve of government funding of religion, they would not have appropriated the funds for the treaty's religious provisions. To make it appear as if Congress had this kind of power over the execution of treaties, Cord and Dreisbach need to play with some dates.

> **According to Dreisbach: "Before formal ratification in December 1803, Jefferson presented both Houses of Congress the treaty in order to secure the necessary**

3. Richard Peters, ed., *The Public Statutes at Large of the United States of America,* vol. 7, (Boston: Charles C. Little and James Brown, 1846), 102.

> **funds to execute the treaty's provisions."**
>
> **According to Cord: "The Proclamation of the Ratified Treaty was issued on December 23, 1803, approximately one month after Jefferson laid it before both Houses of Congress 'in their legislative capacity' on November 25, 1803, presumably for the appropriation of necessary funds to execute the treaty commitments."**

What Cord and Dreisbach do here is use the *proclamation* date to make it look as if the Kaskaskia treaty wasn't ratified until December 23, 1803. They need the ratification date to be after November 25, the date the treaty was laid before Congress, in order to give the impression that Congress had the power to reject it. Cord cleverly makes a practice of using the proclamation dates, rather than the ratification dates, for other treaties in his book so that this one won't stand out.

The Kaskaskia treaty, of course, would not have been laid before Congress until it was ratified. The actual ratification date was November 24, 1803. The following was Jefferson's November 25 message to Congress.

> To the Senate and House of Representatives of the United States:
>
> The treaty with the Kaskaskia Indians being ratified, with the advice and consent of the Senate, it is now laid before both Houses in their legislative capacity. It will inform them of the obligations which the United States thereby contract, and particularly that of taking the tribe under their future protection; and that the ceded country is submitted to their immediate possession and disposal.[4]

Robert Cord does two other things to strengthen the impression that Congress could have rejected the religious treaty provisions by withholding the funding for them.

4. *Journal of the House of Representatives of the United States, 1801-1804,* vol. 4, 8th Cong., 1st Sess., (Washington D.C.: Gales and Seaton, 1826), 458.

The first, which is also used by Daniel Dreisbach, is to imply that the primary reason the treaty was laid before Congress was for the appropriation of funds. Cord's speculation that this was *"presumably for the appropriation of necessary funds to execute the treaty commitments"* is deliberately misleading. Of course this would be *presumed.* That Congress would appropriate the necessary funds to execute the treaty's provisions was a given. The treaty was laid before Congress to *"inform them of the obligations which the United States thereby contract,"* not to get their opinion or approval.

The second is making a point of quoting the words *"in their legislative capacity"* from Jefferson's message. By stating that the treaty was *"laid before* ***both*** *houses in their legislative capacity,"* Jefferson was merely making the distinction between the Senate acting in its executive, or *"advice and consent"* capacity, and the Senate acting in its legislative capacity. In other words, the Senate's opportunity to object to the treaty had come and gone, and their role from this point on was to make any laws necessary to execute the treaty's provisions. Cord, whose story requires that Congress have the power to refuse to fund the treaty's religious provisions, uses the words *"in their legislative capacity"* to give his readers the impression that Congress had some legislative power to do this.

To understand why Robert Cord's notion that Congress could have withheld the funds for the Kaskaskia treaty is so far-fetched, it's helpful to look at a debate in the House of Representatives seven years earlier. This lengthy debate, which took place in March and April of 1796, came about as the result of the very unpopular Jay Treaty with Great Britain. Up until this time, the treaty making process as laid out in the Constitution had gone smoothly. But the unpopularity, as well as the secrecy, of the Jay Treaty raised questions over what right, if any, Congress had to refuse to make the laws necessary execute a treaty.

Shortly after the Jay Treaty was made public, the House of Representatives began to receive petitions from all over the country, some urging the House to pass the laws necessary for its execution, but just as many urging them to refuse to pass these laws. It was obvious from these petitions that the people thought that Congress had the authority, or at least should have the authority, to refuse to execute this treaty. Up until this point, nobody had given the possibility of such a power much thought because no other treaty had ever been opposed. Other treaties that had been laid before the House had simply been referred to a committee of the whole, which, after little or no debate, had voted in favor of a resolution to pass the laws, considering the whole business to be little more than a formality. The Jay Treaty changed this, and raised some important questions about the separation of powers.

The Jay Treaty was a partisan issue. Republicans opposed it because it unfairly favored trade with Great Britain. Some Republican newspapers even went as far as calling George Washington a sellout for signing it. Federalists, many of whom benefited from trade with Great Britain, supported it. The Republicans questioned not only the treaty itself, but the negotiations that had led to it. The secrecy of these negotiations raised suspicions among the House Republicans partly because the Senate, which had given its *"advice and consent,"* was dominated by Federalists. A majority of the House wanted to see the same papers regarding the negotiations that had been laid before the Senate, and thought they had the right to request this. A motion was made by Edward Livingston to petition President Washington for these papers.

Livingston's motion began a debate that would continue for weeks, and address virtually every aspect of the treaty making process, and the role and rights of Congress in this process. Two things came up in this debate that are relevant to the 1803 treaty with the Kaskaskia.

The first was that Indian treaties were unquestionably treaties with foreign nations. These treaties could not be considered anything else because a treaty could not be made with any entity other than a sovereign power. While the Constitution made a distinction between foreign nations and Indian tribes in regard to the power of Congress to regulate commerce, this distinction did not exist in making treaties.

The second is found in a statement made by Abraham Baldwin, a delegate from Georgia at the Constitutional Convention. By the time Baldwin spoke up in the debate, the original question of whether or not the House should request the papers related to the Jay Treaty had become almost incidental to the broader issue of the right of Congress to deliberate on and refuse to execute treaty provisions, specifically those provisions that involved exercising certain powers delegated to Congress by the Constitution.

In an effort to get the House to *"at least agree what they were talking about,"* Baldwin tried to sum up the arguments of both sides, and, at the same time, steer the debate back to the original question of the papers. In doing this, Baldwin emphasized that even those who thought that Congress should have at least some power over treaties were talking about exercising this power only in the most extreme circumstances. The example used by many on this side of the debate, including James Madison, involved the part of Article I, Section 8 of the Constitution giving Congress the power to *"raise and support armies,"* and, more specifically, that no appropriation made for an army could extend for more than two years. This clause gave Congress the power to disband an army and, in effect, prevent an endless war, by simply not reappropriating the funding for the army at the end of the two years. William Giles explained how the president, by a treaty provision, could usurp this power from Congress.

> What security have we that he [the president] will not agree with Great Britain, that if she will keep up an Army of ten thousand men in Canada, he will do the same here? How could such a stipulation be got over by the House, when they were told that in matters of Treaty they must not pretend to exercise their will, but must obey? How will this doctrine operate upon the power of appropriation? A Military Establishment may be instituted for twenty years, and as their moral sense is to prevent their withholding appropriations, they can have no power over its existence.[5]

Although it had not yet been brought up by anyone else, Abraham Baldwin, in describing the extremely limited power that was being considered, included an extreme that might justify Congress in not executing a treaty provision regarding religion – the *"introduction of an established religion from another country."*

> If it were allowed that there might be any possible or extraordinary cases on the subject of Treaty-making in which it might ever be proper for that House to deliberate—as, for

5. *The Debates and Proceedings in the Congress of the United States,* vol. 5, 4th Cong., 1st Sess., (Washington D.C.: Gales and Seaton, 1855), 512.

> instance, offensive Treaties which might bring the country into a war—subsidies and support of foreign armies—introduction of an established religion from another country, or any other of those acts which are by the Constitution prohibited to Congress, but not prohibited to the makers of Treaties; if it were allowed that there might possibly exist any such case, in which it might ever be proper for Congress to deliberate, it would seem to be giving up the ground on which the discussion of the present question has been placed; what agency the House should take, and when would be other questions. Whether a case would probably occur once in a hundred years that would warrant the House in touching the subject, is of no consequence to the debate.[6]

This 1796 debate, most of which was irrelevant to the original question, was considered so important to those involved that they made sure an accurate record of it was kept, proofreading and correcting their speeches to ensure that no errors were made. This was something that was rarely done. At this time, the accounts of debates printed in the newspapers were often better than the records kept by Congress itself. The House knew that if this debate needed to be referred to by any future Congress, it would likely mean that a treaty had been ratified containing something so obnoxious that Congress was considering refusing to execute it.

The House did eventually decide to petition Washington for the papers, a request which Washington denied. The following excerpt from Washington's reply clearly shows that he was of the opinion that Congress had no right whatsoever to do anything other than obey a treaty and make the necessary laws for its execution.

> Having been a member of the General Convention, and knowing the principles on which the Constitution was formed, I have ever entertained but one opinion on this subject, and from the first establishment of the Government to this moment, my conduct has exemplified that opinion, that the power of making Treaties is exclusively vested in the

6. *The Debates and Proceedings in the Congress of the United States,* vol. 5, 4th Cong., 1st Sess., (Washington D.C.: Gales and Seaton, 1855), 535-536.

> President, by and with the advice and consent of the Senate, provided two-thirds of the Senators present concur and that every Treaty so made, and promulgated, thenceforward becomes the law of the land. It is thus that the Treaty-making power has been understood by foreign nations, and in all the Treaties made with them, *we* have declared, and *they* have believed, that when ratified by the President, with the advice and consent of the Senate, they become obligatory. In this construction of the Constitution, every House of Representatives has heretofore acquiesced; for until now, without controverting the obligation of such Treaties, they have made all the requisite provisions for carrying them into effect.[7]

After receiving Washington's denial of their request, the question in the House became how, or even if, they should respond to it. It was pointed out that if no statement indicating their disagreement was entered in the House Journal along with Washington's message, it would appear to their constituents, and also to future Congresses, that Washington's message had caused them to change their opinion, and that they were in full agreement that they should in every case, no matter how harmful they thought it might be to the American people, submit to the Executive and pass all laws necessary to execute every treaty. The following is from James Madison's speech in favor of considering and voting on a proposed resolution to be entered in the House Journal.

> On the whole, it appeared that the rights of the House on the two great Constitutional points had been denied by a high authority in the Message before the Committee. This Message was entered on the Journals of the House. If nothing was entered in opposition thereto, it would be inferred that the reasons in the Message had changed the opinion of the House, and that their claims on those great points were relinquished. It was proper, therefore, that the questions, brought fairly before the Committee in the propositions of

7. *The Debates and Proceedings in the Congress of the United States,* vol. 5, 4th Cong., 1st Sess., (Washington D.C.: Gales and Seaton, 1855), 761.

> the gentleman [Mr. Blount] from North Carolina, should be examined and formally decided. If the reasoning of the Message should be deemed satisfactory, it would be the duty of this branch of the Government to reject the propositions, and thus accede to the doctrines asserted by the Executive. If, on the other hand, this reasoning should not be satisfactory, it would be equally the duty of the House, in some such firm, but very decent terms, as are proposed, to enter their opinions on record.[8]

The majority of the House agreed with Madison that an official statement for the record was necessary, and the following resolution was passed on April 7, 1796.

> Resolved, That, it being declared by the second section of the second article of the Constitution, "That the President shall have power, by and with the advice and consent of the Senate, to make treaties, provided two-thirds of the Senators present concur," the House of Representatives do not claim any agency in making treaties; but that when a Treaty stipulates regulations on any of the subjects submitted by the Constitution to the power of Congress, it must depend for its execution, as to such stipulations, on a law or laws to be passed by Congress. And it is the constitutional right and duty of the House of Representatives, in all such cases, to deliberate on the expediency or inexpediency of carrying such Treaty into effect, and to determine and act thereon, as, in their judgment, may be most conducive to the public good.[9]

It is clear from the debate over the Jay Treaty that the 1796 House of Representatives in no way considered itself to have the right to object to a treaty, unless it contained something so harmful to the American people that they felt justified in encroaching on the power

8. *The Debates and Proceedings in the Congress of the United States,* vol. 5, 4th Cong., 1st Sess., (Washington D.C.: Gales and Seaton, 1855), 4th Congress, 1st Session, 781.

9. *Journal of the House of Representatives of the United States, 1793-1797,* vol. 2, 4th Cong., 1st Sess., (Washington D.C.: Gales and Seaton, 1826), 499.

of another branch of the government. This makes it just plain silly to imply, as Robert Cord and Daniel Dreisbach do, that the Congress of 1803 could possibly have imagined itself to have the right to refuse to appropriate the funds for the religious provisions in the Kaskaskia treaty. These provisions would have absolutely no effect on the American people. A few hundred dollars towards building a church and supporting an Indian tribe's priest wasn't even close to Abraham Baldwin's extreme example of the *"introduction of an established religion from a foreign country."*

Something to note about Cord's and Dreisbach's other argument, that the religious provisions in the Kaskaskia treaty could have been avoided by not specifying what the money was for, is that this is exactly what Congress ended up doing anyway. This wasn't because they thought there was anything unconstitutional about these provisions, but because, at this time, the purpose of the funds for Indian treaties was almost never specified in an appropriations bill. The early Congresses simply added up the payments due for the annuities and other provisions from all the treaties and included enough money to cover them in the annual appropriations bills for the expenses of the government. This lump sum was included in the appropriation for the Department of War, with no description other than it being the part of this appropriation designated for the Indian Department.

Daniel Dreisbach ends his story about the Kaskaskia treaty with the following sentence: "It is significant that Jefferson did not register any doubts about this treaty violating the No Establishment clause."

There is nothing significant about this at all. Jefferson knew for sure that this treaty didn't violate anything. The provisions in the Kaskaskia treaty fell into the category of *"those acts which are by the Constitution prohibited to Congress, but not prohibited to the makers of Treaties,"* as Abraham Baldwin put it in the Jay Treaty debate.

Jefferson, who had a great deal of confidence in the ability of the American people to understand the Constitution, no doubt assumed that the people understood the treaty making process, and would not perceive these provisions as unconstitutional. In the first draft of his 1803 annual message, he described the Kaskaskia treaty in detail, including the provisions for the church and the priest. But, Secretary of State James Madison, when he read Jefferson's draft, wasn't quite so confident that the people would understand this. He had been in the House of Representatives in 1796 when it received the petitions from people who assumed that Congress had a power that it did not have, and certainly remembered that even the House itself debated the various aspects of the treaty power for weeks. Madison advised Jefferson to limit his description of the treaty to the large land acquisition and omit the details of the religious provisions, which in the final speech became *"other articles of their choice."*

> May it not be as well to omit the detail of the stipulated considerations, and particularly that of the Roman Catholic Pastor. The jealousy of some may see in it a principle, not according with the exemption of Religion from Civil power. In the Indian Treaty it will be less noticed than in a President's speech.[10]

Like Robert Cord, Chief Justice William Rehnquist made no distinction between an appropriation for a treaty provision and a regular appropriation by Congress, using the Kaskaskia treaty as an example of an appropriation by Congress for sectarian Indian education.

> **According to Justice Rehnquist, in his dissenting opinion, Wallace v. Jaffree, 1985: "As the United States moved from the 18th into the 19th century, Congress appropriated time and again public moneys in support of sectarian Indian education carried on by religious organizations. Typical of these was Jefferson's treaty with the Kaskaskia Indians, which provided annual cash support for the Tribe's Roman Catholic priest and church."**

The religious provisions in the Kaskaskia treaty weren't even typical of Indian treaty provisions, let alone typical of, or even an exam-

10. James Madison to Thomas Jefferson, October 1, 1803, James Morton Smith, ed., *The Republic of Letters: The Correspondence Between Thomas Jefferson and James Madison 1776-1826,* vol. 2, (New York and London: W.W. Norton & Company, 1995), 1298.

ple of, an appropriation by Congress for sectarian Indian education. Out of the hundreds of Indian treaties made during the first fifty years following the ratification of the First Amendment, only nine, including the Kaskaskia treaty, contained provisions related in any way whatsoever to religion. Several of these were nothing more than provisions compensating missionaries for the churches and other buildings they lost when Indian land was ceded. Only four of the nine, including the Kaskaskia treaty, contained an explicit provision for the building of a church or the salary of a religious teacher. The other three were a 1794 treaty with the Oneida and other tribes, an 1830 treaty with the Chickasaw, and an 1832 treaty with the Kickapoo.

The 1794 treaty with the Oneida and other tribes included a provision to build a church. This was to replace a church that the British had burnt down when these tribes sided with the Americans during the Revolutionary War. The 1830 Chickasaw treaty provided for two houses of worship and the salary of religious teachers. The 1832 Kickapoo treaty provided a lump sum of money to build both a mill and a church. One other treaty, an 1836 treaty with the Ottawa and Chippewa, provided for a less specific annuity for missions, along with monetary compensation for any church and mission buildings that fell within the land cession.

In this same fifty year period, only one treaty provided direct funding to schools run by a religious organization. This was an 1827 treaty with the Creeks, which provided funding for the tribe's three existing schools, which had been established by missionaries. Other tribes did use money obtained through treaties for sectarian schools, but this came from tribal education funds and annuities. Treaties with tribes that did not already have schools usually included provisions to create education funds by investing the proceeds from the sale of a reserved section of the ceded land. The money from these education funds, as well as annuities for education, belonged to the Indians and could be used as they wished to educate their children, including educating them in religious schools.

The remaining three of the nine are used by Robert Cord in a section of his book called *"Direct Support of Religion by Treaties."*

According to Robert Cord: "President James Monroe, Madison's former Secretary of State, in a treaty with

> **the Wyandots and other Indian tribes, because of their attachment to the 'Catholic religion,' granted United States land—by the terms of Article I of that treaty—'*to the rector of the Catholick church of St. Anne* of Detroit, for the use of the said church, and to the corporation of the college at Detroit, for the use of the said college, to be retained or sold, *as the said rector* and corporation may judge expedient, each, one half of three sections of land, to contain *six hundred and forty acres,...*"**

First of all, it was not James Monroe who granted this land to the Catholic church. Monroe signed the treaty, but the land was actually granted by three Indian tribes out of land reserved to them in an earlier treaty. Cord omits the beginning of the sentence because it shows that this land was being granted by the Indians, and the end of the sentence because it shows that it was the Indians who gave the authorization to the Superintendent of Indian Affairs to select land for this purpose. The following are the omitted parts of the sentence.

> Some of the Ottawa, Chippewa, and Potawatomy tribes, being attached to the Catholick religion, and believing they may wish some of their children hereafter educated, do grant to the rector of the Catholick church of St. Anne of Detroit...
>
> ...the superintendent of Indian affairs, in the territory of Michigan, is authorized, on the part of the said Indians, to select the said tracts of land.[11]

This land had to be granted in a treaty for two reasons. One was a 1793 law which made any grant or sale of land within the boundaries of the United States by an Indian nation invalid if it was not done by treaty, regardless of whatever claim the Indians had to the land. The other was that the land was being granted by only three of

11. Richard Peters, ed., *The Public Statutes at Large of the United States of America,* vol. 7, (Boston: Charles C. Little and James Brown, 1846), 166.

the four tribes that it was reserved to in the earlier treaty, so the consent of the fourth tribe was necessary.

> **According to Cord: "Van Buren's treaty with the Oneida in 1838 called not only for 'the erection of a church' but also for a 'parsonage house.'"**

This treaty did not *call for* the erection of a church or a parsonage house. It put a limit on how much of the money from the treaty could be spent on these buildings, and whose part of the money this had to come out of. There were two groups of Oneida Indians involved in this treaty, the *First Christian* party, who were Episcopalians, and the *Orchard* party, who were Methodists. It was only the Episcopalian Oneida who wanted to use money from the treaty to build a church, so the treaty stated that this had to be paid for out of their part of the money. The limit put on the amount that could be spent on the church was to ensure that enough money would be left to pay all of the members of the First Christian party who had individual claims to part of this money. The following is from Article 3 of the treaty.

> In consideration of the cession contained in the 1st article of this treaty, the United States agree to pay to the Orchard party of the Oneida Indians three thousand (3000) dollars, and to the First Christian party of Oneida Indians thirty thousand five hundred (30,500) dollars, of which last sum three thousand (3,000) dollars may be expended under the supervision of the Rev. Solomon Davis, in the erection of a church and parsonage house, and the residue apportioned, under the direction of the President among the persons having just claims thereto; it being understood that said aggregate sum of thirty-three thousand five hundred (33,500) dollars is designed to be in reimbursement of monies expended by said Indians and in remuneration of the services of their chiefs and agents in purchasing and securing a title to the land ceded in the 1st article.[12]

12. Richard Peters, ed., *The Public Statutes at Large of the United States of America*, vol. 7, (Boston: Charles C. Little and James Brown, 1846), 567.

According to Cord: "...President John Quincy Adams, Monroe's former Secretary of State, in a treaty with the Osages and other tribes—proclaimed on December 30, 1825—provided for a 'Missionary establishment' on ceded United States land, to teach, civilize, and improve the Indians."

The following is Article 10 of the Osage treaty, which Cord does include in his book.

> It is furthermore agreed on, by and between the parties to these presents, that there shall be reserved two sections of land, to include the Harmony Missionary establishment, and their mill, on the Marias des Cygne; and one section, to include the Missionary establishment, above the Lick on the West side of Grand river, to be disposed of as the President of the United States shall direct, for the benefit of said Missions, and to establish them at the principal villages of the Great and Little Osage Nations, within the limits of the country reserved to them by this Treaty, and to be kept up at said villages, so long as said Missions shall be usefully employed in teaching, civilizing, and improving, the said Indians.[13]

Cord's wording that this treaty *"provided for a 'Missionary establishment' on ceded United States land"* is very misleading, and the sentence from the treaty itself is just confusing enough for Cord to include without being concerned that it doesn't actually mean what he says it means. A mission was not being established on ceded United States land. An established mission existed on the land that the Osages were ceding to the United States, and the government agreed to *re*-establish the mission on the land reserved in this treaty if the missionaries wanted to relocate with the Indians.

The mission referred to in the Osage treaty was the Harmony Mission, established in Missouri by the United Foreign Missionary Society of New York in 1821. By 1825, this mission was a settlement

13. Richard Peters, ed., *The Public Statutes at Large of the United States of America*, vol. 7, (Boston: Charles C. Little and James Brown, 1846), 242-243.

with quite a few buildings and a mill. In addition to ministers and school teachers, Harmony Mission included a physician, blacksmith, carpenter, shoemaker, several farmers, and their families. The treaty provision guaranteed that the missionaries would be compensated for their buildings, regardless of what they decided to do after the Osages ceded their land.

The first part of the provision, ending where it states that the land would *"be disposed of as the President of the United States shall direct, for the benefit of said Missions,"* meant that a portion of the proceeds from the sale of a reserved section of the ceded land would be used to compensate the missionaries for the loss of their buildings. This did not depend on anything else that followed it, and would be done even if the missionaries did not choose to reestablish their mission on the new Osage reservation. The rest of the provision is contingent upon the missionaries relocating with the Indians. If they decided to do this, the government would *"establish them at the principal villages of the Great and Little Osage Nations."* The money expended by the government to do this would obviously have been considered as payment towards any compensation owed to the missionaries for their buildings.

The last part of the provision is also conditional. The mission would *"be kept up at said villages, so long as said Missions shall be usefully employed in teaching, civilizing, and improving, the said Indians."* Since the provision stated that the funding to keep up the mission had to come from the proceeds of a single land sale, but that this funding would be for an indefinite length of time, the government clearly intended to create an education fund like those described earlier. If the mission was reestablished, it would be maintained with the interest from this fund, but only if it continued to operate a school.

From the time it was established in 1821, until the time of the 1825 treaty, the Harmony Mission had made little progress in educating the Osages. At one point the school had over fifty students, but most only attended sporadically. The missionaries had also been completely unsuccessful in converting these Indians to Christianity. The following was written by Rev. Benton Pixley, after seven years of trying to convert the Osages. Pixley, who was one of the original missionaries at the Harmony Mission in 1821, and also helped establish a second Osage mission in Kansas in 1824, wrote the following in 1828.

> When I tell them I came to teach them the word of God, they sometimes sneeringly ask, "Where is God? Have you seen him?" – and then laugh that I should think of making them believe a thing so incredible, as a being who sees and takes knowledge of them, while they cannot see him. They indeed call the earth, the sun and moon, thunder and lightning, God; but their conceptions on this subject are altogether indefinite and confused. Some old men, who are more given to seriousness and reflection, frankly declare that they know nothing about God – what he is, or where he is, or what he would have them do.
>
> They speak of him as hateful and bad, instead of being amiable and good. They often say, "They hate him; he is of a bad temper; they would shoot him, if they could see him."[14]

Because the Harmony Mission had not been successful, the missionaries decided not to relocate with the Osages. Some of them left right away for the Kansas mission, others left over the next few years, and the mission was finally closed in 1836 when the government began surveying and selling the public lands in Missouri. The remaining missionaries, of course, had no right to this land, and would have been forced to leave as soon as the government decided to use or sell it.

In the end, the reserved land was kept for government use, and the mission was paid $8,000 for its buildings. In 1838, Harmony Mission was renamed Batesville for Missouri's second governor, Frederick Bates, and the Batesville Post Office was opened. From 1841 to 1847, the mission buildings were used as a temporary county seat for the newly formed Bates County. The land itself was valued at $69,000. Since the intent of reserving this land had been the education of the Osages, this $69,000 was invested to create an education fund for them.

As already mentioned, the 1836 treaty with the Ottawa and

14. *Missionary Herald,* Boston, Vol. 24, March 1828, 80.

Chippewa also provided for compensation to a mission for its buildings.

> If the church on the Cheboigan, should fall within this cession, the value shall be paid to the band owning it. The net proceeds of the sale of the one hundred and sixty acres of land, upon the Grand River upon which the missionary society have erected their buildings, shall be paid to the said society, in lieu of the value of their said improvements.[15]

Unlike the confusing provision in the Osage treaty, this provision is spelled out too clearly to twist or selectively quote, so none of the Liars for Jesus mention it in their books.

To give the impression that new appropriations for sectarian Indian education were regularly made and steadily increased throughout the 1800s, Justice Rehnquist began his lie with an example from the beginning of the century, the 1803 Kaskaskia treaty, and ended with a misleading statement about the end of the century.

> **According to Justice Rehnquist: "It was not until 1897, when aid to sectarian education for Indians had reached $500,000 annually, that Congress decided thereafter to cease appropriating money for education in sectarian schools."**

Annual appropriations for Indian education, sectarian and secular combined, did not reach anything even close to $500,000 until the 1880s, long after anyone who could be considered a founder was out of the picture. The only appropriation made for Indian education by any of the early Congresses was in *An Act making provision for the civilization of the Indian tribes adjoining the frontier settlements,* passed in 1819. This appropriation was for $10,000 annually, an amount that did not change for over fifty years. And, it was not, as

15. Richard Peters, ed., *The Public Statutes at Large of the United States of America,* vol. 7, (Boston: Charles C. Little and James Brown, 1846), 494, 497.

This article was amended by the Senate prior to ratification. The original article appears in the treaty on page 494. "The Mission establishments on the Grand River shall be appraised and the value paid to the proper board." The amendment, paying the society the value of the land in lieu of the value of the buildings, appears on page 497.

Justice Rehnquist implied, the amount of money that caused Congress to discontinue the appropriations in the 1890s. They were discontinued because of a sectarian battle for control of the funding.

The following is the 1819 *Act making provision for the civilization of the Indian tribes adjoining the frontier settlements.* No further appropriations were made for Indian education until 1870.

> *Be it enacted by the Senate and House of Representatives of the United States of America in Congress assembled,* That for the purpose of providing against further decline and final extinction of the Indian tribes, adjoining the frontier settlements of the United States, and for introducing among them the habits and arts of civilization, the President of the United States shall be, and he is hereby authorized, in every case where he shall judge improvements in the habits and condition of such Indians practicable, and that the means of instruction can be introduced with their own consent, to employ capable persons of good moral character, to instruct them in the mode of agriculture suited to their situation; and for teaching their children in reading, writing, and arithmetic, and in performing other such duties as may be enjoined, according to such instructions and rules as the President may give and prescribe for the regulation of their conduct, in the discharge of their duties.
>
> SEC. 2. *And be it further enacted,* That the annual sum of ten thousand dollars, and the same is hereby appropriated, for the purpose of carrying into effect the provisions of this act; and an account of the expenditure of the money, and proceedings in execution of the foregoing provisions, shall be laid annually before Congress.[16]

Funding under this act did go to Indian schools run by missionary societies, but only as a means of accomplishing the object of the act – instructing the Indians in agriculture. Only those schools that provided agriculture education could apply for this money.

16. Richard Peters, ed., *The Public Statutes at Large of the United States of America,* vol. 3, (Boston: Charles C. Little and James Brown, 1846), 516-517.

$10,000 a year was not enough money to establish even a few public schools for the Indians. To put this in perspective, in a report listing the twenty-one Indian schools receiving a portion of this money in 1823, one school, established in 1822 with sixty-six students, had annual expenses totalling over $15,000. Two schools established about five years earlier, each with around eighty students, had expenses of over $7,000 and $9,000. The only way that a $10,000 appropriation could be put to any good use was to cooperate with existing schools, and the only schools that existed at the time were mission schools. President Monroe had the Department of War send a circular to the missionary societies that were already running Indian schools, and those that were in the process of raising money to establish new ones. The circular informed these societies that they could apply for a portion of this funding, but only under certain conditions. One condition, as already mentioned, was that the school's curriculum include instruction in agriculture, as well as reading, writing, and arithmetic. The other was that the schools had to be in Indian territory. The ultimate goal of promoting agriculture education was to encourage the Indians, particularly those closest to the white settlers on the frontier, to stop wandering by turning them into farmers rather than hunters.

Obviously, since these schools were outside the boundaries of the United States, the students were not American citizens, the teachers were not employees of the government, and the object of the act was completely secular, nobody saw these grants as a violation of the First Amendment. In addition to this, the act required that the *means* of instruction, which would be a mission school, could only be introduced with the Indians' consent.

The following, from the circular sent to the missionary societies by the Department of War on September 3, 1819, clearly stated that this grant money was to be used *"to effect the object contemplated by the act of Congress."*

> In order to render the sum of $10,000 annually appropriated at the last session of Congress for the civilization of the Indians, as extensively beneficial as possible, the President is of the opinion that it ought to be applied in co-operation with the exertions of the benevolent societies, or individuals, who may choose to devote their time or means to effect the object

> contemplated by the act of Congress. But it will be indispensable, in order to apply any of the sum appropriated in the manner proposed, that the plan of education, in addition to reading, writing, and arithmetic, should, in the instruction of the boys, extend to the practical knowledge of the mode of agriculture, and such of the mechanic arts as are suited to the condition of the Indians; and in that of the girls, to spinning, weaving, and sewing. It is also indispensable that the establishment should be fixed within the limits of those Indian nations who border on our settlements. Such associations or individuals who are already actually engaged in educating the Indians, and who may desire the co-operation of the government, will report to the Department of War, to be laid before the president, the location of the institutions under their superintendence, their funds, the number and kind of teachers, the number of youths of both sexes, the objects which are actually embraced in their plan of education, and the extent of the aid which they require; and such institutions as are formed, but have not gone into actual operation, will report the extent of their funds, the places at which they intend to make their establishments, the whole number of youths of both sexes which they intend to educate, the number and kind of teachers to be employed, the plan of education adopted, and the extent of the aid required.[17]

In 1824, the House of Representatives considered repealing the 1819 appropriation act, and referred the issue to the Committee on Indian Affairs. The committee recommended that the appropriation be continued for the following reasons – the schools receiving the grants were complying with the condition of teaching agriculture, and the goal of getting the Indians to settle down on farms was gradually being accomplished because of this.

> All the schools are increasing; and so urgent is the wish of the Indians to have their children educated, that numerous applications are refused, from the limited means which the

17. *American State Papers: Indian Affairs*, vol. 2, (Washington D.C.: Gales and Seaton, 1834), 201.

> schools possess. The time of the children is not wholly devoted to their books while at school; the girls are instructed in such arts as are suited to female industry in civilized life, and the boys are required to devote a part of their time in acquiring a knowledge of husbandry. The advances of males and females in these branches are most satisfactory, and have already had no small influence in inducing their parents to become less fond of an erratic life, and more inclined to have fixed residences, and rely for their support on the cultivation of the ground. Such has been the effect of the above circumstances, combined with some others not more influential, that, at many of the places where schools have been established, the Indians have already constructed comfortable dwellings, and now cultivate farms of considerable extent. They have become the owners of property necessary to agricultural pursuits, and for the convenience of life.[18]

The committee also concluded that the reason for the failure of most Indian missions was that they only taught religion, while ignoring general education and instruction in agriculture.

> The attempts which have heretofore been made, many of which have failed, omitted this essential part. Many zealous but enthusiastic persons, who have been most conspicuous in endeavoring to reclaim the Indians, persuaded themselves to believe that, to secure this object, it was only necessary to send missionaries among them to instruct them in the Christian religion. Some of their exertions failed, without producing any salutary effect, because the agents employed were wholly unfitted for the task. Others, though productive of some good effect at first, eventually failed, because to their missionary labors were not added the institutes of education and instruction in agriculture.[19]

The government grants to individual mission schools were small,

18. *American State Papers: Indian Affairs,* vol. 2, (Washington D.C.: Gales and Seaton, 1834), 458.
19. *ibid.*

some schools receiving as little as $50 a year. To the missionary societies, however, the amount of the grants was unimportant. They knew that any appropriation for Indian education would spark an increase in private donations to their schools. People who considered efforts to educate the Indians frivolous might reconsider this if they saw that the government was taking it seriously enough to provide funding for it. In their 1824 report, the Indian Affairs Committee reported that private donations to Indian missions had, in fact, increased dramatically as a result of the appropriation. The committee's only interest in this was whether these donations were aiding or undermining the goals of the appropriation act. In other words, Congress did not want the appropriations to encourage donations to missions whose only goal was to spread religion. The committee, however, found no signs that this was happening.

> No fanciful schemes of proselytism seem to have been indulged. They formed a correct estimate of the importance of their undertaking, and pointed to the most judicious means for the accomplishment of their wishes. Since the passage of the law, hundreds and thousands have been encouraged to contribute their mite in aid of the wise policy of the government. However the various denominations of Christians may differ in their creeds and general doctrines, they all unite in their wishes that our Indians may become civilized. That this feeling almost universally prevails, has been declared in language too unequivocal to admit of doubt. It has been seen in their words and in their actions.
>
> The committee believe that such demonstrations are not to be regarded lightly; that the National Legislature will treat them with the highest respect. If a sectarian zeal had had any agency to produce this general interest, it would be less entitled to serious consideration.[20]

As described in the previous chapter, a common tactic of the Liars for Jesus is to take one action of the government, which is usually a

20. *American State Papers: Indian Affairs,* vol. 2, (Washington D.C.: Gales and Seaton, 1834), 458-459.

half-truth to begin with, and imply that this one action is representative of many similar actions. Justice Rehnquist, of course, did this in his Wallace v. Jaffree dissent by claiming that *"Congress appropriated **time and again** public moneys in support of sectarian Indian education,"* using the word *"typical,"* and indicating a long span of time – *"As the United States moved from the 18th into the 19th century,"* and then *"It was not until 1897..."*

Robert Cord, using this same tactic, also creates an extremely misleading statement about appropriations for Indian education.

> **According to Cord: "...under the guise of bringing 'Civilization to the Indians,' many United States Congresses and Presidents provided hundreds of thousands of dollars of federal money, for more than a century, to support ministers of many religions, missionaries, and religious schools which, I am sure none would dispute, might have taught 'just a bit' of religion along with reading, writing, and Western culture."**

Cord follows this with several reports from the 1820s about the expenditure of funds from the act of 1819, and page after page of the charts that were included with these reports. Nine of these pages are charts showing what portion of the $10,000 appropriation went to each of the mission schools in two different years. Cord just leaves out one small detail in this part of his book. He neglects to reveal, in this chapter titled *"Revelations,"* that these charts had anything to do with the appropriation act of 1819. Without this part of the story, it would appear to anyone looking at these charts that forty different religious schools were granted money by a whole bunch of individual acts, rather than these schools each receiving a portion of the single $10,000 appropriation. And, of course, since the act of 1819 was for an annual appropriation, this money was appropriated every year until this appropriation was repealed in 1873. Without knowing this, the charts and reports from several different years imply that new acts were passed year after year to fund these religious schools.

Because Cord neglects to mention the act of 1819, the purpose of this act and the conditions for receiving the funding are, of course, also omitted. Agriculture instruction is mentioned nowhere in Cord's description of what this money was used for. According to Cord, it was used *"to support ministers of many religions, missionaries, and religious schools which, I am sure none would dispute, might have taught 'just a bit' of religion along with reading, writing, and Western culture."* Cord also exaggerates a bit for the time frame element of his story. He claims that money was provided to sectarian schools *"for more than a century."* The first appropriation for Indian education was the act of 1819. The last appropriation for any sectarian school was in 1899. That's only eighty years in which it was even possible for any funding to go to sectarian schools.

Cord eventually gets around to mentioning the appropriation act of 1819 – in another chapter of his book, and not in any way that would connect it to the nine pages of charts of mission schools that received the funding. In fact, by selectively quoting a footnote from the 1908 Supreme Court case, *Reuben Quick Bear v. Leupp, Commissioner of Indian Affairs,* he deliberately separates the 1819 act from the schools funded by it in 1820, even while mentioning both within the same paragraph.

> **According to Cord, referring to Justice Rutledge's dissent in Everson v. Board of Education, 1947: "Justice Rutledge does not mention, for example, that the footnotes in the *Reuben Quick Bear* Case indicate that 'Catholic mission schools were erected at the cost of charitable Catholics' and with the approval of the United States Government and, that to aid these schools under an 'Act of 1819, ten thousand dollars was appropriated for the purpose of extending financial help' to those engaged in these enterprises to help educate and civilize the Indians through the work of religious organizations. Neither does Justice Rutledge mention the *Quick Bear* footnote indicating that in 'In 1820, twenty-one schools conducted by *different religious societies* were given $11,838 by the United States government and from that date until 1870 the principal educational work in relation to the Indians was under the auspices of these bodies' with financial aid by the national government."**

In his first sentence, Cord uses the phrases *"to aid **these** schools"* and *"engaged in **these** enterprises,"* giving the impression that there was an act in 1819 that appropriated $10,000 separately and specifically for these Catholic mission schools, rather than that these schools were among the many schools to receive a portion of the single $10,000 appropriation. In his second sentence, taking another part of the *same* footnote from *Quick Bear,* he says twenty-one schools were given $11,838, misquoting this in a way that hides the fact that these were actually the schools receiving money from the 1819 appropriation. Cord is aided in his deception by the fact that, in 1820, the amount paid out exceeded the $10,000 appropriation. The extra $1,138 was just money left over from the $10,000 appropriated for 1819. Little of the funding was actually used in 1819, so the balance was carried over into 1820 and 1821. Congress did not appropriate anything above the usual $10,000 for 1820, and some members even objected to applying unused funds from one year in another.

The following are the actual sentences from the *Quick Bear* footnote.

> 12. The Catholic missions schools were erected many years ago at the cost of charitable Catholics, and with the approval of the authorities of the government of the United States, whose policy it was then of encourage [sic] the education and civilization of the Indians through the work of religious organizations. Under the provisions of the act of 1819, ten thousand dollars ($10,000) were appropriated for the purpose of extending financial help 'to such associations or individuals who are already engaged in educating the Indians,' as may be approved by the War Department.
>
> In 1820, twenty-one schools conducted by different religious societies were given eleven thousand eight hundred and thirty-eight dollars ($11,838), and from that date until 1870 the principal educational work in relation to the Indians was under the auspices of those bodies, aided more or less by the government.[21]

21. Reuben Quick Bear v. Leupp, Commissioner of Indian Affairs, 210 U.S. 50 (1908).

Two paragraphs later, Cord again lists all of the missionary societies from the charts in his previous chapter whose schools received funding under the act of 1819, and, again, completely omits that there was any connection between this act and these schools, keeping up the impression that all of these schools received funding through individual acts.

> **According to Cord: "Rather than recognizing the historical fact that during the early years of 1824-1831 alone, the *Annual Reports of the Commissioner of Indian Affairs* document that the U.S. Government supported church schools run by the Society of the United Brethren, the American Board of Foreign Missions, the Baptist General Convention, the Hamilton Baptist Missionary Society, the Cumberland Missionary Board, the Synod of South Carolina and Georgia, the United Foreign Missionary Society, the Methodist Episcopal Church, the Western Missionary Society, the Catholic Bishop of New Orleans, the Society for Propagating the Gospel among the Indians, the Society of Jesuits, the Protestant Episcopal Church of New York, the Methodist Society and the Presbyterian Society for Propagating the Gospel..."**

After fifty-one years in which the only money appropriated for Indian education was the annual $10,000 from the act of 1819, a new appropriation of $100,000 was made in 1870. By this time, however, many tribes had their own education funds from treaties. The $100,000 appropriated in 1870 was only for those tribes that did not have any other education funds. An additional $40,000 was appropriated in 1871 for one of the five districts, or superintendencies, that the country had been divided into. These two appropriations were one-time appropriations, not an annual amount. In 1873, the $10,000 annual appropriation from 1819 was repealed.

When President Grant took office in 1869, one of his top priorities was a complete overhaul of the country's Indian policies. A big part of what was known as Grant's *"Peace Policy"* was to rid the Indian agent system of corruption. One of the causes of Indian hostilities was the widespread problem of corrupt Indian agents stealing and selling the food and other goods intended as treaty payments. The military was doing little to stop this because they knew that Grant was reducing the size of the army, and retaliation by Indians who didn't receive their treaty payments meant job security for soldiers.

Grant's plan to end this corruption can best be described as a faith-based initiative gone bad. His idea was to have missionaries who were already established among the Indians oversee the Indian agencies. The missionary societies would nominate men to fill the Indian agent and other positions within their agencies, submitting the names to the Secretary of the Interior. This plan was first tested on a small scale by putting a few of the Indian agencies under the control of the Quakers. While this experiment was going on, the rest of the agencies were turned over to the military. Once the Quaker experiment was deemed a success, a law was passed that had the effect of removing military control over the other agencies. As part of an act reducing the size of the military, army officers were made ineligible to perform the duties of any civil position, which included the position of Indian agent. This meant that any army officer who was temporarily in control of an Indian agency could only continue to act in that capacity if he resigned his commission, something no officer was likely to do. This cleared the way to put the rest of the agencies under the control of missionaries.

As soon as they began to implement this plan, Congress made a mistake that pretty much guaranteed its failure. Of the large numbers of Indians who had converted to Christianity, the majority were Catholic, and were as attached to their religion as any other Catholics. Based on the religious make-up of each tribe and the locations of the missions that already existed, thirty-eight of the seventy-three Indian agencies should have been put under the control of the Catholics. Completely disregarding this, the Board of Indian Commissioners, an advisory board appointed by Congress to oversee the program, and composed entirely of Protestants, recommended that all but seven of the agencies be assigned to Protestants. This went against President Grant's guideline that each agency be assigned to the mission already established there, but the Board of Indian Commissioners found a way to get around this. In all of the many cases in which a well established Catholic mission and a newer, competing Protestant mission existed within the same agency, they picked the Protestant one.

This whole plan, particularly considering that it involved schools, was very out of character for Grant, who, in one of his annual messages, urged Congress to pass a constitutional amendment prohibiting the teaching of any sectarian tenets in any public school in any state. The following remarks were made by Grant in an 1876 speech.

> Encourage free schools and resolve that not one dollar of the money appropriated to their support shall be appropriated to the support of any sectarian school; that neither the state or nation, nor both combined, shall support institutions of learning other than those sufficient to afford to every child in the land the opportunity of a good common-school education, unmixed with sectarian, pagan, or atheistic dogma.
>
> Leave the matter of religion to the family altar, the church, and private schools entirely supported by private contributions. Keep the church and state forever separate.[22]

Whatever the reason for Grant's inconsistency when it came to Indian schools, the result was that this part of his Peace Policy fueled an increase in Indian hostilities. Because of the sectarian favoritism of Congress and the Board of Indian Commissioners, thousands of Catholic Indian children were suddenly transferred from Catholic to Protestant schools. Complaints from parents who wanted their children in Catholic schools were completely ignored by the Indian agents, who, of course, were almost always members of whatever Protestant denomination controlled their agency. The agents were also loyal to the missionary societies because the same societies that had nominated them for their jobs also had the power to recommend their removal.

Grant's plan did little to improve the Indian agent system. The agents chosen by the religious denominations weren't much better than the old agents. Some were just as corrupt, while others were honest, but incompetent. The only good thing to come out of the new

22. *The Annals of America*, vol. 10, (Encyclopedia Britannica, 1976), 365.

system was a bit of public outrage at the government's infringement on the Indians' right to religious freedom. Prior to the Indian agencies being put under denominational control, agents assigned where there were missions of religions other than their own often interfered with and tried to undermine the work of the missionaries. In some cases, they even succeeded in driving these missions out of their agencies. Grant's plan, under which the agents were almost exclusively members of whatever denomination controlled their agency, solved this problem, but created a new problem. On a number of occasions, Catholic missionaries, attempting to visit Catholic Indians, were expelled from the grounds of Protestant agencies. When reports of these incidents began appearing in the newspapers, the government's policy of forcing Indian children into sectarian schools against their parents' wishes became widely known, and the right of the Indians to religious freedom became a big issue among the American people, Catholic and Protestant alike. Eventually, in 1881, the government ordered that all missionaries have access to all agencies.

In 1874, the Catholic church opened an office in Washington D.C. called the *Bureau of Catholic Indian Missions* to collect and disburse funds from private donations, and, more importantly, to lobby for a fair proportion of the Indian schools. At this point, Congress had not appropriated any money for Indian education since the appropriations of 1870 and 1871. For the most part, the schools were funded by private donations, and in some cases by treaty payments or tribal education funds. Not long after it opened, the Bureau of Catholic Indian Missions began lobbying for what became known as the contract school system. Under this system, the government paid a certain amount for the living expenses of each student in a contracted private school. The government had already entered into contracts with a few schools, and the Catholics immediately saw that a per capita contract system would give them an edge. Before applying for a contract, a school had to be built and students enrolled, and the Catholics had the resources to build more schools and attract more students than the other denominations.

In 1876, Congress made its first appropriation for Indian education in five years – $20,000 *"for the support of industrial schools and other educational purposes for the Indian tribes."* The part of this and subsequent appropriations that went to contract schools was intended for the room, board, and supplies of the students. An act of 1871 had made Indian tribes within the territory of the United States no longer independent nations, so students from these tribes were considered wards of the United States. Students born in Indian territory could not receive this aid. All other money to operate the contract schools – for teachers, buildings, etc. – still came from private donations, as did the living expenses of the students who didn't qualify for the government aid.

Appropriations for Indian education increased gradually over the next few years, reaching $75,000 in 1880. Over the next decade, they became much larger, going from $125,000 in 1881 to $1,300,000 in 1890. These dramatic increases, however, had little to do with the sectarian contract schools. Most of this additional funding was for the growing system of government-run schools.

Justice Rehnquist's claim that it *"was not until 1897, when aid to sectarian education for Indians had reached $500,000 annually, that Congress decided thereafter to cease appropriating money for education in sectarian schools"* was a bit off. Appropriations for sectarian contract schools peaked from 1889 and 1891, the only years in which they reached $500,000.[23] The total appropriations for contract schools exceeded $500,000 in a few other years, but not all contract schools were sectarian. These other years, however, were also prior to 1897. The last year in which the total amount appropriated was $500,000 or more was 1893. In 1897, the total appropriation was only $212,954, of which $156,754 went to sectarian schools.[24]

Religious right authors have a reason for placing the high point for sectarian contract school funding later than it actually was, usually making it 1897, sometimes 1896. This allows them to imply that this funding was discontinued because of the amount of money being spent, rather than giving the real reason, which, as already mentioned, was sectarian rivalry. The Indian appropriation acts of 1896 and 1897 both declared it to be *"the settled policy of the government to hereafter make no appropriation whatever for education in any sectarian school."* If these authors gave the real date of 1891 as the

23. These appropriations were for the fiscal years 1890, 1891, and 1892, i.e. the appropriation made in 1889 was for the fiscal year ending June 1890.

24. *Annual Reports of the Department of the Interior for the Fiscal Year Ended June 30, 1897, Report of the Commissioner of Indian Affairs,* (Washington D.C.: Government Printing Office, 1897), 15.

high point for the funding, they would need to explain why Congress suddenly found it necessary to make this new policy in 1896. By this time, sectarian school funding had already been reduced by more than forty percent from its high point in 1891. The claim that the funding was discontinued because the amount of funding had become too high doesn't make sense unless the date of the government's policy change coincides with the date that the funding was at its highest.

The amount of funding was never an issue. In fact, it cost far less for the government to pay the living expenses of a student in a contract school than it cost to keep a student in a government-run school where the government had to pay for the buildings, teachers, and everything else. Funding to sectarian contract schools ended because the Catholics started getting more of the funding than the Protestants, and the Protestants didn't like this.

Three major factors contributed to the increase in contracts to Catholic Indian schools. First, as already mentioned, the Catholics were able to build more schools than any other denomination; second, many of the Protestants lost interest in the whole business; and third, the Catholic schools were just better.

When senators and other officials visited some of the contract schools in the early 1880s, they found the Catholic schools to be far superior to the Protestant. The success of the few existing Catholic contract schools led even some of the most anti-Catholic members of Congress to support giving more contracts to the Catholics. When the 1884 Indian Appropriation Bill was under consideration in the Senate, Senator George Vest of Missouri, who had personally visited a number of the schools, described what he had seen at the Catholic schools on the Flathead Reservation.

> To-day the Flathead Indians are a hundred per cent. advanced over any other indians in point of civilization, at least in Montana. Fifty years ago the Jesuits went amongst them, and to-day you see the result. Among all those tribes, commencing with the Shoshones, the Arapahoes, the gros-Ventres, the Blackfeet, the Piegans, the river crows, the Bloods and Assiniboines, the only ray of light I saw was on the Flathead Reservation at the jesuit mission schools, and there were boys and girls – fifty boys and fifty girls. They

> raise cattle; the Indian boys herd them. They have mills; the Indian boys attend them. They have blacksmith-shops; the Indian boys work in them. When I was there they were building two school-houses, all the work done by the scholars at the mission. They can not raise corn to any extent in that climate, but they raise enough vegetables and enough oats to support the whole school, and I never saw in my life a finer herd of cattle or horses than they had at that mission.
>
> Five nuns, sisters, and five fathers constitute the teachers in the respective schools. We had a school examination there which lasted through two days. I undertake to say now that never in the States was there a better examination than I heard at that mission, of children of the same age with those I saw there. The girls are taught needlework; they are taught to sew and to teach; they are taught music; they are taught to keep house. The young men are taught to work upon the farm, to herd cattle, to be blacksmiths and carpenters and millwrights.[25]

Senator Vest went on to give some possible reasons for the success of the Catholic schools, then added the following remarks.

> I do not speak with any sort of denominational prejudice in favor of Jesuits. I was taught to abhor the whole sect; I was raised in that good Old-School Presbyterian Church that looked upon a Jesuit as very much akin to the devil; but I now say, if the senator from Massachusetts, the chairman of the Committee on Indian Affairs, will find me any tribe of 'blanket' Indians on the continent of North America – I do not speak of the five civilized tribes, because they got their civilization in Georgia and Alabama, and by immediate contact with the whites – but if he will find me a single tribe of Indians on the plains, "blanket" Indians, that approximate in civilization to the Flatheads who have been under control of the Jesuits for fifty years, I will abandon my entire theory on this

25. *The Catholic World,* Vol. 40, No. 239, February 1885, 601.

> subject. I say that out of eleven tribes that I saw – and I say this as a Protestant – where they had Protestant missionaries they had not made a single, solitary advance towards civilization, not one.[26]

Within a few years, Catholic contract schools greatly outnumbered the Protestant schools, and in 1888, the Catholics, for the first time, received more in contract payments than the Protestants. In 1889, the first of the three years in which the total amount appropriated for sectarian schools reached $500,000, the Catholics got $356,957 of the $508,600.

Beginning in 1883, representatives of the various Protestant Indian mission societies had been holding yearly conferences with the all-Protestant Board of Indian Commissioners at a Lake Mohonk, New York resort. These conferences also included various government officials and politicians, and members of anti-Catholic organizations like the Indian Rights Association. The idea of abolishing the contract school system had been discussed at these conferences since the first signs that the Catholics were pulling ahead, but those who wanted to put an end to the whole system were in the minority until the end of the 1880s.

The Protestants found plenty of things on which to blame the increase of Catholic Indian schools, but the most popular was Grover Cleveland's Democratic administration, under which more Catholics were appointed to the Indian Bureau. Most assumed that this Catholic *favoritism* would end when Republican Benjamin Harrison was elected in 1888, and that the contract school system would shift back to Protestant control. What the Protestants got from President Harrison, however, was a Commissioner of Indian Affairs who wanted to completely reform the Indian education system. The new Commissioner, Thomas Morgan, was a Baptist minister and educator who, like some of the Protestants, wanted to abolish contract schools altogether. Morgan attended the 1889 Lake Mohonk conference, where he proposed his plan, which called for a gradual replacement of the contract schools with a school system run entirely by the government. All of the Protestant groups, whether they had previously opposed contract schools or not, got behind Morgan's plan. This universal support, of

26. *The Catholic World,* Vol. 40, No. 239, February 1885, 602.

course, was only universal among the Protestants.

The Catholics, led by Father Joseph Stephan of the Bureau of Catholic Indian Missions, opposed Morgan's appointment as Commissioner, as well as that of Daniel Dorchester, a Methodist minister appointed by Harrison as Superintendent of Indian Schools. Morgan and Dorchester both opposed Catholic schools of any kind. In 1888, Dorchester had published *Romanism versus the Public School System*, and Morgan, that same year, had publicly attacked Catholic schools at a meeting of the National Education Association. Aided by the Democratic press, the Catholics unsuccessfully fought against the Senate confirmations of both men. Harrison had appointed Morgan in July 1889 during a Senate recess, giving him time to propose his plan at the Mohonk conference in October and get the support of the influential Protestant groups and the Board of Indian Commissioners before his name was sent to the Senate for confirmation in December. By this time, Morgan and Dorchester had already begun removing Catholics appointed to the Indian Bureau during the Cleveland administration, claiming that they were incompetent, or charging them with insubordination or intemperance. The Senate confirmed both Morgan and Dorchester in February 1890.

Shortly after President Harrison took office in 1889, representatives of the Protestant Indian mission societies went to Washington to meet with him and his Secretary of the Interior, John W. Noble. At this point, which was prior to Morgan's appearance at the Lake Mohonk conference, few members of these societies wanted to abolish the contract school system. Most, as already mentioned, just wanted the Protestants to get more contracts than the Catholics, and thought this would happen now that a Republican administration was in power. Since it was unlikely that any existing contracts would be taken away from the Catholics, they wanted the government to increase the number of contract schools and give the new contracts to Protestants. The recommendations made to Noble by the societies were printed in the May 1889 issue of the Congregationalist magazine *The American Missionary*. One of these recommendations was that the contract school system be expanded.

> 3. That the co-operation of the Government with the missionary societies in what are known as *Contract* schools

> should be continued and enlarged. We believe that no better teaching has been afforded to the Indians than that given in these Contract schools. The educational qualifications of the teachers, together with their disinterested and self-denying characters and their religious influence and instruction, render them pre-eminently fit for their places and successful in their work. The experience of the past and the testimony of all unprejudiced persons bear witness to this fact.[27]

A few months later, of course, at the October 1889 Mohonk conference, the leaders of these same societies agreed to support Thomas Morgan's plan, under which there would be no new contracts, and the contract schools would be gradually replaced by government schools. Rumors about Morgan's plan had been in the newspapers prior to the conference, and the leaders of the missionary societies no doubt anticipated that the decision of the conference would be to support the plan. But, they had just reported to their church memberships a few months earlier that they supported enlarging the contract school system. They couldn't just suddenly report their support of a plan that opposed this, so they began by raising some questions about the system, and slowly worked their way up to calling for an end to contract schools.

The following is how the story progressed over the next few years in *The American Missionary*, beginning with a hint in the October 1889 issue that the system *might be* unfair to Protestants.

INDIAN CONTRACT SCHOOLS.

> The public has been made aware through the press recently that the United States government aids the Roman Catholics to support 2,098 Indian pupils and assists all Protestant denominations in the support of only 1,146 pupils. Why is this discrimination, and who is to blame for it? If the Roman Catholics give for plant, teachers' salaries, etc., an amount proportionately greater than given by the Protestants, then the Protestants have themselves only to

27. *The American Missionary,* Vol. 43, No. 5, May 1889, 127.

> blame, and the difficulty can be remedied by their giving an equal amount. But if, on the other hand, the Government gives in proportion more to the Roman Catholics than it does to the Protestants, then the Government is showing a wholly unjustifiable partiality. Figures are in order on this subject. Who will furnish them?[28]

In September 1890, they began broaching the subject of withdrawing from the contract school system because of the Senate's favoritism towards Catholics.

> **SECTARIAN LEGISLATION.**
>
> The recent action of the United States Senate on the Indian Appropriation Bill presents a marked instance of denominational favoritism. In 1889, the Roman Catholics received from the government for Indian Schools $356,000 as against $204,000 for *all other denominations.*
>
> Not content with this, the Roman Catholics recently urged the appropriation of large sums to three additional schools. The Indian Bureau, anxious to avoid sectarian discussion by still farther increasing the disparity, declined to enter into contract for those schools. But the Roman Catholics maintain an active Bureau of Missions in Washington which has been constantly pushing their schools upon government support; and when the Indian office declined, this Mission bureau went to the House of Representatives and obtained the insertion of amendments granting aid to these three schools. The Senate Committee, unwilling to increase the existing preponderance of appropriations to Roman Catholic schools, struck out two of these amendments, but the Senate itself adopted them all, and the bill was passed in that form, thus granting in full the added demands of the Roman Catholics.
>
> If this is not sectarian favoritism, we know not what is. Why

28. *The American Missionary,* Vol. 43, No. 10, October 1889, 279.

> should this one denomination be aided beyond all others? Is a Roman Catholic Mission Bureau to dictate measures to the House of Representatives and dominate the Senate? We believe in "contract schools," but rather than have a foreign hierarchy rule in National legislation, we should prefer to receive no Government aid for our Indian schools. Impartial legislation is better than money.[29]

In 1892, the Methodists, Episcopalians, and Presbyterians all announced that they would no longer be accepting any government funding. The Congregationalists soon joined them, publishing the following resolutions in the December 1892 issue of *The American Missionary*.

> *Whereas,* The system known as "contract schools," in connection with Indian work, is open to very serious abuse; and
>
> *Whereas,* Government schools have now reached a position as to equipment, methods and general efficiency, where the common school education among the Indians may be safely and wisely entrusted to them; therefore
>
> *Resolved,* First, that public money expended upon the education of Indians ought to be expended exclusively by government officers upon government schools.
>
> *Resolved,* Second, that the practice of appropriating public money for the support of sectarian schools among the Indians ought henceforth to cease.
>
> *Resolved,* Third, that it is wise for the A.M.A. to join in the purpose expressed by other great ecclesiastical bodies, the Methodist General Conference, convened at Omaha, May 9th, 1892, the Presbyterian General Assembly, which met at Portland, Ore., May 23d, 1892, and the Episcopal Convention at Baltimore October 19th, 1892, to decline to seek or accept

29. *The American Missionary*, Vol. 44, No. 9, September 1890, 267-268.

> any subsidy from the government, and that henceforth this Society act in conformity with this purpose.[30]

An 1893 appeal to the Congregational churches for donations to replace the government funding gave *"obedience to the principle of separation between Church and State"* as the very noble reason that the societies were giving up this funding.

> It was felt at Hartford that a question of principle was at issue. The great Methodist, Presbyterian and Episcopal Communions had taken a stand against Government aid to denominational schools. It was felt to be time that Congregationalists took the same American position. *The Association took it,* trusting God and the churches. We gave up money for the sake of a principle. Congregationalists are not the men to repudiate that principle, or let our grand work suffer because we have taken that position. If every man will give to our A.M.A. treasury this year, one quarter more than he gave last year, our work will not suffer, and we pledge ourselves that it shall even advance in the Indian department as well as others.
>
> The emergency is peculiar and peremptory. The logic of it is decisive upon this point of special obligation. You, yourselves, brethren of the ministry and of the churches, have voiced a command by your special committees, a command for advance in the Indian work. But on the very threshold of such advance we find ourselves counseled and compelled by the action at Hartford to surrender twenty-two thousand dollars in obedience to the principle of separation between Church and State.[31]

30. *The American Missionary,* Vol. 46, No. 12, December 1892, 427.

31. *ibid.,* Vol. 47, No. 3, March 1893, 85.

Contrary to what was reported in *The American Missionary,* only the Methodists appear to have immediately *"taken a stand against Government aid,"* receiving no funding from fiscal year 1893 on, with the exception of $600 in 1896. According to the Annual Reports of the Commissioner of Indian Affairs, the Presbyterians, Episcopalians, and Congregationalists all accepted some funding for fiscal years 1893 and 1894, and the Episcopalians were still receiving a small amount in 1896. The denominations also turned a few small schools over to individuals. Although these schools only amounted to a few thousand dollars in contracts, and were no longer officially under denominational control, they were run by members of the denominations.

Congress first addressed the contract school issue in 1894, in reaction to the public opposition to contract schools stirred up by the various Protestant denominations, as well as pressure from powerful anti-Catholic organizations like the *American Protection Association,* which, by this time, had joined in with the anti-Catholic Indian organizations. In the 1894 Indian Appropriations Bill, the Secretary of the Interior was directed to study the feasibility of discontinuing the contract school system. The Secretary recommended that contract school funding be cut gradually, but by at least twenty percent a year, giving both the government and the missionary societies time to make other arrangements.

The Indian appropriation act of 1895 limited sectarian contract school funding for fiscal year ending June 1896 to eighty percent of that spent in 1895.[32] The act of 1896 limited the funding for 1897 to fifty percent of that spent in 1895, and prohibited contracts with sectarian schools where non-sectarian schools were available. The act of 1896, as already mentioned, also declared it to be *"the settled policy of the government to hereafter make no appropriation whatever for education in any sectarian school."* The act of 1897, the act cited by Justice Rehnquist, also contained this declaration, and cut funding to existing contract schools for the year 1898 to forty percent of that spent in 1895. The act of 1898 cut the funding for 1899 to thirty percent. The act of 1899 cut it to fifteen percent, and stated that this appropriation, for the year 1900, was *"the final appropriation for sectarian schools."*

Although these acts applied only to public appropriations, the Commissioner of Indian Affairs also prohibited the use of tribal funds for sectarian schools. The only exception made was for the Osages, whose contracts with Catholic schools had always been paid from their tribal funds, and who specifically petitioned for these payments to continue.

The government's goal was to get all Indian children into government schools, and cutting off public appropriations alone was not going to accomplish this. The Catholics, in particular, were determined to keep their schools open, and were capable of doing this

32. The 1895 amount on which these funding cuts were based was $398,815. This was the amount appropriated for sectarian schools for that year, not the total amount for all contract schools, which was $463,505. Payments to non-sectarian contract schools, and contracts paid with tribal funds rather than public appropriations, were not included.

through private donations. The Bureau of Catholic Indian Missions determined that a minimum of $140,000 a year was needed to replace the contract funding. Some of this was raised through special collections and donations from various organizations, but most of it came from one individual. Katharine Drexel, founder of the Sisters of the Blessed Sacrament, and now a Catholic saint, made up the difference, which was usually about $100,000 a year. Over the course of her life, Katharine Drexel, daughter of a wealthy Pennsylvania businessman, gave away an inheritance of over $20 million, much of it to establish and support Indian schools. It was due in large part to her donations during the 1880s that the Catholics were able to build the schools they needed to get the government contracts.

Prohibiting the use of tribal funds for sectarian schools was only one of several measures taken to force all Indian children into government schools. In 1901, food and clothing rations, due to the Indians through treaties, were cut off to all students attending non-government schools. The most significant measure, however, was the 1896 ruling of Commissioner of Indian Affairs Daniel M. Browning that Indian parents had no right to choose which schools their children would attend. Browning contended that because the Indian children, as well as their parents, were wards of the United States, it was the government's right to decide where the children went to school. Under the Browning ruling, Indian children could only attend non-government schools if the government schools were filled to capacity.

The Bureau of Catholic Indian Missions urged President McKinley to abrogate the Browning ruling, and also to allow the use of tribal funds for sectarian schools. McKinley ordered the Browning ruling abrogated, which took effect in January 1902. All this did, however, was allow the Indians to choose their schools. The issue of using tribal funds was referred to the new Commissioner of Indian Affairs, William A. Jones, who decided against it.

In 1904, the Bureau of Catholic Indian Missions brought the tribal fund issue to the attention of President Roosevelt, who referred the matter to the Department of Justice. The following is from an executive order issued by Roosevelt on February 3, 1905.

> This new request was submitted to the Department of Justice, and the Department decided, as set forth in the

> accompanying report, that the prohibition of the law as to the use of public moneys for sectarian schools did not extend to moneys belonging to the Indians themselves, and not to the public, and that these moneys belonging to the Indians themselves might be applied in accordance with the desire of the Indians for the support of the schools to which they were sending their children. There was, in my judgment, no question that, inasmuch as the legal authority existed to grant the request of the Indians, they were entitled, as a matter of moral right, to have the moneys coming to them used for the education of their children at the schools of their choice....[33]

Roosevelt's order required that the funds be properly petitioned for by members of the tribe, and that the amount for any one school could not exceed the proportion of the tribe's funds that petitioners for that school were entitled to. Based on this executive order, the next Commissioner of Indian Affairs, Francis Leupp, began making contracts with mission schools for the following year.

The Protestants, of course, were not happy about the return of contract schools. The Catholics had managed to keep nearly all of their schools open after the appropriations were stopped, and even non-Catholic Indians preferred these schools to those run by the government. Treaty rations for students in non-government schools had been restored in 1904, so this deterrent was also gone. Francis Leupp made nine contracts with sectarian schools in 1905 – eight with Catholic schools, two of which were the Osage schools that were already using their tribal funds, and one with a Lutheran school.

Protestant missionaries from the agencies where these schools were located immediately began urging the Indian Rights Association to do something to get the contracts cancelled. The missionaries were advised to seek out Protestant members of the tribes whose funds were being used, and get as many of them as possible to write letters and petitions protesting the contracts. Meanwhile, the Indian Rights Association contacted the various missionary societies, asking that they write to President Roosevelt and the Secretary of the Interior, and launched a campaign in the press to stir up public opposition.

33. Reuben Quick Bear v. Leupp, Commissioner of Indian Affairs, 210 U.S. 50 (1908).

None of this was successful. Roosevelt responded to the few letters he received by politely replying that letters on the subject should be sent to the Commissioner of Indian Affairs. The Department of the Interior responded by telling the Protestant missionary societies that they could also apply for contracts.

Eventually, the Indian Rights Association decided to challenge the contracts in the courts. In order to do this, however, they needed a plaintiff. They chose Reuben Quick Bear, who, along with other Protestant members of the Sioux tribe at the Rosebud Agency in South Dakota, had written a letter objecting to the contract with the St. Francis Mission Boarding School. Quick Bear was chosen by the Indian Rights Association mainly because his letter was addressed to them, and appealed specifically to them for help. In order to be able to dismiss accusations of being anti-Catholic, the Indian Rights Association needed some other reason to explain their involvement in the case. Quick Bear's solicitation of their help gave them their reason.

The 1908 case of *Reuben Quick Bear v. Leupp* involved both tribal fund payments and treaty payments. Tribal funds, as explained earlier in this chapter, were the education funds created by investing the proceeds from the sale of a reserved section of ceded land. Tribal fund payments were payments of the interest on these investments, and did not require an appropriation by Congress. Treaty payments, on the other hand, did require an appropriation, but were considered to be installment payments for the land ceded by the Indians, not public appropriations. In the mid-1800s, when Indian appropriations bills became more complicated than simply adding up the treaty payments due and covering them in the general appropriation for the operating expenses of the Indian department, Congress began differentiating treaty payments from public appropriations by listing them separately under a *"Fulfilling Treaty Stipulations"* heading. The court ruled in favor of Francis Leupp, deciding once and for all that tribal funds and treaty payments were not public appropriations, but were monies that belonged to the Indians, which could be used by them to educate their children in whatever schools they chose.

Although the court confirmed in *Quick Bear* that tribal funds and treaty payments were not public appropriations, religious right authors still do everything possible to imply that they were. Robert Cord, for example, calls them *"federal monies earmarked"* as trust funds, says that they *"grew out of federal treaties,"*and were *"controlled by the United States Government."*

> **According to Cord: "No court was declaring the use of these federal funds or the use of additional federal monies earmarked as 'Indian trust funds,' which grew out of federal treaties, and which supported church schools for over a century under the regime of the First Amendment, unconstitutional. Why not?"**
>
> **Cord follows this with some more questions: "Lest it be counterargued that the money belonged to the Indians pursuant to treaties, it ought to be asked: 'Can the Senate and the President violate the First Amendment by treaty although the President and entire Congress by passage of national legislation may not?' It should not go unnoticed that these "Indian Funds" were controlled by the United States Government acting through the Commissioner and the Bureau of Indian Affairs. Presumably these people were employees and agents of the United States Government. As such, were their actions not subject to the authority of the *Constitution* of the United States and its First Amendment?"**

Cord's questions, like his assertion that Congress had the power to reject the religious provisions in the 1803 Kaskaskia treaty, are just a continuation of the same blurring of the separation of powers. Again, he equates the *"Senate and the President"* when making a treaty to *"the President and entire Congress"* when passing legislation. These questions, of course, were answered in the 1796 Jay Treaty debate in the House of Representatives.

James M. O'Neill, in his 1949 book *Religion and Education Under the Constitution,* completely omitted any mention of tribal funds in his section on *Quick Bear.* The reason for this, of course, is that tribal funds did not require an appropriation by Congress. By claiming that *Quick Bear* involved only treaty payments, O'Neill was able to argue that, because these payments did require an appropriation, they *"required the Congress of the United States to pass a law about 'religion or religious institutions'"* when used for sectarian schools. Therefore, according to O'Neill, the court, by ruling that treaty payments could be used for these schools, ruled that not all laws respecting religion were necessarily unconstitutional.

O'Neill's version of the story is included here because his book, although published over half a century ago, is still used as a source by today's religious right authors, and was also one of Justice Rehnquist's sources for his Wallace v. Jaffree dissent.

> **By 1896, Congress was appropriating annually over $500,000 in support of sectarian Indian education carried on by religious organizations. This expenditure of public money appropriated by act of Congress for over a century following the ratification of the First Amendment constitutes absolute proof that for over a century neither Congress nor the religious leaders interpreted the First Amendment to mean a prohibition of the use of public funds by Congress in aid of religion and religious education.**
>
> **In 1897, Congress decided on another policy. They declared by the act of June 7, 1897 that it should be the settled policy of the government hereafter to make no appropriation whatever for education in any sectarian school. This was a declaration of policy by Congress. Whether or not a Congressional resolution can settle the policy of the government in a way to be binding on succeeding Congresses, is not a matter that should concern us here. The point is that in declaring this policy, there was no contention that Congress had been committing unconstitutional acts for the last century.**
>
> **This is clearly demonstrated by the fact that in this act declaring the change of policy, Congress provided for continuous appropriations for another three years, tapering off the appropriations to end in 1900.**

> **We have not only Congressional evidence that this was considered only a question of wisdom and expediency, and not a question of constitutionality, but the declaration of the Supreme Court of the United States in a lawsuit that grew out of the Act of 1897. This was the famous Quick Bear lawsuit, decided by the Supreme Court in 1908. It resulted from a protest against public money being paid to the Catholic board of Indian Missions. The contention was that such payments violated the declared policy of the Act of June 7, 1897. The Supreme Court ruled that the payment was not a violation of this Act because the money that was paid to the Catholic Board of Indian Missions was not tax money by 'treaty funds' which belonged to the Indians. The United States was only the custodian of the treaty funds and Congress could appropriate such funds to the Catholic Board of Indian Missions. This, of course, required Congress to pass a law about 'religion or religious institutions,' and the action would have been clearly unconstitutional under the Rutledge doctrine. The Supreme Court, however, in 1908 did not see it that way; in fact, it was not even argued that it was unconstitutional. The modern slogan [separation between church and state] had not been adopted at that time. Chief Justice Fuller speaking for the Supreme Court in handing down the decision said in regard to the action they were passing upon, 'It is not contended that it is unconstitutional, and it could not be.'"**

By setting up an appropriation of treaty funds for sectarian education as *"a law about 'religion or religious institutions,'"* and quoting Justice Fuller out of context, O'Neill made it appear that the court did not contend that *"a law about 'religion or religious institutions'"* was unconstitutional. The sentence misquoted by O'Neill appears in a paragraph in which Justice Fuller was disagreeing with one of the arguments from the Quick Bear side. In this argument, the lawyer for the Quick Bear side did not go as far as saying that this use of treaty payments was unconstitutional, but merely asserted that an 1897 declaration of Congress ending public appropriations for sectarian schools was *in the spirit of* the Constitution, and, in this same spirit, should also be applied to treaty payments. Justice Fuller, before giving his reasons why this use of treaty funds was not unconstitutional, simply acknowledged that it was never actually contended by the Quick Bear side that it was unconstitutional. The following was the context of Justice Fuller's statement.

> Some reference is made to the Constitution, in respect to this contract with the Bureau of Catholic Indian Missions. It is not contended that it is unconstitutional, and it could not be....But it is contended that the spirit of the Constitution requires that the declaration of policy that the government 'shall make no appropriation whatever for education in any sectarian schools' should be treated as applicable, on the ground that the actions of the United States were to always be undenominational, and that, therefore, the government can never act in a sectarian capacity, either in the use of its own funds or in that of the funds of others, in respect of which it is a trustee; hence, that even the Sioux trust fund cannot be applied for education in Catholic schools, even though the owners of the fund so desire it. But we cannot concede the proposition that Indians cannot be allowed to use their own money to educate their children in the schools of their own choice because the government is necessarily undenominational, as it cannot make any law respecting an establishment of religion or prohibiting the free exercise thereof.[34]

34. Reuben Quick Bear v. Leupp, Commissioner of Indian Affairs, 210 U.S. 50 (1908).

— CHAPTER FOUR —

Propagating the Gospel Among the Heathen?

As mentioned at the end of chapter two, in the companion book to the *Religion and the Founding of the American Republic* Exhibit, James H. Hutson, Chief of the Manuscript Division at the Library of Congress, follows his comments about the Northwest Ordinance with what he describes as *"a little noticed action two weeks later"* in which Congress offered *"financial support to a church."* This little noticed action, used by Hutson as an example of *"Congress's broad program to promote religion,"* was a land grant which, for reasons that had nothing to do with religion, was put in trust in the name of a society of Moravian missionaries by the Continental Congress.

> **According to Hutson: "In response to a plea from Bishop John Ettwein (1721-1802), Congress voted, July 27, 1787, that ten thousand acres on the Muskingum River in the present state of Ohio 'be set apart and the property thereof be vested in the Moravian Brethren...or a society of the said Brethren for civilizing the Indians and promoting Christianity.'"**

Hutson uses this story to *vindicate* the Continental Congress for neglecting to provide financial support for churches in the Northwest Ordinance, claiming that *"rhetorical encouragement for religion was all that was possible on that occasion."* He follows this claim with a misleading version of the Moravian land grant story, presenting this as evidence that the omission of financial support for churches in the Northwest Ordinance didn't mean that Congress was opposed to the government financially supporting them.

Because the real story of the Moravian land grant spans four decades, it is sometimes used, as by Hutson, to create lies about the Continental Congress, but it is also used for lies about later Congresses and several presidents. In the majority of religious right American history books it is used for a lie about Thomas Jefferson, and almost always follows the story about the Kaskaskia Indian treaty. This lie is based solely on the titles of certain acts signed by Jefferson. Besides the fact that none of these acts actually had anything to do with this land grant, the grant, as already mentioned, didn't even have anything to do with religion in the first place.

> **According to William Federer, in his book *America's God and Country Encyclopedia of Quotations*: "President Thomas Jefferson also extended, three times, a 1787 act of Congress in which special lands were designated:**
>
> > **For the sole use of Christian Indians and the Moravian Brethren missionaries for civilizing the Indians and promoting Christianity."**

It is unclear exactly what Federer is quoting here in his *"Encyclopedia of Quotations,"* but it is not a 1787 act of Congress. This *act,* (a resolution of the Continental Congress), can be found on page 133.

> **According to Mark Beliles, in the introduction to his version of the *Jefferson Bible*: "On April 26, 1802, Jefferson signed into law the Act of Congress which assisted the Society of the United Brethren 'for propagating the Gospel among the Heathen' in the Northwest territory."**

The first thing that needs to be understood about any mention of *The Society of the United Brethren for Propagating the Gospel Among the Heathen* in any act of Congress or other official document is that this was the legal name of an incorporated society. Every act of Congress referring to this society, whatever its purpose, contains the words *"propagating the Gospel among the Heathen"* because it was part of the society's name, not because the government was propagating the Gospel. Mark Beliles, like many Liars for Jesus, puts only the words *"propagating the Gospel among the Heathen"* in quotation marks to make it appear that this was the purpose of the act. Others take advantage of a convenient printing error to achieve this effect. In the title of one of the several acts related to this land trust, a comma was mistakenly inserted in the society's name after the word *"Brethren,"* inadvertently giving the impression that what followed the comma was the purpose of the act. This, of course, is the act that most religious right authors choose to quote.

Although the United Brethren were a religious society, and *their* purpose was to propagate the Gospel, Congress's reason for putting a land grant in their name had nothing to do with religion. It was done to protect the land granted to a group of Indians.

At the beginning of the Revolutionary War, a declaration of Congress promised that any Indians who did not aid the British would have *"all the lands they held confirmed and secured to them"*[1] when the war was over. In the years following the war, the United Brethren, concerned that a particular group of Indians, who not only remained neutral throughout the war, but had been both displaced by the British and attacked by American militiamen, might lose the lands they were entitled to. Because these Indians were unable to return at this time to claim the land themselves, the United Brethren petitioned the Continental Congress on their behalf. Congress agreed that these Indians had a right to the land, but, in order to secure their claim, the land had to be put in someone's name. The solution that Congress agreed to was that the United Brethren form an incorporated society to hold the land in trust.

The Indians involved in this story, who, for reasons explained later, were referred to by Congress as the *"Christian Indians,"* were permanently settled in 1772 by the great council of the Delaware nation on land along the Muskingum River, in what is now Ohio. With

1. Walter Lowrie, ed., *American State Papers: Indian Affairs*, vol. 2, (Washington D.C.: Gales and Seaton, 1834), 373.

the help of Moravian missionaries, these Indians, numbering about three hundred and seventy at that time, built three settlements, Gnadenhutten, Schoenbrun, and Salem, which became thriving agricultural communities.

Shortly after settling on the Muskingum, the Christian Indians adopted a constitution of sorts, laying down the rules that everyone had to follow in order to live at their settlements. In 1778, although the Delaware nation was still officially neutral in the war, many Delawares were attaching themselves to other tribes, joining the fight on the British side. That year, at their annual public meeting, the mostly Delaware Christian Indians voted to add the following articles to their constitution.

> 19. No man inclining to go to war—which is the shedding of blood—can remain among us.
>
> 20. Whosoever purchases goods or articles of warriors, *knowing* at the time that such have been stolen or plundered, must leave us. We look upon this as giving encouragement to murder and theft.[2]

Throughout the war, the Christian Indians and their Moravian missionaries, suspected of spying for the Americans, were harassed by British Indian allies. In August 1781, a group of British Indians, led by a British Indian agent, broke up their settlements. The Christian Indians were forcibly moved to Sandusky, more than a hundred miles from their settlements, and left there with no food or supplies. The Moravians were taken to Detroit for questioning. The following spring, nearly a third of the Christian Indians were murdered – not by the British, but by American militiamen.

In February 1782, some of the Christian Indians returned to their settlements to gather whatever food and supplies they could find to take back to Sandusky. Shortly after the Christian Indians returned, another band of Indians from Sandusky attacked a frontier family, killing a woman and taking her children captive. Under the guise of pursuing the Indians who attacked this family, several hundred Pennsylvania

2. James W. Taylor, *History of the State of Ohio, First Period, 1650-1787,* (Cincinnati: H.W. Derby & Co., 1854), 234-235.

militiamen,[3] commanded by Lieutenant Colonel David Williamson, headed straight for the Christian Indian settlements. Upon hearing of Williamson's plan, Colonel John Gibson, the temporary commander at Fort Pitt, immediately dispatched messengers to warn the Indians, but they arrived too late.

When Williamson and his men appeared at the settlements on March 7, the Indians, having no reason to fear Americans, believed the story that they had come to help. The militiamen told the Indians that because the British, their common enemy, had caused them to be in their current situation, they had been sent to take them to Fort Pitt to get supplies. Prior to their removal by the British, these Indians had been supplying Fort Pitt with corn and beef, so this offer of help did not seem strange at all. To keep the Indians from becoming suspicious as they were gathered into two houses in Gnadenhutten, the militiamen kept up constant discussions about religion, between themselves and with the Indians, and claimed that the Moravians from Bethlehem would be expecting them at Fort Pitt.

Once the Indians were rounded up, the men in one house and the women and children in another, the militiamen turned on them, accusing them of stealing horses, aiding the enemy, and other crimes. The officers then had their men vote on whether to kill them on the spot or take them to Fort Pitt as prisoners. All but eighteen of the several hundred militiamen voted to kill them. On March 8, ninety-six unarmed Indians – sixty-two adults and thirty-four children – were murdered. Strangely enough, Colonel Williamson, the leader of the expedition, was one of the eighteen to vote against the killing, but either did not or could not stop it.

All of the Indians who were in Salem and Gnadenhutten were killed, except for two boys who managed to escape, one by hiding, and one by playing dead until the militiamen left. Those who were at Schoenbrun, however, were able to get away. A messenger sent from Sandusky by one of the Moravians, on his way from Schoenbrun to Gnadenhutten, came across the body of an Indian boy who had been murdered the day before by the approaching militiamen. The

3. Estimates of the number of militiamen involved in the massacre have varied greatly, ranging from 70 to over 400. The first list, published in the Pennsylvania Archives in 1888, put the number at "at least 160," listing 57 by name. The actual number was probably closer to 300, about 200 of whom can currently be named with some certainty.

messenger returned to Schoenbrun to warn the others, who had been visited by the militiamen and were preparing to go to Gnadenhutten.

When the British heard about the 1782 massacre, they were appalled by the actions of the Pennsylvania militiamen. The British had driven the Christian Indians from their settlements the year before because they were suspected of spying for the Americans, and their settlements were in a strategic location to do this. Their Indian agent had been instructed only to move the Indians, but not to physically harm them. After the massacre, Major Arent Schuyler DePeyster, the British commander at Detroit, decided to protect the remaining Christian Indians. DePeyster, the same officer who had questioned and released the Moravians in 1781, helped David Zeisberger, one of the missionaries he had questioned, set up a temporary settlement for the remaining Indians. An empty British army barracks was turned over to Zeisberger while DePeyster negotiated with the Chippewa to lease some of their land north of Detroit to the Moravians. Zeisberger gathered as many of the remaining Christian Indians as he could find, and built the town of New Gnadenhutten on the leased land, where they stayed from 1782 until 1786. It was during this time that the United Brethren, represented by Bishop John Ettwein, first petitioned Congress on the Indians' behalf.

In October 1783, six months after the end of hostilities with Great Britain was officially declared, Bishop Ettwein personally delivered a memorial to Charles Thomson, the Secretary of Congress.[4] Ettwein made two requests in this memorial. First, he wanted an investigation of the 1782 massacre. This had been promised by Congress, as well as the assemblies of both Pennsylvania and Virginia, but, as far as he knew, had never been carried out. Second, he wanted to ensure that the remaining Christian Indians, although temporarily displaced, would not lose the legal right to their land. This memorial was referred to a committee, but no immediate action was taken on it.

In March 1784, Bishop Ettwein wrote to Thomas Mifflin, the President of Congress, to see if anything was being done.[5] On March 31, 1784, Bishop Ettwein's 1783 memorial was favorably reported on by the committee.

4. *Papers of the Continental Congress,* National Archives Microfilm Publication M247, r49, i41, v3, p73.

5. *ibid.,* M247, r94, i78, v8, p409.

The next year, in the land ordinance of May 20, 1785, Congress included, among the various reservations in the Northwest Territory for military service and other purposes, a provision reserving the Christian Indians' land. Congress had no way of knowing at this time that it would later become necessary to put the Indians' land in someone else's name, so the United Brethren were not mentioned in the 1785 ordinance. At this point, the society's only involvement was that of petitioning Congress on the Indians' behalf. In the ordinance, however, Congress did need to designate in some way who the land was being reserved for. Having nothing more specific than Bishop Ettwein's description – *"the Christian Indians now on Huron River or such trustees as they shall appoint"*[6] – Congress, in the ordinance and subsequent documents, just called them the Christian Indians. The following was the provision in the 1785 ordinance reserving the Christian Indians' land.

> And be it further Ordained, That the towns of Gnadenhutten, Schoenbrun and Salem, on the Muskingum, and so much of the lands adjoining to the said towns, with the buildings and improvements thereon, shall be reserved for the sole use of the Christian Indians, who were formerly settled there, or the remains of that society, as may, in the judgment of the Geographer, be sufficient for them to cultivate.[7]

All this 1785 provision did was reserve the Christian Indians' land from the lands that could be sold under the ordinance. This alone did not reserve the land forever. It only meant that Congress, for the time being, was promising not to sell it to anyone else. If the Indians did not take the steps necessary to legally take possession their land, Congress, after a reasonable amount of time, might assume they didn't want it and extinguish their claim. In fact, this almost happened a few years later, when Secretary of State Thomas Jefferson, having information that the remaining Christian Indians had moved to Canada, listed their reservation in a report as unclaimed land that could be sold.

6. *Papers of the Continental Congress,* National Archives Microfilm Publication, M247, r49, i41, v3, p73.

7. John C. Fitzpatrick, ed., *Journals of the Continental Congress, 1774-1789,* vol. 28, (Washington D.C.: Government Printing Office, 1933), 381.

In 1786, after receiving the news that Congress had reserved their land, Zeisberger and the Christians Indians started making their way home. Many of these Indians did not want to return to the site of the 1782 massacre, but the Chippewa, who considered the lease negotiated by Major DePeyster to have expired when the war ended, had already been asking them to leave for some time.

The Christian Indians crossed Lake Erie to the mouth of the Cuyahoga in the spring of 1786, but, because the ongoing Northwest Indian War[8] made this the most dangerous time of year to travel, they stopped ten miles down the river to wait out the summer in an abandoned Ottawa village. It was here, about seventy-five miles north of their former settlements, that the Christian Indians encountered the problem that led Congress to put their land in trust with the United Brethren.

By 1786, land in the area of the Christian Indians' settlements was in great demand, and white settlers wanted to be able to buy the land reserved by Congress. Some of these settlers figured that if they could keep the Indians away long enough, Congress would extinguish their claim and offer their land for sale. The settlers' plan was to make the Indians afraid to return, and Congress inadvertently played right into their hands.

Upon being informed by Bishop Ettwein in August 1786 that the Indians were at the Ottawa village and planning to return to their land in the fall, Congress passed the following resolution.

> *Resolved,* That the secretary at war give orders to lieutenant-colonel Harmar, that he signify to the Moravian Indians, lately come from the river Huron to Cuyahoga, that it affords pleasure to Congress to hear of their arrival, and that they have permission to return to their former settlement on the Muskingum, where they may be assured of the friendship and protection of the United States; and that lieutenant colonel Harmar supply the said Indians, after their arrival at

8. The Northwest Indian War, between a confederation of Indian tribes and the United States for control of the Northwest Territory, lasted from 1785 to 1795. Often referred to as Little Turtle's War, and known by a variety of other names, it was officially called the Miami Campaign in army records. The war was ended by the Treaty of Greenville, in which the Indian confederation ceded territory that included much of present day Ohio, establishing the boundary line between Indian territory and that open to white settlers.

> Muskingum, with a quantity of Indian corn, not exceeding five hundred bushels, out of the public stores on the Ohio, and deliver the same to them at fort Mcintosh, as soon after next Christmas as the same may be procured; and that he furnish the said Indians with twenty Indian axes, twenty corn hoes, and one hundred blankets; and that the board of treasury and Secretary at War take order to carry the above into effect.[9]

The white settlers, through local Delaware Indians, had already sent warnings to the Christian Indians, telling them that the militiamen who murdered their friends intended to finish the job if they returned. The resolution of Congress, of course, sounded just like what the militiamen had said in 1782 to trick their friends and family members into gathering in Gnadenhutten. The remaining Christian Indians were easily convinced that the soldiers from Fort McIntosh were also trying to trick them. At the end of the summer, they did not continue south to their land, but instead went sixty miles to the west and built their next temporary settlement, New Salem.

When Congress found out why the Indians were not returning, they decided that the best way to solve the problem was to permanently take the Indians' land off the market by putting the deed to it in someone's name. Once this was done, the white settlers would know they had no chance of getting this land, no matter how long they kept the Indians away. This is why Congress put the land in trust with the United Brethren.

Many years later, when the Senate was investigating allegations that the United Brethren had mismanaged this trust, C.G. Hueffel, then president of the society's board of directors, submitted a report on the history and present condition of the Christian Indians and their land grant. The following, from that report, was Hueffel's explanation of the events of 1786.

> On a representation of their distressed condition, laid before Congress by Bishop Ettwein, through the instrumentality of Charles Thompson, Esq., Secretary of Congress, that honor-

9. John C. Fitzpatrick, ed., *Journals of the Continental Congress, 1774-1789*, vol. 31, (Washington D.C.: Government Printing Office, 1934), 562-563.

> able body passed a resolution, directing Lieutenant Colonel Harmar to furnish the Indians at Fort McIntosh with five hundred bushels of Indian corn, one hundred blankets, and other necessaries. Unfortunately, this benevolence of Congress could not be carried into effect, notwithstanding the active friendship of the gentlemen concerned, as it proved impossible to bring on the Christian Indians far enough; the reports which reached them of the threats of the murderers of their friends intending to complete their destruction filling their minds with the utmost apprehension. It was believed that these threats were uttered in hopes of thereby preventing the return of the Christian Indians upon their land, and thus extinguishing the reservation thereof in the ordinance of May 20, 1785, as by this time these lands began to be an object of cupidity.
>
> Representations of these impediments thrown in the way of the Christian Indians having again been submitted to Congress, together with an exposition of the nature of the fears operating upon these persecuted sufferers, that honorable body, *in order at once to cut off all hopes of the aforementioned unprincipled persons of ever acquiring the lands, even if they should succeed, by their threats, in preventing the return of the Christian Indians,* determined, by an ordinance dated 27th July, 1787, "that the property of ten thousand acres, adjoining to the former settlements of the Christian Indians, should be vested in the Moravian Brethren at Bethlehem, Pennsylvania, *or a society of the said Brethren, for civilizing the Indians and promoting Christianity,* in trust, and for the uses expressed in the ordinance of May 20, 1785, including Killbuck and his descendants, and the nephew and descendants of the late Captain White-eyes, Delaware chiefs, who have distinguished themselves as friends of the cause of America."[10]

The "ordinance" of July 27, 1787 referred to by Hueffel was actually a resolution, attached to Congress's authorization for the Board of

10. Walter Lowrie, ed., *American State Papers: Indian Affairs*, vol. 2, (Washington D.C.: Gales and Seaton, 1834), 373.

Treasury to complete Ohio Company land sale. Because the land reserved for the Indians land fell within the boundaries of the lands being purchased by the Ohio Company, it needed to be excluded from the purchase in their contract.

> Whereas the United States in Congress Assembled have by their ordinance passed the 20th May 1785 among other things Ordained "that the Towns Gnadenhutten, Schoenbrun and Salem on the Muskingum and so much of the lands adjoining to the said Towns with the buildings and improvements thereon shall be reserved for the sole use of the Christian Indians who were formerly settled there, or the remains of that society, as may in the judgement of the Geographer be sufficient for them to cultivate."
>
> *Resolved* That the board of treasury except and reserve out of any Contract they may make for the tract described in the report of the Committee which on the 23d instant was referred to the said board to take order, a quantity of land around and adjoining each of the before mentioned Towns amounting in the whole to ten thousand acres, and that the property of the said reserved land be vested in the Moravian Brethren at Bethlehem in Pennsylvania, or a society of the said Brethren for civilizing the Indians and promoting Christianity, in trust, and for the uses expressed as above in the said Ordinance, including Killbuck and his descendants, and the Nephew and descendants of the late Captain White Eyes, Delaware Chiefs who have distinguished themselves as friends to the cause of America.[11]

Because they were now defining the Christian Indians' reservation for the purpose of excluding it in an actual contract, Congress had to be more specific about the amount of land being reserved than they had been in the ordinance of 1785. At this point, they decided that the amount of land described in that ordinance as *"sufficient for them to cultivate"* would be ten thousand acres.

11. Roscoe R. Hill, ed., *Journals of the Continental Congress, 1774-1789*, vol. 33, (Washington D.C.: Government Printing Office, 1936), 429-430.

In this resolution, Congress also named two individuals, Killbuck and the nephew of Captain White Eyes, as having a claim in the reservation. These were two Delaware chiefs who, at the beginning of the Revolutionary War, tried to keep the Delaware nation at peace with the United States. Both were commissioned as Lieutenant Colonels,[12] and later awarded land grants in the same amount as other officers of this rank for their military service. Captain White Eyes was killed in November 1778 while serving as a guide for American troops in Pennsylvania,[13] so his grant went to his nephew.[14] Killbuck remained on the American side when the Delaware, in reaction to Congress's failure to supply the clothing, tools, and weapons promised in a September 1778 treaty, joined the war on the side of the British.

Because of his actions during the war, it was not safe for Killbuck to return to the Delaware. When he heard about the reservation made for the Christian Indians, he requested that, for the protection of his and Captain White Eyes's families, Congress include them in this grant, allowing them to settle on land adjoining the Moravian community. Killbuck had previously lived with the Christian Indians, and Captain White Eyes had been on the Delaware council that first settled the Christian Indians on this land in 1772, so there were no objections to this arrangement from either side.

The July 27, 1787 resolution of Congress is often quoted in religious right American history books, chosen because it contains the words *"promoting Christianity."* John Eidsmoe, in his book *Christianity and the Constitution,* not only quotes this resolution, but implies that there were two separate land grants, one for the use of Christian Indians, and another for the Moravians. He also omits the word *"the"* before Christian Indians, and all other words indicating that Congress was referring to a specific group known as *"the Christian Indians,"*

12. "Captain" was not White Eyes's rank in the army, but the title adopted by the Delaware for members of their council who decided on questions of war.

13. Although the widely accepted story at the time was that Captain White Eyes died of small pox, the truth is that he was murdered by American troops. Colonel George Morgan, a United States Indian commissioner, covered up the murder, keeping the real story secret from all but a handful of members of Congress. The cover up was considered necessary to maintain good relations with the Delaware, whose neutrality in the war, which was largely due to the efforts and influence of Captain White Eyes, was already on very shaky ground.

14. George White Eyes later contested the nephew being named his father's heir, and hired a lawyer to get his family's land separated from the Christian Indians' land and put in his name. On his way to Washington in 1798, however, George, while intoxicated, attacked a white boy in Pennsylvania, and was killed.

giving the impression that land was granted to Christian Indians in general.

> **According to Eidsmoe: "In 1787, another act of Congress ordained special lands 'for the sole use of Christian Indians' and reserved lands for the Moravian Brethren 'for civilizing the Indians and promoting Christianity.'**

The reason for this particular wording in the 1787 resolution was that Congress did not yet know what the Moravians were going to call their society. In order for Congress to convey the Indians' land to them, the Moravians, or a society of them, had to be incorporated. While Bishop Ettwein was in Pennsylvania taking care of this, Congress had to proceed with the Ohio Company contract. Congress assumed that the Moravians were going to name their society something similar to the names of the many other Indian missionary societies of the time, which were all called something to the effect of societies *"for civilizing the Indians and promoting Christianity."* This, along with the description of the Indians, was specific enough to leave no question as to who they were referring to in the 1787 resolution. In the September 3, 1788 act conveying the land to the society, it was clarified in two places that the society described in the 1787 resolution and *"The Society of the United Brethren for propagating the Gospel among the Heathen"* were one and the same.[15]

As mentioned at the beginning of the chapter, most religious right authors attribute the United Brethren land trust to Thomas Jefferson, in an attempt to turn the president who was least likely to grant land to a religious society into the one who did. There is no truth whatsoever to this claim. It is a lie based on a 1796 act for creating the United States Military District, and locating and surveying the military land grants within this district. Because of a 1795 decision to confirm the trust created by the Continental Congress, the surveying of the Christian Indians' land was tagged onto this act. This was just a matter of expediency, due to the fact that the Christian Indian's land grant fell within the boundaries of the Military District, and needed to

15. Roscoe R. Hill, ed., *Journals of the Continental Congress, 1774-1789,* vol. 34, (Washington D.C.: Government Printing Office, 1937), 485-486.

be reserved from it. By confirming that this land had been appropriated by the Continental Congress in one section of the act, and then excluding from the military district any lands previously appropriated in another section of the same act, Congress killed two birds with one stone.

This act of 1796 was, of course, signed by George Washington, not Thomas Jefferson. The lie about Jefferson is created by using the titles of the later acts amending this act that were signed by him. According to the act of 1796, the deadline to register and locate military land grants was January 1, 1800. This time limit was extended once by John Adams, and three times by Thomas Jefferson. By the time of these extensions, however, the section in the original act regarding the Christian Indians' land grant was a dead letter. Everything ordered to be done in this section had been carried out by 1798, and the parts of the original act that were later extended had not applied to this land grant to begin with.

The following is the section regarding the Christian Indians' land from the act of 1796.

> Sec. 5. *And be it further enacted,* That the said surveyor general be, and he is hereby, required to cause to be surveyed three several tracts of land, containing four thousand acres each, at Schoenbrun, Gnadenhutten, and Salem; being the tracts formerly set apart, by an ordinance of Congress of the third of September, one thousand seven hundred and eighty-eight, for the society of United Brethren for propagating the gospel among the heathen; and to issue a patent or patents for the said three tracts to the said society, in trust, for the uses and purposes in the ordinance set forth.[16]

Because this section was tagged onto the military land grant act, the name of the United Brethren's society appeared in the act's title. The original 1796 act was called *An Act regulating the grants of land appropriated for Military services, and for the Society of the United Brethren, for propagating the Gospel among the Heathen.*[17] The

16. Richard Peters, ed., *The Public Statutes at Large of the United States of America*, vol. 1, (Boston: Charles C. Little and James Brown, 1845), 491.
17. *ibid.*, 490.

extensions of this act, although containing nothing that applied to the United Brethren's trust, still had the name of the society in their titles. This is simply because they were acts amending the original act. In April 1802, the act extending Adams's 1799 extension of the act of 1796 was called ***An Act in addition to an act, intituled "An act, in addition to*** *an act regulating the grants of land appropriated for military services, and for the society of the United Brethren for Propagating the gospel Among the Heathen."*[18] The next extension, in March 1803, was called ***An act to revive and continue in force an Act in addition to an act, intituled "An act, in addition to*** *an act regulating the grants of land appropriated for military services, and for the Society of the United Brethren for Propagating the Gospel among the Heathen,"* ***and for other purposes.***[19] The titles of these acts are the sole basis of the religious right claim that Thomas Jefferson granted land to religious societies.

Many Liars for Jesus, in addition to lying about the purpose of these acts, imply that the United Brethren land trust originated with Jefferson by making vague statements like the following.

> **According to David Barton, in his book *Original Intent*: "...Jefferson signed into law three separate acts setting aside government land for the sole use of Christian missionaries to evangelize the Indians and others."**

Others, although still lying about the purpose of the acts, do mention the earlier acts of the Continental Congress, or that the acts signed by Jefferson were extensions of the act of 1796. The goal of these lies, however, is the same – to make it appear that Thomas Jefferson approved of government land grants to religious organizations.

> **John Eidsmoe, following his story about the 1787 resolution, claims: "This was renewed in 1796 with a new law entitled 'An Act regulating the grants of land appropriated for Military services, and for the Society of the United Brethren, for propagating the Gospel**

18. Richard Peters, ed., *The Public Statutes at Large of the United States of America*, vol. 2, (Boston: Charles C. Little and James Brown, 1845), 155.
19. *ibid.*, 236.

> **among the Heathen.' Congress extended this act three times during Jefferson's administration and each time he signed the extension into law."**

> **According to Daniel Dreisbach, in his book *Real Threat and Mere Shadow:* "The United States government during Washington's administration employed a Christian missionary society and granted it control over vast tracts of land as part of a broader scheme to develop western lands and proselytize and 'civilize' the 'heathen' Indians. The Fifth through Eighth Congresses each reviewed the 'Act,' making some minor alterations and extending the life of the Act as provided for in the original Act of 1796. The last three extensions an April 26, 1802, March 3, 1803, and March 19, 1804, were approved during the administration of President Jefferson. Jefferson, like his predecessors Washington and Adams, signed the Act into law without registering any misgivings concerning the constitutionality of the Act's provisions."**

Robert Cord, in his book *Separation of Church and State,* presents some of the most creative lies about the act of 1796 and its subsequent extensions. Cord begins with the Continental Congress, but omits the circumstances that led them to put the land in trust. According to Cord's story, Congress vested this land in *"this newly created evangelical arm of the United Brethren"* for no other reason than *"to facilitate that these lands be used for the good of the Christian Indians."* Nowhere does he mention why it was necessary for Congress to do this.

Cord, cited by Dreisbach as the source of his similar lie, then claims that the United Brethren trust was the equivalent of the federal government paying a religious society to proselytize.

> **According to Cord: "Even if this proselytizing arm of the United Brethren was not financially successful—a matter of no consequence here—most significant is the fact that, after the adoption of the Establishment**

> **of Religion Clause, the United States Government in effect purchased, with grants of land amounting up to 12,000 acres placed in a controlling trust, the services of a religious evangelical order to settle in western U.S. lands to aid the Christian Indians. This action was tantamount to underwriting the maintenance and spreading of Christianity among the Indians...."**

Cord then goes out of his way to point out something that would be assumed anyway – that the United Brethren didn't have to pay for the land grant put in their trust. Cord's sole reason for focusing on the act of 1796 is to place the date of the grant after the ratification of the First Amendment.

> **According to Cord: "After the adoption of the federal *Constitution* in 1788 and the addition in 1791 of the First Amendment with its Establishment of Religion Clause, the Fourth Congress in 1796 enacted at least two 'Land Statutes.' The first, 'An Act providing for the *Sale* of the Lands of the Unites States, in the territory northwest of the river Ohio, and above the mouth of the Kentucky river," was a comprehensive land enactment which became law on May 18, 1796. This act detailed, among other things, the public lands available for sale by the United States Government, modes of payment, and the method of authorization for granting patents (titles) to the lands purchased. The second law, approved June 1, 1796 and entitled 'An Act regulating *the grants of land* appropriated for Military services and for the Society of the United Brethren, for propagating the Gospel among the Heathen,' was distinctly different. Like the preceding federal statute, this one detailed the lands to be granted; Section Two, however, provided, in part, that 'the patents for all lands located under the authority of this act, shall be granted...*without requiring any fee therefor.*'**

Section Two of this act didn't even apply to the United Brethren's trust. With the exception of one section regarding the free navigation of rivers, Section Five was the only section of this act that applied to the Christian Indians' land. Sections One through Four applied only to military land grants. The following is the Section Two provision, with the part omitted by Cord restored.

> And the patents for all lands located under the authority of this act, shall be granted in the manner directed by the before mentioned act, without requiring any fee therefor.[20]

The *"before mentioned act"* was the act of May 18, 1796 referred to by Cord. This act regarding the sale of lands was passed two weeks prior to the military land grant act, which was passed on June 1. The provision from the June 1 act quoted by Cord meant nothing more than that the surveying and paperwork for military land grants would be carried out in the same manner as specified in the act of May 18 for land that was sold, with the exception that the fees for these services would be waived. Cord, by misquoting the act of June 1 and italicizing certain words, makes it appear as if waiving the fee for issuing the patent meant waiving the cost of the land itself. It didn't. A patent was the piece of paper a purchaser received when their land was paid for in full; a certificate was the piece of paper a purchaser received if they were paying for the land in installments. The following were the fees for these documents, from the May 18 act for the sale of lands.

> Sec. 11. *And be it further enacted,* That the following fees shall be paid for the services done under this act, to the treasurer of the United States, or to the receiver in the western territory, as the case may be; for each certificate for a tract containing a quarter of a township, twenty dollars; for a certificate for a tract containing six hundred and forty acres, six dollars; and for each patent for a quarter of a township, twenty dollars; for a section of six hundred and forty acres, six dollars: And the said fees shall be accounted for by the receivers, respectively.[21]

20. Richard Peters, ed., *The Public Statutes at Large of the United States of America,* vol. 1, (Boston: Charles C. Little and James Brown, 1845), 491.
21. *ibid.,* 468.

These fees were what Section Two of the act of June 1 waived for military land grants. In addition to not meaning what Cord implies it meant, this section, as already mentioned, didn't even apply to the Christian Indians' grant. Obviously, since this was a grant that was put in their trust, the United Brethren didn't pay for the land. Cord just invents a different reason for this to fit his story that land was granted to a religious society, and places the date of this grant after the First Amendment by incorporating a completely irrelevant act of 1796.

Chief Justice Rehnquist, in his 1985 dissent in Wallace v. Jaffree, also played with the dates, omitting any mention of the Continental Congress and beginning the story in 1789. Rehnquist misleadingly called the trust an *"endowment,"* gave no reason for the land being put in trust, and, going even further than Cord, actually claimed that the act of June 1, 1796 was the act *"creating this endowment."*

> **According to Justice Rehnquist: "From 1789 to 1823 the United States Congress had provided a trust endowment of up to 12,000 acres of land 'for the Society of the United Brethren, for propagating the Gospel among the Heathen.'...The Act creating this endowment was renewed periodically and the renewals were signed into law by Washington, Adams, and Jefferson."**

In addition to the acts of 1802 and 1803, Jefferson signed a third act extending parts of the military land grant act of June 1, 1796. Most Liars for Jesus don't bother with this third act, signed by Jefferson in 1804, because, unlike the acts of 1802 and 1803, the title of this one didn't contain the words *"propagating the gospel among the heathen."* This act is usually only counted in the vague claims, like David Barton's *"...Jefferson signed into law three separate acts setting aside government land for the sole use of Christian missionaries to evangelize the Indians and others."* Robert Cord, on the other hand, tries to squeeze a religious purpose out of the act of 1804.

> **According to Cord: "This, the last renewal, had a new statutory name: 'An Act granting further time for**

> **locating military land warrants, and for other purposes.' The 'other purposes' were in part the propagating of 'the gospel among the heathen.'"**

Cord's claim is based on nothing more than the fact that the titles of the three prior extensions, the one signed by Adams and the two signed by Jefferson, appear in this act. The reason for this is that the *"other purposes"* were amendments to or continuations of various provisions from each of these earlier acts. The other purposes were related to the location of new warrants, and the requirement that the Secretary of War endorse all new warrants, certifying that they didn't duplicate any warrants already issued. This act, like the others, had no purpose that had anything whatsoever to do with propagating the gospel.

The 1796 order to survey the Christian Indians' land was not the first attempt to survey this land. Bishop Ettwein had obtained the warrants to have it surveyed in 1788, and wanting to have this done as quickly as possible, had even offered to pay for it and be reimbursed by Congress later. John Heckewelder, appointed by the United Brethren as their agent for the Indians' land, made three separate attempts to have it surveyed, all of which were halted by the Indian war. The first attempt was stopped when the area became so dangerous that the Governor of the Northwest Territory temporarily forbid all surveying. A second attempt was made as soon as it was allowed, but the surveying party was stopped by Indians who stole their surveying equipment. A third attempt was called off when information was received that the Indian confederation had put out an order to treat surveyors as enemy combatants.

During the time that Heckewelder was trying to get their land surveyed, the Christian Indians were still living at New Salem, where they had gone in 1786 after being scared away by the white settlers. When the Indian war escalated in 1791, they evacuated New Salem and fled to British Territory, building temporary village in Ontario. Because of this move, Thomas Jefferson, as already mentioned, almost made the Christian Indians' land available for sale.

In November 1791, Jefferson submitted a report to Congress in response to their request for an estimate of the amount and location of unclaimed lands in the territories. Since the Indians for whom the grant was intended had chosen to leave the country, Jefferson categorized their reservation as unclaimed land belonging to the United States. Jefferson obviously considered the United Brethren's trust to be irrelevant because, without the Indians, the purpose of this trust could not be carried out. The following is the section of Jefferson's report regarding the Christian Indians' land.

> 7th. The same ordinance of May 20th, 1785, appropriated the three towns of Gnadenhutten, Schoenbrunn, and Salem, on the Muskingum, for the christian Indians formerly settled there, or the remains of that society, with the grounds round about them; and the quantity of the said circumjacent grounds for each of the said towns was determined by the resolution of Congress of September 3d, 1788, to be so much as, with the plat of its respective town, should make up four thousand acres. This reservation was accordingly made out of the larger purchase of Cutler and Sargent, which comprehended them. The Indians, however, having chosen to emigrate beyond the limits of the United States; so the lands reserved for them still remain to the United States.[22]

Within a month of Jefferson's report, Bishop Ettwein petitioned Congress, requesting that the grant made by the Continental Congress be confirmed by the new government, and that new warrants be issued to survey it. This was referred to the committee on establishing land grant offices. The committee tended to agree with Jefferson that the trust created by the Continental Congress required the *"occupation"* of the land by the Christian Indians. However, no actual decision was made at this point because the Indian war caused Congress to put any legislation regarding land grants on the back burner.

Meanwhile, the Christian Indians, still in Canada, were granted fifty thousand acres of land by the British. In 1793, the community of a hundred and fifty-nine, some from the original group that had been driven from their land in 1781, and others who had joined them, built a permanent settlement at Fairfield. In spite of some problems with

22. Walter Lowrie, ed., *American State Papers: Public Lands*, vol. 1, (Washington D.C.: Duff Green, 1834), 20.

white settlers and passing Indian war parties on their way to defend Indian land in the United States, the Christian Indians lived in relative peace and safety in Canada, developing a somewhat profitable business selling corn and maple sugar.

In 1794, with the end of the Indian war in sight, Congress resumed its work on establishing land grant offices, appointing a new committee for this purpose. Bishop Ettwein immediately submitted a new petition, repeating the request made in 1791. This time, he filled the committee in on the history and current situation of the Indians, and explained that by not confirming the trust, this Congress would recreate the problem that caused the Continental Congress to put the land in trust in the first place. As soon as the Indians tried to return, they would be driven away by white settlers who would once again have hopes of getting their land. Those Indians who wanted to return would be far fewer than the number successfully driven away in 1786, and would not even consider leaving the safety of Canada until they knew their land was secured. The problem was that their land would not be secured until it was surveyed and the patents issued.

Despite Bishop Ettwein's explanation of the situation, the committee was still reluctant to confirm the United Brethren's trust. Several members of the committee proposed alternatives, such as giving the Indians money in lieu of their land grant. The argument in favor of this was that, based on their past problems with white settlers, the Indians might be safer in Indian territory. Another proposal was that the land remain the property of the United States, but that the Indians be allowed to occupy it. Eventually, however, after it was suggested that the Moravian settlements on the frontier might be useful to the United States in the event of another Indian war, the committee decided in favor of confirming the trust, and Congress, of course, did this in the act of 1796.

The Christian Indians' land was surveyed in 1797, and the patents were issued to the United Brethren in February 1798. That spring, John Heckewelder traveled to Fairfield with the news that the Indians could return. Of the hundred and seventy Christian Indians at Fairfield, only seven families, totalling thirty people, chose to leave. This group of thirty, accompanied by David Zeisberger and one other missionary, included only a few of the original Christian Indians.

According to the society's plan, which had been approved by the

Continental Congress in 1788, and reluctantly agreed to, with some revisions, by the Congress of 1795, the Indians would settle on only one of their three tracts. The other two would be leased to white tenant farmers, carefully screened by the Moravians, with the rents from these lands going to support the Indians. The Indians picked the Schoenbrun tract, where they built the town of Goshen.

The next lie about this story is that the United Brethren, with the approval of Congress, used the money from the leased land to go out and evangelize other Indians.

> **According to Robert Cord: "As is evident from its name, this Society was concerned with more than merely controlling and using land set aside, in trust, for the Indians who were already Christians. In addition to exercising their trust in the interest of the Christian Indians living on portions of this land, the Society used some of the resources derived from the cultivation of these lands, and the land leases sold to white tenant farmers, to convert souls 'from among the neighboring heathen' and to send out missionaries to proselytize."**

The source that Cord cites and quotes out of context to create this lie is the report submitted by C.G. Hueffel to Congress in 1822, when the United Brethren were under suspicion of mismanaging the trust. Hueffel, after stating that only thirty of the Indians returned from Canada in 1798, gave the following account of Goshen's population from that time until 1820.

> ...Their number was augmented by some new converts from among the neighboring heathen, and a family or two joined them from Fairfield; so that, at the close of the year 1800, they amounted to about sixty souls. In the following year, the Brethren there were induced, by the pressing solicitations of the Delaware on the Wabash, to send a missionary thither, accompanied by some of the best of their flock from Goshen, who hoped thus to gain their relations there; and it was not till after some time that it became apparent that these solici-

> tations were part of a plan to draw all the Christian Indians thither for their destruction.
>
> This removal caused a dimunition of the number at Goshen, never replenished; a number which, from 1801 to the close of 1810, continued vacillating between forty-five and thirty-five souls; some returning to Fairfield, as before observed, and several of the most respectable completing their course here below by a happy death. From that year to the end of the year, their number was still further reduced by deaths and removals; so that, at the close of this year, there were but twenty-six persons left.[23]

Cord completely disregards the fact that Hueffel made a point of clearly explaining elsewhere in the same report that it was not the practice of the Moravians to go out evangelizing, and plucks a few words from this account to support his lie. The Moravians never established more than a few small communities, and, even then, only when invited to do so by the Indians. Other Indians who joined these communities were not solicited by the Moravians. Some were local Indians who approached the communities on their own. Others were friends and relatives invited by those Indians who were already there.

Hueffel explained in his report that, although the published histories of the Christian Indians at Goshen described numerous settlements, these were all successive settlements of this one particular community, not a number of separate communities that had existed concurrently or continued to exist. This explanation, of course, was included by Hueffel to show Congress that the money from the leases on the trust land had not been used to fund other missions.

> It, however, becomes proper to remark, in the outset, that this success of the united Brethren was, at all times, a limited one; and that they never attempted to convert or civilize whole nations. The inadequacy of their means, depending exclusively on the voluntary contributions of *the members of their church,* and such other friends as, *without solicitation,*

23. Walter Lowrie, ed., *American State Papers: Indian Affairs,* vol. 2, (Washington D.C.: Gales and Seaton, 1834), 376.

> thought proper to render them aid; and the tenor of their principles, which require a vital conversion from heathenism, not unto a professed *belief* in the Christian doctrine alone, but chiefly unto a practically moral Christian life and demeanor, at all times forbade extensive attempts, and necessarily confined their endeavors to planting and preserving one or more select communities of Christian Indians.
>
> Hence, it is evident that they never pretended to such an extension of missions as some have been induced to represent, from overlooking the circumstance that the numerous stations of which their missionary histories make mention were not *contemporary* establishments, but *successive* abodes of one and the same community of persons.[24]

It was also pointed out to Congress that it was strictly against the Moravians' principles to use any money for a purpose other than that for which it was intended. This was made very clear by John Heckewelder in the statement he supplied for Hueffel's report.

> Neither do the United Brethren, as a body, amass to themselves any thing that belongs to others, or is intended for the benefit of others; nor beguile their consciences, or bring a reproach upon themselves, by appropriating gifts of benevolence intrusted to them for others, to themselves, or for their interest or use. All acts of this kind are held sacred with them.[25]

The only money from the Christian Indians' land that was spent to support religion was used to support the religion of the Indians in the community. There was absolutely nothing unconstitutional about this, of course. The Indians had the same right to have their church supported by money earned from their lands as recipients of military land grants had to support their churches with money earned from theirs.

24. Walter Lowrie, ed., *American State Papers: Indian Affairs*, vol. 2, (Washington D.C.: Gales and Seaton, 1834), 372.
25. *ibid.*, 390.

Only a few religious right versions of the Moravian land trust story mention that the United Brethren were eventually divested of this trust. None of these, however, mention that this was prompted by allegations that the trust had been mismanaged and a Senate investigation into these charges. Although the United Brethren were cleared of any wrongdoing, this investigation doesn't fit very well into the story that Congress granted the society this land to aid them in their missionary efforts, particularly since one of the things the society had to prove to Congress was that they *hadn't* used any of the proceeds from this land to fund missionary efforts.

The religious right version of this part of the story is that the United Brethren, due solely to financial problems, asked Congress to divest them of the trust, and Congress quickly granted this request.

> **According to Robert Cord: "Due to the unreliability of white tenant farmers—who incurred debts and then abandoned them and their leased farms—the Society, over a period of years, lost large sums of money. Increased expenses for the Society also resulted from Ohio state land taxes. Because of continuing growth of indebtedness, the Society asked to be divested of its 'trust Estate' in the early 1820s. Shortly thereafter an agreement was reached on August 4, 1823 whereby the Society of the United Brethren, for Propagating the Gospel Among the Heathen agreed to 'retrocede to the United States the three several tracts of lands...which had been patented to the Society by the United States' in consideration of $6,654.25 and several tracts of land on which existed churches, parsonages and graveyards.**

It is true that the United Brethren lost a great deal of money because of this trust, but the unreliable tenant farmers and Ohio state land taxes accounted for only part of this. By 1822, the trust had cost the society over $32,000 that they could provide receipts for, and a significant amount beyond this that they had not kept records of. Only about $2,000 of this was due to unpaid tenant farm rents. Much more of it was from the expenses incurred by the society between

1788, when the trust was first created, and 1800, when the first farms were leased. These initial expenses, for which the society had to borrow money, included the roads and mills that had to be built before any of the land could be leased to farmers. The society had also borrowed the money to pay for the early surveying attempts. According to the act of 1788, the money spent by the society to survey the grant was to be reimbursed by Congress, but this was never done.

From 1800 to 1806, the society sold a number of twenty-one year leases to tenant farmers. The terms of these leases were that no rent would be charged for the first year, and after that the rent would increase gradually over the time of the lease, anticipating that the farmers' incomes would increase proportionally over this time. The other condition was that at the end of the twenty-one years, the society would reimburse the tenants for their investments in buildings and other improvements on the land. Some of the tenant farmers did skip out on their leases, mainly because Congress, in 1804, made it easier for them to buy their own land by reducing the minimum number of acres that an individual was required to purchase. Although this contributed to the society's financial problems, most of their losses up until this point were the result of borrowing money for their initial expenses, and the interest on those debts.

The situation was made worse in 1814, when the state of Ohio began taxing the land. The taxes on the two tracts that were being leased were not the problem. The society, when it leased these lands, had anticipated that they might be taxed, and had included a clause in the leases stating that any future taxes would be the responsibility of the lessees. They had not, however, anticipated that the tract the Indians were living on, none of which, according to the terms of the trust, could be leased, would also be taxed.

Adding to the society's expenses was the fact that they were also supporting the original Christian Indians, the majority of who had remained at Fairfield. Although these were the Indians that the land grant on the Muskingum was intended to support, the Moravians, throughout this entire time, had been supporting them with their own funds. In 1814, the same year that the state of Ohio began taxing the trust lands, the settlement at Fairfield, which was in British territory, was destroyed by American troops in the War of 1812, and a new settlement had to be built there.

In 1821, the United Brethren petitioned the Ohio legislature, asking that the tract that the Indians were living on be exempted from taxes, but their request was denied. By this point, in violation of the trust, the society had already been forced to lease part of this tract. The income from leasing only part of this tract, however, was not enough to cover the taxes on the entire tract. The combined rents from all three tracts were not enough to pay the interest on the existing debts, let alone the interest on the new debts that resulted from the society then having to borrow more money just to supply the Indians at Goshen with necessities.

It was the society's 1821 petition for tax relief that led to the 1822 Senate investigation. The Ohio legislature didn't understand how anyone with eight thousand acres of farmland to lease could be having problems paying their taxes. The opinion of the committee that reviewed the society's petition was that the property must be yielding *"a considerable revenue,"* and that they had *"no means of ascertaining whether that revenue is faithfully disbursed in effecting the original object of the grant."*[26] This prompted the Governor of Ohio, Ethan Allen Brown, to pay a visit to Goshen. What he found there made him understandably suspicious that the income from the leases was not being used to carry out the purpose of the trust.

When Governor Brown made his 1821 visit, there were only twenty Indians at Goshen, all of them living in poor conditions, and most of them drunk. Most of the twenty were members of the families of Killbuck and Captain White Eyes, and one was a member of original group of Christian Indians that the land was granted to. The others were a handful of individuals who had joined the Christian Indians sometime after they were driven from their settlements in 1781. The few original Christian Indians who had returned in 1798 or afterwards had either died or gone back to Fairfield. All but one of the missionaries had also gone to Fairfield. This one remaining missionary was recalled to Bethlehem by the United Brethren later in 1821, but was still there at the time of Governor Brown's visit. Unaware of the United Brethren's debts and the circumstances that had led to the decline of the Goshen settlement, Governor Brown naturally suspected that the income from the leases was being used by the society for

26. Walter Lowrie, ed., *American State Papers: Indian Affairs,* vol. 2, (Washington D.C.: Gales and Seaton, 1834), 391.

purposes other than that intended by the trust.

In January 1822, Governor Brown was elected to fill a vacant seat in the Senate. One of the first things he did when he got to Washington was to bring what he had seen at Goshen to the attention of the Chairman of the Committee on Indian Affairs, Senator Thomas Hart Benton of Missouri. In February 1822, Senator Benton launched an investigation, moving the following resolutions, which were passed on February 22.

> *Resolved,* That the Secretary of the Treasury be directed to lay before the Senate a copy of the patent (if any such there be in the Treasury Department) which issued under an act of Congress of June 1st, 1796, conveying to the Society of United Brethren for propagating the Gospel among the Heathen, three tracts of land, of four thousand acres each, to include the towns of Gnadenhutten, Schoenbrunn, and Salem, on the Muskingum, in the state of Ohio, in trust to said society, for the sole use of the Christian Indians formerly settled there.
>
> *Resolved,* That the President of the United States be requested to cause to be collected and communicated to the Senate at the commencement, of the next session of Congress, the best information which he may be able to obtain relative to the said Christian Indians, and the lands intended for their benefit in the above-mentioned grant; showing, as correctly as possible, the advance or decline of said Indians in numbers, morals, and intellectual endowments; whether the said lands have inured to their sole benefit; and, if not, to whom, in whole or in part, have such benefits accrued.
>
> *Resolved,* That the Secretary of the Senate furnish a copy of the above resolutions to the Society of United Brethren for propagating the Gospel among the Heathen, addressed to the President of the Society, at Bethlehem, in Northampton county, in the state of Pennsylvania.[27]

27. *The Debates and Proceedings of the Congress of the United States of America,* vol. 38, 17th Cong., 1st Sess., (Washington D.C.: Gales & Seaton, 1855), 229.

In answer to these resolutions, C.F. Hueffel, in September 1822, submitted the report referred to throughout this chapter. In the statement he provided for Hueffel's report, John Heckewelder, who lived at Goshen from 1798 to 1810, explained how the settlement deteriorated. According to Heckewelder, the problems began in 1802. With Ohio about to become a state, new settlers quickly began pouring into the area. Because the three tracts in the grant were not contiguous, the lands lying between them were sold, placing all sorts of settlers between the Goshen tract and the tracts where the tenants were selected by the Moravians, and bound by their leases not to interfere with the Indians. Back in 1788, when the Continental Congress first created the trust, the United Brethren had tried to buy the lands in between the three grant tracts, intending to keep undesirable white settlers away from the Indians. The society, however, which had to pay Congress the same price for land as anyone else, could not afford these other tracts.

By 1810, the Indians were surrounded by white settlers, some of whom wanted to lease land on the Goshen tract. The Moravians, although later leasing this land to raise money for taxes, would not lease it at that time. Knowing that the Indians didn't fully understand what a trust was, the white settlers convinced them that they would be rich if the Moravians weren't cheating them out of rent money that was rightfully theirs. The Indians were told that they could lease any part of their land to anybody they wanted to, collect the rent money themselves, and never have to work again. Believing that they were being taken advantage of by the Moravians, the Indians refused to continue working. Many began drinking, and what little interest, if any, they still had in the Moravians' religion was gone.

The United Brethren, after explaining what happened, and presenting the Senate with the society's books from 1800 to 1821, and documentation of all expenses going back to the early surveying attempts in 1788, were cleared of any wrongdoing.

After the investigation was over, the United Brethren asked to be divested of the trust. Here, however, they ran into a bit of a problem. The Committee on Public Lands reported on February 7, 1823 that Congress, without the permission of the Indians for whose benefit the trust was created, did not have the authority to put an end to it.[28]

28. Walter Lowrie, ed., *American State Papers: Public Lands,* vol. 3, (Washington D.C.: Duff Green, 1834), 537.

On March 3, 1823, *An act making further appropriation for the military services of the United States for the year 1823, and for other purposes* was passed, which included an appropriation of $1,000 to enable the President to take the necessary measures to purchase the tracts.[29] Lewis Cass, the Territorial Governor of Michigan, was appointed to negotiate with the United Brethren for the purchase of the land, and then to negotiate with representatives of the Christian Indians to get their assent to the sale.

The date of August 4, 1823 given by Robert Cord was the date of the contract made between Cass and the United Brethren. Cord, minimizing the fact that this land was granted to the Christian Indians, and only in trust with the United Brethren, omits that there was a second agreement, between Cass and the Indians on November 8, 1823. At this time, the representatives of the Christian Indians agreed to give up the right to their land in exchange for an annuity of $400, to be paid from the sale of the land. The Indians were also given the option to apply to the President for a reservation of twenty-four thousand acres in exchange for this annuity if they wished to return to the United States at any time in the future.

It was determined by Congress that the society, although having lost well over $30,000 on the trust, was only entitled to repayment of those expenses that the Continental Congress had promised to reimburse in their act of 1788, and the interest on this amount. These expenses totalled, with interest, about $18,500. As mentioned by Cord, the society retroceded the land *"in consideration of $6,654.25 and several tracts of land on which existed churches, parsonages and graveyards."* This religion related property alone did not, of course, account for the difference of almost $12,000. The United Brethren also kept a few non-religious properties. The United States, by taking over the existing leases, became responsible for other expenses, such as reimbursing certain tenants, as stipulated in their leases, for their houses and other buildings when their leases expired. These future expenses, as well as the cost of the deed conveying the land back to the United States, were also deducted from the money owed to the United Brethren.

The agreements made by Lewis Cass were approved by the

29. Richard Peters, ed., *The Public Statutes at Large of the United States of America*, vol. 3, (Boston: Charles C. Little and James Brown, 1846), 749-750.

Committee on Public Lands on April 2, 1824.[30] *An Act providing for the disposition of three several tracts of land in Tuscarawas county, in the state of Ohio, and for other purposes,* passed on May 26, 1824, authorized the contract with the United Brethren and the agreement with the Christian Indians to be executed.[31]

Another popular United Brethren story, found in several religious right American history books, involves a letter written to the society by George Washington.

> **According to William Federer, in his book *America's God and Country*: "In July of 1789, in a letter to the Director of the Society of the United Brethren for Propagating the Gospel among the Heathen, President Washington committed that the government should:**
>
> > **Co-operate, as far as circumstances may admit, with the disinterested endeavors of your Society to civilize and Christianize the Savages of the Wilderness."**

Washington didn't commit the government to anything in this letter. He knew the role the Moravians had played in keeping the Delaware neutral as long as possible during the Revolutionary War, and considered their relationship with the Indians to be extremely valuable for the protection of the United States. This was also the argument, as mentioned earlier, that convinced Congress to confirm the United Brethren's trust in 1795.

The following is one example of how the Moravians were used in the Revolutionary War. Early in the war, the Continental Congress decided that the best way to keep the Delaware from joining the British was to make them think the British were losing. The only problem was that the British were actually winning. Knowing that the Delaware council trusted the Moravians, Congress used them in a propaganda campaign. Whenever the United States won a battle,

30. Walter Lowrie, ed., *American State Papers: Public Lands,* vol. 3, (Washington D.C.: Duff Green, 1834), 615.

31. Richard Peters, ed., *The Public Statutes at Large of the United States of America,* vol. 4, (Boston: Charles C. Little and James Brown, 1846), 56-59.

Congress sent the Moravians newspapers reporting the victory to read to the Delaware council. Congress couldn't ask the Moravians to lie, so they were only asked to report the real victories. When the United States lost a battle, Congress sent an Indian agent to lie and tell the Delaware that the United States had won, making it the Indian agent's word against that of any British soldiers the Delaware came into contact with. But, because the Delaware were hearing about enough real victories from the Moravians, who never lied to them about anything, the Indian agents' lies sounded more believable, and the Delaware were convinced for quite a while that the United States were winning every battle.

The quote used by William Federer is taken out of context from Washington's reply to a letter from the United Brethren congratulating him on being elected president in 1789. In this letter, the society took the opportunity to inform Washington of the situation of the Christian Indians, who were then at their New Salem settlement in the middle of the Indian war. The following was the context of the quote, in which Washington clearly said that his reason for offering to cooperate with the society was the protection of the United States.

> In proportion as the Government of the United States shall acquire strength by duration, it is probable that they may have it in their power to extend a salutary influence to the Aborigines in the extremities of their territory. In the meantime, it will be a desirable thing for the protection of the Union to co-operate, as far as circumstances may admit, with the disinterested endeavors of your Society to civilize and christianize the Savages of the Wilderness.[32]

32. George Washington to Directors of the Society of the United Brethren for Propagating the Gospel among the Heathen, July 10, 1789, *George Washington Papers at the Library of Congress, 1741-1799: Series 2, Letterbooks;* Letterbook #38.

— CHAPTER FIVE —

Thomas Jefferson and Public Education

Over the course of almost five decades, Thomas Jefferson was involved with a number of educational institutions and plans for education, beginning in 1778 with his proposed plan for public schools in Virginia in his *Bill for the More General Diffusion of Knowledge,* and ending with the University of Virginia, which opened in 1825, a year before his death. In order to support their position that religion belongs in public schools, the Liars for Jesus have invented tales of Jefferson including, encouraging, and even requiring religious worship and religious instruction in every school and education plan he was connected with.

The Geneva Academy Proposal...

> **According to D. James Kennedy, in his book *What if America were a Christian Nation Again?*: Jefferson "wanted to bring the entire faculty of Calvin's theological seminary over from Geneva, Switzerland, and establish them at the University of Virginia."**

There are two things wrong with Kennedy's claim. The first is the time frame. Jefferson did consider a proposal to move the Geneva Academy to the United States, but this was in 1794 and 1795, thirty years before the University of Virginia opened. The second is that, although the Geneva Academy was originally founded by John Calvin in 1559 as theological seminary, by the late 1700s it had been transformed into an academy of science. The plan considered by Jefferson was not to import a religious school. It was to import a group of Europe's top science professors.

In 1794, François D'Ivernois, an economist and political writer from Geneva, wrote to Thomas Jefferson and John Adams. Political upheaval in Geneva had forced D'Ivernois into exile in England, and was threatening the future of the Geneva Academy. D'Ivernois, who had met both Jefferson and Adams when they were foreign ministers in Europe, wrote separately to each of them proposing that the faculty of the academy be relocated to the United States.

In a letter to George Washington, who was also anxious to establish a public university in America, Jefferson described the Geneva Academy and its faculty.

> ...the revolution which has taken place at Geneva has demolished the college of that place, which was in a great measure supported by the former government. The colleges of Geneva & Edinburgh were considered as the two eyes of Europe in matters of science, insomuch that no other pretended to any rivalship with either. Edinburgh has been the most famous in medicine during the life of Cullen; but Geneva most so in the other branches of science, and much the most resorted to from the continent of Europe because the French language was that which was used. a Mr. D'Ivernois, a Genevan, & man of science, known as the author of a history of that republic, has proposed the transplanting that college in a body to America. he has written to me on the subject, as he has also done to Mr. Adams, as he was formerly known to us both, giving us the details of his views for effecting it. probably these have been communicated to you by Mr. Adams, as D'Ivernois desired should be done; but lest they should not have been communicated I will take the liberty of doing it. his plan I think would go to about ten or twelve professorships. he names to me the following professors as likely if not certain to embrace the plan.

Monchon, the present President, who wrote the Analytical table for the Encyclopedists, & which sufficiently proves his comprehensive science.

Pictet, known from his admeasurements of a degree, & other works, professor of Natural philosophy.

his brother, said by M. D'Ivernois to be also great.

Senebier, author of commentaries on Spallanzani, & of other works in Natural philosophy & Meteorology; also the translator of the Greek tragedies.

Bertrand } both mathematicians, and said to be inferior to
L'Huillier } nobody in that line except La Grange, who is without an equal.

Prevost, highly spoken of by D'Ivernois.

De Saussure & his son, formerly a professor, but who left the college to have more leisure to pursue his geological researches into the Alps, by which work he is very advantageously known.[1]

Like many of D. James Kennedy's lies about Thomas Jefferson, the version of the story about the Geneva Academy in *What If America Were A Christian Nation Again?* is borrowed from Mark Beliles's introduction to his version of the *Jefferson Bible*, and then changed a bit. In his chapter about Jefferson, Kennedy paraphrases dozens of lies from Beliles's book, changing them just enough to reveal his complete ignorance of the actual events on which Beliles based the original versions of the lies. In his version of the Geneva Academy story, Beliles does connect John Calvin with this school to imply that Jefferson wanted to import a theological seminary, but Beliles claims only that the proposed relocation was to *"form the foundations of a state university,"* not that the decades away University of Virginia was the destination. Kennedy's addition of this anachronism makes it pretty clear that he has no idea that the lie he is copying is about something that happened thirty years before the University of Virginia opened. This doesn't make Beliles's version of the story any less of a lie. It just shows that, unlike Kennedy, Beliles knows what he's lying about.

1. Thomas Jefferson to George Washington, February 23, 1795, *The Thomas Jefferson Papers, Series 1, General Correspondence, 1651-1827*, Library of Congress Manuscript Division, #16799.

According to Beliles's version of the story: Jefferson "attempted to move the entire faculty of John Calvin's University of Geneva to form the foundations of a state university (but was thwarted by the legislature)."

Beliles mentions that the plan was thwarted by the legislature, but the truth is that it never even got as far as being proposed to the legislature. Of course, since the Geneva Academy was not a religious school, this had nothing to do with religion.

Jefferson wanted to find out if the Virginia legislature would be receptive to the plan before actually proposing it, but didn't want his name associated with it, so he asked Wilson Nicholas, a friend and member of the legislature, to run the idea by a few of his colleagues to see if they thought it stood any real chance of passing.[2] Nicholas reported back to Jefferson that, although the members he spoke to liked the idea, they didn't think the majority of the legislature would go for it. Nicholas gave three reasons for this, which Jefferson listed in his reply to D'Ivernois.

> The reasons which they thought would with certainty prevail against it, were 1, that our youth, not familiarized but with their mother tongue, were not prepared to receive instructions in any other; 2, that the expense of the institution would excite uneasiness in their constituents, and endanger its permanence; and 3, that its extent was disproportioned to the narrow state of the population with us. Whatever might be urged on these several subjects, yet as the decision rested with others, there remained to us only to regret that circumstances were such, or were thought to be such, as to disappoint your and our wishes.

> I should have seen with peculiar satisfaction the establishment of such a mass of science in my country, and should probably have been tempted to approach myself to it, by procuring a residence in its neighborhood, at those seasons

2. Thomas Jefferson to Wilson Nicholas, November 22, 1794, Andrew A. Lipscomb and Albert Ellery Bergh, eds., *The Writings of Thomas Jefferson,* vol. 9, (Washington D.C.: Thomas Jefferson Memorial Association, 1904), 291-293.

> of the year at least when the operations of agriculture are less active and interesting.[3]

After Jefferson informed D'Ivernois that the plan would not succeed in Virginia, he pursued one more possibility. This was the reason for his letter to George Washington describing the Geneva Academy's faculty. Washington had been given shares in the James River and Potomac Companies by the Virginia Assembly, and had previously discussed with Jefferson the idea of using these shares to fund a public university.

Because Jefferson had resigned as Secretary of State and returned to Monticello, he was unaware that Washington was already working on a plan to establish a national university in the District of Columbia, and had promised the revenue from his shares in the Potomac Company to Congress for this purpose. Washington had also written to the Virginia legislature, offering his shares in the James River Company to fund a university in that state. Washington was actually hoping that the Virginia legislature wouldn't take him up on this offer, but felt obliged to make it because the shares had been given him to by Virginia. He thought it would be better to apply the shares from both companies to the university in the District of Columbia, knowing that it would be difficult enough to establish one university, let alone two at the same time.

Nowhere in any of the letters written by Jefferson or Washington about either of these early plans for a public university is religion mentioned even once.

The Geneva Academy lie has been around for a long time. Mark Beliles didn't invent this one – he only revived it. Beliles's source is William Eleroy Curtis's 1901 book *The True Thomas Jefferson.* Although Curtis is long gone, the lies from his highly inaccurate biography of Jefferson are included here because a reprinted edition of this book is currently being recommended and sold on many Christian American history and homeschooling websites. Curtis's version of the Geneva Academy story is found in two places in his book – first, in a chapter about the founding of the University of Virginia, and again in

3. Thomas Jefferson to François D'Ivernois, February 6, 1795, Andrew A. Lipscomb and Albert Ellery Bergh, eds., *The Writings of Thomas Jefferson*, vol. 9, (Washington D.C.: Thomas Jefferson Memorial Association, 1904), 298-299.

a chapter about Jefferson's religious views. Curtis, like today's Liars for Jesus, completely disregarded the fact that the Geneva Academy had become a scientific institution, and that the proposal was to import science professors, not theologians. He even claimed that religious opinion was one of the reasons the plan failed in the Virginia legislature, although, as already mentioned, the plan was never proposed to that body. Curtis also added a concern about religious differences to George Washington's objections to the idea, although this was not among the objections Washington listed in his reply to Jefferson's letter.

The following are two excerpts about the Geneva Academy proposal from Curtis's *The True Thomas Jefferson.*

> **From the chapter about the founding of the University of Virginia: "Jefferson's first idea of a university for Virginia was to transform his venerable alma mater, William and Mary College, which was under the care of the church, into a non-sectarian State institution, and in 1795 he corresponded with Washington on the subject. He also asked Washington's coöperation in bringing the faculty of the Calvinistic Seminary of Geneva en masse to the United States, and proposed the plan to the Legislature. It was considered too grand and expensive an enterprise for the feeble colony, and Washington's practical mind questioned the expediency of importing a body of foreign theologians and scholars who were not familiar with the language or the customs of the people. Jefferson then suggested the faculty of the University of Edinburgh, but similar objections were heard from every direction, and the plan was reluctantly abandoned."**
>
> **From the chapter about Jefferson's religious views: "In 1794, as related in another chapter, he endeavored to arrange for the removal to America of the Calvinistic college of Geneva, Switzerland, and planned to establish the entire faculty at Charlottesville as the nucleus of a States university. This was the first step in the**

> **development of the idea that afterwards found form and substance in the present University of Virginia. But French Calvinism did not commend itself to the practical-minded Virginians. Jefferson appealed to General Washington for support and encouragement, and urged him to dedicate the property presented to him by the Legislature as an endowment for such an institution. Washington's practical mind questioned the expediency of importing a faculty of theologians unfamiliar with the language and unsympathetic with the religious opinion prevailing in Virginia, and suggested to Jefferson that if teachers were to be brought from abroad it would be better to seek them in the English universities. Acting upon his advice, Jefferson turned to Edinburgh, and endeavored to obtain a faculty there. This, however, was only one of his many inconsistencies, and those who are familiar with the incidents of his life will not be surprised to learn that in a letter to a friend he commended a nursery of the gloomiest and cruelest sort of Presbyterianism and a seminary of Calvinists as the two best institutions of learning in the world."**

By the time Washington received Jefferson's letter about the Geneva Academy, he had already heard about the proposal from John Adams, and had already decided against it. The following is the part of Washington's reply to Jefferson in which he listed his objections, none of which had anything to do with religion.

> Hence you will perceive that I have, in a degree, anticipated your proposition. I was restrained from going the whole length of the suggestion, by the following considerations: 1st, I did not know to what extent, or when any plan would be so matured for the establishment of an University, as would enable any assurance to be given to the application of Mr. D'Ivernois. 2d, the propriety of transplanting the Professors in a body, might be questioned for several reasons; among others, because they might not be all good

> characters; nor all sufficiently acquainted with our language; and again, having been at variance with the levelling party of their own country, the measure might be considered as an aristocratical movement by more than those who, without any just cause that I have been able to discover, are continually sounding the alarm bell of aristocracy. and 3d, because it might preclude some of the first Professors in other countries from a participation; among whom some of the most celebrated characters in Scotland, in this line, I am told might be obtained.[4]

Curtis's claim that "*Jefferson then suggested the faculty of the University of Edinburgh, but similar objections were heard from every direction, and the plan was reluctantly abandoned*" is completely untrue. Curtis took the reference to Scotland in Washington's reply to Jefferson, and Jefferson's mention of Edinburgh in his letter to Wilson Nicolas, the "*letter to a friend*" referred to by Curtis, and twisted them into a claim that Jefferson "*commended a nursery of the gloomiest and cruelest sort of Presbyterianism.*" Jefferson's reason for mentioning Edinburgh had nothing to do with its religious affiliation. Because he was writing to people who were unlikely to be familiar with the Geneva Academy, he made the comparison to point out that this was an institution as advanced in science as Edinburgh, a school they would be familiar with.

Jefferson did attempt to recruit one professor from Edinburgh, but this was thirty years later, when he sent Francis Gilmer to Europe to recruit professors for the University of Virginia, giving him very specific instructions as to which particular professors were to be sought out at which particular universities. Jefferson's only interest in Edinburgh was its medical school, and the only professor Gilmer was instructed to look for there was a professor of anatomy.[5] There actually was a fairly widespread objection at that time to Jefferson importing professors from Europe, but, like the objections to the Geneva Academy proposal, this had nothing to do religion.

4. George Washington to Thomas Jefferson, March 15, 1795, John C. Fitzpatrick, ed., *The Writings of George Washington from the Original Manuscript Sources, 1745-1799*, vol. 34, (Washington D.C.: Government Printing Office, 1931), 147-148.

5. Agenda for the University of Virginia, April 26, 1824, *The Thomas Jefferson Papers, Series 1, General Correspondence, 1651-1827*, Library of Congress Manuscript Division, #40400.

The objections came from members of the American academic community who considered it an insult to all American universities that Jefferson didn't think qualified professors could be found in the United States. In an 1825 letter thanking British Parliament member John Evelyn Denison for a donation of books for the university, Jefferson mentioned the objections to his recruitment of European professors.

> Your favor of July 30th was duly received, and we have now at hand the books you have been so kind as to send to our University. They are truly acceptable in themselves, for we might have been years not knowing of their existence; but give the greater pleasure as evidence of the interest you have taken in our infant institution. It is going on as successfully as we could have expected; and I have no reason to regret the measure taken of procuring professors from abroad where science is so much ahead of us. You witnessed some of the puny squibs of which I was the butt on that account. They were probably from disappointed candidates, whose unworthiness had occasioned their applications to be passed over. The measure has been generally approved in the South and West; and by all liberal minds in the North.[6]

The College of William and Mary...

> **In his book *Americas Christian History: The Untold Story,* Gary DeMar claims: "Jefferson advocated the tax-supported College of William and Mary maintain a perpetual mission among the Indian tribes which included the instruction of the principles of Christianity."**

Jefferson did not advocate a mission to instruct the Indians in the principles of Christianity. He was stuck with it because it was written

6. Thomas Jefferson to John Evelyn Denison, November 9, 1825, Andrew A. Lipscomb and Albert Ellery Bergh, eds., *The Writings of Thomas Jefferson,* vol. 16, (Washington D.C.: Thomas Jefferson Memorial Association, 1907), 129.

into the charter of the college. What Jefferson proposed was to turn this into an anthropological, rather than a religious, mission.

The mission, called the Brafferton Professorship, was established with a private donation from the will of English scientist Robert Boyle. The funding was provided by the rental of Brafferton, an estate in England purchased by the executors of Boyle's will. The 1693 charter of William and Mary had specified that the college was to train young Indian boys in the Anglican religion to become missionaries to their people, and, in 1697, the income from the Brafferton estate was earmarked for this purpose.

The Indian school at the college was a failure from the start. The biggest problem was that the Indians didn't want to send their children to a white school. In fact, the school's first six students were actually boys who were purchased from enemy tribes that had captured them. Although the college's charter called for twenty Indian students at a time, in 1721 there were none at all. Nevertheless, the Brafferton building was built in 1723 as a permanent home for the school, which struggled along for the next fifty years. The last Indian student was admitted in 1775. There is no evidence that any student who attended this school ever became a Christian missionary.

Benjamin Franklin, who in some ways considered the Indians to be more civilized and sensible than white men, and found the idea of sending Indian children to white schools ridiculous, wrote the following satirical account of one attempt to recruit students for the Brafferton School.

> ...Our laborious manner of Life compared with theirs, they esteem slavish and base; and the Learning on which we value ourselves; they regard as frivolous and useless. An Instance of this occurred at the Treaty of Lancaster in Pennsylvania, Anno 1744, between the Government of Virginia & the Six Nations. After the principal Business was settled, the Commissioners from Virginia acquainted the Indians by a Speech, that there was at Williamsburg a College with a Fund for Educating Indian Youth, and that if the Chiefs of the Six-Nations would send down half a dozen of their Sons to that College, the Government would take Care that they should be well provided for, and instructed in

> all the Learning of the white People. It is one of the Indian Rules of Politeness not to answer a public Proposition the same day that it is made; they think it would be treating it as a light Matter; and that they show it Respect by taking time to consider it, as of a Matter important. They therefore deferred their Answer till the day following; when their Speaker began by expressing their deep Sense of the Kindness of the Virginia Government, in making them that Offer; for we know, says he, that you highly esteem the kind of Learning taught in those Colleges, and that the Maintenance of our Young Men while with you, would be very expensive to you. We are convinced therefore that you mean to do us good by your Proposal, and we thank you heartily. But you who are wise must know, that different Nations have different Conceptions of things; and you will therefore not take it amiss, if our Ideas of this Kind of Education happen not to be the same with yours. We have had some Experience of it: Several of our Young People were formerly brought up at the Colleges of the Northern Provinces; they were instructed in all your Sciences; but when they came back to us, they were bad Runners, ignorant of every means of living in the Woods, unable to bear either Cold or Hunger, knew neither how to build a Cabin, take a Deer, or kill an Enemy, spoke our Language imperfectly; were therefore neither fit for Hunters, Warriors, or Counsellors; they were totally good for nothing. We are however not the less obliged by your kind Offer, tho we decline accepting it; and to show our grateful Sense of it, if the Gentlemen of Virginia will send us a dozen of their Sons, we will take great Care of their Education, instruct them in all we know, and make *Men* of them.[7]

In 1779, Thomas Jefferson became both Governor of Virginia and a member of William and Mary's Board of Visitors. He immediately set to work on reorganizing the college, with the goal of turning it into a non-sectarian state university. The main problem Jefferson faced was

7. J.A. Leo Lemay, ed., *Benjamin Franklin, Writings,* (New York: Literary Classics of the United States, 1987), 969-970.

that the Board of Visitors did not have the authority to make changes that required amending the college's constitution, something that could only be done by the legislature. Jefferson did propose the changes he wanted to make in his *Bill for Amending the Constitution of the College of William and Mary, and Substituting More Certain Revenues for Its Support,* but this bill was never acted on.

Among the changes that the Board of Visitors could not make was to increase the number of professors. They could, however, change what each professor taught. William and Mary's constitution limited the number of professorships to five, plus the Brafferton. At the time that Jefferson joined the board, the college had a divinity school with two professors, teaching theology and what Jefferson called "*oriental*" languages, meaning Hebrew and Aramaic. There was also a professor of Latin and Greek. Jefferson got rid of all three of these and replaced them with professorships of law and police, anatomy and medicine, and modern languages. Jefferson's reason for abolishing the school of Latin and Greek, which he referred to as the "*grammar*" school, was that it attracted very young students whom he considered disruptive to the college. Jefferson's opinion was that students who were old enough for college should already be proficient in these languages, making this school unnecessary.

While the purpose of the Brafferton Professorship could not be changed completely, Jefferson's idea was to take advantage of it to study the Indians' culture and languages. The phrases that Gary DeMar takes out of context to create his lie come from Jefferson's *Notes on the State of Virginia.* DeMar omits the part of the sentence in which Jefferson explained his plan for the Brafferton Professorship, and also the part where he made a point of noting that instruction in Christianity as part of this position could not be eliminated because it was required by its founder.

> The purposes of the Brafferton institution would be better answered by maintaining a perpetual mission among the Indian tribes, the object of which, besides instructing them in the principles of Christianity, as the founder requires, should be to collect their traditions, laws, customs, languages, and other circumstances which might lead to a discovery of their relation with one another, or descent from other nations.

> When these objects are accomplished with one tribe, the missionary might pass on to another.[8]

In addition to providing an opportunity to learn about the Indians, Jefferson's idea of sending the Brafferton professor among them would remove the Indian school from the grounds of William and Mary, getting rid of the only remaining religious school at the college.

In his *Bill for Amending the Constitution of the College of William and Mary,* Jefferson proposed that the number of professorships be increased to eight, plus the Brafferton. He also specified the duties of the Brafferton Professorship, and made it very clear that it was for these specified duties, and not whatever religious instruction this professor might engage in, that college funds would be used. In the bill, he called the position "*Missionary for Indian History, etc.*"

> The said Professors shall likewise appoint, from time to time, a missionary, of approved veracity, to the several tribes of Indians, whose business shall be to investigate their laws, customs, religions, traditions, and more particularly their languages, constructing grammars thereof, as well as may be, and copious vocabularies, and, on oath, to communicate, from time to time to the said president and professors the materials he collects to be by them laid up and preserved in their library, for which trouble the said missionary shall be allowed a salary at the discretion of the visitors out of the revenues of the college.[9]

Although he was able to make a number of significant changes to William and Mary, Jefferson eventually realized that this college could never be transformed into the kind of state university he envisioned, as he explained to Joseph Priestley in 1800.

> We have in that State a College (William and Mary) just well enough endowed to draw out the miserable existence to

8. Andrew A. Lipscomb and Albert Ellery Bergh, eds., *The Writings of Thomas Jefferson,* vol. 2, (Washington D.C.: Thomas Jefferson Memorial Association, 1904), 210.

9. Julian P. Boyd, ed., *The Papers of Thomas Jefferson,* vol. 2, (Princeton, NJ: Princeton University Press, 1950), 540.

> which a miserable constitution has doomed it. It is moreover eccentric in its position, exposed to all bilious diseases as all the lower country is, and therefore abandoned by the public care, as that part of the country itself is in a considerable degree by its inhabitants. We wish to establish in the upper country, and more centrally for the State, an University on a plan so broad and liberal and modern, as to be worth patronizing with the public support, and be a temptation to the youth of other States to come and drink of the cup of knowledge and fraternize with us.[10]

The University of Virginia...

The plan that would eventually evolve into the University of Virginia was hatched in 1803, when a group of Albemarle County citizens revived a twenty year old plan to establish a college in Charlottesville. Although a charter was obtained from the legislature at this time, nothing more was done towards establishing this school until a decade later, when five of the trustees from 1803 decided to revive the plan once again. Jefferson had supported the original 1783 plan for a school in Charlottesville, but was not around in 1803 when the plan was revived because he was busy running the country.

Jefferson got involved in 1814, allegedly by accident. The story, which may or may not be true, is that Jefferson happened to be riding past the tavern in Charlottesville where the five trustees of Albemarle Academy were meeting. The trustees, one of whom was Jefferson's nephew Peter Carr, saw Jefferson and invited him to sit in on their meeting. Whether or not this story is true, Jefferson did attend this meeting, was named a trustee, and within six months had pretty much taken over the project. Jefferson didn't actually have any interest in establishing the local college that the other trustees were planning. He did, however, see the existing Albemarle Academy charter as the vehicle he needed to establish his university.

At the request of the other trustees, Jefferson outlined a plan of

10. Thomas Jefferson to Dr. Joseph Priestley, January 18, 1800, Andrew A. Lipscomb and Albert Ellery Bergh, eds., *The Writings of Thomas Jefferson*, vol. 10, (Washington D.C.: Thomas Jefferson Memorial Association, 1907), 140.

education for the academy, which he sent to Peter Carr in September 1814. This outline is the source of a very popular religious right lie.

> **Mark Beliles, in the introduction to his version of the *Jefferson Bible*, presents a list of things he claims Jefferson supported the government being involved in, which includes: "establishing professional schools of theology."**

D. James Kennedy, putting his own twist on this lie, once again demonstrates that he has no idea what Beliles is lying about. In *What If America Were A Christian Nation Again?*, Kennedy copies Beliles's list of things "*Jefferson supported the government being involved in,*" but makes a few changes, including calling it a list of "*Jefferson's actions as president.*" Kennedy apparently doesn't know enough about Jefferson, or history in general, to recognize that many of the items on Beliles's are lies about things that occurred either long before or long after Jefferson's presidency, such as the 1814 plan for Albemarle Academy. Kennedy's changes also turn what Beliles claims Jefferson merely supported into things that Jefferson actually did. So, according to Kennedy, Jefferson not only established schools of theology, but did so while he was president.

Jefferson neither established nor supported government involvement in any theological school – before, during, or after his presidency. Beliles's claim is based on the fact that Jefferson, in the outline he sent to Peter Carr, listed a school of theology and ecclesiastical history among nine possible professional schools that might be added to Albemarle Academy as the school grew.

What needs to be remembered here is that Jefferson had no intention of there ever being an Albemarle Academy, let alone this school getting to a point where these professional schools would be added. Jefferson was planning from the start to hijack the schools charter and use it to establish his university. In order to do this, however, he first had to revive Albemarle Academy to a point where he could get its charter changed. The first step was to fill the vacant board seats. Jefferson wanted to reduce the number of trustees called for in the charter from eighteen to six, but couldn't petition the legislature to change the charter because there weren't enough trustees to take a vote. A board of eighteen was quickly assembled, most of whom had no idea what Jefferson was planning to do. Although Jefferson intended to get rid of this board as soon as he could, he had to watch his step because, while it existed, this was a real board with the power to put an end to his plan.

The outline Jefferson prepared for the trustees was really just a list compiled from the plans of the best universities in Europe, and was described by Jefferson as *"an authority for us to select from their different institutions the materials which are good for us, and, with them, to erect a structure, whose arrangement shall correspond with our own social condition..."* [11] The European universities that Jefferson drew from included theological schools, and he did not omit this from his outline. Jefferson had no intention of having a theological school in his university, but it would have been unnecessary, as well as stupid, to bring the subject up at this stage in the game. He couldn't risk opposition from the temporary board of trustees, and there was no reason he couldn't just wait until after the charter was changed and his plan was further along to delete the theological school.

Jefferson explained this in a letter to Dr. Thomas Cooper. Jefferson already had his eye on Cooper as a potential professor for his future university, and sent him a copy of the Albemarle Academy outline for his comments. Cooper objected to the theological school, and was a bit surprised that Jefferson had included it. Jefferson's provided the following explanation in his reply to Cooper's comments.

> I agree with yours of the 22d, that a professorship of Theology should have no place in our institution. But we cannot always do what is absolutely best. Those with whom we act, entertaining different views, have the power and the right of carrying them into practice. Truth advances, and error recedes step by step only; and to do to our fellow men the most good in our power, we must lead where we can, follow where we cannot, and still go with them, watching always the favorable moment for helping them to another step.[12]

11. Thomas Jefferson to Peter Carr, September 7, 1814, Andrew A. Lipscomb and Albert Ellery Bergh, eds., *The Writings of Thomas Jefferson,* vol. 19, (Washington D.C.: Thomas Jefferson Memorial Association, 1907), 212.

12. Thomas Jefferson to Dr. Thomas Cooper, October 7, 1814 , *ibid,* vol. 14, 200.

By 1816, Jefferson had accomplished the first part of his plan. The charter was changed, reducing the number of trustees to six, which now included James Madison and James Monroe, and the name of the school was changed from Albemarle Academy to Central College.

The name Central College was insisted on by Jefferson for a reason. The next step of his plan was to get the *Bill for Establishing a System of Public Education* through the legislature. This bill, written by Jefferson himself, called for establishing a state university in a *central* part of the state. He wanted his college to be chosen as the site of the university, so he wanted it to sound more central than any other colleges that might be proposed, and nothing sounded more central than Central College. In 1819, Central College, then under construction, became the University of Virginia, which opened in 1825.

When the University of Virginia was established, it had no school of theology, or any other religious instruction. This, of course, doesn't stop the Liars for Jesus from claiming that religion was taught there. Almost every religious right American history book and website contains some story about Thomas Jefferson encouraging, and even requiring, religious instruction or religious worship at the university. Although James Madison was also on the university's original Board of Visitors, Jefferson is singled out as the target of these lies.

> **According to William J. Federer, in his book *America's God and Country*: "In establishing the University of Virginia, Thomas Jefferson not only encouraged the teaching of religion, but set aside a place inside the Rotunda for chapel services."**
>
> **Mark Beliles, in the introduction to his version of the *Jefferson Bible*, claims that Jefferson: "arranged for organized chapel services and nondenominational religious instruction in schools and at his university in Virginia."**

No religious activities whatsoever took place at the University of Virginia while Jefferson was alive, and it wasn't until about five years after Madison's death that any religious activities occurred that would be considered unconstitutional even by today's standards.

The most popular stories about religion at the University of Virginia come from the *Report of the Commissioners appointed to fix the site of the University of Virginia,* more commonly known as the *Rockfish Report.* The Liars for Jesus base their claims solely on this one report, which was carefully written by Jefferson in 1818 to ensure that the Virginia Assembly would approve his plan, and completely disregard what was actually done at the university once it was established.

In August 1818, six months after the Assembly passed the bill to establish a state university, a commission appointed by the governor met at a tavern in Rockfish Gap. The commission consisted of one representative from each of Virginia's voting districts, with Jefferson and Madison representing their districts. The commissioners were instructed to submit their recommendations for the university's site, as well as plans for the buildings, faculty, and courses of education, but the only thing they really needed to do was decide on the site. Jefferson had already written the plan of education, and, if Central College was chosen from among the three proposed sites, he'd had his building plan since about 1810.

Joseph C. Cabell, a state senator who was on board of Central College, and later on the first board of the University of Virginia, did everything he could to tip the scales in favor of the college. It was Cabell who proposed that the commission be made up of a representative from each voting district, ensuring a majority from the more populated eastern part of the state who would naturally favor Charlottesville over the other more western sites. Cabell also used his influence to make sure that the governor, who had recently moved to Albemarle County himself, would be appointing the commissioners, assuming that he would choose men who were likely to vote for Central College, regardless of what part of the state they were from.

Right from the start, Cabell wanted both Jefferson and Madison to be on the commission, but Jefferson thought it would be better if Cabell himself, who also lived in his district, went as its representative. Jefferson was afraid that his presence would make his association with Central College too obvious, and might actually hurt the college's chances of being being approved by the legislature, even if it was the site recommended by the commission. The following is what Jefferson wrote to Cabell.

> You seem to doubt whether Mr. Madison would serve if named a commissioner for the location, &c. of the University? but there can be no doubt that he would, and it is most important that he should. As to myself, I should be ready to do anything in my power for the institution; but that is not the exact question. Would it promote the success of the institution most for me to be in or out of it? Out of it, I believe. It is still to depend ultimately on the will of the Legislature; and that has its uncertainties. There are fanatics both in religion and politics, who, without knowing me personally, have long been taught to consider me as a raw head and bloody bones, and as we can afford to lose no votes in that body, I do think it would be better that you should be named for our district.[13]

Jefferson not only ended up representing his district, but was chosen as president of the commission. Although he knew that Cabell's groundwork had made the choice of Central College almost certain, Jefferson arrived at the meeting with a few things to sway anyone who might be in favor of one of the other proposed sites. He made a cardboard map of the state showing that the college's location was the most central, both geographically and by population. He also compiled a list of the large number of Albemarle County residents who were over eighty years old, presenting this as evidence of the area's healthy climate. This was a good selling point because, although it wasn't a serious contender for the university, it was well known that William and Mary's location made it prone to outbreaks of disease at certain times of the year. It's interesting that, a decade later, religious fanatics would attribute a deadly outbreak of typhoid at the University of Virginia to divine retribution brought on by the absence of religious worship at the school, while accepting that the regular outbreaks of disease at William and Mary, which were just as common when it was a theological seminary as they were after Jefferson's reorganization, were nothing more than the result of the unhealthy climate in that part of the state.

13. Thomas Jefferson to Joseph C. Cabell, February 26, 1818, *Early History of the University of Virginia, as Contained in the Letters of Thomas Jefferson and Joseph C. Cabell*, (Richmond, VA: J.W. Randolph, 1856), 128.

The Rockfish Commission appointed a committee of six members, including Jefferson and Madison, to write the plan of education for the university. Jefferson, of course, had already done this. There is no indication that there were any objections from the other committee members, or the commission as a whole, to the omission of religious instruction in Jefferson's plan. But, as Jefferson mentioned in his letter to Joseph Cabell, the commission was only the first hurdle. It was the approval of the legislature that he was worried about.

Jefferson knew that the absence of a theological school in his plan would be less likely to raise an alarm among the religious members of the legislature, or be used as ammunition by his political enemies, if he threw a few other things into the report that sounded somewhat accommodating to religion, so this is exactly what he did. This tactic was used by Jefferson and Madison on several other occasions, not only to avoid and diffuse rumors that the university was an enemy of religion, but also to prevent accusations that it was a partisan institution.

Jefferson and Madison actually did have every intention of using the university to inculcate their political principles in the next generation of Virginians, and to spread those principles to the rest of the country by attracting students from other states, as Jefferson wrote in one of his last letters to Madison.

> It is in our Seminary that the Vestal flame is to be kept alive; it is thence it is to spread anew over our own and the sister states. If we are true and vigilant in our trust, within a dozen or 20. years a majority of our own legislature will be from our school, and many disciples will have carried its doctrines home with them to their several States, and will have leavened thus the whole mass.[14]

While the choice of texts for all other subjects was left entirely up to the professors, Jefferson and Madison decided that they should be the ones to select the texts for law and government. Jefferson sent Madison a list of his choices, which included the *Virginia Resolutions,*

14. Thomas Jefferson to James Madison, February 17, 1826, James Morton Smith, ed., *The Republic of Letters: The Correspondence Between Thomas Jefferson and James Madison 1776-1826,* vol. 3, (New York and London: W.W. Norton & Company, 1995), 1965.

a document written by Madison against the *Alien and Sedition Acts* of 1798, in which he pretty much accused the Federalists of the Adams administration of wanting to turn the country into a monarchy. Madison wasn't sure that including this document was such a great idea, given that they were trying to attract students from the remaining federalist parts of Virginia, as well as students from the northern states.

> ...With respect to the Virginia Document of 1799, there may be more room for hesitation. Tho corresponding with the predominant sense of the Nation; being of local origin and having reference to a state of Parties not yet extinct, an absolute prescription of it, might excite prejudices against the University as under Party Banners, and induce the more bigoted to withhold from it their sons, even when destined for other than the studies of the Law School....[15]

Madison's solution was not to omit the *Virginia Resolutions,* but to throw in a few documents that the Federalists would approve of – George Washington's Inaugural Speech and Farewell Address. He also suggested that their text choices be presented merely as "*selected Standards*" rather than making them mandatory, confident that their selection alone would be enough to "*give them authority with the students*" and "*controul or counteract deviations of the professor.*"

> ...I have, for your consideration, sketched a modification of the operative passage in your draught, with a view to relax the absoluteness of its injunction, and added to your list of Documents the Inaugural Speech and Farewell Address of President Washington. They may help down what might be less readily swallowed, and contain nothing which is not good; unless it be the laudatory reference in the Address to the Treaty of 1795 with G.B. which ought not to weigh against the sound sentiments characterizing it.[16]

15. James Madison to Thomas Jefferson, February 8, 1825, James Morton Smith, ed., *The Republic of Letters: The Correspondence Between Thomas Jefferson and James Madison 1776-1826,* vol. 3, (New York and London: W.W. Norton & Company, 1995), 1925.

16. *ibid.*

To *"help down what might be less readily swallowed"* in the Rockfish Report, namely the omission of a theological school, Jefferson listed religious worship among the possible uses for the Rotunda, and made the proposed Professorship of Ethics sound as if it might include some religious instruction. The following sentence from the report, found at the end of a section describing and estimating the cost of the buildings that needed to be finished before the university could open, is the sole source of the claim that Jefferson *"arranged for organized chapel services"* at the university.

> It is supposed probable, that a building of somewhat more size in the middle of the grounds may be called for in time, in which may be rooms for religious worship, under such impartial regulations as the Visitors shall prescribe, for public examinations, for a library, for the schools of music, drawing, and other associated purposes.[17]

Before the University even opened, a request to hold a religious service in one of the finished pavilions was denied by the Board of Visitors. Because the Rockfish Report had specified only the Rotunda as a possible place for religious worship, the board was able to fend off requests to hold services in other buildings by making it an unwritten policy to prohibit the use of university buildings for anything other than university purposes. Of course, this policy wasn't going to work once the Rotunda was completed because the Rockfish Report did list religious worship as a possible use for that building. But, until that time, such requests could be, and were, denied. Obviously, if Jefferson and Madison had really wanted religious services to be held at the university, they could have allowed them in another building until the Rotunda was finished, rather than using the wording of the Rockfish Report to avoid them as long as possible.

The board's building use policy, which does not appear to have been used to deny anything other than requests for religious services, was invoked by Jefferson in April 1825, a month after the university opened. This time it was used to deny a request by the university's proctor, Arthur S. Brockenbrough, to allow Sunday services in one of

17. Edgar W. Knight, ed., *A Documentary History of Education in the South Before 1860*, vol. 3, (Chapel Hill, NC: University of North Carolina Press, 1952), 164.

the pavilions. This is an interesting letter because, in order to use the board's policy to deny Brockenbrough's request, Jefferson had to be a little less than honest about a few things.

> In answer to your letter proposing to permit the lecturing room of the Pavilion No. 1. to be used regularly for prayers and preachings on Sundays, I have to observe that some 3. or 4. years ago, an application was made to permit a sermon to be preached in one of the pavilions on a particular occasion, not now recollected, it brought the subject into consideration with the Visitors, and altho they entered into no formal and written resolution on the occasion, the concurrent sentiment was that the buildings of the University belong to the state that they were erected for the purposes of an University, and that the Visitors, to whose care they are committed for those purposes have no right to permit their application to any other. and accordingly, when applied to, on the visit of General Lafayette, I declined at first the request of the use of the Rotunda for his entertainment, until it occurred on reflection that the room, in the unfinished state in which it then was, was as open and uninclosed, and as insusceptible of injury, as the field in which it stood. In the Rockfish report it was stated as probable that a building larger than the Pavilions might be called for in time, in which might be rooms for a library, for public examinations, and for religious worship *under such impartial regulations as the Visitors should prescribe,* the legislature neither sanctioned nor rejected this proposition; and afterwards, in the Report of Oct 1822, the board suggested, as a substitute, that the different religious sects should be invited to establish their separate theological schools in the vicinity of the University, in which the Students might attend religious worship, each in the form of his respective sect, and thus avoid all jealousy of attempts on his religious tenets. among the enactments of the board is one looking to this object, and superseding the first idea of permitting a room in the Rotunda to be used for religious worship, and of undertaking to frame a set of

> regulations of equality and impartiality among the multiplied sects....[18]

The sentence in this letter about allowing the use of the Rotunda for General Lafayette's dinner, which was added by Jefferson in the margin of his draft, is not true. Jefferson apparently realized after writing the rest of the letter that if he was going to use the board's building policy to deny this request, he had to make up an excuse for allowing Lafayette's dinner, an event five months earlier that had clearly violated that policy. If anyone had wanted to question Jefferson's decision to deny the request to hold religious services, this dinner would have been their best argument, so Jefferson beat them to it and let them know that bringing it up wasn't going to make him change his mind.

Jefferson's claim that he initially denied a request to use the Rotunda for Lafayette's dinner is very hard to believe, mainly because the dinner was his idea. When Lafayette toured America in 1824 and 1825, he was nothing short of a rock star. Everyone wanted to meet him, and every town wanted to have him as their guest. The town of Charlottesville was no exception. Jefferson, who hadn't seen Lafayette in thirty-five years and wanted to spend as much time with him as possible, didn't want the people of Charlottesville to plan a bunch of events that would keep him away from Monticello, so he suggested instead that they hold one big public dinner. On September 3, 1824, Jefferson wrote to Lafayette that the dinner was being planned, and that it had been his idea.

> Our little village of Charlottesville insists also on receiving you. They would have claimed you as their guest, were it possible I could have seen you the guest of any other than myself in the vicinage of Monto. I have reduced them therefore to the honor of your accepting from them a dinner, and that, thro me, they beseech you to come & accept. I suppose in fact that either going to or returning from the South, the line by Monto. & Montpellier will be little out of your way. Come then, my dear friend, suit the time to yourself, make your

18. Thomas Jefferson to Arthur S. Brockenbrough, April 21, 1825, *The Thomas Jefferson Papers, Series 1, General Correspondence, 1651-1827,* Library of Congress Manuscript Division, #40962.

> headquarters here from whence the ride to Charlottesville & its appendage our university will not be of an hour.[19]

The reason given by Jefferson for deciding to allow the use of the Rotunda for Lafayette's dinner wasn't true either. According to the records of the building's construction, the board's reports to the legislature, and Jefferson's own correspondence, the Rotunda was far from being "*as open and uninclosed...as the field in which it stood*" at the time the dinner was being planned. The exterior walls had been completed in 1823, and the roof put on in the summer of 1824. Much of the interior was still unfinished, but the only major exterior work that remained to be done consisted of the steps, which at the time were temporary and made out of wood, the columns, whose caps and bases were being carved in Italy, and the installation of some of the glass, which had not yet arrived from Boston. On October 12, 1824, Jefferson even remarked in a letter to Francis Gilmer, who had been in Europe recruiting professors, and would have been unaware of the progress made during that year's building season, that the Rotunda was "*sufficiently advanced*" to use for the dinner.

> The public papers will have informed you of the universal delirium into which all orders of our citizens are thrown, by the visit of Genl Fayette...he is to visit Montpellier and Monticello within about 3 weeks, and to accept a public dinner in our University. The Rotunda is sufficiently advanced to receive him.[20]

The other problem with Jefferson's unfinished building excuse is that a second dinner for Lafayette was held in the Rotunda when he visited Virginia again before returning to France. This was in August 1825, four months *after* Jefferson denied Brockenbrough's request. By this time even the interior of the building was nearly completed. Beginning in 1826, public dinners in the Rotunda became a regular

19. Thomas Jefferson to the Marquis de Lafayette, September 3, 1824, Paul Leicester Ford, ed., *The Works of Thomas Jefferson, Federal Edition*, vol. 12, (New York and London: G.P. Putnam's Sons, 1905), 376-377.

20. Thomas Jefferson to Francis Walker Gilmer, October 12, 1824, Richard Beale Davis, ed., *Correspondence of Thomas Jefferson and Francis Walker Gilmer, 1814-1826*, (Columbia, SC: University of South Carolina Press, 1946), 109.

occurrence on occasions like Washington's birthday and the 4th of July. The dinner for Lafayette in 1824 was clearly not a one time thing allowed because of the unfinished state of the Rotunda.

Jefferson wouldn't actually have expected Arthur Brockenbrough to buy his unfinished building excuse. Brockenbrough, whose job as proctor of the university included purchasing the building materials and hiring the workmen, would have known better than anyone exactly how far along the Rotunda was at any given time. But, Jefferson's excuses weren't meant to convince Brockenbrough of anything. They were for Brockenbrough to use on the members of the two Charlottesville congregations who had asked him to make the request. Jefferson knew his excuses would be good enough for the congregations in his neighborhood. He did not, however, want his enemies in other parts of the state to get a hold of his letter, and was clearly relieved when Brockenbrough, who thought of publishing it in the local newspaper, asked for his permission before doing so.

> With your permission I will publish in the Cent Gaz: your letter of the 21 April last seting forth your objections to permiting the lecture rooms of the Pav: to be used for prayer & reading on sundays your objections I have no doubt are perfectly satisfactory to all but the Bigoted part of the community and to correct any false statements that they may make, I wish it to go to the public [21]

This was Jefferson's reply to Brockenbrough.

> You have done very right in not publishing my letter of Apr. 21. I should have had immediately a whole kennel of Scriblers attacking me in the newspapers, insisting on their right to use a public building for any public exhibition, and drawing me into a paper war on the question. [22]

21. Draft of letter from Brockenbrough to Jefferson, written on the back of Jefferson's June 13, 1825 letter to Brockenbrough, Frank Edgar Grizzard, Jr., *Documentary History of the Construction of the Buildings at the University of Virginia, 1817–1828,* (Ph.D. Dissertation, University of Virginia, 1996).

22. Thomas Jefferson to Arthur S. Brockenbrough, June 20, 1825, *The Thomas Jefferson Papers, Series 1, General Correspondence, 1651-1827,* Library of Congress Manuscript Division, #41042.

It wasn't only the board's unwritten policy and his excuses for allowing Lafayette's dinner that Jefferson was worried about. There was another lie in his letter that his enemies would have jumped on – his claim that a proposal in the October 1822 Board of Visitors report to the legislature had superceded the proposal in the Rockfish Report allowing religious worship in the Rotunda.

The proposal in the board's October 1822 report was an effort to stop the clergy's attacks on the university, particularly a rumor that the university was an enemy to all religions except Unitarianism. To make it more difficult for the clergy to accuse the board of being enemies of religion, Jefferson came up with the idea of inviting all the religious sects to establish their own theological schools adjacent to, but independent of, the university.

The invitation to the religious sects, and the rumors that prompted it, are described in more detail later in this chapter. It is only mentioned here because Jefferson's claim in his letter to Brockenbrough that this invitation superceded the proposal in the Rockfish Report wasn't true. In fact, the 1822 invitation actually included the possibility of allowing the professors of the theological schools to use a room in the Rotunda *because of* the proposal in the Rockfish Report.

The board's October 1824 report to the legislature, the last report before Jefferson's letter to Brockenbrough, contained the decisions about the use of the Rotunda's rooms as of that date. In this report, no room was designated solely for religious worship, but religious worship was still listed among the possible uses of a room designated for exams and lectures that required a larger room. Both the 1822 and 1824 reports were written by Jefferson himself, so he was completely aware when he wrote his letter to Brockenbrough in April 1825 that nothing in the Rockfish Report had been superceded by the board's invitation to the religious sects. Jefferson's enemies, who were scrutinizing every word written by the board looking for things to complain about, would also have been aware of this.

Jefferson's reason for adding this lie to his letter isn't hard to figure out. Nor is the fact that he thought he could get away with it, at least among the people he intended to hear it. None of the religious congregations in Charlottesville had a church in 1825. Four different denominations held their services in the courthouse, each getting one Sunday a month. This is why two of the congregations asked to use a building at the university. While the board's building policy could be used to deny this request, Jefferson obviously anticipated that these same congregations would just make another request as soon as the Rotunda was completed – unless he gave them reason to believe that the part of the Rockfish Report allowing services in that building no longer applied. Jefferson took a gamble that the members of these local congregations hadn't paid much attention to what was decided at later board meetings, and, unlike his enemies who were watching every move he made, would simply take his word for it that the 1822 proposal superceded the one in the Rockfish Report.

Another popular story in the religious right American history books, which almost always follows the lie that Jefferson arranged for organized chapel services at the University of Virginia, has to do with the use of the Charlottesville courthouse by the four religious congregations. These stories are coupled not because of the request by two of these congregations to hold services at the university, but because Jefferson mentioned both the courthouse services and the university's invitation to religious sects in the same 1822 letter to Dr. Thomas Cooper.

According to David Barton, in his book *Original Intent,* Thomas Jefferson "praised the use of the Charlottesville courthouse for religious services."

Jefferson did not "*praise*" the use of the courthouse for religious services. He merely mentioned that the different sects used the courthouse. Dr. Cooper had written to Jefferson about the rise of religious fanaticism in America. Jefferson, in response to Cooper's comments on the subject, told him that the problem had not yet reached his part of Virginia. To illustrate this, Jefferson noted that the four different religious sects in Charlottesville, none of which had a church, were able to amicably share the courthouse for their services. Jefferson's only point was that the different sects in his area were still getting along well enough to share a building, not that he was happy that the building they were sharing was the courthouse. The following is the part of Jefferson's letter to Cooper in which the courthouse is mentioned.

> ...The atmosphere of our country is unquestionably charged with a threatening cloud of fanaticism, lighter in

some parts; denser in others, but too heavy in all. I had no idea, however, that in Pennsylvania, the cradle of toleration and freedom of religion, it could have arisen to the height you describe. This must be owing to the growth of Presbyterianism. The blasphemy and absurdity of the five points of Calvin, and the impossibility of defending them, render their advocates impatient of reasoning, irritable, and prone to denunciation. In Boston, however, and its neighborhood, Unitarianism has advanced to so great strength, as now to humble this haughtiest of all religious sects; insomuch, that they condescend to interchange with them and the other sects, the civilities of preaching freely and frequently in each others meeting-houses. In Rhode Island, on the other hand, no sectarian preacher will permit an Unitarian to pollute his desk. In our Richmond there is much fanaticism, but chiefly among the women. They have their night meetings and praying parties, where, attended by their priests, and sometimes by a henpecked husband, they pour forth the effusions of their love to Jesus, in terms as amatory and carnal, as their modesty would permit them to use to a mere earthly lover. In our village of Charlottesville, there is a good degree of religion, with a small spice only of fanaticism. We have four sects, but without either church or meeting-house. The court-house is the common temple, one Sunday in the month to each. Here, Episcopalian and Presbyterian, Methodist and Baptist, meet together, join in hymning their Maker, listen with attention and devotion to each others preachers, and all mix in society with perfect harmony. It is not so in the districts where Presbyterianism prevails undividedly. Their ambition and tyranny would tolerate no rival if they had power. Systematical in grasping at an ascendency over all other sects, they aim, like the Jesuits, at engrossing the education of the country, are hostile to every institution which they do not direct, and jealous at seeing others begin to attend at all to that object. The diffusion of instruction, to which there is now so growing an attention, will be the remote remedy to this fever of fanaticism; while the more

> proximate one will be the progress of Unitarianism. That this will, ere long, be the religion of the majority from North to South, I have no doubt.[23]

Jefferson also mentioned the courthouse situation in his 1825 letter to Arthur Brockenbrough denying the request to hold Sunday services at the university. Jefferson ended this letter by saying that he wanted all of the congregations to build their own buildings, and that allowing any of them to use the university would hinder this. Independent of his reasons for not allowing the services at the university, Jefferson explained to Brockenbrough that the inconvenience of sharing the courthouse was what would motivate the congregations to build churches. As long as they were using the courthouse, each sect could only have a service with a minister of their denomination once a month. If two of the sects moved to the university and were able to have their type of services more often, they would have less incentive to build churches. Jefferson also foresaw that not all of the members of the congregations making the request would be willing to travel to the university for their services, splitting each of those congregations into two groups, neither of which would be large enough to support a minister, let alone raise money to build a church. The following is the last paragraph of Jefferson's letter to Brockenbrough.

> ...that place has been in long possession of the seat of public worship, a right always deemed strongest until a better can be produced. there too they are building, or about to build, proper churches and meeting houses, much better adapted to the accommodation of a congregation than a scanty lecturing room. are these to be abandoned, and the private room to be preferred? if not, then the congregations, already too small, would by your proposition be split into halves incompetent to the employment and support of a double set of officiating ministers. each of course would break up the other, and both fall to the ground. I think therefore that, independant of our declining to sanction this application, it will

23. Thomas Jefferson to Dr. Thomas Cooper, November 2, 1822, Andrew A. Lipscomb and Albert Ellery Bergh, eds., *The Writings of Thomas Jefferson*, vol. 15, (Washington D.C.: Thomas Jefferson Memorial Association, 1903), 403-405.

> not, on further reflexion, be thought as advantageous to religious interests as their joint assembly at a single place.[24]

At the time Jefferson wrote this letter, the Episcopalians were the only sect that had started building a church in Charlottesville. The design of this church, although long attributed to Jefferson and claimed to be evidence of his devotion to religion, was actually the work of John Neilson, a builder who was working on the university. The other three sects all built churches over the next decade – the Presbyterians in 1827, the Baptists in 1833, and the Methodists in 1834.

The Board of Visitors' 1822 invitation to the religious sects to establish their own schools near the University of Virginia is the source of a number of lies, all of which contain some combination or variation of the following three claims: that the invitation was extended by Jefferson to promote religious instruction at the university; that religious schools were invited to build on state property; that these schools were actually built and were attended by university students.

According to David Barton, in his book *Original Intent*: Jefferson "expected students to participate in the various religious schools which he personally had invited to locate adjacent to and upon the University property..."

David Barton, like most Liars for Jesus, completely ignores all of the letters in which Jefferson and Madison, as well as Joseph Cabell, made it perfectly clear that the reason for the invitation was to stop the clergy's attacks on the university. Cabell, as mentioned earlier, was a member of the university's Board of Visitors as well as a member of the Virginia legislature. Jefferson did see some good that could come from the sects accepting the invitation, but it wasn't that university students would attend their religious schools. It was that future ministers might attend classes at the university and study science, which he saw as the best remedy for religious fanaticism.

The following is from one of the many letters in which Jefferson

24. Thomas Jefferson to Arthur S. Brockenbrough, April 21, 1825, *The Thomas Jefferson Papers, Series 1, General Correspondence, 1651-1827,* Library of Congress Manuscript Division, #40962.

gave the real reason for invitation. This particular letter was written to Thomas Cooper in April 1823, shortly after Jefferson learned from Joseph Cabell that the invitation had, in fact, been effective in stopping the use of the clergy's rumors by the university's enemies in the legislature.

> ...we disarmed them of this calumny however in our last report by inviting the different sects to establish their respective divinity schools on the margin of the grounds of the University, so that their students might attend its schools & have the benefit of its library, to be entirely independent of it at the same time, and no ways incorporated with it. one sect, I think, may do it, but another, disdaining equality, ambitioning nothing less than a soaring ascendancy, will despise our invitation. they are hostile to all educ^{n} of which they have not the direction, and foresee that this inst^{n}, by enlightening the minds of the people and encouraging them to appeal to their own common sense is to dispel the fanaticism on which their power is built....[25]

The sect that Jefferson knew would despise the invitation was the Presbyterians. The sect he thought might accept it was the Episcopalians. For reasons explained later in this chapter, Jefferson wasn't even concerned about Virginia's other two significant sects, the Baptists and the Methodists. When Jefferson came up with the idea of the invitation in October 1822, he knew there wasn't much chance that any of the sects would actually accept it. Making a public statement that this idea had been suggested by "*some pious individuals,*" and that the board was "*disposed to lend a willing ear*" to such suggestions, was simply a way to let the air out of the clergy's accusations that the university was excluding them. By the time Jefferson wrote to Cooper in April 1823, things had changed. From 1820 to 1822, the Episcopalians had been trying to reestablish the theological school at William and Mary that Jefferson had abolished forty years earlier. There was no possibility that they would attempt to establish a second school in the same state. In the spring of 1823, however, Jefferson found out that

25. Thomas Jefferson to Dr. Thomas Cooper, April 12, 1823, *The Thomas Jefferson Papers, Series 1, General Correspondence, 1651-1827,* Library of Congress Manuscript Division, #39995.

their attempt to establish the school at William and Mary had failed, and that they were considering a plan to relocate it to another part of the state. Since they had not yet decided on a new location, there was suddenly a real possibility that they might accept the invitation and relocate near the university.

The Board of Visitors needed to stop the clergy's rumors for two reasons. The first was that they were interfering with the board's selection of professors. The second was that the university's enemies in the legislature were effectively using these rumors, in conjunction with their accusations that Jefferson was being extravagant and wasting public money, to block the funding needed to finish the university's buildings.

The first wave of rumors, sparked by the absence of religious instruction in the 1818 Rockfish Report, had been expected, and was described by James Madison as "*manageable.*" These initial rumors, which were confined to the clergy of certain sects and a handful of religious fanatics, were ignored by most Virginians and did little to change the favorable public opinion of the university. One particular accusation, however, made a year and a half after the Rockfish Report, became a real problem.

In January 1820, John Holt Rice, a Presbyterian minister and editor of the *Virginia Literary and Evangelical Magazine,* published an article that, among other things, accused the university of promoting Unitarianism, while excluding trinitarian Christianity. Rice's accusation was based on the appointment of Thomas Cooper as the university's first professor. Dr. Cooper was a Unitarian, and had a reputation for being outspoken about his religious opinions. Dr. Rice, assuming that clergymen were to be excluded from professorships at the university, claimed that the appointment of Dr. Cooper, although not a clergyman, was an unfair promotion of Unitarianism. In his preface to an 1806 edition of *The Memoirs of Dr. Joseph Priestly,* Cooper had made some unfavorable statements about trinitarianism. Rice included the most shocking of these statements in his article as proof of Cooper's animosity towards all trinitarian sects.

Dr. Rice's article was very effective. It not only united the clergy and religious people of Virginia's rival sects in a common cause, but raised opposition to Cooper's appointment among those who weren't religious. Many non-religious people, believing Rice's accusation that the appointment of Cooper was an effort to promote Unitarianism, objected on the grounds that promoting any religious beliefs in a public university violated the state's constitution. According to Joseph Cabell, even the *"free-thinkers"* of Richmond, most of whom probably agreed with Cooper's opinions, objected to his appointment, not only for constitutional reasons, but because they feared that the controversy would hurt the university's reputation.

Joseph Cabell, a state senator as well as a member of the university's board, wrote regularly to Jefferson, and occasionally to Madison, keeping them up to date on what was going on in the legislature between board meetings. On March 10, 1821, a little over a year after Dr. Rice's first article appeared, Cabell wrote to Madison, describing how out of control the Dr. Cooper situation had become.

> The enemies of the institution are gaining ground with the Bulk of the people generally thro the state. The Appointment of Dr. Cooper has enlisted all the religious orders of society against the institution. You have not an idea how excessively unpopular Doctor Cooper now is in Virginia. I verily believe that 99/100s of the people of Virginia would now vote against him. Even all the free-thinkers of my acquaintance in Richmond protest against his being made a Professor of the University: all on the ground of policy, & some on the ground of principle. I sincerely believe that if Doctor Cooper should be made President, it will cause the entire overthrow of the institution. Possibly he may be sustained as a Professor, if he comes in with others, after a time. I doubt whether he would get any votes except yours, Mr. Jefferson's, & mine. If he should, the further support would be reluctant homage to yourself and Mr. Jefferson. This state of things vexes & distresses me: and I apprize you of it to prevent you and Mr. Jefferson from being taken unaware, & from committing yourselves to Doctr Cooper.[26]

While waiting for the University of Virginia to open, Dr. Cooper had taken a temporary position teaching chemistry at South Carolina College. This is where he was when he first heard about Dr. Rice's

26. Joseph C. Cabell to James Madison, March 10, 1821, *The James Madison Papers at the Library of Congress, Series 1, General Correspondence,* Library of Congress Manuscript Division.

article, receiving an extract from it from a friend in Richmond. Cooper had already been the subject of an attack by the clergy in Pennsylvania and knew from experience how ugly the attack in Virginia was likely to get. He wrote to Jefferson in March 1820, a full year before Cabell became concerned enough about the situation to write his letter warning Madison about it, offering to resign from the university if Jefferson thought he should. Jefferson, who had only heard about Rice's accusation a few days before receiving Cooper's resignation offer, greatly underestimated the damage it was going to do, and replied to Cooper that the article, in what he considered an obscure periodical, would soon be forgotten. The following, from his reply to Cooper, was Jefferson's initial assessment of the situation.

> ...The Baptists are sound republicans and zealous supporters of their government. The Methodists are republican mostly, satisfied with their government meddling with nothing but the concerns of their own calling and opposing nothing. These two sects are entirely friendly to our university. The anglicans are the same. The Presbyterian *clergy* alone (not their followers) remain bitterly federal and malcontent with their government. They are violent, ambitious of power, and intolerant in politics as in religion and want nothing but license from the laws to kindle again the fires of their leader John Knox, and to give us a 2d blast from his trumpet. Having a little more monkish learning than the clergy of the other sects, they are jealous of the general diffusion of science, and therefore hostile to our Seminary lest it should qualify their antagonists of the other sects to meet them in equal combat. Not daring to attack the institution with the avowal of their real motives, they Peck at you, at me, and every feather they can spy out. But in this they have no weight, even with their own followers, excepting a few old men among them who may still be federal & Anglomen, their main body are good citizens, friends to their government, anxious for reputation, and therefore friendly to the University.[27]

27. Thomas Jefferson to Dr. Thomas Cooper, March 13, 1820, Adrienne Koch and William Peden, eds., *The Life and Selected Writings of Thomas Jefferson*, (New York: Random House, 1944), 697.

Jefferson also assumed, based on previous experience, that the other sects would band together against the Presbyterians, regardless of the issue, if it appeared that that sect was in any way trying to get control of the university. He soon realized he was wrong about this, writing the following to William Short only a month after his letter to Cooper.

> The serious enemies are the priests of the different religious sects, to whose spells on the human mind its improvement is ominous. Their pulpits are now resounding with denunciations against the appointment of Dr. Cooper, whom they charge as a monotheist in opposition to their tritheism. Hostile as these sects are in every other point, to one another, they unite in maintaining their mystical theogony against those who believe there is one God only.…[28]

At the April 1820 meeting of the Board of Visitors, a committee, consisting of Jefferson and John Hartwell Cocke, was appointed to contact Dr. Cooper regarding his contract. This actually had more to do with the delay in opening the university and lack of funding from the legislature than Dr. Rice's article, and probably would have happened anyway. According to his contract, Cooper was to be paid $1,500 in advance while he was waiting for the university to open. This arrangement was decided on when the board thought the university would be opening in the spring of 1821. By 1820, however, it was obvious that the earliest it could possibly open was 1822, and even that was being optimistic. The board couldn't expect Cooper to put his life on hold for another year without offering him some additional compensation, but they didn't have the funds to do this. They hadn't even paid him the initial $1,500 yet. Although a few of the board members, including Cocke, saw the university's financial situation as an excuse to get rid of the Cooper problem, Cooper had a contract and terminating it had to be a mutual decision. The following was the resolution of the board.

> Resolved that the committee of superintendence be authorised to communicate to Doctor Thomas Cooper the delay

28. Thomas Jefferson to William Short, April 13, 1820, Andrew A. Lipscomb and Albert Ellery Bergh, eds., *The Writings of Thomas Jefferson,* vol. 15, (Washington D.C.: Thomas Jefferson Memorial Association, 1903), 246.

> and uncertainty now unavoidable in regard to the time of opening the University, and to make such change in the contracts with him as to them may seem advisable.[29]

Jefferson didn't let Cocke know until a week after the board meeting that Cooper had already offered to resign. He wanted to handle the situation in a way that would allow the board to simply rehire Cooper when the university did open. Before doing anything official, Jefferson wanted to write to Cooper unofficially to explain that his lack of concern about Rice's article had been a mistake, and to find out if he still wanted to resign. Jefferson, always a stickler for procedure, thought it necessary to clear this course of action with his fellow committee member. This meant he had to explain to Cocke why he wanted to write this unofficial letter, and inform him that Cooper had heard about Dr. Rice's article and offered to resign. Cocke agreed to let Jefferson write the letter. Cooper, like Jefferson, didn't want to rule out any future possibilities, so he didn't actually resign. He simply informed the board that the $1,500 originally promised would be sufficient to cover his expenses and that he wouldn't expect any further compensation. That Jefferson had no intention of letting Cooper go is clear from their correspondence over the next year. The following, for example, is what Jefferson wrote to Cooper four months later.

> In the consultations of the Visitors of the University on the subject of releasing you from your engagement with us, although one or two members seemed alarmed at this cry of fire from the Presbyterian pulpits, yet the real ground of our decision was that our funds were in fact hypotheticated for five or six years to redeem the loan we had reluctantly made; and although we hoped and trusted that the ensuing legislature would remit the debt and liberate our funds, yet it was not just, on this possibility, to stand in the way of your looking out for a more certain provision....
>
> The legislature meets on the 1st Monday of December, and before Christmas we shall know what are their intentions. If

29. Andrew A. Lipscomb and Albert Ellery Bergh, eds., *The Writings of Thomas Jefferson*, vol. 19, (Washington D.C.: Thomas Jefferson Memorial Association, 1907), 389.

> such as we expect, we shall then immediately take measures to engage our professors and bring them into place the ensuing autumn or early winter. My hope is that you will be able and willing to keep yourself uncommitted, to take your place among them about that time; and I can assure you there is not a voice among us which will not be cordially given for it. I think, too, I may add, that if the Presbyterian opposition should not die by that time, it will be directed at once against the whole institution, and not amuse itself with nibbling at a single object. It did that only because there was no other, and they might think it politic to mask their designs on the body of the fortress, under the [feint] of a battery against a single bastion. I will not despair then of the avail of your services in an establishment which I contemplate as the future bulwark of the human mind in this hemisphere.[30]

It wasn't until March of 1821 that Dr. Cooper informed Jefferson and Madison that he had accepted a permanent position at South Carolina College. Although Jefferson had done his best to assure Cooper that the clergy's attacks against him would die down and that the Board of Visitors would be behind him, the trustees of South Carolina College had already unanimously pushed for the legislature of that state to increase his salary, and had elected him president of the college. Cooper, whose family had been waiting in Philadelphia this entire time because they weren't sure where they should move to, couldn't pass up this guaranteed position, particularly after finding out on a visit to Jefferson a few months earlier that the opening date of the university was still as uncertain as ever. A decade later, Cooper was attacked by the Presbyterian clergy of South Carolina, but the legislature exonerated him of all charges and, although stepping down as president, he remained at South Carolina College as a professor until 1834.

Very few religious right authors acknowledge that there was a connection between the clergy's attack on Dr. Cooper and the university's invitation to the religious sects. How, or even if, the attack on

30. Thomas Jefferson to Dr. Thomas Cooper, August 14, 1820, Andrew A. Lipscomb and Albert Ellery Bergh, eds., *The Writings of Thomas Jefferson,* vol. 15, (Washington D.C.: Thomas Jefferson Memorial Association, 1903), 267-269.

Cooper is mentioned depends on how each particular author portrays Thomas Jefferson. Those who claim that Jefferson was a devout Christian who promoted Christianity at the university have to omit this story. It would obviously be a bit hard to explain why the clergy would have been accusing Jefferson of excluding their religion if, as these authors claim, he was promoting their religion by inviting them to open schools, requiring that university students attend these schools, and organizing chapel services.

Authors who portray Jefferson as a bit irreligious or at best only sort of a Christian can admit that he supported Cooper in spite of, or even because of, his religious opinions. These authors, however, usually claim that Jefferson was the oddball, and that the rest of the university's board opposed Cooper. One such version of the story is found in Jennings L. Wagoner's book *Jefferson and Education.* Wagoner's book, unfortunately published by the Thomas Jefferson Foundation, doesn't contain many flat out lies. For the most part, Wagoner only goes as far as toning down some of Jefferson's actions and statements, but in his version of the Dr. Cooper story, Wagoner lies and takes quotes out of context just like any of the more obvious Liars for Jesus.

> **According to Wagoner: "...Cooper was considered by many to be an atheist, although he sometimes contended 'Unitarian' was a more appropriate appellation for one holding his beliefs—or disbeliefs. Jefferson admired Cooper for his scientific researches, unorthodox religious beliefs, and strong Republican loyalties, but Joseph Cabell tended to agree with the widely held view that Cooper was 'defective' in manners, habits, or character and was 'certainly rather unpopular in the enlightened part of society.' Cabell considered an invitation to Cooper to be a matter of 'great delicacy' and urged Jefferson to pause and reconsider the implications of offering Cooper a professorship. Enemies of the institution, Cabell warned, would seize upon Cooper's appointment as another occasion to 'keep it down.' Although Cabell was proven correct,...Jefferson refused to back away from this candidate, a decision that one historian termed 'the biggest**

mistake [Jefferson] made in founding the university.'"

Wagoner continues in a later chapter: "Moreover, his [Jefferson's] failure to provide for a professor of divinity, his rejection of compulsory chapel, and his earlier move to hire the free-thinking Thomas Cooper combined to arouse considerable controversy and opposition. Jefferson refused to back away from his support of Cooper and persuaded a reluctant board of the newly chartered University of Virginia that it should respect the earlier offer made to him. John Holt Rice, both a Presbyterian minister and an early supporter of the university, led a campaign against Cooper. This placed the institution in an embarrassing situation until Cooper, aware of the resentment against him, removed himself from candidacy in 1820. Jefferson branded the Presbyterian clergymen as the loudest and 'most intolerant of all' sectarian leaders and asserted they opposed the university because 'they wish to see no instruction of which they have not the exclusive direction.' But Presbyterians were not alone in questioning Jefferson's beliefs and decisions with respect to religion—and Cooper—at the university. Madison did not agree with Jefferson regarding Cooper's appointment, nor did fellow visitors John Hartwell Cocke, Chapman Johnson, and Joseph Cabell. As Cocke put the dilemma, 'I think our old friend went a little too far...[but] we must stand around him...and extricate him as well as we can.' It is understandable then that his invitation to the leading denominations to erect their seminaries near (but not on) the university grounds naturally was suspect in the minds of many...."

The main problem with Wagoner's story is that the letters he uses to construct it are from February and March of 1819, nearly a year before the religious attacks on Dr. Cooper even began. These letters were not written in response to the clergy's attacks, as Wagoner implies, but were about two earlier issues that had nothing to do with Cooper's religious opinions.

The first was a difference of opinion between Jefferson and a few of the other board members regarding the status of Cooper's initial agreement, which was made with Central College before it became the university. Wagoner mentions this dispute, but, like the rest of his story, in a way that implies it had something to do with the religious opposition to Cooper. The second was a rumor that Cooper was a drunk who was prone to violence. This rumor was spread by friends of the other Virginia colleges who saw the university as a threat to their schools. They knew that having such a well known scientist on its faculty would make the university even more popular, so they were determined to keep him away. Wagoner doesn't mention this at all, letting his readers to assume that Cabell's reference to Cooper being considered *"'defective' in manners, habits, or character"* had something to do with his religious opinions.

The 1819 disagreement over Cooper's contract was not about whether or not he should be appointed, but the manner in which Jefferson was handling the situation. This disagreement was caused by some erroneous information that Joseph Cabell got from his friend, Isaac Coles. Cabell was told by Coles in the fall of 1818 that Cooper had backed out of his 1817 agreement with Central College, and that Jefferson was through with him. Believing this to be true, Cabell misunderstood Jefferson's reference in a February 1819 letter to the university's *"engagements with Dr. Cooper,"* and thought that Jefferson had entered into a new arrangement with Cooper without consulting the rest of the board. At the same time, Cabell was becoming concerned about the rumors of Cooper's drunkenness and temper, not because he believed them, but because he was afraid they might hurt the university's reputation. Cabell did not *"agree with the widely held view that Cooper was 'defective,'"* as Jennings Wagoner claims. He merely reported to Jefferson what he was hearing around Richmond, considering the fact that so many people there seemed to believe it to be *"worthy of notice."* Wagoner simply ignores the part of the letter in which Cabell said that Cooper's unpopularity among the people of Richmond might just be because they didn't know him as well as Jefferson and Madison did.

Wagoner also claims that *"Cabell considered an invitation to Cooper to be a matter of great delicacy and urged Jefferson to pause and reconsider the implications of offering Cooper a professorship."* Cabell didn't urge Jefferson to do anything of the kind. The *"pause"* referred to by Cabell was nothing more than waiting a month to make a final decision regarding Cooper's contract. Cabell wrote this on February 22, 1819, and March 29 was the date on which power was to be transferred from the old board of Central College to the new board of the university. Cabell and Chapman Johnson, one of three new university board members who had not been on the board of Central College, agreed that it would be best to wait until the first meeting of the new board to vote on Cooper, preventing any chance that the validity of his appointment could later be questioned. Johnson was also a member of the state senate, so, as soon as he was appointed to the board, Cabell began consulting with him about university matters and including his opinions in his letters to Jefferson. Wagoner apparently gets his claim that Cabell *"urged Jefferson to pause and reconsider"* from the part of Cabell's letter in which he informed Jefferson that Johnson thought *"it would be advisable to pause, in the manner, and for the reasons"* stated in the letter. The reasons stated in this letter, however, were based on the misinformation that Cooper had backed out of his original agreement with Central College. As soon as Cabell found out that Cooper had not backed out of this agreement, he wrote to Jefferson that a *"course may be taken, which will preserve essentially your engagements with Dr. Cooper."* This was on March 8, three weeks before the board was to meet.

The following are the relevant parts of Cabell's February 22, 1819 letter to Jefferson.

> You speak of our engagements with Doctor Cooper. I did not know that any engagements existed. The last information I received on this subject was either from Gen. Cocke or Col. Coles, during my illness last fall. I was then told that *you* had been under the impression that Doctor Cooper had laid himself under an obligation to come to the Central College; but that *he* had written you a letter from Fredericksburg, apprising you that he did not consider himself bound in any way whatsoever. I confess I was not mortified at the occurrence;

for whilst Dr. Cooper's talents and acquirements are unquestioned, I find the impression very general, that either in point of manners, habits, or character, he is defective. He certainly is rather unpopular in the enlightened part of society. This may be because he is not as well known to the world as he is to you and Mr. Madison. The fact, however, is worthy of notice....

...This furnishes with me a strong reason not only to lay out all the money at present in building, but convinces me of the importance of rather keeping the houses empty till a sufficient number can be got into a state of readiness to receive some half dozen eminent professors, than to fill them successively as they are finished, with perhaps here and there a man obnoxious to public prejudice. If Doctor Cooper comes, let him come unaccompanied by other professors. But if he is to come alone, permit me to recommend that no final decision to that effect shall be taken till the meeting of the Visitors of the University, when Generals Taylor and Breckenridge may be fully informed of the reasons for and against the appointment, and *their* acquiescence *previously* secured. I have spoken with Mr. Johnson on this point. He, like myself, has the highest opinions of the abilities of Doctor Cooper; but he considers the appointment one of great delicacy and importance and thinks it would be advisable to pause, in the manner, and for the reasons, I have stated. I have devoted two winters and one summer of my life to the most sincere co-operation with you in getting this measure through the Assembly. I think I am well apprised of the state of the public mind; and, believe me, the contest is not over. The very same interests and prejudices which arrayed themselves against the location at Charlottesville, will continue to assail that establishment. They will seize upon every occasion, and avail themselves of every pretext, to keep it down. On the motion for leave to bring in a bill to repeal the $20,000, these interests were visible in the opposition. I write to you in haste, as the mail is about to leave town. Perhaps I may

> have taken up erroneous views, but I thought it my duty to state them.[31]

Unaware of the misinformation that Cabell had gotten from Isaac Coles, Jefferson was clearly confused that Cabell didn't remember the agreement they had made with Dr. Cooper in 1817, and sent him transcripts of the meeting at which Cooper was elected. Jefferson also told Cabell that he already knew about the rumor that Cooper was a drunk, and that there was no truth to it. The following excerpts are from Jefferson's reply to Cabell, dated March 1, 1819.

> On the subject of engagements, I must quote a passage in your letter to me, to wit: "you speak of our engagements with Dr. Cooper. I did not know that any engagements existed." In answer to this, I have made transcripts from our journals, which I now enclose, and which you will recollect the more satisfactorily, as the original is in your own hand writing....

> ...By this time the expectation that the Legislature would adopt the College for the University, had induced us to enlarge our scale, to purchase more lands, make our buildings larger, &c., so that if that hope failed, it was doubtful whether the state in which our funds would be left, would not make it desirable to be off with Dr. Cooper. In answering his paper, therefore, I availed myself of the opportunity to premise to the articles agreed to, that they were to be considered by him as founded on the hypothesis of the Legislatures adopting our institution, and entitling us consequently to the additional funds of $15,000 a year. I considered his not replying to this paper as evidence of a tacit acceptance, and so spoke of it to Mr. Correa, although assuredly he had not, by word or writing, signified an acceptance. Learning this on the journey from Correa, he immediately wrote back to correct me, and said he had supposed he was to hold the thing under advisement until the legislative decision should be known, and in the

31. Joseph C. Cabell to Thomas Jefferson, February 22, 1819, *Early History of the University of Virginia, as Contained in the Letters of Thomas Jefferson and Joseph C. Cabell*, (Richmond, VA: J.W. Randolph, 1856), 165-166.

> mean time to weigh our propositions with others; for, besides that of New York, he had a most liberal offer from New Orleans. As soon as I heard of the first vote of our Legislature on the site of the University, carried by so large a majority, I informed Cooper of it, and that as soon after the passage of the law as a meeting of the visitors could be procured, I would write to him finally, and request his decision, and expect him, if he accepted, to come on in early spring. From all this it appears to me that we are bound, not only in consistency and reputation, but in law, if Dr. Cooper accepts our propositions. And why should we wish otherwise? Cooper is acknowledged by every enlightened man who knows him, to be the greatest man in America, in the powers of mind, and in acquired information; and that, without a single exception. I understand, indeed, that a rumor unfavorable to his habits, has been afloat, in some places, but never heard of a single man who undertook to charge him with either present or late intemperance; and I think rumor is fairly outweighed by the counter-evidence of the great desire shown at William & Mary to get him, that shown by the enlightened men of Philadelphia to retain him (which was defeated by family influence alone), the anxiety of New York to get him, that of Correa to place him here, who is in constant intercourse with him, the evidence I received in his visit here, that the state of his health permitted him to eat nothing but vegetables, and drink nothing but water, his declarations to me at table, that he dared not to drink ale or cider, or a single glass of wine, and this in the presence of Correa, who, if there had been hypocrisy in it, would not have failed to tell me so.[32]

Cabell replied to Jefferson on March 8, explaining why he had misunderstood his earlier letter.

> My last letter to you was written under considerable pain, (arising from an eruption on my side,) and I wrote more con-

32. Thomas Jefferson to Joseph C. Cabell, March 1, 1819, *Early History of the University of Virginia, as Contained in the Letters of Thomas Jefferson and Joseph C. Cabell*, (Richmond, VA: J.W. Randolph, 1856), 167-169.

cisely, and perhaps abruptly, than I should have written in a different situation. I had, by no means, forgotten the proceedings of the Visitors of the Central College, as stated in the copy of the record which you have had the kindness to send me. You will recollect, that I was prevented by a severe spell of sickness from attending the meeting of the Visitors last fall, and I can assure you I was entirely ignorant, till the receipt of your favor of 1st instant, of the nature of the communications between yourself and Dr. Cooper, about that time. I not only did not know of any new engagements with that gentleman, but had been led to believe that the obligations under which he had had it in his power to place us by the acceptance of our proposals of former dates, had been dissolved by a course of conduct on his part, with which you were by no means satisfied. My information was derived from Col. Coles or Gen. Cocke, but to the best of my-recollection from the former, during my illness last fall. I was told that Dr. Cooper's letter, from Fredericksburg, was not satisfactory to you; that you were so disgusted you would not answer it, and that your engagements with him were at an end. Hence, I observed, I did not know that any engagements existed. As you must have been misunderstood by that one of these two friends who gave me this information; or, if not misunderstood, as you must have been subsequently satisfied by other communications from Dr. Cooper, the statement of these circumstances is not made with any other view than to account to you for what must appear to you a strange inconsistency or want of recollection on my part....

...As I shall probably have an opportunity of conversing with you before the meeting of the Visitors, I will not now trouble you with unnecessary remarks on this subject. A course may be taken, which will preserve essentially your engagements with Dr. Cooper, and guard against the injurious consequences of the prejudices existing against him.[33]

33. Joseph C. Cabell to Thomas Jefferson, March 8, 1819, *Early History of the University of Virginia, as Contained in the Letters of Thomas Jefferson and Joseph C. Cabell*, (Richmond, VA: J.W. Randolph, 1856), 171-172.

Cabell, although not completely certain that Jefferson was right about the university being legally bound by the terms of an agreement made by the board of Central College, continued to support Dr. Cooper, both at this time and throughout the later attacks by the clergy.

During this exchange between Cabell and Jefferson, Cabell also received a letter from John Hartwell Cocke, one of the old board members who would also be on the new board. Although the new board was to meet on March 29, Jefferson called a meeting of the Central College board for February 26. The reason for this was that the end of March would be too late to make decisions about hiring workmen for that year's building season. Cocke almost didn't make it to this meeting, which was held at James Madison's house, because of a blizzard. He made a stop on the way and considered staying put, but when he heard that Jefferson, seventy-five years old and on horseback, had kept going, he decided he couldn't use the weather as an excuse. Cocke, Jefferson, and Madison were the only three members who attended.

Cocke expected this meeting to be strictly about the buildings, and was taken by surprise when Jefferson brought up his latest plan for Dr. Cooper. The plan was to open a grammar school in Charlottesville that May, which would be under the patronage of but not financially supported by the university, and have Cooper teach the higher classes in that school. This would allow Cooper, who was going to teach both law and science at the university, to open his law school before the rest of the university opened. Madison already knew about this plan, as did Cabell, and most likely Johnson, but it was a complete surprise to Cocke, who ended up feeling like he had been ambushed by Jefferson and Madison. The following is what Cocke wrote to Cabell on March 1.

> You are already informed that M^{r} J– called a meeting of the Visitors of the Central College under the Clause of the Univer*** continuing our power until the 1st meeting of the University Visitors. – The time was Friday last, & the place Mr Madison's – Watson was prevented from attending by the bad weather and I only met Mr J. & Mr M. – and in the whole course of my life never have I encountered a severer trial – Knowing that the progress of the buildings wou'd be materially retard^{d} if there was no meeting before the 29 March, I

> went up expecting only that subjects connected with this object wou'd be presented to the meeting – but M[r] J. had previously arranged a plan not only for this purpose, but for the election of D[r] Cooper to fill two professorships & to go into immediate operation without a coadjutor in any other branch of the sciences. Such a step at this period seemed to me so injudicious for a variety of reasons, that I felt myself bound to withhold my assent, and the thought of opposing my individual opinion upon a subject of this nature against the high authority of M[r] J. & M[r] M. has cost me a conflict which has shaken the very foundation of my health (for I feel now as if I shou'd have a spell of illness), but I cou'd not acct otherwise, for the convictions of my judgment were so clear – that if I had expired under the trial I shou'd have held out to the last. From something that dropt from M[r] J. after he had withdrawn the propositions in relation to Cooper I am induced to infer you wou'd have supported me in the course I took in this business & that he was in possession of this information. Shou'd it be the case, do hasten to give me all the consolation you can on the subject, for even now, when I think of what I have done, I am half inclined to suppose it tensivly.[34]

Neither Joseph Cabell nor Chapman Johnson appear to have liked Jefferson's grammar school plan. Their opinion was that Dr. Cooper should be confirmed by the new board in March, but that he shouldn't come to the university until the end of the year.

The quote attributed by Jennings Wagoner to John Cocke, that *"our old friend went a little too far,"* was not written by Cocke, but by Cabell *to* Cocke. What Cabell was referring to was something in Jefferson's March 1 letter to him. Jefferson told Cabell in that letter that when he sent the terms agreed to by the Central College board to Cooper in 1817, he had taken it upon himself to make those terms contingent upon the college being chosen by the legislature as the university. This was why Jefferson considered the university bound to the terms of that agreement. Cabell didn't think that Jefferson had had a right to do this without the approval of the board. But, what was

34. John Hartwell Cocke to Joseph Cabell, March 1, 1819, *Cabell Family Papers,* University of Virginia.

done, was done, so Cabell told Cocke that they *"must not insist on points of right"* and that they should *"extricate him as well as we can."* All Cabell meant by this was that they should try to get the new board to honor as much of the original agreement as they could. He knew that confirming Cooper's appointment already had a majority, even if both of the other new board members voted against it. But, simply confirming the appointment would not completely *"extricate"* Jefferson. The new board was not going to agree to Cooper coming to Charlottesville immediately. Cabell and Johnson didn't want him to come until the end of the year, and Cocke would most likely side with them, so, unless both of the other new members sided with Jefferson and Madison, Jefferson would be left having to explain to Cooper that he had overstepped his authority when he promised this.

The following is an excerpt from Cabell's March 6 letter to Cocke, containing the quote taken out of context and wrongly attributed to Cocke by Jennings Wagoner.

> I concur entirely in opinion with you in regard to Doct^r^ Cooper's being immediately engaged for the University by the Visitors of the Central College. So does Chapman Johnson. At the time of your meeting at Mr Madison's Mr J. had received a letter from me stating it as my opinion that for the first year the funds should be applied altogether to buildings; and another letter from me was there at Monticello, written with the hope that it would arrive before Mr Jefferson's departure, in which I ex-pressed many doubts about Doct: Cooper, & expressed it as my positive opinion that should he be employed, it should be by the Visitors of the University, & in that case it would be better to defer his arrival till some other professors could come along with him. To this last letter I have received a long reply from Mr Jefferson. He thinks we are bound in law & reputation to receive Doct: Cooper, if he should accept the terms we formerly offered him. I was not at the meeting last fall, & from information rec^d^ from Col: Coles, I thought the Visitors of the Central College were absolved from all their obligations to Doct: Cooper by a letter he wrote to Mr Jefferson from Fredericksburg. If the Visitors had actually engaged him, I should not think the Visitors of

> the University bound to receive him. Mr Jefferson seems not only to be entirely satisfied with Cooper, but actually to have engaged him provisionally last fall for the University. I think our old friend went a little too far:— but we must not insist on points of right – if from the best motives he has committed himself, we must stand around him and extricate him as well as we can. But let the *Visitors of the University* sanction the transaction. I wish Genls Taylor & Breckenridge to assent to the appointment in the first instance: and that Cooper should be engaged to come on at the end of this year. He is unquestionably a very able man, & perhaps we may be very wrong to lose him. Johnson seems to be in favor of his appointment ultimately, and from Mr Richard H. Lee of Staunton, who was one of Cooper's pupils, he has had the most favorable view of his character. Let us keep our minds open till our meeting on last Monday in March. I am consulting confidentially some of our ablest friends on this subject.[35]

The most ridiculous part of Jennings Wagoner's story is that *"Madison did not agree with Jefferson regarding Cooper's appointment."* Madison's support for Cooper never wavered for a minute. Madison's biggest concern about Cooper was that his feelings would be hurt if he found out that people in Virginia were spreading rumors about him. The following are excerpts from the correspondence between Jefferson and Madison during March of 1819.

Jefferson to Madison, March 3:

> I also enclose you a letter from Mr. Cabell which will shew you that the sour grapes of Wm. and Mary are spreading; but certainly not to the enlightened part of society as the letter supposes. I have sent him a transcript from our journals that he may see how far we are under engagements to Dr. Cooper.[36]

35. Joseph Cabell to John Hartwell Cocke, March 6, 1819, *Cabell Family Papers,* University of Virginia.

36. Thomas Jefferson to James Madison, March 3, 1819, James Morton Smith, ed., *The Republic of Letters: The Correspondence Between Thomas Jefferson and James Madison 1776-1826,* vol. 3, (New York and London: W.W. Norton & Company, 1995), 1807-1808.

Madison to Jefferson, March 6:

> I return Mr. Cabell's letter. I hope his fears exaggerate the hostility to the University; though, if there should be a dearth in the Treasury, there may be danger from the predilection in favor of the popular schools. I begin to be uneasy on the subject of Cooper. It will be a dreadful shock to him if serious difficulties should beset his appointment. A suspicion of them, even, will deeply wound his feelings and may alienate him from his purpose.[37]

Jefferson to Madison, March 8:

> In consequence of the doubts discovered on the subject of Cooper, I wrote to Mr Cabell, to Correa, and to Cooper himself, and inclose you copies of my letters for perusal that you may see on what ground I place the matter with each.[38]

Madison to Jefferson, March 11:

> I know not any course better to be taken in relation to Dr. Cooper, than your letter to him and Correa. I have not a particle of doubt that the answer of the latter will completely remove the objection brought forward agst. the former; and I hope if there are others not disclosed, that they will evaporate before the moment for decision.[39]

The letter to Correa referred to in these letters was a letter from Jefferson to his friend Jose Correa de Serra, a Portuguese diplomat and botanist who was well acquainted with Cooper. On March 2, Jefferson wrote to Correa and asked him to write a letter refuting the rumor that Cooper was a drunk in case the new board members wouldn't take his word for it.

37. James Madison to Thomas Jefferson, March 6, 1819, James Morton Smith, ed., *The Republic of Letters: The Correspondence Between Thomas Jefferson and James Madison 1776-1826*, vol. 3, (New York and London: W.W. Norton & Company, 1995), 1808.

38. Thomas Jefferson to James Madison, March 8, 1819, *ibid.*, 1809.

39. James Madison to Thomas Jefferson, March 11, 1819, *ibid.*

> I must now mention to you a subject so confidential that I must not only pray it never be repeated to any mortal, but that this letter may be burnt as soon as read. at a meeting of our visitors called the other day, I proposed to invite Dr. Cooper to come on immediately for the purpose of opening our classical school, and was mortified to find one or two of our members in doubt of employing him; alledging that they had heard he was in habits of drinking. I unhesitatingly repelled the imputation, and, besides other presumptative evidence, stated my own observation of his abstenuousness during his short visit to Monticello, not venturing to take a glass of wine nor to drink of the common beverages of beer or cyder; and added that the state of his health threatened to render this abstinence necessarily permanent. Mr. Madison was equally urgent as myself, but we found it prudent to let the matter lie until the 1st meeting of the new board of visitors on the 29th inst. but, in this, three new members are added to four of the old ones, and we know not therefore whether the majority of the new board may entertain the same views as that of the old one. Some testimony may therefore be necessary to rebut this suggestion with them, & none would be more satisfactory than yours; and the more so as your intercourse with Dr. Cooper enables you to speak on your own knolege, and not on rumor. will you then write me a letter, as in answer to enquiry from me, stating what you know of our friends habits & temperance, and write it so that you can permit me to read it to the visitors. I would not have Dr. Cooper know anything of this enquiry because the very thought is an injury. and if you wish to trust what you say no further than myself alone, say so, and using your information for my own government only, I will burn your letter as I have requested you do to this.[40]

Correa's reply to Jefferson, dated March 22:

> I was very glad you had thought of Mr. Cooper, to whom you could find no equal in America, in point of science and zeal

40. Thomas Jefferson to Jose Correa da Serra, March 2, 1819, *The Thomas Jefferson Papers, Series 1, General Correspondence, 1651-1827,* Library of Congress Manuscript Division, #38304.

> to spread it, and in point of sound and manly morals too, fitter perhaps for the Virginian climate, than for that in which he now lives, but from my knowledge of mankind, as far as it goes, I am apt to believe that since the news of the spirited acts of your Legislature have been known as well as your intention which is not a secret, all the aspiring mediocrity has been speculating, and their first step will be to try by all means to put him out of their way. The first three years of my residence in America, it is incredible, the *but* with which such people of a certain description mixed when they spoke of him to me, the praises which they could not well deny to his superior talents and knowledge. I have passed the last four years in acquaintance and intimacy with him, remarking the direct opposition, between his real character and all the *but,* I had heard before. They had represented him as nearly an infidel, of a violent temper, and of intemperate habits, and I have found him only a bitter enemy of hypocrites, no violent man, but by no means an enduring one, and have not seen a single solitary instance of intemperance.[41]

Jefferson didn't receive Correa's letter until the day after the March 29 Board of Visitors meeting, but Correa's testimony wasn't necessary. The majority of the new board already knew that the rumors weren't true, and Cooper was appointed Professor of Chemistry and Law at that meeting. As soon as Cooper was officially appointed, the rumors of his drunkenness suddenly stopped. Since the purpose of these rumors was to deter the new board from appointing him, there wasn't any point in keeping them up once he was appointed.

Unlike the drunk rumor, the religious attacks, begun in 1820 by John Holt Rice to get rid of Cooper, did not end once they had accomplished their purpose. This continued even after Cooper decided in 1821 to stay in South Carolina. The rumor that the university was an enemy to all trinitarian sects was just too useful to those who opposed it for other reasons, particularly those who opposed it out of loyalty to the state's other colleges.

The real issue driving the friends of the other colleges was the

41. Jose Correa da Serra to Thomas Jefferson, March 22, 1819, *The Thomas Jefferson Papers, Series 1, General Correspondence, 1651-1827,* Library of Congress Manuscript Division, #38340.

amount of money Jefferson was asking the legislature for. The rumors they started about Jefferson being extravagant and wasting public money would probably never have become popular with the public if it hadn't been for the damage done to the university's reputation by the attack on Cooper, so they wanted to keep the clergy's rumors alive long as possible.

Jefferson was asking for funding from two sources. One was the money still owed to Virginia by the federal government for debts from the War of 1812. The other was the surplus in the state's Literary Fund, resulting from several years of unused appropriations to the counties for elementary schools for the poor. The reappropriation of this surplus to build the university was opposed by several factions in the legislature. One faction opposed redirecting this money on the grounds that it was appropriated for elementary schools and shouldn't be used for any other purpose. Another supported reappropriating the surplus, but thought it should be divided between the university and the state's other colleges. This group also wanted the money from the 1812 war debt to be similarly divided. A third faction, although small, disliked Jefferson so much that they wanted to abolish the Literary Fund altogether rather than see him get any of it for the university. The idea of dividing the money among the state's colleges was supported mainly by the representatives of the areas where the other colleges were located, but also by some of Jefferson's political enemies, simply because one of these other colleges had strong ties to what remained of the Virginia's Federalist party.[42]

Splitting the money among the colleges was also supported by the clergy. The Presbyterians were firmly in control of Hampden-Sidney College, and had plans to establish a theological seminary there. At the same time, as mentioned earlier in this chapter, the Episcopalians were attempting to establish their divinity school at William and Mary. Jefferson wasn't overly concerned about the William and Mary supporters in the legislature. It was the supporters of the other colleges, particularly Hampden-Sidney, who were gaining ground, in large part by keeping the clergy's rumors about the university alive.

On August 5, 1821, Joseph Cabell wrote to Jefferson, updating him

42. This was Washington College, later renamed Washington and Lee. In 1796, this school, then called Liberty Academy, was the recipient of the shares offered to the Virginia legislature by George Washington, and was also supported by the Society of the Cincinnati.

on the situation.

> You, doubtless, observe the movements of the Presbyterians at Hampden Sidney, and the Episcopalians at William & Mary. I learn that the former sect, or rather the clergy of that sect, in their synods and presbyteries, talk much of the University. They believe, as I am informed, that the Socinians are to be installed at the University for the purpose of overthrowing the prevailing religious opinions of the country. They are therefore drawing off, and endeavoring to set up establishments of their own, subject to their own control. Hence the great efforts now making at Hampden Sidney, and the call on all the counties on the south side of James River to unite in support of that college.[43]

In January 1822, Joseph Cabell, after consulting with Chapman Johnson, decided to try to smooth things over with the clergy. Cabell wrote to Jefferson on January 7 that he intended to talk to Dr. Rice, and also to Bishop Moore, the Episcopalian Bishop who was trying to reestablish the divinity school at William and Mary.

> In reflecting on the causes of the opposition to the University, I cannot but ascribe a great deal of it to the clergy. William & Mary has conciliated them. It is represented that they are to be *excluded* from the University. There has been no decision to this effect; and, on full reflection, I should suppose that religious opinions should form no test whatever. I should think it improper to exclude religious men, and open the door to such as Doctor Cooper. Mr. Johnson concurs with me in this view. And I have publicly expressed the opinion. The clergy have succeeded in spreading the belief of their intended exclusion, and, in my opinion, it is the source of much of our trouble. I am cautious not to commit yourself, or Mr. Madison, or the board. I have also made overtures of free communication with Mr. Rice, and shall take occasion to call

43. Joseph C. Cabell to Thomas Jefferson, August 5, 1821, *Early History of the University of Virginia, as Contained in the Letters of Thomas Jefferson and Joseph C. Cabell*, (Richmond, VA: J.W. Randolph, 1856), 215-216.

> on Bishop Moore. I do not know that I shall touch on this delicate point with either of them. But I wish to consult these heads of the church, and ask their opinions.[44]

It doesn't appear that Joseph Cabell ever met with Bishop Moore, but he did meet with Dr. Rice, and wrote the following to Jefferson on January 14, 1822 about the meeting.

> I have had a very long interview with Mr. Rice. He and myself differed on some points; but agreed in the propriety of a firm union between the friends of the University and the Colleges, as to measures of common interest, and of postponing for future discussion and settlement points on which we differ. I think this safe ground. We shall be first endowed; and have the vantage ground in this respect....
>
> ...They have heard that you have said they may well be afraid of the progress of the Unitarians to the South. This remark was carried from Bedford to the Synod, beyond the Ridge, last fall. The Bible Societies are in constant correspondence all over the continent, and a fact is wafted across it in a few weeks. Through these societies the discovery of the religious opinions of Ticknor and Bowditch was made. Mr. Rice assured me that he was a warm friend of the University; and that, as a matter of policy, he hoped the Visitors would, in the early stages of its existence, remove the fears of the religious orders. He avowed that the Presbyterians sought no peculiar advantage, and that they and the other sects would be well satisfied by the appointment of an Episcopalian. I stated to him that I knew not what would be the determination of the board; but I was sure no desire existed any where to give any preference to the Unitarians; and, for my own part, I should not vote against any one on account of his being a professor of religion or free-thinker.[45]

44. Joseph C. Cabell to Thomas Jefferson, January 7, 1822, *Early History of the University of Virginia, as Contained in the Letters of Thomas Jefferson and Joseph C. Cabell*, (Richmond, VA: J.W. Randolph, 1856), 230.
45. Joseph C. Cabell to Thomas Jefferson, January 14, 1822, *ibid*, 233-237.

When Rice wrote his article attacking Dr. Cooper in January 1820, he made the assumption the university's Board of Visitors intended to exclude clergymen from the professorships. This accusation was still a favorite of the university's enemies two years later, although the Board of Visitors had never made any official decision to exclude clergymen. Jefferson actually did oppose hiring clergymen, but remained silent on the subject until 1824, when the recruitment of professors had actually begun and there was a reason to bring it up. In April 1824, Jefferson met with Francis Gilmer, who was being sent to Europe to recruit professors. In his notes for this meeting, Jefferson listed "*no clergymen*" among the selection criteria that Gilmer was instructed to follow.[46] A few of the other board members probably would have disagreed with this, but Jefferson did it anyway.

It should be noted that, in 1817, the board of Central College did vote to offer a professorship to a Presbyterian minister, Rev. Samuel Knox. Rev. Knox, however, would probably have caused nearly as big a problem with the Presbyterians as Thomas Cooper did. Knox had been an outcast among the Presbyterian clergy since the presidential campaign of 1800, when he had opposed them at the General Assembly of their church, which was held in Virginia that year as part of the church's agenda to turn southern Presbyterians against Jefferson. Jefferson had known since 1810 that Knox had authored of one of the anonymous pamphlets published during the 1800 campaign defending him against the attacks of the clergy. Jefferson also knew that Knox did not think religion should be mixed with public education. Knox never even knew that he had been considered for a professorship by the board of Central College. Jefferson was wrongly informed by his friend John Patterson that Knox had retired from teaching, so the board never bothered contacting him.

Knox actually wrote to Jefferson in 1818 asking for a job at the university, but Jefferson completely blew him off. Knox's lengthy letter detailed the tactics the Federalists had used in their attempts to ruin his teaching career in Maryland, and it's possible that Jefferson, after reading this letter, just didn't think Knox was worth the kind of risk that he was later willing to take to get a scientist like Thomas Cooper. Jefferson got rid of Knox with a lie, claiming that, because of

46. Agenda for the University of Virginia, April 26, 1824, *The Thomas Jefferson Papers, Series 1, General Correspondence, 1651-1827,* Library of Congress Manuscript Division, #40400.

his age and health, he was only helping Central College get established by the legislature as the university, but that once this was accomplished, he would no longer be involved enough to make any decisions regarding the faculty.[47]

The information that Joseph Cabell obtained in his January 1822 meeting with Dr. Rice was probably a bit alarming to Jefferson, particularly that the Presbyterian clergy had heard of his comment about Unitarians from someone in Bedford in the fall. Bedford was the location of Jefferson's second home, Poplar Forest, where he spent time each fall. Jefferson wrote in numerous letters around this time that Unitarianism was spreading to the south and would soon be the predominant religion of the country, so it's entirely possible that he said something to this effect that was heard by, or heard about by, someone in Bedford that the clergy was using as an informant.

Cabell's other piece of information, that the religious opinions of George Ticknor and Nathaniel Bowditch had been investigated, was a pretty good sign that every candidate the university was even considering was going to be subjected to a religious test by the Presbyterians. At their October 1820 meeting, the Board of Visitors had passed a resolution to begin negotiations with Ticknor, who was then a professor at Harvard, a school that had been under Unitarian control since 1805, and Bowditch, who was a member of a Unitarian church in Massachusetts. While the brand of Unitarianism practiced in New England was not as radical as the Unitarianism of Dr. Priestley and Dr. Cooper, and probably wouldn't ordinarily have raised an alarm among Virginians, hiring any Unitarian in the wake of the Dr. Cooper controversy might be used by the clergy as confirmation of their suspicion that the university was showing a preference for Unitarians.

Cabell's letter, which made it clear that Cooper's resignation had not made the clergy back off, was almost certainly what prompted Jefferson to cook up the idea of inviting the religious sects to open their own schools near the university. There is no doubt that this invitation was entirely Jefferson's idea, although he claimed in the October 1822 report to the legislature that it was "*suggested by some pious individuals.*" Joseph Cabell even referred to it in a letter to Jefferson as "*your suggestion.*" Claiming that the idea was suggested by some-

47. Thomas Jefferson to Rev. Samuel Knox, December 11, 1818, *The Thomas Jefferson Papers, Series 1, General Correspondence, 1651-1827,* Library of Congress Manuscript Division, #38188.

one else would prevent the clergy from being able to claim that the invitation was another plan designed by Jefferson to keep religion separated from the university, even though this is exactly what it was.

To battle the other problematic rumor, that Jefferson was being extravagant and wasting public money, Cabell suggested that the board have a set of books prepared for the legislature, accounting for every penny that had been spent.

The combination of the invitation to the religious sects and the account books worked. In February 1823, the University Loan Bill was passed by the legislature, which meant that the construction of the Rotunda could finally proceed. Cabell wrote the following to Jefferson on February 3, when it looked certain that this important bill was going to pass.

> I was, from the first, confident that no weapon could be wielded by us with more efficacy than this annual rendition of accounts which seemed to be a rod in pickle for us. I think also that your suggestion respecting the religious sects has had great influence. It is the Franklin that has drawn the lightning from the cloud of opposition. I write you, dear sir, with a heart springing up with joy, and a cheek bedewed with tears of delight. Accept, I beseech you, my cordial congratulations at this evidence of the returning good sense of the country, and of its just appreciation of your labors.[48]

As already mentioned, Jefferson was reasonably certain when he came up with the idea of the invitation that none of the religious sects would actually accept it.

Bishop Moore and the other Episcopalians, who, from 1820 to 1822, were trying to reestablish the divinity school at William and Mary didn't even have the support of their own church. The Bishops of the surrounding states, as well as the more orthodox Episcopalians in Virginia, were opposed to the idea of ministers being trained anywhere other than their General Seminary in New York. Moore was having enough problems trying to establish one school in Virginia, so

48. Joseph C. Cabell to Thomas Jefferson, February 3, 1823, *Early History of the University of Virginia, as Contained in the Letters of Thomas Jefferson and Joseph C. Cabell*, (Richmond, VA: J.W. Randolph, 1856), 273.

there was almost no chance, at least in 1822, that they would attempt to establish a second school in response to the university's invitation.

The reestablishment of the Episcopalians at William and Mary, a school only partially supported by the state, also met with opposition from the public. James Madison mentioned this in a letter to Edward Everett, a Unitarian minister and Professor of Greek Literature at Harvard, who had written to Madison about the problems that Harvard was experiencing since opening a divinity school.

> A late resolution for establishing an Episcopal school within the College of William & Mary, tho in a very guarded manner, drew immediate animadversions from the press, which if they have not put an end to the project, are a proof of what would follow such an experiment in the University of the State, endowed and supported as this will be, altogether by the Public authority and at the common expense.[49]

By the end of 1822, the attempt to establish the divinity school at William and Mary was deemed a failure, having attracted only one student in two years. Nevertheless, Bishop Moore was determined to try again. This, as already mentioned, is why Jefferson, in the spring of 1823, thought it was possible that the Episcopalians might accept the university's invitation. The location eventually selected by Moore for the second attempt, however, was not Charlottesville, but Alexandria.

Moore's plan was so unpopular among members of his own church that he actually got a little taste of the kind of stuff Jefferson had to put up with. Orthodox Episcopalians labeled the Virginia school schismatic, accused Moore of trying to break away from the church, and even tried to intimidate him with threatening letters. Bishop Moore doesn't appear to have had any motive for trying to establish this school other than wanting to reopen the many Episcopalian churches in Virginia that had been closed for decades due to a shortage of ministers. Moore just thought that Virginians considering the ministry would be more likely to pursue it if there was a seminary in their own state. The Alexandria plan eventually gained the support of the Episcopal Convention of Virginia, and the new seminary was far more

49. James Madison to Edward Everett, March 19, 1823, *Letters and Other Writings of James Madison,* Vol. 3, (New York: R. Worthington, 1884), 308.

successful than the school at William and Mary, receiving about a dozen students in its first year.

Although Jefferson never saw any real chance of the Presbyterians accepting the university's invitation, he did think his plan through, considering what might happen if they did. He knew that if the Presbyterians did decide to establish a school, the other sects would be more likely to do the same simply to keep an eye on them and prevent them from attempting to take over the university.

Jefferson's accusation in his April 1823 letter to Dr. Cooper that the Presbyterians were *"hostile to all educn of which they have not the direction"* was well founded. The Presbyterians had a long track record of abandoning any school that they were losing control over, then establishing another that they could control. By 1823, they were already on their third college in Kentucky. They withdrew their support of Transylvania Seminary, which had been founded by a Presbyterian minister in 1783, when a Baptist was elected president in 1788. In 1797, they established Kentucky Academy, but this school merged with Transylvania Seminary for economic reasons to form Transylvania University. The Presbyterians were unable to maintain a majority on the board of this university, and in 1818, Horace Holley, a Unitarian minister was elected president. The Presbyterians quickly began working on another school, Centre College in Danville, which opened in 1823. Even though they had a new college to control, the Presbyterians kept up their campaign against Holley, forcing him to resign a few years later.

The Presbyterians' attack on Holley would not have surprised John Adams a bit. The following is from the letter of introduction Adams wrote to Jefferson for Holley, who planned to stop in Virginia on his way from Massachusetts to Kentucky in 1818.

> ...He is indeed an important Character; and if Superstition Bigotry, Fanaticism and Intolerance will allow him to live in Kentucky, he will contribute Somewhat to the illumination of the darkest and most dismal Swamps in the Wilderness. I shall regret his Removal from Boston because that City ought always to have one Clergyman at least who will compell them to think and enquire: but if he can be supported in Kentucky I am convinced he will be more extensively usefull.

> If upon conversing with him Your Conscience will allow you to give him a Line to any of your Friends in Kentucky where all are your Friends, you will do him more Service and perhaps more Service to our Country and our kind than you or I may be aware....[50]

As already mentioned, Jefferson didn't give much thought to Virginia's other two sects, the Baptists and the Methodists. For one thing, neither of these sects had ever shown the kind of interest in establishing schools that the Presbyterians and Episcopalians had, and weren't suddenly going to want to establish them just because they were invited to. The Baptists and Methodists also had strong convictions against mixing religion with public institutions. Their temporary alliance with the other sects over Dr. Cooper had not changed their long held opinion that a state supported university should be secular.

In the end, none of the sects accepted the university's invitation, a detail rarely mentioned in the religious right versions of the story. It wasn't until 1859, when the Presbyterians considered, but abandoned, a plan to locate a school near the university, that any of the sects even showed an interest in the idea. Authors who imply that university students were expected to attend the invited theological schools, of course, have to omit the fact that these schools never actually existed.

> **David Barton, as mentioned earlier, claims that Jefferson "expected students to participate in the various religious schools which he personally had invited to locate adjacent to and upon the University property..."**

Barton's source for this claim is the following sentence in the rules and regulations of the university, written at the October 1824 meeting of the Board of Visitors.

> Should the religious sects of this State, or any of them, according to the invitation held out to them, establish within,

50. John Adams to Thomas Jefferson, January 28, 1818, Lester J. Cappon, ed., *The Adams-Jefferson Letters: The Complete Correspondence Between Thomas Jefferson and Abigail and John Adams,* (Chapel Hill and London: The University of North Carolina Press, 1988), 523.

> or adjacent to, the precincts of the University, schools for instruction in the religion of their sect, the students of the University will be free, and expected to attend religious worship at the establishment of their respective sects, in the morning, and in time to meet their school in the University at its stated hour.
>
> The students of such religious school, if they attend any school of the University, shall be considered as students of the University, subject to the same regulations, and entitled to the same rights and privileges.[51]

What's interesting about this sentence is not what it says, but why it was included. This was obviously another case of adding something to *"help down what might be less readily swallowed."* By 1824, it was clear that none of the religious sects were going to accept the university's invitation. In the two years that had elapsed since the invitation was extended, the Episcopalians had chosen Alexandria for their seminary, and the Presbyterians had established theirs at Hampden-Sidney, turning their attention to promoting that school. There was absolutely no reason in 1824 for the board to write a rule about religious schools. These schools didn't exist then, and would probably never exist. The only logical explanation for the religious school rule is the nature of the rules that preceded and followed it. Preceding it is a rule that any testimony required from a student would always be voluntary, and never under oath, something that the clergy and religious fanatics would surely object to. Following it is a list of the purposes assigned to each of the rooms in the Rotunda, in which religious worship is reduced to sharing the room designated for large lectures and annual examinations. Adding this pointless rule would remind everyone of the invitation to the religious sects, making it much more difficult for anyone to revive the old rumors by claiming that the other rules were evidence of the university's goal to undermine religion.

Even with the religious school rule, however, the board was apparently still a little worried that the no oath rule might cause problems. At their next meeting they toned it down a bit, removing the part of

51. Andrew A. Lipscomb and Albert Ellery Bergh, eds., *The Writings of Thomas Jefferson*, vol. 19, (Washington D.C.: Thomas Jefferson Memorial Association, 1907), 449.

the original version about reasoning with students to get them to see that they had a moral obligation to testify. The following is the no oath rule, with the part that was deleted in parentheses.

> When testimony is required from a student, it shall be voluntary, and not on oath. And the obligation to give it shall–(if unwilling to give it, let the moral obligation be explained and urged, under which every one is bound to bear witness, where wrong has been done, but finally let it)–be left to his own sense of right.[52]

In addition to simply reminding everyone of the university's invitation, this rule also kept the ball in the court of the religious sects. If they wanted the university students of their sect to attend religious services, all they had to do was accept the invitation and open a school. They couldn't complain that theology students were being discriminated against either, because, if they opened a school, its students could take advantage of all the benefits of the University.

If any of the religious sects did happen to surprise the board and open a school, the part of the rule limiting students to attending it only in the morning before classes would have made doing so nearly impossible. Classes at the university began at 7:30 a.m., with very strict attendance and tardiness rules. If Jefferson really expected students to attend these theoretical religious schools, it certainly seems a bit odd that he would deliberately make this so difficult, and it is completely inconceivable, of course, that he would have allowed the possibility that a university rule might have the effect of governing what time a religious institution held its services.

Another popular lie that comes from this same 1824 rule is that Jefferson invited the religious sects to build schools on university property. This was not the case. Establishing schools "*within*" the precincts of the university referred only to allowing a religious sect to teach in the room in the Rotunda where religious worship was to be allowed, not to a physical school building. The use of the Rotunda by the professors of the religious schools was part of the original 1822 invitation, included at that time because of the original proposal in

52. Andrew A. Lipscomb and Albert Ellery Bergh, eds., *The Writings of Thomas Jefferson*, vol. 19, (Washington D.C.: Thomas Jefferson Memorial Association, 1907), 449.

the 1818 Rockfish Report. Any actual religious school buildings were to be built "*on the confines*" of the university, which means adjacent to, not within, the borders of the university. This is clear in the board's report to the legislature, and in every letter in which Jefferson or Madison described the invitation. Jefferson described the intended location as "*on the confines of the university, so near as that their students may attend the lectures there.*"[53] and "*in the vicinity of the university*"[54] Madison described it as "*so near that the students of the University may respectively attend the religious exercises in them.*"[55] The only place where this is not clear is the 1824 religious school rule, so the Liars for Jesus base their story on that alone, disregarding every other description. The idea that Jefferson would allow religious schools to be built on university property is ridiculous. Prior to Madison's retirement in 1834, the Board of Visitors wouldn't allow a chaplain, paid for with private funds raised by a group of students, to live in an unused building on the university's grounds, considering even that to be pecuniary support of religion by the state.

> **According to Gary DeMar, in his book *America's Christian History: The Untold Story*: "Jefferson's proposed curriculum for the University of Virginia included a provision for a 'professor of ethics' who would present 'the Proofs of the being of God, the Creator, Preserver, and Supreme Ruler of the universe, the Author of all the relations of morality, and of the laws and obligations these infer.' While Jefferson was against ecclesiastical control of education, he was not against the teaching of religion."**

What DeMar quotes here are a few bits of the sentence in the Rockfish Report about the university having no professor of divinity. In addition to splitting up and rearranging the order of the phrases to

53. Thomas Jefferson to Dr. Thomas Cooper, November 2, 1822, Andrew A. Lipscomb and Albert Ellery Bergh, eds., *The Writings of Thomas Jefferson,* vol. 15, (Washington D.C.: Thomas Jefferson Memorial Association, 1903), 405.

54. Thomas Jefferson to Arthur S. Brockenbrough, April 21, 1825, *The Thomas Jefferson Papers, Series 1, General Correspondence, 1651-1827,* Library of Congress Manuscript Division, #40962.

55. James Madison to Edward Everett, March 19, 1823, *Letters and Other Writings of James Madison,* Vol. 3, (New York: R. Worthington, 1884), 306-307.

imply that a large part of the ethics professor's job was to teach religion, DeMar alters Jefferson's wording a bit, changing "*the being of **a** God*" to "*the being of God.*" He also completely ignores the fact that the actual position created once the university was established did not include any religious instruction. Just like proposing religious worship in the Rotunda, implying that the ethics professor would be teaching some religion was intended to offset the absence of a divinity school and get the Rockfish Report approved by the legislature.

> ...we have proposed no professor of divinity; and the rather as the proofs of the being of a God, the creator, preserver, and supreme ruler of the universe, the author of all the relations of morality, and of the laws and obligations these infer, will be within the province of the professor of ethics...[56]

In the same paragraph, Jefferson also implied that the teaching of ancient languages had a religious purpose, although the only reason given by Jefferson anywhere else for teaching Latin and Greek was to read the classics in their original languages, and Hebrew, although listed in the report, was not actually going to be taught at all.

The 1824 correspondence between Jefferson and Madison regarding the selection of an ethics professor makes it very clear that they were not looking for a religion teacher. Nowhere in any of Jefferson's or Madison's letters about this professorship is a knowledge of religion, or even having a religion, ever considered as a qualification for the position. Being limited by the university's charter to ten professors, and by finances to even fewer than that, what they were really looking for was a professor who was qualified to teach some other subject, but could also teach a few ethics courses. The following is from Jefferson's first letter to Madison on the subject.

> I am quite at a loss for a Professor of Ethics, This subject has been so exclusively confined to the clergy, that when forced to seek one, not of that body, it becomes difficult. But it is a branch of science of little difficulty to any ingenious man. Locke, Stewart, Brown, Tracy for the general science of the

56. Saul K. Padover, ed., *The Complete Jefferson,* (New York: Duell, Sloan & Pearce, Inc., 1943), 1104.

> mind furnish material abundant, and that of Ethics is still more trite. I should think that any person, with a general education rendering them otherwise worthy of a place among his scientific brethren might soon qualify himself.[57]

Madison replied by suggesting George Tucker, a lawyer, political economist, and member of Congress.

> What are the collateral aptitudes of George Tucker the member of Congress. I have never seen him, and can only judge him by a volume of miscellaneous Essays published not very long ago. They are written with acuteness and elegance; and indicate a capacity and taste for Philosophical literature.[58]

The two candidates that Jefferson was considering before Madison suggested Tucker were also lawyers. It's obvious from their correspondence that neither Jefferson of Madison knew enough about Tucker to have any idea whether he was religious or not. Their opinion that he was qualified for the professorship was based solely on a collection of fifteen essays that had nothing to do with religion. The wide variety of topics covered in this essay collection included the evolution of language, why Americans were not advancing in literature as quickly as they were advancing in science, why Greek architecture had remained so popular through the centuries, whether or not poetry should rhyme, the pros and cons of an increase in population, and a justification of the practice of dueling. His essays on ethics addressed such questions as whether or not a representative always had an obligation to follow the instructions of his constituents, even if they had knowledge or information that told them it was the wrong decision. The collection also included essays on national banks and national debts, which, interestingly, disagreed with Jefferson's opinions on these subjects. What was undoubtedly more important to Jefferson than whether or not he agreed with all of Tucker's opinions was that Tucker

57. Thomas Jefferson to James Madison, November 30, 1824, James Morton Smith, ed., *The Republic of Letters: The Correspondence Between Thomas Jefferson and James Madison 1776-1826*, vol. 3, (New York and London: W.W. Norton & Company, 1995), 1909.

58. James Madison to Thomas Jefferson, December 3, 1824, *ibid.*, 1910.

wrote about every one of his topics specifically in relation to American society and government.

Tucker's philosophical ideas were thoroughly secular and scientific, based only on the faculties of the human mind. This science of *mental philosophy,* as it was commonly called at the time, was essentially psychology, although that term didn't catch on until later in the nineteenth century. Tucker's areas of research while a professor at the University of Virginia included memory, the association of ideas, the similarities and differences between waking thought and dreams, and a nature vs. nurture study using the famous Siamese twins, Chang and Eng, as subjects.

When Tucker was offered the professorship in January 1825, he didn't immediately accept it. The previous summer he had written *Valley of the Shenandoah,* a tragic novel about a southern plantation family. Tucker had hoped to begin a career as a full-time novelist when his term in Congress was up, but this plan wasn't going very well. Although his novel was later reprinted in England and translated into German, only a hundred copies were printed in America, and Tucker himself had to put up half the money for the printing. When Congress let out in March 1825, he decided to accept the professorship, which would give him a house and a salary, while leaving him enough time to write. Two years later, under the pseudonym Joseph Atterley, Tucker published his second novel, *A Voyage to the Moon with Some Account of the Manners and Customs, Science and Philosophy, of the People of Morosofia, and Other Lunarians,* a satirical science fiction story about a trip to the moon in a spaceship coated with an anti-gravity metal, in which Tucker *"aimed to notice the errors of the day in science and philosophy."*

Because of the limited number of professors they could hire, the Board of Visitors assigned several subjects to each professorship, but allowed for the subjects to be rearranged in the future, based on the particular qualifications of each professor. As of 1824, the ethics professor, who was by then being called the Professor of Moral Philosophy, would teach *"mental science generally, including ideology, general grammar and ethics,"*[59] Because the distribution of subjects had been decided on before Madison thought of George Tucker, Political

59. Andrew A. Lipscomb and Albert Ellery Bergh, eds., *The Writings of Thomas Jefferson,* vol. 19, (Washington D.C.: Thomas Jefferson Memorial Association, 1907), 434.

Economy, a field in which Tucker was an expert, had been assigned to the professor of law. When the law school opened in July 1826, however, its professor, John Lomax, agreed to hand Political Economy over to Tucker. He also picked up Rhetoric and Belles Lettres, which had been assigned to the Professor of Ancient Languages. Tucker wanted these courses not only so he could teach his favorite subjects, but because he wanted an income closer to that of the other professors. Because of Jefferson's elective system, which allowed students to take only those courses that they wanted to take, the professors, who were paid according to the number of students in their schools, made more money if they happened to teach the more popular courses. Since mental science and ethics weren't very high on the popularity scale, adding these other courses to his school gave Tucker a more equal share of the students.

George Tucker was Professor of Moral Philosophy and Political Economy for twenty years. When he retired in 1845, the university lost the last of its original professors. It was Tucker's successor, William Holmes McGuffey, who would play a major role in undermining the secular policies that Jefferson had worked so hard to put in place. McGuffey, a Presbyterian minister best known for his McGuffey Readers, was the first clergyman to become a professor at the university. McGuffey was everything Jefferson had tried to avoid by keeping clergymen out of the professorships. He blatantly promoted his religious opinions, taught weekly Bible classes in his lecturing room, and supported the opening of a university branch of the Young Men's Christian Association, an organization that eventually took over so many aspects of student affairs that it became impossible for any student to avoid it, or its religious influence.

Although a complete disregard of the university's original policies regarding religion didn't begin to take hold until the 1840s, the first signs of what was to come began within two years of Jefferson's death. When George Long, the Professor of Natural Philosophy, announced in 1827 that he planned to resign, Chapman Johnson, who had always opposed Jefferson's exclusion of clergymen, made it clear that he wanted Long's replacement to be a clergyman. But, even with Jefferson gone, Johnson knew he would have to get either Joseph Cabell or James Madison to go along, so he wrote to John Hartwell Cocke, the other board member he knew would side with him, and asked him to work on Cabell.

> Tell Cabell...it is time to give up his old prejudice upon this subject, the offspring of the French Revolution, long since a bastard by a divorce of the unnatural alliance between liberty and atheism.[60]

Johnson also wrote to Madison, apparently trying to trick him into stating his position on hiring clergymen by claiming that he had reason to suspect that a particular candidate for the professorship might be a clergyman. Madison didn't buy this, and didn't give Johnson a definite answer. He then listed all the problems that allowing clergymen into the professorships could cause. Madison knew that Johnson was scheming to bring religion into the university by putting clergymen on the faculty, so he ended his letter by making it clear that he wanted religious worship and instruction to be initiated by the students, not the school.

> I have indulged more particularly the hope, that provision for religious instruction & observances among the Students, would be made by themselves or their parents & guardians, each contributing to a fund, to be applied in remunerating the services of Clergymen of denominations corresponding with the preference of Contributors. Small contributions would suffice, and the arrangements would become more adequate and more efficient as the Students become more numerous, whilst being altogether voluntary, it would interfere neither with the characteristic peculiarity of the University, the consecrated principle of the law, nor the spirit of the Country.[61]

Up until 1828, no religious services at all were held at the university, leaving the students, as well as the faculty who lived on campus, with no other option than to walk to the services in Charlottesville. In

60. Philip Alexander Bruce, *History of the University of Virginia 1818-1819,* vol. 2, (New York: The Macmillan Company, 1920), 150.

61. James Madison to Chapman Johnson, May 1, 1828, *The James Madison Papers at the Library of Congress, Series 1, General Correspondence,* Library of Congress Manuscript Division.

1828, two clergymen from Charlottesville were invited to preach on alternate Sunday afternoons in the room in the Rotunda where religious worship was allowed, but this arrangement didn't last long. It was too inconvenient for the clergymen to leave their own congregations on Sundays to travel to the university, and the students and faculty who were religious enough to want worship services in the first place wanted more than just one service a week.

In 1829, a chaplain was hired with private contributions, but a lack of contributions from 1830 until 1833 made this impossible during those years. At this time, chaplains were not permitted to live within the precincts of the university, which meant a chaplain couldn't be hired unless enough money was raised to pay them a salary that would cover renting a place to live. Between 1830 and 1833, there was no regular religious worship, but various guest ministers were invited to give sermons in the Rotunda. In 1833, there were also some services led by a minister who happened to be attending courses at the university.

What Madison described in his 1828 letter to Chapman Johnson is exactly what eventually did happen. During the 1832-1833 school year, a student named McClurg Wickham took charge and organized a group of about thirty students, all of whom signed a pledge that between them they would contribute enough money to pay the salary of a chaplain. Wickham's plan was approved by the chairman of the faculty and presented to the Board of Visitors, who approved it at their July 1833 meeting. Members of the faculty and the board also contributed to the students' chaplain fund, but strictly as individuals in a private capacity.

In addition to hiring a chaplain, Wickham wanted to start a Sunday school, and requested the use of the room in the Rotunda for his classes. This request was denied by the chairman of the faculty, who thought it went beyond what was allowed by both the Rockfish Report, which allowed the use of the room for worship services, and the board's 1822 invitation, which allowed for its use by teachers of the various religious sects for lectures. The Board of Visitors, however, decided to allow Wickham the use of a room in one of the pavilions. By allowing this student run religious group the use of a room, the board did exactly what is required in today's public schools. Other student groups, such as debating and academic societies, had been given the use of rooms in the pavilions and the basement of the Rotunda, so denying the same privilege to another group of students simply because their activities were religious would be considered unconstitutional by today's standards.

Because no religious activities at all took place at the University of Virginia while Jefferson was alive, and what was allowed during Madison's rectorship wouldn't even be challenged in today's public schools, the Liars for Jesus have a problem. The solution for many is to find later promotions of religion by the university, some as late as the early 1900s, pretend they happened while Jefferson was alive, and use them as evidence that he never intended to exclude religion. This trick has been around since 1901, when William Eleroy Curtis came up with the idea of quoting University of Virginia catalogs from the late 1800s and omitting the dates. As noted earlier, a reprinted edition of Curtis's 1901 book *The True Thomas Jefferson* is currently being sold on religious right websites and recommended to Christian homeschoolers.

> **According to Curtis: "The catalogue of the institution says that morality and religion are recognized as the foundation and indispensable concomitants of education. Great efforts are made to surround the students with religious influences, but experience having proved that it is best to forbear the employment of coercion, the attendance upon religious exercises is entirely voluntary. Prayers are held every evening and divine service is conducted twice on Sunday in the University Chapel by clergymen invited from the principal religious denominations."**

The first year in which anything like this appeared in the university's catalog was 1865. Because this appeared with only slight wording changes for many years, and there is no way of knowing if Curtis even quoted whatever catalog he was using accurately, it is impossible to say exactly which year's catalog he used. Of course, the exact date of the catalog used by Curtis really doesn't matter because the earliest possible date was nearly forty years after Jefferson's death.

> **Curtis continued: "The rules permit all ministers and**

students who are preparing for the ministry to enjoy free of cost all of the privileges of the University, including tuition, attendance at the lectures and recitations, and the privileges of the libraries and laboratories. Very few if any other institutions are so liberal."

What Curtis quoted here was a later version of a practice begun by the professors in 1841. This was not a university rule at that time. It was only a resolution of the faculty, by which the professors waived their own fees. This did not exempt ministers and theological students from the fees of the university. The following is how it appeared in the *Expenses,* not the *Regulations,* section of the 1841 university catalog.

> Ministers of the Gospel, and young men preparing for the ministry, may attend any of the schools of the University, without payment of fees to the Professors. [62]

An advertisement for the university in an 1845 magazine clearly stated that this was only a resolution of the faculty.

> And by a resolution of the faculty, ministers of the Gospel may attend any of the schools, without the payment of fees to the professors. The same privilege is extended to young men who are preparing for the ministry, upon their presenting to the Faculty satisfactory evidence of decided merit. [63]

Nothing in the original university rules of 1824 exempted clergymen from any fees, and the original rule that theological students would be considered as students of the university applied only to students of schools that might locate near the university according to the boards 1822 invitation. This rule said that students of those schools would have the same rights and privileges, and be subject to the same rules, as students of the university, meaning only that they would be

62. *University of Virginia Catalog,* 1841, 18. Coincidentally, 1841 was also the first year in which Sunday religious services were listed in the catalog.

63. Advertisement for the University of Virginia, *Southern Literary Messenger,* Vol. XI, Issue 12, December 1845.

able to attend the university's schools without paying the university's tuition fee. It said nothing about them being exempt from the professors' fees for the courses they took.

> **Curtis also quoted this from a later catalog: "In the regular course each term are lectures on religious and scriptural subjects such as Bible History, the Holy Land, the Mosaic Code of Laws, the Life of Christ, the Life of St. Paul, the Lives of the Apostles, the Kings of Israel, the Literary Features of the Bible, the Poetry of the Bible, the History of Prophecy, and similar topics."**

Lists of lectures like these began appearing in the university catalog in the 1890s, when the Y.M.C.A., at the height of its control over student affairs, was given several pages to list its activities. These were lectures sponsored by the Y.M.C.A., not part of a university course.

As already mentioned, the university branch of the Y.M.C.A., established in 1858, eventually took over so many aspects of student affairs that no student, whatever their religion, could avoid it, or its overt promotion of evangelical Protestantism. When the Y.M.C.A. first opened, it was completely independent of the university, and merely provided religious activities for those students who wanted to participate. By the end of the 1800s, however, students had no choice but to go to the Y.M.C.A. for virtually every kind of information, from student handbooks and dormitory assignments to employment information. In 1897, the following official endorsement of the Y.M.C.A. by the Board of Visitors and faculty appeared in the university catalog.

> The Visitors and Faculty of the University heartily commend the work of the Association, and it is earnestly desired that every parent or guardian see to it that the student under his care is encouraged to join the Association as soon as he reached the University.[64]

In the 1906 catalog, Y.M.C.A. information appeared not only in the

64. *University of Virginia Catalog*, 1897, 155.

Religious Worship section, but several pages of additional information were included in a new section with the title of *Religious Work*. In the same catalog, it was announced that the entire northwest wing of the Rotunda had been assigned by the university to the Y.M.C.A. to be used *"for its various purposes in Christian work."* [65]

If Jefferson wasn't already rolling in his grave by this point, what appeared in the 1907 catalog certainly would have made him start. Out of the security deposit paid by students at the beginning of the school year for things like library fines and damage to university property, a fee for the support of religious work was to be automatically deducted. Students who did not want to contribute to this religious work had to specifically request that this fee not be deducted from their deposit.

> From this deposit there will be deducted the sum of $2 for the support of the Chapel Services and General Religious Work of the University, *unless within one month after registration the student shall request the Bursar not to deduct this contribution.* It will be observed that this amount also (which is less than the average contribution made by the students who have given towards the Chapel Fund in past years) is not a necessary expense, as the support of the religious work of the University is left entirely to the option of the students and professors. [66]

This policy was, in principle, exactly what the Danbury Baptists had complained to Jefferson about over a century earlier, prompting his famous *"separation between church and state"* letter. The Baptists didn't *have to* pay the tax to support Connecticut's established church, but in order to be exempted from it they had to single themselves out as dissenters by filing a special certificate, a practice that they described as degrading.

Lies about Jefferson promoting religious instruction at the University of Virginia sometimes mention the fact that he included books on religion in the original catalog for the university's library. This is usually combined with the misleading description of the duties

65. *University of Virginia Catalog*, 1906, 146.
66. *University of Virginia Catalog*, 1907, 91.

of the Professor of Ethics from the Rockfish Report and/or the Board of Visitors 1822 invitation to the religious sects to invent a *"policy of non-sectarian education,"* as William Eleroy Curtis called it in *The True Thomas Jefferson.*

> **Curtis ends his not too accurate version of the Dr. Cooper story with the following: "This is all set forth in Jefferson's own handwriting in the records of the Board of Visitors, and led to a declaration of the policy of the University of Virginia with reference to religious instruction which was offered jointly by Jefferson, Madison, and Monroe on October 7, 1822. It was prepared by Jefferson and appears in his handwriting, announcing the intention of the Board of Visitors to place all religious sects upon an equal footing in the University, and to allow each to establish and maintain a divinity school under its care, 'provided the same should be financially independent and were not a burden upon the endowment of the institution.' It was resolved that the library should be supplied promptly upon publication with the writings 'of the most respected authorities of every sect, and that courses of ethical lectures should be delivered at regular intervals for the education of the students in those moral obligations in which all of the sects agreed.'"**
>
> **"In explanation of this policy of non-sectarian education Jefferson prepared a paper which was made public at the same time. 'It is not to be understood,' he said, 'that instruction in religious opinion and religious duties is precluded because of indifference on the part of the board of visitors to the best interests of society. On the contrary, in the opinion of the board, the relations which exist between man and his Maker and the duties resulting from those relations, are among the most interesting and important to every human being, and the most incumbent upon his study and investigation.'"**

Curtis crammed quite a few lies into these two paragraphs. He even added an extra president, James Monroe, to the 1822 Board of Visitors, although Monroe, who had been on the board of Central College, did not join the board of the university until after he left the presidency in 1825.

There was no resolution to supply the library with religious books, promptly upon publication or otherwise. The quotes used by Curtis in the first paragraph to connect religious books to ethical lectures, and to make proposed religious schools only *financially* independent of the university rather than completely independent, do not come from anything written by the Board of Visitors or Thomas Jefferson. What Curtis claimed in the second paragraph to be from a separate paper prepared by Jefferson as an *"explanation of this policy of non-sectarian education"* actually *is* from the October 7, 1822 report of the board referred to by Curtis in the first paragraph. This report was written four years after the Rockfish Report description of the Professor of Ethics, and two years before Jefferson began working on the catalog for the library, and had absolutely nothing to do with either.

Of course, Jefferson did include books on religion in the university library. He wouldn't have considered an academic library complete without them. He also didn't consider a religion section complete without books on religions other than Christianity, as well as books disputing Christian doctrines, which were also included. While Jefferson didn't think anyone was as qualified as himself to compile a catalog for the library, he made an exception when it came to the religion section. Jefferson seemed to think that Madison, who had at least had some theological education at Princeton fifty years earlier, would be better qualified for this task. On August 8, 1824, Jefferson wrote the following to Madison.

> I have undertaken to make out a catalogue of books for our library, being encouraged to it by the possession of a collection of excellent catalogues, and knowing no one, capable, to whom we could refer the task. It has been laborious far beyond my expectation, having already devoted 4. hours a day to it for upwards of two months, and the whole day for some time past and not yet in sight of the end. It will enable us to judge what the object will cost. The chapter in which I

> am most at a loss is that of divinity; and knowing that in your early days you bestowed attention on this subject, I wish you could suggest to me any works really worthy of a place in the catalogue. The good moral writers, Christian as well as Pagan I have set down; but there are writers of celebrity in religious metaphysics, such as Duns Scotus etc. alii tales [and others of such kind] whom you can suggest.[67]

Jefferson apparently overestimated Madison's knowledge of the subject, as Madison noted in his reply.

> I will endeavor to make out a list of Theological Works, but am less qualified for the task than you seem to think...[68]

After receiving a letter from Jefferson a few weeks later asking him to hurry up and finish the list, Madison realized that Jefferson hadn't meant for him to compile anything as extensive as what he was working on.

> On the rect of yours of Aug. 8, I turned my thoughts to its request on the subject of a Theological Catalogue for the Library of the University; and not being aware that so early an answer was wished, as i now find was the case, I had proceeded very leisurely in noting such Authors as seemed proper for the collection. Supposing also, that altho Theology was not to be taught in the University, its Library ought to contain pretty full information for such as might voluntarily seek it in that branch of Learning, I had contemplated as much of a comprehensive and systematic selection as my scanty materials admitted; and had gone thro the first five Centuries of Xnity when yours of the 3d instant came to hand which was the evening before last. This conveyed to me more distinctly the limited object your letter had in view, and relieved me from a task which I found extremely tedious;

67. Thomas Jefferson to James Madison, August 8, 1824, James Morton Smith, ed., *The Republic of Letters: The Correspondence Between Thomas Jefferson and James Madison 1776-1826,* vol. 3, (New York and London: W.W. Norton & Company, 1995), 1897.

68. James Madison to Thomas Jefferson, August 16, 1824, *ibid.,* 1898.

> especially considering the intermixture of the doctrinal and controversial part of Divinity with the moral and metaphysical part, and the immense extent of the whole.[69]

Madison's list included the Koran, works by the leading Unitarian writers, and books by all the authors that John Adams claimed in an 1812 letter to Benjamin Rush had influenced the young Jefferson and Madison to abolish the religious establishment in Virginia.[70]

> **Mark Beliles, in his list of things Jefferson supported government being involved in, includes the following item: "Purchasing and stocking religious books for public libraries."**

> **D. James Kennedy's version of Beliles's list, in which Beliles's claims are turned into "Jefferson's actions as President," includes: "Funding religious books for public libraries."**

Beliles's claim, which implies that Jefferson made some effort to get religious books into many public libraries, is based on nothing other than Jefferson asking Madison to compile the list of religious books for the University of Virginia library. In fact, while Jefferson did think theology books had a place in a university library, he listed them among the least necessary when establishing a library for the general public. In 1823, when the town of Charlottesville was planning a library, Jefferson recommended that they limit their purchases to *"books of general instruction,"* and exclude professional books, theological books, and novels.[71] Jefferson didn't think novels were worthy of a place in any library. Like most libraries of the time, the library being planned in Charlottesville wasn't truly a public library,

69. James Madison to Thomas Jefferson, September 10, 1824, James Morton Smith, ed., *The Republic of Letters: The Correspondence Between Thomas Jefferson and James Madison 1776-1826,* vol. 3, (New York and London: W.W. Norton & Company, 1995), 1898-1899.

70. John Adams to Benjamin Rush, September 4, 1812, John A Shultz and Douglass Adair, eds., *The Spur of Fame: Dialogues of John Adams and Benjamin Rush, 1805-1813,* (Indianapolis: Liberty Fund, 1999), 267.

71. Thomas Jefferson to F. W. Hatch, March 13, 1823, *The Thomas Jefferson Papers, Series 1, General Correspondence, 1651-1827,* Library of Congress Manuscript Division, #39915.

but was funded by annual subscriptions from the citizens of the town.

Another common trick to make the university look like it was religious at its founding is to point out religious wording and symbols on university structures, ignoring the fact that these structures weren't built until generations after the days of Jefferson and Madison. The most popular, the inscription on Cabell Hall, was first used by William Eleroy Curtis, and is still being used today.

> **According to Curtis: "There is a popular impression that Jefferson forbade religious instruction at the University of Virginia, but the contrary is the case. That institution is usually coupled with Girard College as an example of atheistic propaganda, but the motto of the University is a passage from St. Paul selected by Jefferson, and by his orders inscribed upon the frieze of the rotunda of the auditorium:**
>
> **'And ye shall know the truth, and the truth shall make you free.'"**

This is not the motto of the university, and was not selected by Jefferson for anything. It appears, in Greek, on the frieze of Cabell Hall, an auditorium built over seventy years after Jefferson's death. Cabell Hall was one of several new buildings designed by architect Sanford White when he was hired to rebuild the Rotunda after it was destroyed by a fire in 1895. The quote on the frieze was chosen by Armistead Gordon, a member of the Board of Visitors at that time. Gordon wanted the words carved in English, but White insisted on Greek lettering to match the classical architecture of the building. The sculptures on the frieze were carved in 1898 by Hungarian artist George Julian Zolnay, who hired local prostitutes as models because none of the women of Charlottesville would pose in the nude.

No motto was chosen for the university when it was founded. The university seal, suggested by Jefferson and adopted by the original Board of Visitors, depicted the goddess Minerva. The only wording on the seal was the name of the university and the date of its founding, 1819.

The most remarkable thing about the Liars for Jesus who claim that Jefferson included religion at the University of Virginia is that they completely contradict the opinions of the religious right of Jefferson's day and the first few decades following his death. The religious groups who began pushing for a chapel to be built at the university in the early 1840s didn't claim that Jefferson was really very religious and never intended to exclude religion. They portrayed him as even more irreligious than he actually was, criticized him for excluding religion at the university, and said his secular policies were a mistake and should be disregarded. The practice of posthumously converting Jefferson to Christianity and claiming that he encouraged religion in public schools didn't catch on until a bit later in the century, when the fight over Bible reading in public schools began to heat up. If anyone had tried this in 1840, nobody would have believed them. Obviously, the reason the religious groups were trying to introduce religion into the university was because of its absence, so claiming that Jefferson had included religion at the university's founding would have been ridiculous.

The following excerpts from an article in the January 1842 issue of the *Southern Literary Messenger* are typical of what was being written about the University of Virginia at the time.

> Experiment has proved that Mr. Jefferson committed one great error[72] in the system of government which he sought to establish in the University. But this was as the dust of the balance to that of banishing religion from her walls. The whole should have been planned and executed in reliance upon Divine aid and direction; for nothing can be truer than except the Lord build the house, they labor in vain who build it. Without being superstitious, the overruling hand of Providence must be acknowledged; and apprehensions sometimes arise lest Heaven has decreed the fall of the University, in order to prove to man the folly and impiety of founding such institutions, without invoking its blessing. Religion cannot be safely separated from any human undertaking. For literature and science to produce their salutary effects upon the mind and heart—to make man better as

72. The omission of a Department of English Literature.

> they make him wiser—they must be associated with, and tempered by, religion; nor should their connection be slight and incidental, but designed and intimate. The system of Mr. Jefferson has been abandoned; and there are now regular religious services twice a-week, and the students pay marked respect to the minister. But the fact of having a chaplain is a small matter. He must not be looked upon as a mere preacher and sermonizer on Sundays, but as pastor and instructor in religious matters; not as a mere appendage, but as an important, an essential part of the institution. Religion must be admitted, not as a secondary matter, but as of primary concern; not as an incident, but an essential; not through complaisance to public opinion, to allay the fears of anxious parents, nor as a compromise between the opposition of Mr. Jefferson, and the convictions of the Visiters....
>
> ...The first thing to be done is to erect a suitable chapel. The faculty are anxious for this to be effected, and presented a memorial to the Visiters on the subject. At the request of the writer, Professor Bonnycastle drew up an eloquent memorial to be presented on the part of the students; but as circumstances prevented the signatures from being obtained, it was not handed in. A chapel is not only necessary for the religious services, but for public occasions, anniversary orations, the use of societies, and for important meetings of the students, when they wish to do honor to the memory of a departed fellow-student or professor. It will also be useful as an ornament, and this dreadful hiatus, so painfully obvious to every Christian friend of the institution, should be speedily supplied....[73]

As this article indicates, by the early 1840s, there had been some increase in religious activity at the university, but not enough to satisfy everyone. Almost as soon as Madison retired, the board began to relax some of the rules. The very first school year that Madison was-

73. "The University of Virginia," *Southern Literary Messenger,* Vol. VIII, Issue 1, January 1842, 53-54.

n't there, the chaplain was allowed to live on the campus. By 1840, with a number of new professors who opposed the university's secular policies, conditions were right for an all out campaign to make religion an integral part of the university. One of the new professors was James Lawrence Cabell, a nephew of Joseph C. Cabell, hired in 1837 as Professor of Anatomy. James Cabell was a leader in the movement to build a chapel and parsonage at the university, and, although not a clergyman, also began leading a weekly Bible study.

Just as Jefferson had predicted two decades earlier, it would be the Presbyterians who would attempt to establish their particular brand of religion at the university as soon as an opportunity presented itself. James W. Alexander, a Presbyterian minister, and brother-in-law of James Lawrence Cabell, noted the progression of religion at the university in several of his letters to fellow Presbyterian minister John Hall. In 1840, when it was beginning to look like a religious takeover might be possible, Alexander wrote the following to Hall.

> The religious prospects of the University of Virginia are really encouraging. It seems as if Providence was throwing contempt on old Jefferson's ashes.[74]

In another letter to Hall, after visiting the university seven years later, he wrote:

> Jefferson knew how to select one of the finest plateaus in the land for this college. His antichristian plans have been singularly thwarted in every way. For example, here is a chapel, (since I was here last;) three professors are communicants, besides Dr. McGuffey, who is a Presbyterian minister; and a proctor and treasurer who are Presbyterian communicants. McGuffey is a West Pennsylvanian, and is second to no man in Virginia for fame as a lecturer and public speaker. He does not preach here, but often in other places. I shall not be surprised if, before ten years, this rich and central institution should have on its very grounds a Presbyterian theological school; as the law founding the university gives leave to any

74. James W. Alexander to John Hall, June 10, 1840, John Hall, D.D., ed., *Forty Years' Familiar Letters of James W. Alexander, D.D.*, vol. 1, (New York: Charles Scribner, 1860), 305.

> Christian sect to build, and to have a theological professor, with freedom of library, apparatus, &c....[75]

Alexander's reference in this 1847 letter to a chapel does not mean that an actual chapel had been built. What Alexander was referring to was a lecturing room in one of the wings of the Rotunda, which had been designated for religious worship in 1841. The Rotunda's wings were originally intended as gymnasiums, but turned out not to be well suited for this purpose. In the mid-1830s, the board decided to divide the wings into lecturing rooms. Because the school had grown, the lecturing room in which religious services were originally held had become too small. The larger room that the services were moved to, which unlike the old room was designated solely for religious worship, was the "chapel" until an actual chapel was built in the late 1880s.

Although Alexander seemed to consider the lecturing room chapel a significant improvement, the author of the 1842 *Southern Literary Messenger* article certainly didn't find it adequate.

> In the university, the services are performed in the lecture-room, which is very inconveniently arranged, and where the mind is diverted by a thousand perceptions and associations. Every thing in connection with the *spirituel* of that institution would show, if we did not know the fact, that the introduction of religion was an afterthought. In all her extensive arrangements, there is not a single accommodation for religion.[76]

Lies about Thomas Jefferson advocating religious instruction at the University of Virginia have been used by certain Supreme Court justices in cases involving religion in public schools, one of these cases involving the University of Virginia itself.

> **Justice Thomas, in his concurring opinion, Rosenberger v. University of Virginia, 1995: "And even Thomas Jefferson, respondents founder and a champion of**

75. James W. Alexander to John Hall, May 27, 1847, John Hall, D.D., ed., *Forty Years' Familiar Letters of James W. Alexander, D.D.*, vol. 2, (New York: Charles Scribner, 1860), 71.

76. "The University of Virginia," *Southern Literary Messenger*, Vol. VIII, Issue 1, January 1842, 54.

disestablishment in Virginia, advocated the use of public funds in Virginia for a department of theology in conjunction with other professional schools."

Here, of course, Justice Thomas is referring to Jefferson's 1814 outline for Albemarle Academy. Besides the fact that Jefferson had no intention of this school ever existing, and only temporarily listed a theological school for the reasons explained earlier in this chapter, Albemarle Academy, if it had come into being, was going to be supported by private, not public, funds. The money was to be raised by subscriptions and a lottery. The only professional school proposed in his Albemarle Academy plan that Jefferson said should be supported by public funds was a school of technical philosophy, a night school to teach the aspects of science useful to those already working in various trades.

Justice Thomas, in the same opinion, also takes the following out of context: "Jefferson advocated giving 'to the sectarian schools of divinity the full benefit [of] the public provisions made for instruction in the other branches of science.'"

When taken out of context as it is by Justice Thomas, this statement from the Board of Visitors 1822 invitation to the religious sects makes it sound as if public funds would be supporting schools of divinity. All it really meant, of course, was that the students of a divinity school located near the university would receive the benefit of the public provisions made for the university by being able to attend lectures in the branches of science taught at the university.

The following is the entire proposition regarding religious schools as it appeared in the October 1822 report of the Board of Visitors.

> A remedy, however, has been suggested, of promising aspect, which, while it excludes the public authorities from the domain of religious freedom, would give to the sectarian schools of divinity the full benefit of the public provisions made for instruction in the other branches of science. These branches are equally necessary to the divine as to the other professional or civil characters, to enable them to fulfill the

> duties of their calling with understanding and usefulness. It has, therefore, been in contemplation, and suggested by some pious individuals, who perceive the advantages of associating other studies with those of religion, to establish their religious schools on the confines of the University, so as to give to their students ready and convenient access and attendance on the scientific lectures of the University; and to maintain, by that means, those destined for the religious professions on as high a standing of science, and of personal weight and respectability, as may be obtained by others from the benefits of the University. Such establishments would offer the further and great advantage of enabling the students of the University to attend religious exercises with the professor of their particular sect, either in the rooms of the building still to be erected, and destined to that purpose under impartial regulations, as proposed in the same report of the Commissioners, or in the lecturing room of such professor. To such propositions the Visitors are prepared to lend a willing ear, and would think it their duty to give every encouragement, by assuring to those who might choose such a location for their schools that the regulations of the University should be so modified and accommodated as to give every facility of access and attendance to their students, with such regulated use also as may be permitted to the other students of the library which may hereafter be acquired, either by public or private munificence, but always understanding that these schools shall be independent of the University and of each other....[77]

Justice Reed, in 1948, used the university's 1824 religious school rule as evidence that Jefferson *"did not exclude religious education from that school."*

> **According to Justice Reed, in his dissenting opinion, McCollum v. Board of Education, 1948: "Mr. Jefferson, as one of the founders of the University of Virginia, a**

77. Andrew A. Lipscomb and Albert Ellery Bergh, eds., *The Writings of Thomas Jefferson*, vol. 19, (Washington D.C.: Thomas Jefferson Memorial Association, 1907), 415-416.

school which from its establishment in 1819 has been wholly governed, managed and controlled by the State of Virginia, was faced with the same problem that is before this Court today: The question of the constitutional limitation upon religious education in public schools. In his annual report as Rector, to the President and Directors of the Literary Fund, dated October 7, 1822, approved by the Visitors of the University of whom Mr. Madison was one, Mr. Jefferson set forth his views at some length. These suggestions of Mr. Jefferson were adopted and ch. II, 1, of the Regulations of the University of October 4, 1824, provided that:

'Should the religious sects of this State, or any of them, according to the invitation held out to them, establish within, or adjacent to, the precincts of the University, schools for instruction in the religion of their sect, the students of the University will be free, and expected to attend religious worship at the establishment of their respective sects, in the morning, and in time to meet their school in the University at its stated hour.' Thus, the 'wall of separation between church and State' that Mr. Jefferson built at the University which he founded did not exclude religious education from that school."

Bible Reading in Public Schools...

What is probably the single most popular religious right lie about Thomas Jefferson and public education is a lie about about schools that Jefferson had virtually nothing to do with – the first public schools in Washington D.C. There are several versions of this lie on the Christian American history websites, and it appears in some form in almost every religious right American history book.

According to William J. Federer, in his book *Americas God and Country*: "Thomas Jefferson,

> **while president (1801-1809), chaired the school board for the District of Columbia, where he authored the first plan of education adopted by the city of Washington. This plan used the Bible and Isaac Watts' Psalms, Hymns and Spiritual Songs, 1707, as the principle books for teaching reading to the students."**

> **D. James Kennedy claims that Jefferson: "Used the Bible and nondenominational religious instruction in the public schools. He was involved in three different school districts, and the plan in each required Bible reading."**

Kennedy's version, although not mentioning the city of Washington by name, is found in his list of claims about Jefferson borrowed from Mark Beliles, and the sources cited by Beliles are two books about the history of Washington D.C. Only the first sentence of Kennedy's claim actually appears in Beliles's list. Kennedy improved upon Beliles's lie, expanding it to three different school districts, and adding the claim that Bible reading was *"required."*

This myth about Jefferson and the Washington D.C. schools is based on two things. One is that, in 1805, Jefferson was elected president of the Board of Trustees of the Washington City Public Schools. The other is a report by the teacher of one of the city's early public schools, showing that the Bible and *Watts's Hymns* were used as reading texts in that school. The problem with the story is that the school that used these books didn't exist until several years after Jefferson left Washington.

The first public schools in Washington D.C. were funded partly by the city, but mostly by donations from about two hundred private contributors. When the Washington City school board was formed in 1805, it consisted of thirteen members. Seven of these were appointed by the City Council, and the other six were elected by the private contributors from among the private contributors. Thomas Jefferson, who had made one of the larger donations, was one of the six elected. At the first meeting of the board, Jefferson was elected board president. Jefferson was not present at either of these elections. He was informed of his election by mail, and accepted the position by mail. It does not appear that Jefferson had much actual involvement with the school board. Other than his election as board president, the only other mention of Jefferson in the minutes of the school board had to do with appropriating public land as the site for a school. But, Jefferson's role in this was in his capacity of President of the United States, not president of the school board.

Between the years of 1806 and 1811, the Washington City school board attempted to establish and maintain two public schools in the city. The board's biggest problem was that they couldn't afford to pay high enough salaries to get and keep qualified teachers. Classes were held in rented buildings until enough money was raised through private donations to build two schoolhouses in 1807. By 1809, the City Council had cut the public funding for these schools nearly in half, and one of the two was closed. These first two schools were the only schools that existed at the time that Jefferson was president of the school board. Neither of these schools, however, is the school referred to in the lie about Jefferson requiring Bible reading. The school in the lie is the Lancasterian school that opened in Washington D.C. in 1812, three years after Jefferson left the presidency and returned to Virginia.

In 1811, the teacher of a Lancasterian school in Georgetown wrote a letter to the Washington City school board suggesting that they might have more success with this type of school. Lancasterian schools were developed by Joseph Lancaster in England as an economical way to educate large numbers of poor children. By using the older students to teach the younger ones, Lancaster's system allowed one teacher to oversee the education of hundreds of children. The school in Georgetown was teaching three hundred and fifty students in one room. In 1812, the Washington City school board decided to open a Lancasterian school. Henry Ould, a teacher trained by Lancaster in England, was brought over to run this school. This, of course, disproves William Federer's claim that Thomas Jefferson authored the plan of education for the public schools in Washington D.C.

Among the books used for reading lessons in Lancaster's schools in England were the Bible and *Watts's Hymns for Children.* These were also used in the Lancasterian school in Washington D.C. Ould's progress report to the school board in 1813 showed the number of children who were able to read from the Bible and *Watts's Hymns* to demonstrate the school's success in teaching reading.

> M. Ould, teacher of the Lancasterian School, submitted the following report, dated February 10, 1813: GENTLEMEN: This day twelve months ago I had the pleasure of opening, under your auspices, the second genuine Lancasterian School in America. The system was set in operation, as far as the nature of the room would admit, in an inconvenient house opposite to the General Post Office; but, notwithstanding, there were 120 scholars entered on the list during the first three months. I was then under the necessity of delaying the admission of scholars, as the room would not accommodate more than 80 to 100 scholars. It now becomes my duty to lay before you an account of the improvement of the scholars placed under my direction: which I shall do in the following order: One hundred and thirty scholars have been admitted since February 10, 1812, 82 males and 48 females; out of which number 2 have died, and 37 have left the school for various employments, after passing through several grades of studies; leaving 91 on the list. Fifty-five have learned to read in the Old and New Testaments, 26 are now learning to read Dr. Watts's Hymns, and 10 are learning words of four or five letters. Out of 59 of the whole number admitted who did not know a single letter, 20 read in the Bible, 29 in Watts's Hymns, and 10 spell words of four and five letters. Fifty-five scholars are able to write on paper, many of them, also, in German text, who never attempted to form such characters before entering the school; 26 write words of two or three syllables on slates, and 10 are writing words of two or five letters. All the scholars who left the school could write a tolerable and many of them a capital hand. Twenty-six scholars are in Reduction, Single and Double Rule of Three, direct and practice, and 23 are rapidly progressing through the first four rules of Arithmetic, both simple and compound.[78]

78. Samuel Yorke At Lee, *History of the Public Schools of Washington City, D.C., from August, 1805, to August, 1875, written at request and published by order of the Board of Trustees of Public Schools, for the National Centennial Year, 1876*, (Washington D.C.: McGill & Witherow, 1876), 11-12.

An interesting thing about this report is that the Bible and *Watts's Hymns* are the *only* books mentioned, although Lancaster's curriculum called for a variety of other reading texts. There is, however, a pretty likely explanation for this – the War of 1812. Virtually all children's books at this time, including all of the other books in Lancaster's curriculum, had to be imported from England. The few textbooks that had been printed in America, such as the first edition of Noah Webster's *Blue Back Speller,* did not contain enough reading passages to be useful as a reading text. As explained in Chapter One, all import duties were doubled in 1812 to fund the war. This would have made any imported books far too expensive for this school. The Bible and *Watts's Hymns,* however, were being printed in America, and printed in large enough editions to make them affordable. The progress reports from this same school from after the War of 1812 do not mention either of these books, indicating that they may just have been used out of necessity.

The best evidence, however, that there was no religious instruction in the early public schools of Washington D.C. are the repeated requests of the city's mayor, Samuel Smallwood, to add non-denominational Christian instruction to the curriculum. Obviously, if there had already been religious instruction in these schools, there would have been no reason for Smallwood to request that it be added. Smallwood's first request appeared in an 1819 message to the school board.

> The schools for the poor need the fostering hand of the Council. Let us not forget that as this is the Metropolis of a great and rising nation, and ought to be the source from which correct principles should emanate, so ought it to be distinguished for the correct deportment of its inhabitants, and afford an example for imitation. This, then, cannot be aided in a better manner than by teaching the poor and indigent the principles of morality, and the knowledge of the goodness of our holy religion.[79]

79. Samuel Yorke At Lee, *History of the Public Schools of Washington City, D.C., from August, 1805, to August, 1875, written at request and published by order of the Board of Trustees of Public Schools, for the National Centennial Year, 1876,* (Washington D.C.: McGill & Witherow, 1876), 17.

Five years later, in 1824, he tried again.

> I conceive the maintenance of the Public Schools to be highly important. We should make them, by every means in our power, the instrument to improve the moral character of our fellow-men. It would have the best tendency to this purpose, if the Trustees of our schools would cause the children to assemble every Sunday morning, at the respective schoolhouses, before the hour of public worship in the churches, and there to lecture them on the principles of morality and religion. I presume that this might be done in such a manner as in no wise to give offense to any denomination of Christians; and the occasional attendance of the Council at these schools with the Trustees, in order to examine the pupils, would be of great advantage. I hope, too, that, before long, by a proper application, we may obtain from Congress some important aid for the laudable object of public instruction. It has been accomplished elsewhere, and why may it not be granted here? [80]

Smallwood's requests were ignored by both the school board and the City Council.

As already mentioned, D. James Kennedy upgrades the Washington D.C. schools claim in Mark Beliles's list to *"three different school districts."* Kennedy gives no indication of what the other two school districts were, although one is certainly Jefferson's 1778 plan for public schools in Virginia. Beliles, elsewhere in his introduction, ends his story about Jefferson including the Bible in the plan he *"drafted"* for the schools in Washington D.C. with a claim that his *"educational proposals for Virginia were based on a similar plan."*

No plan of education written by Thomas Jefferson ever included, let alone required, Bible reading. In fact, in his proposed plan for public schools in Virginia in 1778, he deliberately excluded Bible reading, specifying in his *Bill for the More General Diffusion of Knowledge* the types of books to be used as reading texts.

80. Samuel Yorke At Lee, *History of the Public Schools of Washington City, D.C., from August, 1805, to August, 1875, written at request and published by order of the Board of Trustees of Public Schools, for the National Centennial Year, 1876,* (Washington D.C.: McGill & Witherow, 1876), 17.

> At every of these schools shall be taught reading, writing, and common arithmetick, and the books which shall be used therein for instructing the children to read shall be such as will at the time make them acquainted with Græcian, Roman, English, and American history.[81]

Describing this bill in his *Notes on the State of Virginia*, Jefferson made it clear that this was a deliberate exclusion of the Bible.

> Instead therefore, of putting the Bible and Testament into the hands of the children at an age when their judgments are not sufficiently matured for religious inquiries, their memories may here be stored with the most useful facts from Grecian, Roman, European, and American history.[82]

There aren't many lies about Jefferson's plan for public schools in Virginia, probably because there nothing in his 1778 bill can be misquoted effectively. David Barton, however, gets around this problem by quoting something that had absolutely nothing to do with the plan for schools in Virginia.

> **According to David Barton, in his book *Original Intent*: "...when Thomas Jefferson authored his plan of education in Virginia, he considered religious study an inseparable component in the study of law and political science. As he explained:**
>
> **[I]n my catalogue, considering ethics, as well as religion, as supplements to law in the government of man, I had placed them in that sequence."**

What Barton is quoting here is a letter from Jefferson to Augustus Woodward regarding the best arrangement for a library catalog, written nearly fifty years after his plan for schools in Virginia. Woodward was

81. Julian P. Boyd, ed., *The Papers of Thomas Jefferson,* vol. 2, (Princeton, NJ: Princeton University Press, 1950), 528.

82. Andrew A. Lipscomb and Albert Ellery Bergh, eds., *The Writings of Thomas Jefferson,* vol. 2, (Washington D.C.: Thomas Jefferson Memorial Association, 1904), 204.

one of the founders of the University of Michigan, as well as a territorial judge. President Monroe, who had planned to appoint Judge Woodward to the Michigan court in 1824, withdrew his name because he was accused of being a drunk. The truth was that, during a typhus outbreak in the summer of 1823, Woodward became ill and his doctor prescribed a treatment that included, among other things, a combination of brandy and opium. That September, Woodward, still not completely well, but not wanting to miss the opening day of court, took an extra dose of his medicine after he arrived at the courthouse. Some of his political enemies saw him do this, and sent letters and affidavits to the White House accusing him of drinking in public and being drunk on the bench. Woodward's accusers later recanted their story, and Monroe gave him a new appointment as a judge in the Florida Territory.

Woodward also shared Jefferson's interest in books, and through numerous visits to libraries in major cities and discussions with various scholars, developed a system of classification for all of the branches of science. This was published in 1816 as *A System of Universal Science*. In the letter quoted by Barton, Jefferson, who had come up with a different system for cataloging his own library, was simply explaining to Woodward how he had arrived at what he thought was the proper place for books on religion.

> The naturalists, you know, distribute the history of nature into three kingdoms or departments: zoology, botany, mineralogy. Ideology or mind, however, occupies so much space in the field of science, that we might perhaps erect it into a fourth kingdom or department. But, inasmuch as it makes a part of the animal construction only, it would be more proper to subdivide zoology into physical and moral. The latter including ideology, ethics, and mental science generally, in my catalogue, considering ethics, as well as religion, as supplements to law in the government of man, I had placed them in that sequence. But certainly the faculty of thought belongs to animal history, is an important portion of it, and should there find its place.[83]

83. Thomas Jefferson to Judge Augustus B. Woodward, March 24, 1824, Andrew A. Lipscomb and Albert Ellery Bergh, eds., *The Writings of Thomas Jefferson,* vol. 16, (Washington D.C.: Thomas Jefferson Memorial Association, 1903), 19.

— CHAPTER SIX —

Did Prayer Save the Constitutional Convention?

According to the religious right version of American history, without the power of prayer, the Constitution would never have been written. This claim is based on a speech made by Benjamin Franklin at the Constitutional Convention on June 28, 1787. Franklin's speech, made at a point when disagreements among the delegates had brought things almost to a standstill, recalled the practice of daily prayers in Congress during the Revolutionary War, and ended with a motion that prayers be held each morning from that point on. Although no action was taken on Franklin's motion, and no prayers were ever held at the Convention, many Liars for Jesus still insist that prayers were held, and that the Constitution never could have been written without them.

Most of the myths regarding Franklin's motion for prayers are not about the motion itself, but what followed the motion. The following are two recent versions of the story from the internet.

> **"Benjamin Franklin then proposed that the Congress adjourn for two days to seek divine guidance. When they returned they began each of their sessions with prayer. The stirring speech of Benjamin Franklin marked a turning point in the writing of the Constitution, complete with a Bill of Rights."**

> **"The Assembly of 55 of America's greatest intellects**

> **and leaders solemnly and humbly adopted Benjamin Franklin's motion, and each session was thereafter begun with prayer for God's guidance and wisdom. The effect on the Convention was nothing short of miraculous. A sense of order and direction emerged resulting in the adoption of what leaders throughout the world have acknowledged as the greatest document ever crafted by the human mind."**

Many versions of the story, like the second example above, contain a claim that, following Franklin's speech, the Convention adjourned for two or three days to pray. A few even say that George Washington immediately got up and marched the entire Convention to a church. Neither of these things happened. The Convention met on both of the next two days, and the subject of prayers was never brought up again.

During the first month of the Constitutional Convention, there were various disagreements and close votes, but things didn't get really ugly until the debate over how much representation each state would have in Congress. While the majority of the delegates agreed that representation in the House of Representatives should be based on population, the question of representation in the Senate divided the Convention, pitting the small states against the large states. The small states thought every state should have an equal representation; the large states thought the Senate should also be based on population. It wasn't until the end of June that the real debate on this began, a debate that came dangerously close to putting an end to the Convention altogether. It was at this critical point that Benjamin Franklin made his famous motion for prayers.

> Mr. President
>
> The small progress we have made after 4 or five weeks close attendance & continual reasonings with each other—our different sentiments on almost every question, several of the last producing as many noes as ays, is methinks a melancholy proof of the imperfection of the Human Understanding. We indeed seem to feel our own want of political wisdom, since we have been running about in search of it. We have

gone back to ancient history for models of Government, and examined the different forms of those Republics which having been formed with the seeds of their own dissolution now no longer exist. And we have viewed Modern States all round Europe, but find none of their Constitutions suitable to our circumstances.

In this situation of this Assembly, groping as it were in the dark to find political truth, and scarce able to distinguish it when presented to us, how has it happened, Sir, that we have not hitherto once thought of humbly applying to the Father of lights to illuminate our understandings? In the beginning of the Contest with G. Britain, when we were sensible of danger we had daily prayer in this room for the divine protection. Our prayers, Sir, were heard, and they were graciously answered. All of us who were engaged in the struggle must have observed frequent instances of a Superintending providence in our favor. To that kind providence we owe this happy opportunity of consulting in peace on the means of establishing our future national felicity. And have we now forgotten that powerful friend? or do we imagine that we no longer need his assistance? I have lived, Sir, a long time, and the longer I live, the more convincing proofs I see of this truth—that God governs in the affairs of men. And if a sparrow cannot fall to the ground without his notice, is it probable that an empire can rise without his aid? We have been assured, Sir, in the sacred writings, that "except the Lord build the House they labour in vain that build it." I firmly believe this; and I also believe that without his concurring aid we shall succeed in this political building no better than the Builders of Babel: We shall be divided by our little partial local interests; our projects will be confounded, and we ourselves shall become a reproach and bye word down to future ages. And what is worse, mankind may hereafter from this unfortunate instance, despair of establishing Governments by Human Wisdom and leave it to chance, war and conquest.

I therefore beg leave to move—that henceforth prayers

> imploring the assistance of Heaven, and its blessings on our deliberations, be held in this Assembly every morning before we proceed to business, and that one or more of the Clergy of this City be requested to officiate in that service.[1]

According to James Madison's records of the Convention, the following is what occurred after Franklin's speech.

> Mr. Sherman seconded the motion.
>
> Mr. Hamilton & several others expressed their apprehensions that however proper such a resolution might have been at the beginning of the convention, it might at this late day, 1. bring on it some disagreeable animadversions. & 2. lead the public to believe that the embarrassments and dissentions within the convention, had suggested this measure. It was answered by Docr. F. Mr. Sherman & others, that the past omission of a duty could not justify a further omission—that the rejection of such a proposition would expose the Convention to more unpleasant animadversions than the adoption of it: and that the alarm out of doors that might be excited for the state of things within. would at least be as likely to do good as ill.
>
> Mr. Williamson, observed that the true cause of the omission could not be mistaken. The Convention had no funds.
>
> Mr. Randolph proposed in order to give a favorable aspect to ye. measure, that a sermon be preached at the request of the convention on 4th of July, the anniversary of Independence, — & thenceforward prayers be used in ye Convention every morning. Dr. Frankn. 2ded. this motion. After several unsuccessful attempts for silently postponing the matter by adjourng. the adjournment was at length carried, without any vote on the motion.[2]

1. Max Farrand, ed., *The Records of the Federal Convention of 1787,* vol. 1, (New Haven, CT: Yale University Press, 1911), 450-452.
2. *ibid.*, 452.

Alexander Hamilton's objection at least made some sense. What would people think if a minister was seen entering the building? Because of the complete secrecy of the Convention, curious people were constantly hanging around outside hoping to get some idea of what was going on. If a minister was suddenly allowed in, it might appear that the Convention was in trouble. Hugh Williamson's objection that they had no money to pay a chaplain is ridiculous. Some of the wealthiest men in the country were there. If they had really wanted prayers, they could have scraped together the small amount of money needed to pay a minister. They were also in a city full of Quakers, whose ministers weren't allowed to accept money. There was even a minister among the delegates. Abraham Baldwin was a former army chaplain who had been offered the professorship of divinity at Yale. If they were really concerned about a minister attracting attention, they could have asked Baldwin to lead their prayers. The delegates were clearly just trying to find excuses to dismiss Franklin's motion. They even avoided voting on Edmund Randolph's motion to postpone prayers until the Fourth of July, which would have provided an excuse for the sudden appearance of a minister. Apparently, neither Randolph, or Franklin, who seconded Randolph's motion, saw a lack of funds as the problem, unless they thought the Convention would be able to come up with money on July 4 that it couldn't on June 28.

Franklin made the following note at the end of his handwritten copy of his speech.

> The convention, except three or four persons, thought prayers unnecessary.[3]

The religious right American history books contain many variations of what occurred after Franklin's motion, most of which end up with prayers being held. In their book *America's Providential History,* for example, Mark Beliles and Stephen McDowell not only claim that a vote was taken, but that the Convention found volunteer chaplains.

According to Beliles and McDowell: "Mr. Sherman sec-

3. Max Farrand, ed., *The Records of the Federal Convention of 1787,* vol. 1, (New Haven, CT: Yale University Press, 1911), 452.

> **onded the motion for prayer, and it was carried with only one negative, but then Mr. Williamson of North Carolina pointed out that they had no funds to pay the salary of a full-time chaplain. This part of Franklin's motion, therefore, failed, but Mr. Randolph then proposed that they obtain clergy who would volunteer their time as much as possible to lead in prayer, and especially 'that a sermon be preached, at the request of the convention, on the Fourth of July, the anniversary of independence.'**
>
> **They were successful in obtaining clergymen to volunteer on some mornings, for Mr. Dayton refers to one opening the session on the first day after the three-day recess."**

William Federer, in his book *America's God and Country* works James Madison into the debate, claiming that he *moved* Franklin's *motion.*

> **According to Federer: "Following the historical address, James Madison moved, seconded by Roger Sherman of Connecticut, that Dr. Franklin's appeal for prayer be enacted."**

Although Franklin's motion was never acted on, and prayers did not save the Constitutional Convention, Franklin's speech may have. It's not likely that Franklin actually thought that prayers would make any difference. He just knew how the delegates would react if he suggested that they might not be capable of getting the job done without some supernatural help. They would be determined to prove him wrong, and the only way to prove him wrong would be to finish writing the Constitution – without any *"foreign aid,"* as Alexander Hamilton allegedly put it.

The myth that the Convention adjourned for several days after Franklin's motion dates back to the 1820s. The source of this myth is a letter written by William Steele in 1825, first published in the *New York Gazette and General Advertiser*, and reprinted in the *National Intelligencer* in August 1826.

Painted Post, September, 1825.

My dear Son: —

I some time ago repeated to you an historical anecdote, in which you felt so much interested that you extorted from me a promise, that I would at some moment of leisure commit it to paper for you. I am now seated for that purpose, and shall relate it as nearly as I can recollect, in the words of General Jonathan Dayton, one of the members of the General Convention, who framed the Constitution, and afterwards Speaker of the House of Representatives, in the Congress of the United States.

I was (said General Dayton) a delegate from New Jersey, in the General Convention which assembled in Philadelphia for the purpose of digesting a constitution for the United States, and I believe I was the youngest member of that body. The great and good Washington was chosen our president, and Dr. Franklin, among other great men, was a delegate from Pennsylvania. A disposition was soon discovered in some members to display themselves in oratorical flourishes; but the good sense and discretion of the majority put down all such attempts. We had convened to deliberate upon, and if possible effect, a great national object—to search for political *wisdom* and *truth;* these we meant to pursue with simplicity, and to avoid everything which would have a tendency to divert our attention, or perplex our scheme.

A great variety of projects were proposed, all republican in their general outlines, but differing in their details. It was, therefore, determined that certain *elementary principles* should at first be established, in each branch of the intended constitution, and afterwards the *details* should be debated and filled up.

There was little or no difficulty in determining upon the *elementary principles* — such as, for instance, that the government should be a *republican-representative* government — that it should be divided into three branches, that is, *legislative, executive, and judicial, &c.* But when the organization of the respective branches of the legislature came under consideration, it was easy to be perceived that the eastern and southern states had *distinct interests,* which it was difficult to reconcile; and that the larger states were disposed to form a constitution, in which the smaller states would be mere appendages and satellites to the larger ones. On the first of these subjects, much animated and somewhat *angry* debate had taken place, when the ratio of representation in the lower house of Congress was before us — the southern states claiming for themselves the *whole* number of their black population, while the eastern states were for confining the elective franchise to *freemen* only, without respect to color.

As the different parties adhered pertinaciously to their different positions, it was feared that this would prove an insurmountable obstacle; — but as the members were already generally satisfied that no constitution could be formed, which would meet the views and subserve the interests of each individual state, it was evident that it must be a matter of *compromise* and mutual *concession.* Under these impressions, and with these views, it was agreed at length that each state should be entitled to one delegate in the House of Representatives for every 30,000 of its inhabitants — in which number should be included *three fifths* of the whole number of their slaves.

When the details of the House of Representatives were disposed of, a more knotty point presented itself in the organization of the Senate. The larger states contended that the same *ratio,* as to states, should be common to both branches of the legislature; or, in other words, that each state should be entitled to a representation in the Senate, (whatever might be the number fixed on,) in proportion to its population, as in the House of Representatives. The smaller states, on the other hand, contended that the House of Representatives might be considered as the guardian of the liberties of the *people,* and therefore ought to bear a just proportion to their numbers; but that the Senate represented the *sovereignty of the States,* and that as each state, whether great or small, was equally an independent and sovereign state, it ought, in this branch of the legislature, to have equal weight and authority; without this, they said, there could be no security for their *equal* rights — and they would, by such a distribution of power, be merged and lost in the larger states.

This reasoning, however plain and powerful, had but little influence on the minds of delegates from the larger states — and as they formed a large majority of the Convention, the question, after passing through the forms of debate, was decided that 'each state should be represented in the Senate in proportion to its population.'

When the Convention had adjourned over to the next day, the delegates of the four smallest states, i.e., Rhode Island, Connecticut, New Jersey, and Delaware, convened to consult what course was to be pursued in the important crisis at which we had arrived. After serious investigation, it was solemnly determined to ask for a *reconsideration* the next morning; and if it was not granted, or if, when granted, that offensive feature of the Constitution could not be expunged, and the smaller states put upon an *equal footing* with the largest, we would secede from the Convention, and, returning to our constituents, inform them that no compact could be formed with the large states, but one which would sacrifice our sovereignty and independence.

I was deputed to be the organ through which this communication should be made — I know not why, unless it be that *young* men are generally chosen to perform *rash* actions. Accordingly, when the Convention had assembled, and as soon as the minutes of the last sitting were read, I arose and stated the view we had taken of the organization of the Senate — our desire to obtain a *reconsideration* and suitable *modification* of that article; and, in failure thereof, our determination to secede from the Convention, and return to our constituents.

This disclosure, it may readily be supposed, produced an immediate and great excitement in every part of the house! Several members were immediately on the floor to express their surprise, or indignation! They represented that the question had received a full and fair investigation, and had been definitively settled by a very large majority. That it was altogether unparliamentary and unreasonable, for one of the *minority* to propose a reconsideration, at the moment their act had become a matter of *record,* and without pretending that any new light could be thrown on the subject. That if such a precedent should be established, it would in future be impossible to say when any one point was definitively settled; as a small minority might at any moment, again and again, move and obtain a reconsideration. They therefore hoped the Convention would express its decided disapprobation by passing silently to the business before them.

There was much warm and some *acrimonious* feeling exhibited by a number of the speeches — a *rupture* appeared almost inevitable, and the bosom of Washington seemed to labor with the most anxious solicitude for its issue. Happily for the United States, the Convention contained some individuals possessed of talents and virtues of the highest order, whose hearts were deeply interested in the establishment of a new and efficient form of government; and whose penetrating minds had already deplored the evils which would spring up in our newly established republic, should the present attempt to consolidate it prove abortive. Among those personages, the most prominent was Dr. Franklin. He was esteemed the *Mentor* of our body. To a mind naturally *strong* and *capacious,* enriched by much reading and the experience of many years, he added a manner of communicating his thoughts peculiarly his own — in which simplicity, beauty, and strength were equally conspicuous. As soon as the angry orators, who preceded him had left him an opening, the doctor rose, evidently impressed with the weight of the subject before them, and the difficulty of managing it successfully.

"We have arrived, Mr. President," said he, "at a very momentous and interesting crisis in our deliberations. Hitherto our views have been as harmonious, and our progress as great, as could reasonably have been expected. But now an unlooked for and formidable obstacle is thrown in our way, which threatens to arrest our course, and, if not skilfully removed, to render all our fond hopes of a constitution abortive. The ground which has been taken by the delegates of the four smallest states, was as unexpected by me, and as repugnant to my feelings, as it can be to any other member of this Convention. After what I thought a full and impartial investigation of the subject, I recorded my vote in the affirmative side of the question, and I have not yet heard anything which induces me to change my opinion. But I will not, therefore, conclude that it is *impossible* for me to be wrong! I will not say that those gentlemen who differ from me are under a delusion — much less will I charge them with an intention of needlessly embarrassing our deliberations. It is *possible* some change in our late proceedings ought to take place upon principles of *political justice;* or that, all things considered, the majority may see cause to recede from some of their just pretensions, as a matter of *prudence* and *expediency.* For my own part, there is nothing I so much dread, as a failure to devise and establish some efficient and equal form of government for our infant republic. The present effort has been made under the happiest auspices, and has promised the most favorable results; but should this effort prove vain, it will be long ere another can be made with any prospect of success. Our *strength* and our *prosperity* will depend on our unity; and the secession of even *four* of the smallest states, interspersed as they are, would, in my mind, paralyze and render useless, any plan which the majority could devise. I should therefore be grieved, Mr. President, to see matters brought to the test, which has been, perhaps too *rashly* threatened on the one hand, and which some of my honored colleagues have treated too *lightly* on the other. I am convinced that it is a subject which should be approached with *caution,* treated with tenderness, and decided on with *candor* and *liberality.*

"It is, however, to be feared that the members of this Convention are not in a temper, at this moment, to approach the subject in which we differ, in this spirit. I would, therefore, propose, Mr. President, that, without proceeding further in this business at this time, the Convention shall adjourn for *three days,* in order to let the present ferment pass off, and to afford time for a more full, free, and dispassionate investigation of the subject; and I would earnestly recommend to the members of this Convention, that they spend the time of this recess, not in associating with their *own* party, and devising *new arguments* to fortify themselves in their *old opinions,* but that they mix with members of *opposite* sentiments, lend a patient ear to their reasonings, and candidly allow them all the weight to which they may be entitled; and when we assemble again, I hope it will be with a determination to form a constitution, if not such an one as we can individually, and in all respects, approve, yet the best, which, under existing circumstances, can be obtained." (Here the countenance of Washington brightened, and a cheering ray seemed to break in upon the gloom which had recently covered our political horizon.) The doctor continued: "Before I sit down, Mr. President, I will suggest *another matter;* and I am really surprised that it has not been proposed by some other member at an earlier period of our deliberations. I will suggest, Mr. President, the propriety of nominating and appointing, before we separate, a *chaplain* to this Convention, whose duty it shall be uniformly to assemble with us, and introduce the business of each day by an address to the *Creator of the universe,* and the Governor of all nations, beseeching Him to preside in our council, enlighten our minds with a portion of heavenly wisdom, influence our hearts with a love of truth and justice, and crown our labors with complete and abundant success!"

The doctor sat down, and never (said Gen. D.) did I behold a countenance at once so *dignified* and *delighted* as was that of

Washington, at the close of this address! Nor were the members of the Convention, generally less affected. The words of the venerable Franklin fell upon our ears with a weight and authority, even greater than we may suppose an oracle to have had in a Roman senate! A silent admiration superseded, for a moment, the expression of that assent and approbation which was strongly marked on *almost* every countenance; I say almost, for *one* man was found in the Convention, Mr. H–, from —, who rose and said, with regard to the first motion of the honorable gentleman, for an *adjournment,* he would yield his assent; but he protested against the second motion, for the appointment of a chaplain. He then commenced a high-strained eulogium on the assemblage of *wisdom, talent,* and *experience,* which the Convention embraced; declared the high sense he entertained of the honor which his constituents had conferred upon *him,* in making him a member of that respectable body; said he was confidently of opinion that *they were competent* to transact the business which had been entrusted to their care — that they were equal to every exigence which might occur; and concluded by saying, that therefore he did not see the necessity of calling in *foreign aid!*

Washington fixed his eye upon the speaker, with a mixture of *surprise* and *indignation,* while he uttered this impertinent and impious speech, and then looked around to ascertain in what manner it affected others. They did not leave him a moment to *doubt;* no one deigned to *reply,* or take the smallest notice of the speaker, but the motion for appointing a chaplain was instantly seconded and carried; whether under the silent *disapprobation* of Mr. H—, *or his solitary negative,* I do not recollect. The motion for an adjournment was then put and carried unanimously, and the Convention adjourned accordingly.

The three days of recess were spent in the manner advised by Doctor Franklin; the opposite parties mixed with each other, and a free and frank interchange of sentiments took place. On the fourth day we assembled again, and if great additional *light* had not been thrown on the subject, every *unfriendly feeling* had been expelled; and a spirit of conciliation had been cultivated, which promised, at least, a *calm* and *dispassionate reconsideration* of the subject.

As soon as the chaplain had closed his prayer, and the minutes of the last sitting were read, all eyes were turned to the doctor. He rose, and in a few words stated, that during the recess he had listened attentively to all the arguments pro and con, which had been urged by both sides of the house; that he had himself said much, and thought more on the subject; he saw difficulties and objections, which might be urged by individual states, against every scheme which had been proposed; and he was now, more than ever, convinced that the constitution which they were about to form, in order to be *just* and *equal,* must be formed on the basis of *compromise* and *mutual concession.* With such views and feelings, he would now move a reconsideration of the vote last taken on the organization of the Senate. The motion was seconded, the vote carried, the former vote rescinded, and by a successive motion and resolution, the Senate was organized on the present plan.

Thus, my dear son, I have detailed, as far as my memory serves me, the information which I received personally from General Dayton. It has been done from a recollection of ten years, and I may have differed much from General Dayton in his phraseology, but I am confident I have faithfully stated the *facts.* I have related this anecdote at different times to gentlemen of information, to all of whom it was entirely *new.* Some of them requested me to furnish them a written copy, but I deemed that improper without the permission of General Dayton; and I intended, the first opportunity I should have, to make the same request of *him* — but the hand of death has removed him.

In committing this anecdote to paper, I have been actuated not only by a wish to gratify *you,* but by a desire to *perpetuate*

> *the facts,* if, as I fear, they are not elsewhere recorded. As they relate to a very important feature in our republican institutions, and to some of the most celebrated individuals who achieved our independence and framed our national government, they will, I am persuaded, be interesting to every lover of this happy country.[4]

The records of the Convention, of course, show much of Steele's account to be incorrect. Completely disregarding this, the Liars for Jesus use Steele's version of the story, usually misrepresenting it as a first hand account of delegate Jonathan Dayton.

There is little doubt that Jonathan Dayton did tell some version of this story to William Steele. Dayton and Steele, both army officers from the same part of New Jersey, were friends, and, according to one local history, were related by marriage. Additionally, certain details in Steele's letter would not have been known to anyone who was not at the Convention. At the time that Steele wrote the letter, there were no published records of the Convention containing these details. It is also possible that Steele, writing the story down ten years after hearing it, was responsible, intentionally or not, for some of its inaccuracies. The basic lies, however, were definitely the work of Dayton, who had a very clear motive for changing the story.

The records of the Convention show that there were several objections to Franklin's motion, and, according to Franklin himself, only three or four of the delegates thought prayers necessary. In Dayton's version of the story, however, Alexander Hamilton was the *only* delegate to object. Hamilton is portrayed as arrogant and irreverent, making *"impertinent and impious"* comments that were ignored by all the other delegates, and even disgusting George Washington. Obviously, Jonathan Dayton was trying to make Alexander Hamilton look bad. Dayton's motive for this not only explains why he made up the story, but the timing of the story's creation.

One of Dayton's closest friends was Aaron Burr. In fact, Dayton had been a co-conspirator in Burr's treason plot. Dayton was arrested for this, but was never prosecuted because an illness had prevented him from accompanying Burr on the actual expedition. The arrest ended

4. "Anecdote of the Federal Convention of 1787," *Littell's Living Age,* Vol. 25, No. 314, May 25, 1850, 357-359.

Dayton's career in national politics, but he remained popular enough in New Jersey to later be elected to some local offices and the state assembly. According to William Steele, Dayton was telling his Franklin story not long after Burr returned from his self imposed exile in Europe. At this time, Burr needed all the help he could get to restore his reputation among his former friends in New York and New Jersey. It wasn't his treason conspiracy, however, that had made Burr an outcast in his home state. It was his duel with Hamilton.

Throughout their political careers, Burr and Hamilton were at opposite ends of the spectrum when it came to speaking out on the subject of their religious opinions. Although Burr came from a family of theologians, most notably his grandfather Jonathan Edwards, he was very evasive about his own beliefs. Hamilton, on the other hand, made a practice of using religion as a political tool.

Hamilton had gone to great lengths to destroy Burr's reputation, both politically and personally, but few things did as much damage as what Hamilton wrote just before their duel. In his final statement, which, of course, would never be seen by anyone unless he was killed, Hamilton claimed to feel no ill will towards Burr. He also said that he intended to throw away his first shot, and possibly even his second, to give Burr an opportunity *"to pause and to reflect."* Hamilton's statement, full of those Christian values that he wanted to be remembered for, was his final attack on the character of Burr. This was extremely effective. Hamilton came out looking like a martyr and, in the opinion of many, Burr was nothing short of a murderer. The following are a few excerpts from Hamilton's statement.

> My religious and moral principles are strongly opposed to the practice of Duelling, and it would ever give me pain to be obliged to shed the blood of a fellow creature in a private combat forbidden by the laws....
>
> I am conscious of no *ill-will* to Col Burr, distinct from political opposition, which, as I trust, has proceeded from pure and upright motives. Lastly, I shall hazard much, and can possibly gain nothing by the issue of the interview....
>
> It is not my design, by what I have said, to affix any odium on

> the conduct of Col Burr, in this case. He doubtless has heard of animadversions of mine which bore very hard upon him; and it is probable that as usual they were accompanied with some falsehoods. He may have supposed himself under a necessity of acting as he has done. I hope the grounds of his proceeding have been such as ought to satisfy his own conscience....
>
> I trust, at the same time, that the world will do me the justice to believe, that I have not censured him on light ground, nor from unworthy inducements. I certainly have had strong reasons for what I may have said, though it is possible that in some particulars, I may have been influenced by misconstruction or misinformation. It is also my ardent wish that I may have been more mistaken than I think I have been, and that he, by his future conduct, may show himself worthy of all confidence and esteem, and prove an ornament and blessing to the country....
>
> As well because it is possible that I may have injured Col Burr, however convinced myself that my opinions and declarations have been well founded, as from my general principles and temper in relation to similar affairs, I have resolved, if our interview is conducted in the usual manner, and it pleases God to give me the opportunity, to reserve and throw away my first fire, and I have thoughts even of reserving my second fire—and thus giving a double opportunity to Col Burr to pause and to reflect.[5]

Jonathan Dayton's account of the proceedings of June 28 at the Constitutional Convention was intended to make Hamilton look like hypocrite. The less Hamilton looked like a sincere Christian, the less genuine his Christian attitude towards Burr in his final statement would appear.

However inaccurate Dayton's story might be, it does indicate that the reaction Franklin anticipated from his prayer motion was exactly

5. Joanne B. Freeman, ed., *Alexander Hamilton, Writings,* (New York: Literary Classics of the United States, 2001), 1019-1021.

the reaction it produced. According to Steele's account of Dayton's story, Hamilton said that the delegates *"were competent to transact the business which had been entrusted to their care"* and that *"he did not see the necessity of calling in foreign aid!"* A number of the delegates probably made comments like this among themselves, although finding other, less impious sounding reasons to object to the motion. In Dayton's story, of course, the irreverent Hamilton was the only delegate to make such a comment, and he stood up and addressed it to the entire Convention. But, whether these were Hamilton's words, something whispered among the delegates, or even Dayton's own reaction to Franklin's motion, doesn't really matter. Dayton got this idea from somewhere, and Franklin's note on his copy of his speech indicates that Hamilton was far from alone in not seeing the necessity of prayers. Franklin didn't note that *"the convention, except three or four persons,"* thought they couldn't afford a chaplain, or were concerned about people seeing a minister entering the building. He noted that they *"thought prayers unnecessary."*

Although Dayton's motive for making up his Franklin story is obvious, Steele's motive for publishing it in 1826 is a matter of speculation, mainly because there is no way of knowing whether or not Steele knew it was a lie. The publication of story like this at the same time that the religious right organizations of the day were scheming to force their religion into the government seems a bit convenient. Dayton's death in 1824 could also account for the timing. Steele claimed in his letter that he had intended to ask Dayton for permission to publish the story, but he may have suspected that Dayton would say no. Spreading a rumor around New Jersey and New York, among people who had no way of knowing it wasn't true was one thing, but Dayton certainly wouldn't have wanted it published where it might be seen by someone who had actually been at the Convention. In fact, on two occasions after Steele's letter was published, James Madison corrected people who had used the story. The first was Jared Sparks, in 1831.

> ...The knot, felt as the Gordian one, was the question between the larger and the smaller States on the rule of voting in the Senatorial branch of the Legislature; the latter claiming, the former opposing, the rule of equality. Great

> zeal and pertinacity had been shown on both sides; and an equal division of votes on the question had been reiterated and prolonged till it had become not only distressing, but seriously alarming. It was during that period of gloom that D[r] Franklin made the proposition for a religious service in the Convention, an account of which was so erroneously given, with every semblance of authenticity, through the National Intelligencer, several years ago.[6]

The second was Thomas S. Grimke, in 1834.

> You wish to be informed of the errors in your pamphlet alluded to in my last. The first related to the proposition of Doctor Franklin in favor of a religious service in the Federal Convention. The proposition was received & treated with the respect due to it; but the lapse of time which had preceded, with considerations growing out of it, had the effect of limiting what was done, to a reference of the proposition to a highly respectable committee. This issue of it may be traced in the printed Journal. The Quaker usage, never discontinued in the State and the place where the Convention held its sittings, might not have been without an influence as might also, the discord of religious opinions within the Convention, as well as among the clergy of the spot. The error into which you had fallen may have been confirmed by a communication in the National Intelligencer some years ago, said to have been received through a respectable channel from a member of the Convention. That the communication was erroneous is certain; whether from misapprehension or misrecollection, uncertain.[7]

Religious right authors like Madison's letter to Grimke because it supports the story that the delegates really wanted to have prayers but just couldn't find a way to do it. It's not surprising that this is what Madison would write to Grimke. He knew how religious Grimke was, and it did no harm to let him believe that the delegates had good rea-

6. James Madison to Jared Sparks, April 8, 1831, *Letters and Other Writings of James Madison,* vol. 4, (New York: R. Worthington, 1884), 169.

7. James Madison to Thomas S. Grimke, January 6, 1834, *ibid.,* 337-338.

sons for deciding against prayers. This part of the story was inconsequential. All that mattered was that Franklin's motion wasn't acted on. It didn't matter why. Madison was only trying to correct the misconception that the dispute between the large and small states had been solved so quickly and easily, and making sure that the right parties were given credit for resolving it. The effect of Franklin's prayer motion on the Convention was one of two myths about how the Convention got past this dispute. The other was that Gouverneur Morris returned to the Convention just in the nick of time, and had a meeting with George Washington that somehow magically changed everything.

Madison was far more concerned about correcting the errors of Jared Sparks than those of Grimke. The reason for this is that Sparks was writing history books that would be around for years to come, so it was important that they be accurate. Grimke, on the other hand, was writing ephemeral pamphlets. What Madison was correcting in his letter to Grimke was a Fourth of July oration for 1833, which Grimke had sent to him along with one of his temperance pamphlets. By the time Madison got around to reading Grimke's oration, the Fourth of July had already come and gone. Madison didn't even bother telling him what the inaccuracies in his oration were when he first wrote back to him. He just politely complimented Grimke on his work, but noted that there were a few errors *"which future lights may correct."*[8] Grimke wrote back to Madison asking him to be more specific, so Madison, who probably wished he hadn't said anything in the first place, had to write something about the Franklin prayer motion story. The other error in Grimke's pamphlet was that it was the plan proposed by Charles Pinckney of South Carolina that had become the Constitution. This was a widespread misconception at the time, caused by the manner in which Pinckney's plan was presented in the printed journal of the Convention. This was a major error that Madison wrote a number of letters correcting.

It was actually Madison's own fault that he was constantly having to correct misconceptions about the Constitutional Convention in the last few years of his life. It was his notes from the Convention that would clear everything up, but he had decided not to let them be published until after his death. Until Madison's notes were published, the

8. James Madison to Thomas S. Grimke, August 10, 1833, *Letters and Other Writings of James Madison,* vol. 4, (New York: R. Worthington, 1884), 305.

only records available were the printed journal, published by an 1818 act of Congress, and the notes of Robert Yates, a delegate from New York, published in 1821. Neither of these contained anything close to the amount of detail that Madison recorded. Madison had been the unofficial secretary of the Convention. As soon as the other delegates realized what good notes he was taking, they began to give him copies of their speeches so they could be included word for word. While Madison's notes contained Benjamin Franklin's entire speech, and exactly what transpired after it, the official journal didn't contain a single word about it, and Yates's notes contained only the following.

> Governor Franklin read some remarks, acknowledging the difficulties of the present subject. Neither ancient or modern history, (said Gov. Franklin,) can give us light. As a sparrow does not fall without Divine permission, can we suppose that governments can be erected without his will? We shall, I am afraid, be disgraced through little party views. I move that we have prayers every morning.[9]

It is possible that William Steele, who, in 1825, could only have had the official journal and Yates's notes, just didn't realize that Dayton's story wasn't true. It is not as easy to give the same benefit of the doubt to Steele's son Jonathan, who had his father's letter reprinted in *Littell's Living Age* in 1850. By this time, Madison's notes from the Constitutional Convention had been in print for ten years. Dolley Madison's sale of these papers to Congress for $30,000 in 1838, and their publication two years later, was big news at the time. It's pretty hard to believe that Jonathan Steele, who wrote in his introduction to the reprinting of his father's letter that *"everything which relates to the formation of our glorious Union is deeply interesting to all those who wish for its perpetuity,"* wouldn't have bothered to read Madison's account of the story his father had written down for him twenty-five years earlier. The fact that he also says in his introduction that the story is *"not elsewhere so minutely recorded"* indicates that he knew where it was recorded, which, with the exception of Robert Yates's brief mention of Franklin's speech, was only in Madison's notes.

9. Max Farrand, ed., *The Records of the Federal Convention of 1787,* vol. 1, (New Haven, CT: Yale University Press, 1911), 457-458.

Apparently, to Jonathan Steele, the addition of a bunch of lies didn't change the story's *"undoubted authenticity."* It just made the story more *"minutely recorded."* The following is the introduction written by Jonathan Steele for the 1850 republication of his father's letter.

> To the Editor of the Living Age:
>
> When I promised last week, in Boston, that I would send you a copy of a letter from my father, received *twenty-five years* ago, narrating a most interesting historical fact, not elsewhere so minutely recorded, I think you concurred with me in the opinion that its publication could not but be useful at this time, when the wisdom and sagacity of our Franklin, and the spirit of conciliation and mutual concession envinced by the convention which adopted our Constitution, are so much needed at Washington.
>
> On Saturday last, I took from my files the original letter, which I now enclose to you, (and which, as I informed you, was published in the Daily Advertiser, in 1825,) and handed it to my clerk to copy. Judge, then, of my surprise, on opening the New York Observer, of the same day, Saturday, 27th, to find that, by a singular coincidence, some ancient reader, and *rememberer,* too, of the paper of my late valued friend, Theodore Dwight, Esq., had, without my knowledge, brought forward from the dark recesses of years long elapsed, this identical letter, in the same spirit in which you proposed to republish it. As everything which relates to the formation of our *glorious Union* is deeply interesting to all those who wish for its perpetuity, I should be gratified to see an historical anecdote of so much interest, and of undoubted authenticity, transferred to the pages of the "Living Age."[10]

10. "Anecdote of the Federal Convention of 1787," *Littell's Living Age,* Vol. 25, No. 314, May 25, 1850, 357.

Steele's story was also published at least one time between its first publications in 1825 and 1826 and its republication in *Littel's Living Age* in 1850. This was in the 1836 book *The Religious Opinions and Character of Washington,* by E.C. McGuire, who described its origin as follows: "The account thereof, in its present authentic form, was written in the year 1825, by an intimate friend of the youngest member of the convention."

In his book *Original Intent,* David Barton omits most of the debate that followed Franklin's motion. The only parts he includes are that Roger Sherman seconded the motion, and that Edmund Randolph proposed that they wait until the Fourth of July to have prayers. Barton then says that *some* opposed the motion, implying, of course, that most were for it, and gives the lack of funds as the only reason for any opposition. Barton, like most religious right authors, claims that prayers did occur at the Convention, but, unlike these other authors, gives something other than Dayton's story as his source.

According to Barton: "...individual delegate accounts suggest that prayer did occur at some point during the Convention."

Barton's source for this claim is *The Genuine Information,* written by Luther Martin. *The Genuine Information* was Martin's report to the Maryland House of Delegates, opposing ratification of the Constitution. Martin was a delegate to the Constitutional Convention, but left before it was over to begin the fight against ratification in his state. One of Martin's big objections to the Constitution was that it did not put an immediate end to the slave trade, but allowed the importation of slaves to continue for another twenty years. Nothing on the page of *The Genuine Information* cited by Barton had anything whatsoever to do with prayers at the Constitutional Convention. What he cites is a statement about the slave trade issue in which Martin made a reference to people appealing to the Supreme Being during the Revolutionary War.

> It was said that we had just assumed a place among independent nations, in consequence of our opposition to the attempts of Great Britain to enslave us; that this opposition was grounded upon the preservation of those rights to which God and nature had entitled us, not in particular, but in common with the rest of all mankind—that we had appealed to the Supreme Being for his assistance, as the God of freedom, who could not but approve our efforts to preserve the rights which he had thus imparted to his creatures—that now, when we scarcely had risen from our knees, from sup-

> plicating his aid and protection, in forming our government over a free people,—a government formed pretendedly on the principles of liberty, and for its preservation,—in that government to have a provision not only putting it out of its power to restrain and prevent the slave trade...[11]

David Barton does not claim that the Convention adjourned immediately after Franklin's motion. Instead, he links Edmund Randolph's motion that prayers be postponed until the Fourth of July to the dates of an actual adjournment from July 2 to July 5. As mentioned at the beginning of this chapter, Randolph's motion was never even voted on. Barton, however, claims that the adjournment the following week was to *"accommodate that proposal."*

> **Referring to Randolph's motion, David Barton makes the following statement: "To accommodate that proposal, on Monday, July 2, the Convention adjourned until Thursday, July 5, so that, as James Madison explained, 'time might be given...to such as chose to attend to the celebrations on the anniversary of Independence.' On July 4, many delegates attended that special service."**

This adjournment had nothing to do with Randolph's proposal, and there was no special service resulting from this proposal. Many of the delegates did attend the Independence Day celebrations at the Race Street Church, but these celebrations were not proposed by the Convention. Similar celebrations, orations, and sermons were going on all over the country, and those in Philadelphia would have been going on whether the Convention was there or not.

The real reason for the adjournment on July 2 was to allow a committee to meet on July 3. Contrary to the myth that, after Franklin's motion, the Convention prayed and suddenly started getting along, the large and small states were still at odds on July 2, so, on that day, a motion was made that a committee be appointed to work on the problem. According to Elbridge Gerry, who spoke in favor of appoint-

11. Jonathan Elliot, ed., *The Debates in the Several State Conventions on the Adoption of the Federal Constitution,* vol. 1, (Washington D.C.: Printed for the Editor, 1836), 373.

ing this committee, the Convention was still in danger of falling apart.

> Mr. Gerry was for the Commitmt. Something must be done, or we shall disappoint not only America, but the whole world. He suggested a consideration of the State we should be thrown into by the failure of the Union. We should be without an Umpire to decide controversies and must be at the mercy of events.[12]

The Convention voted to appoint a committee consisting of one member from each state, to meet on July 3. The delegates, like anybody else, wanted to take the Fourth of July off, so they adjourned until July 5, as Madison recorded in his notes.

> That time might be given to the Committee, and to such as chose to attend to the celebrations on the anniversary of Independence, the Convention adjourned till Thursday.[13]

Barton next quotes a passage from George Washington's diary, in which Washington wrote that he attended an oration at the Calvinist Church. In Barton's book, this passage from Washington's diary is immediately followed by an excerpt from the prayer that concluded the events at the church. What Barton omits is that Washington didn't stay at the church long enough to hear this prayer. Washington only stayed long enough to hear a Fourth of July oration given by a law student, and did not attend whatever religious service or celebrations followed. After the oration, he left to spend the rest of the day with fellow Revolutionary army officers at the Pennsylvania chapter of the Society of the Cincinnati.

William Federer, in his book *America's God and Country,* gets very confused about the dates of the adjournment. In his version of the story, prayers that didn't begin until July 4 caused a profound change in the Convention by July 2.

Federer quotes Randolph's motion that prayers begin

12. Max Farrand, ed., *The Records of the Federal Convention of 1787,* vol. 1, (New Haven, CT: Yale University Press, 1911), 515.
13. *ibid.,* 516.

> **on July 4, and follows it with: "The clergy of the city responded to this request and effected a profound change in the convention, when they reconvened on July 2, 1787, as noted in Jonathan Dayton's records:**
>
> > **We assembled again; and...every unfriendly feeling had been expelled, and a spirit of conciliation had been cultivated."**

In April 1788, an article written by Benjamin Franklin entitled *A Comparison of the Conduct of the Ancient Jews and of the Anti-Federalists in the United States of America* appeared in the *Federal Gazette.* Although Franklin's article really didn't have anything to do with his motion for prayers, Max Farrand, for some reason, included the last paragraph of it in the appendix of the *Records of the Federal Convention of 1787,* and noted to see it in reference to the motion. Misquotes created from this paragraph are found in many religious right American history books.

> **The following is the typical misquote, as it appears in *America's Providential History* by Mark Beliles and Stephen McDowell: "Our General Convention...when it formed the new Federal Constitution, [was]...influenced, guided, and governed by that omnipotent and beneficent Ruler in whom all...live, and move, and have their being."**

Franklin's article was one of many articles published throughout the states by both federalists and anti-federalists during the time between the writing of the Constitution and its ratification. Writings in favor of ratification, such as the *Federalist Papers,* explained the Constitution in an effort to allay any fears or suspicions about it. Franklin was a little more creative in his attempt to convince people that the anti-federalists were wrong. His way of getting the point across was to satirically demonstrate that, according to the Bible, even the *constitution* of the ancient Jews, although said to be handed down to Moses by God himself, had met with suspicion.

The following are some excerpts from Franklin's story, with the often misquoted last paragraph at the end.

> A zealous Advocate for the propos'd Federal Constitution, in a certain public Assembly, said, that "the Repugnance of a great part of Mankind to good Government was such, that he believed, that, if an Angel from Heaven were to bring down a Constitution, form'd there for our Use, it would nevertheless meet with violent Opposition." He was reprov'd for the suppos'd Extravagance of the Sentiment; and he did not justify it. Probably it might not have immediately occur'd to him, that the Experiment had been try'd, and that the Event was recorded in the most faithful of all Histories, the Holy Bible; otherwise he might, as it seems to me, have supported his Opinion by that unexceptionable Authority.
>
> The Supreme Being had been pleased to nourish up a single Family, by continued Acts of his attentive Providence, till it became a great People; and, having rescued them from Bondage by many Miracles, performed by his Servant Moses, he personally deliver'd to that chosen Servant, in the presence of the whole Nation, a Constitution and Code of Laws for their Observance; accompanied and sanction'd with Promises of great Rewards, and Threats of severe Punishments, as the Consequence of their Obedience or Disobedience.
>
> This Constitution, tho' the Deity himself was to be at its Head (and it is therefore call'd by Political Writers a *Theocracy*), could not be carried into Execution but by the Means of his Ministers; Aaron and his Sons were therefore commission'd to be, with Moses, the first establish'd Ministry of the new Government.
>
> One would have thought, that the Appointment of Men, who had distinguish'd themselves in procuring the Liberty of their Nation, and had hazarded their Lives in openly opposing the Will of a powerful Monarch, who would have retain'd that Nation in Slavery, might have been an Appointment acceptable to a grateful People; and that a Constitution fram'd by

the Deity himself might, on that Account, have been secure of an universal welcome Reception. Yet there were in every one of the *thirteen Tribes* some discontented restless Spirits, who were continually exciting them to reject the propos'd new Government, and this from various Motives.

Many still retained an Affection for Egypt, the Land of their Nativity; and these, whenever they felt any Inconvenience or Hardship, tho' the natural and unavoidable Effect of their Change of Situation, exclaim'd against their Leaders as the Authors of their Trouble; and were not only for returning into Egypt, but for stoning their deliverers....

...In Josephus and the Talmud, we learn some Particulars, not so fully narrated in the Scripture. We are there told, "That Corah was ambitious of the Priesthood, and offended that it was conferred on Aaron; and this, as he said, by the Authority of Moses only, *without the Consent of the People.* He accus'd Moses of having, by various Artifices fraudulently obtain'd the Government, and depriv'd the People of their Liberties; and of *conspiring* with Aaron to perpetuate the Tyranny in their Family. Thus, tho' Corah's real Motive was the Supplanting of Aaron, he persuaded the People that he meant only the *Public Good;* and they, moved by his Insinuations, began to cry out, 'Let us maintain the Common Liberty of our *respective Tribes;* we have freed ourselves from the Slavery impos'd on us by the Egyptians, and shall we now suffer ourselves to be made Slaves by Moses? If we must have a Master, it were better to return to Pharaoh, who at least fed us with Bread and Onions, than to serve this new Tyrant, who by his Operations has brought us into Danger of Famine.' Then they called in question the *Reality of his Conferences* with God, and objected the *Privacy of the Meetings,* and the *preventing any of the People from being present* at the Colloquies, or even approaching the Place, as Grounds of great Suspicion...."

To conclude, I beg I may not be understood to infer, that our General Convention was divinely inspired when it form'd the new federal Constitution, merely because that Constitution has been unreasonably and vehemently opposed; yet I must own I have so much Faith in the general Government of the world by *Providence,* that I can hardly conceive a Transaction of such momentous Importance to the Welfare of Millions now existing, and to exist in the Posterity of a great Nation, should be suffered to pass without being in some degree influenc'd, guided and governed by that omnipotent, omnipresent, and beneficent Ruler, in whom all inferior Spirits live, and move, and have their Being.[14]

14. J.A. Leo Lemay, ed., *Benjamin Franklin, Writings,* (New York: Literary Classics of the United States, 1987), 1144-1148.

— CHAPTER SEVEN —

Treaties with the Barbary States

One of the most often used arguments that the United States was *not* founded as a Christian nation is Article 11 of the 1797 *Treaty of Peace and Friendship between the United States and the Bey and Subjects of Tripoli of Barbary.* This is a pretty good argument, considering that the first sentence of that article begins with the words, *"As the government of the United States of America is not in any sense founded on the Christian Religion..."* Because the authors of the religious right version of American history can't deny that these words are there, they attempt to dismiss them, usually using one, or a combination of, several popular arguments.

The first argument is really just a diversion, created by pointing out a mistake sometimes made by those who bring up this treaty. The mistake is attributing the words of Article 11 to George Washington. Because the treaty is dated January 4, 1797, two months before Washington left office, an assumption has often been made that he was the president who signed it. The treaty, however, did not reach the United States until after Washington left office, so it was actually signed by John Adams. It really doesn't matter, of course, whether it was Washington or Adams who signed the treaty. This doesn't change what it said.

Instances of this treaty being attributed to Washington can be found as early as the mid-1800s, not only in arguments about the separation of church and state, but also in articles about the Barbary conflict or treaties in general. With the exception of appearing on the websites of a few overzealous separationists who, like their religious right counterparts, copy quotes without checking their sources, the wrong attribution isn't seen much anymore. Nevertheless, the Liars for Jesus continue to use it as evidence that secularists are trying to rewrite history. This serves two purposes. First, of course, pointing out this error provides a way to dismiss the treaty. Second, there are only two separationist misquotes that have ever appeared with any frequency, and this is one of them. The second is an out of context sentence from a letter written by John Adams. Religious right authors who claim that there are many such secularist misquotes need to use both of these because they just can't find any other examples, although David Barton implies that he has found a third.

> **According to David Barton, in his book *Original Intent*: "Those who advance the notion that this was the belief system of the Founders often publish information attempting to prove that the Founders were irreligious. Some of the quotes they set forth include:**
>
> > **This would be the best of all possible Worlds, if there were no Religion in it. JOHN ADAMS**
> >
> > **The government of the United States is in no sense founded on the Christian religion. GEORGE WASHINGTON**
> >
> > **I disbelieve all holy men and holy books. THOMAS PAINE**
>
> **Are these statements accurate? Did these prominent Founders truly repudiate religion? An answer will be found by an examination of the sources of the above statements."**

Barton throws in the Thomas Paine misquote to fill out his meager list of *some* of the quotes used by separationists, only to pretend, five pages later, that he thinks it might possibly be genuine, saying that *"the real story is not the accuracy of Paine's quote, but rather how the other Founders reacted to Paine's declarations."* Barton's source for this Paine misquote is an obscure document from the *Society of Separationists,* a document that is never actually used or copied by anyone. A search on Google for this misquote, for example, does not produce a single hit. Yet Barton implies that this is a commonly used misquote by presenting it along with the two misquotes that are actually used. Barton's main reason for adding this virtually unheard of Paine misquote, however, is to give him a reason to present several pages of quotes from founders who denounced Paine and his writings.

Barton's footnote for his three misquote examples says to *"see also"* an op-ed piece by Steven Morris entitled *America's Unchristian Beginnings,* which appeared in the Los Angeles Times on August 3, 1995. Morris, however, did not misquote Paine, and did not wrongly attribute the quote from the Treaty of Tripoli to George Washington. He accurately quoted a passage from Paine's *Age of Reason* – *"I do not believe in the creed professed by the Jewish church, by the Roman church, by the Greek church, by the Turkish church, by the Protestant church, nor by any church that I know of...Each of those churches accuse the other of unbelief; and for my own part, I disbelieve them all"* – and correctly said of the Treaty of Tripoli that it *"was during Adams' administration that the Senate ratified the Treaty."*

There is no great number, or widespread use, of separationist misquotes. In fact, there are far more religious right websites pointing out and correcting the Adams and Washington misquotes than separationist websites that use them. Similarly, a search for Barton's sources turns up only rebuttals of the Steven Morris's op-ed piece and copies of Barton's citation of the *Society of Separationists* document, but no instances of anybody actually using or quoting from either. The only part of Barton's straw argument that has any merit is the use of the out of context quote from John Adams, which was, in fact, used by Morris in his 1995 article. This misquote still appears on a significant number of websites, and is occasionally seen elsewhere. The majority of separationists, however, know that this quote is taken out of context, and not only do not use it, but point it out to others as a misquote. For example, the foreword to one popular collection of separationist quotes, which is available in print and on the internet, contains the following statement: *"All of these quotes have been throughly researched. None are 'out of context' or otherwise misleading. For example, the bogus John Adams quote, '...this would be the best of all possible worlds if there were no religion in it ...' is not included."*[1]

> **According to Barton: "The John Adams quote is taken from a letter he wrote to Thomas Jefferson on April 19, 1817, in which Adams illustrated the intorlerance often manifested between Christians in their denominational disputes. Adams recounted a comversation between two ministers he had known:**
>
> > **[S]eventy years ago....Lemuel Bryant was my parish priest, and Joseph Cleverly my Latin schoolmaster. Lemuel was a jocular [humorous] and liberal scholar and divine. Joseph a scholar and a gentleman....The Parson and the Pedagogue lived much together, but were eternally disputing about government and religion. One day, when the schoolmaster [Joseph Cleverly] had been more than commonly fanatical and declared 'if he were a monarch, he would have but one religion in his dominions;' the Parson [Lemuel Bryant] cooly replied, 'Cleverly! you would be the best man in the world if you had no religion.'**
>
> **Lamenting these types of petty disputes, Adams declared to Jefferson:**
>
> > **Twenty times, in the course of my late reading**

1. *Quotations that Support the Separation of State and Church,* compiled by Ed and Michael Buckner, foreword by Clark Davis Adams. Other examples include the Positive Atheism website, on which the Adams misquote is described as an *"Oft-Misquoted Adams Quip."* Another popular separationist website includes it in a list of six *"Problematical Separationist Quotes."* The other five items on this list are the wrong attribution of the Treaty of Tripoli quote to George Washington, a Jefferson quote which is authentic, but sometimes attributed to the wrong letter, a Jefferson quote to which some words from an editor's commentary were accidentally added at some point and copied by others as part of the quote, and two other Jefferson quotes which this website suggests should not be used because they haven't been traced to primary sources.

> **have I been on the point of breaking out, 'This would be the best of all possible worlds, if there were no religion in it!!!' But in this exclamation I would have been as fanatical as Bryant or Cleverly. Without religion this world would be something not fit to be mentioned in polite company, I mean hell."**

Barton, in the process of putting the separationist misquote back in context, omits a few words himself, and does not indicate that he is cutting off the end of the second paragraph. The following are the entire two paragraphs from Adams's letter, with the words omitted by Barton in the first paragraph in bold.

> At that Period Lemuel Bryant was my Parish Priest; and Joseph Cleverly my Latin School Master. Lemuel was a jolly jocular and liberal schollar and Divine. Joseph a Schollar and a Gentleman; **but a biggoted episcopalian of the School of Bishop Saunders and Dr. Hicks, a down right conscientious passive Obedience Man in Church and State.** The Parson and the Pedagogue lived much together, but were eternally disputing about Government and Religion. One day, when the Schoolmaster had been more than commonly fanatical and declared *"if he were a Monarck, He would have but one Religion in his Dominions"* the Parson cooly replied, "Cleverly! you would be the best Man in the World, if You had no Religion."
>
> Twenty times, in the course of my late Reading, have I been upon the point of breaking out, "This would be the best of all possible Worlds, if there were no Religion in it." ! ! ! But in this exclamati[on] I should have been as fanatical as Bryant or Cleverly. Without Religion this World would be Something not fit to be mentioned in polite Company, I mean Hell. So far from believing in the total and universal depravity of human Nature; I believe there is no Individual totally depraved. The most abandoned Scoundrel that ever existed, never Yet Wholly extinguished his Conscience, and while Conscience

> remains there is some Religion. Popes, Jesuits and Sorbonists and Inquisitors have some Conscience and some Religion. So had Marius and Sylla, Caesar Cataline and Anthony, and Augustus had not much more, let Virgil and Horace say what they will.[2]

Barton then says that Jefferson, in his reply to Adams, *"declared that he agreed."* The following was Jefferson's declaration of agreement.

> If, by *religion,* we are to understand *Sectarian dogmas,* in which no two of them agree, then your exclamation on that hypothesis is just, 'that this would be the best of all possible worlds, if there were no religion in it.' But if the moral precepts, innate in man, and made a part of his physical constitution, as necessary for a social being, if the sublime doctrines of philanthropism, and deism taught by Jesus of Nazareth in which all agree, then, without it, this would be, as you say, 'Something not fit to be named, even indeed a hell.'[3]

The discussion of this subject in this particular exchange of letters between Adams and Jefferson had nothing to do with Adams lamenting *"petty disputes"* between members of different denominations, as Barton claims. They were discussing the events taking place in Connecticut, which, in 1817, fifteen years after Jefferson's famous letter to the Danbury Baptists, was finally separating church from state.

While Barton and other religious right authors are quick to point the finger at those who quote from Adams's letter only the sentence *"This would be the best of all possible Worlds, if there were no Religion in it,"* they don't seem to have any problem at all with people who quote only the sentence that follows it. Barton, on his *WallBuilders* website, even provides a link to a website that quotes the second sen-

2. John Adams to Thomas Jefferson, April 19, 1817, Lester J. Cappon, ed., *The Adams-Jefferson Letters: The Complete Correspondence Between Thomas Jefferson and Abigail and John Adams,* (Chapel Hill and London: The University of North Carolina Press, 1988), 509.

3. Thomas Jefferson to John Adams, May 5, 1817, *ibid.,* 512.

tence by itself – James H. Hutson's *Religion and the Founding of the American Republic* exhibit on the Library of Congress website.

> **The following is Hutson's commentary, which appears beside a link to images of the handwritten letter: "John Adams, a self-confessed 'church going animal,' grew up in the Congregational Church in Braintree, Massachusetts. By the time he wrote this letter his theological position can best be described as Unitarian. In this letter Adams tells Jefferson that 'Without Religion this World would be Something not fit to be mentioned in polite Company, I mean Hell.'"**

After successfully disproving the almost never seen assertion that Adams was a deist, agnostic, or atheist by putting the separationist misquote back in context, Barton moves on to the Treaty of Tripoli quote and its wrong attribution to George Washington.

> **Barton writes: "Amazingly, while the assertion concerning Adams was completely inaccurate, the words attributed to Washington are totally false ('The government of the United States is in no sense founded on the Christian religion'). The 1797 Treaty of Tripoli is the source of Washington's supposed statement."**

Barton points out that Washington did not write these words or sign this treaty, which is absolutely correct, but he also claims these words are out of context. While it is true that the words quoted are not the entire sentence, and are often followed by a period instead of an ellipsis, their meaning is not changed by this. Barton, however, attempts to prove that this does change the meaning.

> **According to Barton: "The 1797 treaty with Tripoli was one of the many treaties in which each country officially recognized the religion of the other in an attempt to prevent further escalation of a "Holy War" between Christians and Muslims. Consequently, Article XI of that treaty stated:**

> **As the government of the United States of America is not in any sense founded on the Christian religion as it has in itself no character of enmity [hatred] against the laws, religion or tranquility of Musselmen [Muslims] and as the said States [America] have never entered into any war or act of hostility against any Mahometan nation, it is declared by the parties that no pretext arising from religious opinions shall ever produce an interruption of the harmony existing between the two countries.**

> **This article may be read in two manners. It may, as its critics do, be concluded after the clause "Christian religion"; or it may be read in its entirety and concluded when the punctuation so indicates...."**

Barton never actually gets around to giving a clear explanation of the difference in meaning when this clause is read by itself or read in the context of the entire article. And, for someone so concerned about what the punctuation indicates, it is very interesting that he removes so much of the punctuation in his own quote of the article. In all official printings of the treaty, the first three clauses of this article are separated by either semicolons or dashes, which were often used like semicolons at the time the treaty was first printed. Removing this punctuation, of course, reinforces the notion that the sentence is *"cut abruptly"* to change its meaning.

The following is how the sentence was punctuated in the original printing of the treaty for the Senate in 1797.

> As the government of the United States of America is not in any sense founded on the Christian religion—as it has in itself no character of enmity against the laws, religion or tranquillity of Mussulmen—and as the said states never have entered into any war or act of hostility against any Mahometan nation, it is declared by the parties, that no pretext arising from religious opinions shall ever produce

an interruption of the harmony existing between the two countries.[4]

The first three clauses of this article said three separate things: 1. that the United States had no *official* reason to attack a Muslim nation because of religion; 2. that the United States had no *unofficial* reason to attack a Muslim nation because of religion; and, 3. that the United States had never entered into a voluntary war with a Muslim nation for religious or any other reasons.

Barton's claim that this treaty was *"one of the many treaties in which each country officially recognized the religion of the other"* is ridiculous. In his footnote for this claim, Barton just lists all of the Barbary treaty articles that mentioned religion in any way. None of these had anything to do with officially recognizing the religion of anybody. Examples of these articles appear later in this chapter.

Although the actual author of Article 11 of the 1797 treaty with Tripoli is not absolutely certain, most historians agree that it was Joel Barlow, the consul who concluded the final negotiations in Algiers and oversaw the translation of the treaty into English. It is also possible, but not nearly as likely, that it was Captain Richard O'Brien, who conducted the preliminary negotiations in Tripoli.

The second argument against the Treaty of Tripoli is that Article 11 in Barlow's English translation doesn't match anything in the original Arabic version, a discrepancy that was revealed when a new translation of the surviving Arabic version was done in 1930. What appears in the treaty book where the Arabic version of Article 11 should be is a letter from the Dey of Algiers to the Bashaw of Tripoli, roughly saying that the treaty had been concluded and recommending that it be observed. How this letter ended up in the treaty book in place of Article 11 is a mystery that will probably never be solved.

The problem with using this discrepancy to dismiss Article 11, however, is that Barlow's translation was the only version of the treaty that the Senate or John Adams ever saw, making its accuracy com-

4. One later printing copied the original punctuation from the 1797 printing – Richard Peters, ed., *The Public Statutes at Large of the United States of America,* vol. 8, (Boston: Little, Brown and Company, 1867), 155. Two used semicolons rather than dashes – Walter Lowrie, ed., *American State Papers: Foreign Relations,* vol. 2, (Washington D.C.: Gales and Seaton, 1832), 19; *The Debates and Proceedings of the Congress of the United States of America,* vol. 9, 5th Cong., Appendix, (Washington D.C.: Gales & Seaton, 1851), 3095-3096.

pletely irrelevant. This was the translation, correct or not, that was unanimously approved by the Senate, and this was the translation that was signed by Adams. It was read aloud in the Senate, and copies were printed and given to each senator. There is no record of any objection to the *not founded on the Christian Religion* statement.

There is also no indication that the people of the United States objected to the wording of Article 11. This wasn't because they were unaware of what it said. A week after Adams signed the treaty it was published in several widely circulated newspapers, accompanied by the following proclamation.

> Now be it known, That I John Adams, President of the United States of America, having seen and considered the said Treaty do, by and with the advice consent of the Senate, accept, ratify, and confirm the same, and every clause and article thereof. And to the End that the said Treaty may be observed and performed with good Faith on the part of the United States, I have ordered the premises to be made public; And I do hereby enjoin and require all persons bearing office civil or military within the United States, and all others citizens or inhabitants thereof, faithfully to observe and fulfil the said Treaty and every clause and article thereof.[5]

So, in 1797, less than a decade after the Constitution was ratified, the President, the Senate, and the people of the United States apparently accepted without question an official statement that *"the government of the United States of America is not in any sense founded on the Christian Religion...."*

When religious right American history authors point out that George Washington did not sign the Treaty of Tripoli, they are, of course, left with the problem that John Adams *did* sign it. Some simply overlook this, confident that their readers will consider the wrong attribution to Washington a sufficient reason to dismiss the treaty altogether. Others attempt to vindicate Adams with a few quotes, edited or taken out of context to make it appear that Adams, on other occasions, did say that the United States was a Christian nation.

5. David Hunter Miller, ed., *Treaties and Other International Acts of the United States of America*, vol. 2, (Washington D.C.: Government Printing Office, 1931), 383.

> **According to David Barton, in his book *Original Intent:* "It would also be absurd to suggest that President Adams (under whom the treaty was ratified in 1797) would have endorsed or assented to any provision which repudiated Christianity. In fact, while discussing the Barbary conflict with Jefferson, Adams declared:**
>
> > **The policy of Christendom has made cowards of all their sailors before the standard of Mahomet. It would be heroical and glorious to restore courage to ours."**

The date alone of the letter quoted by Barton makes it impossible that Adams was including the United States when referring to Christendom. By the *"policy of Christendom,"* Adams meant the practice of the Christian nations of Europe paying annual tribute to the Barbary States to protect their merchant vessels from pirates. The United States did not begin to engage in this practice until a decade after Adams wrote this letter. Adams also referred to the sailors of Christendom as *"their"* sailors, and the sailors of the United States as *"ours,"* a distinction that Barton apparently doesn't think his readers will notice.

As colonies of Great Britain, the United States had been covered by the tribute paid by Great Britain. But, when Great Britain officially recognized the United States as an independent nation in 1783, so did the Barbary States. The first American ship was captured in 1784 by Morocco, and several more were soon captured by Algiers. American merchants soon stopped sailing to the Mediterranean, opting for less profitable but safer markets. This began to drive down the price of American produce, the biggest export to the region, in an economy that was barely beginning to recover from the Revolutionary War. In their correspondence during the summer of 1786, foreign ministers Adams, in England, and Jefferson, in France, were debating whether it would be better to solve this problem by giving in and paying tribute to the Barbary States, or raising a navy and fighting them. Congress had already instructed Adams and Jefferson to negotiate a peace, so their opinions really didn't matter. Nevertheless, they engaged in a friendly debate about it for a while.

Both Adams and Jefferson wished the United States could fight the pirates, but only Jefferson considered this to be a realistic option. Jefferson even went as far as calculating how much the war would cost, and planning a possible coalition of smaller European powers to share the burden. The reason this coalition would consist of small nations only was that the larger powers like Great Britain didn't really want the piracy to end. The constant attacks on their smaller commercial rivals more than made up for what they spent on tribute payments.

As foreign ministers in the 1780s, Adams and Jefferson were finding out that not all of the nations of Europe were ready to recognize the United States as a world power. This made the job of negotiating treaties of commerce difficult. There were some nations that wanted to wait and see if the United States was even going to survive, and a few that weren't even aware that a bunch of English colonies halfway around the world had had a revolution. Defeating the Barbary pirates would quickly elevate the status of the young United States in the eyes of the world. This is one thing that Adams and Jefferson were in complete agreement on. But, as much as Adams liked to imagine a United States navy heroically sailing into the Mediterranean and standing up to an enemy that the great powers of Europe had given in to, he thought it would be more practical just to pay the tribute like everyone else.

The following excerpt from Adams's letter includes the quote used by David Barton – along with the sentences leading up to it.

> At present we are Sacrificing a Million annually to Save one gift of two hundred Thousand Pounds. This is not good Œconomy. We might at this hour have two hundred ships in the Mediterranean, whose Freight alone would be worth two hundred Thousand Pounds, besides its Influence upon the Price of our Produce. Our Farmers and Planters will find the Price of their Articles Sink very low indeed, if this Peace is not made. The policy of Christendom has made cowards of all their sailors before the standard of Mahomet. It would be heroical and glorious to restore courage to ours....[6]

6. John Adams to Thomas Jefferson, July 3, 1786, Lester J. Cappon, ed., *The Adams-Jefferson Letters: The Complete Correspondence Between Thomas Jefferson and Abigail and John Adams,* (Chapel Hill and London: The University of North Carolina Press, 1988), 139.

Adams wasn't talking about a religious war in which the United States was fighting on the side of Christendom. He was talking about the United States showing up the nations of Christendom by standing up to an enemy that they were all giving in to.

The third argument against the Treaty of Tripoli is that Joel Barlow and/or John Adams were forced to agree to the *not founded on the Christian religion* statement because the Bashaw of Tripoli had to be reassured that the United States wouldn't try to force the Muslims to convert to Christianity. The problem with this argument is that it contradicts their other argument – that Article 11 didn't appear in the Arabic version of the treaty. If Article 11 never appeared in the Arabic version, how would the Bashaw of Tripoli have been reassured by it?

Because their authors make up the *facts* to fit their stories, religious right American history books often contradict each other. A good example of this is how Joel Barlow, the likely author of Article 11, is portrayed in these books. Reading David Barton's *Original Intent,* one would think that Barlow was, above all else, a Christian minister. In contrast, Gary DeMar, in *America's Christian History: The Untold Story,* claims that Barlow *"deceptively altered"* the Treaty of Tripoli to remove all religious references, and describes his beliefs as *"radical deistic views."*

> **According to Gary DeMar: "Joel Barlow oversaw the original translation process from Arabic to English. In 1930 the original Arabic version was retranslated into English by Dr. Hurgronje. Barlow's translation and Dr. Hurgronje's retranslation bear faint resemblance to each other. For example, in Article 12 of Barlow's version, all religious references have been removed: 'Praise be to God!'; 'May God strengthen [the Pasha of Tripoli], and the Americans'; 'May God make it all permanent love and a good conclusion between us'; and, 'by His grace and favor, amen!'**
>
> **It seems that Barlow's translation deceptively altered the treaty. The deception does not end with Article 12. There was even more tampering with the document in its translation process. In fact, the controversial Article 11 simply does not exist in the original Arabic text."**

To say that Barlow's and Dr. Hurgronje's translations *"bear faint resemblance to each other"* is extremely misleading. Barlow's translation was not a word for word translation of the Arabic text, but this was nothing unusual. Literal translations of the Arabic and Turkish versions of even the simplest articles were often long, confusing, and grammatically incorrect. When these articles were translated into English, they were rewritten in clearer, more concise statements that meant the same thing as their Arabic or Turkish counterparts. With the exception of the missing Arabic version of Article 11, Barlow's translation of the Treaty of Tripoli was no different than translations of other treaties. The following is an example of Dr. Hurgronje's literal translation of an article from the Treaty of Tripoli, and Barlow's translation of the same article.

> Praise be to God! Declaration of the fourth article. We have also agreed concerning all the ships sailing out from the well-preserved Tripoli, that they [evidently the Tripolitans] are not allowed to take any of the American ships until a term of eighteen months shall have expired, and likewise there shall not be taken any of the Tripolitan ships until the condition of eighteen months shall be fulfilled, because the country of the Americans is at a great distance. This stipulation is connected with the passports; when the number of months of the term that we have mentioned shall be complete, and we have observed the term of one year and a half, beginning by the date which we have mentioned, then all the ships of the Americans must have passports. Thus.[7]

> ARTICLE 4. Proper passports are to be given to all vessels of both parties, by which they are to be known. And, considering the distance between the two countries, eighteen months from the date of this treaty shall be allowed for procuring such passports. During this interval the other papers belonging to such vessels shall be sufficient for their protection.[8]

7. David Hunter Miller, ed., *Treaties and Other International Acts of the United States of America,* vol. 2, (Washington D.C.: Government Printing Office, 1931).

8. Richard Peters, ed., *The Public Statutes at Large of the United States of America,* vol. 8, (Boston: Little, Brown, and Company, 1867), 154.

Omitting the exclamations *"Praise be to God!"* and *"Thus,"* which, in the literal translation are found at the beginning and end of almost every article, and putting the actual content of the article into understandable English, can hardly be considered a deceptive alteration of the treaty.

Barlow also omitted other superfluous phrases, some religious and some not. This was also nothing unusual. For example, in Arabic documents, the name of a ruler was almost always followed by the words *"may God strengthen."* A similar customary religious phrase was used in Turkish documents. These phrases were always omitted in the English translations, by both Barlow and other consuls.

The following examples are from two different treaties with Algiers, one negotiated in 1795 by Joseph Donaldson, and the other in 1816 by Isaac Chauncey and William Shaler. In the English translations of both, the religious phrase following the Dey's name was removed, as were any unnecessary non-religious words.

In the literal translation from the Turkish of Article 1 of the 1795 treaty, the treaty was between:

> ...the ruler of America, George Washington, President, our friend and actually the Governor of the States of the island of America, and the lord of our well-preserved garrison of Algiers, His Highness Hassan Pasha—may God grant to him what he wishes—the Dey, together with the Agha of his victorious army, his minister, all the members of the Divan, and all his victorious soldiers, and equally between the subjects of both parties.[9]

In the English translation it was between:

> ...the President and Citizens of the United States of North-America, and Hassan Bashaw, Dey of Algiers, his Divan and Subjects...[10]

In the literal translation from the Turkish of the introductory state-

9. David Hunter Miller, ed., *Treaties and Other International Acts of the United States of America,* vol. 2, (Washington D.C.: Government Printing Office, 1931).

10. Richard Peters, ed., *The Public Statutes at Large of the United States of America,* vol. 8, (Boston: Little, Brown, and Company, 1867), 133.

ment in the 1816 treaty, the parties were:

> ...the President and ruler of the American people, living in the island called America, belonging to the islands of the ocean [and] His Excellency, the strong Vizier and the noble Marshal, Omar Pasha—may God grant to him what he desires—as President of the Divan...[11]

In the English translation they were simply:

> The President of the United States [and] His Highness Omar Bashaw, Dey of Algiers.[12]

Most religious right American history authors actually want Joel Barlow to be an atheist or a deist. This gives them someone to blame the *not founded on the Christian religion* phrase on. For some, the entire argument is that the words were just the opinion of one infidel, and don't reflect the opinion of the rest of the founders.

David Barton, on the other hand, not only wants Barlow to be a Christian, but wants him to be a minister. In fact, in his book *Original Intent,* Barton never even mentions that Barlow had anything to do with the Treaty of Tripoli. Barlow doesn't appear until about ten pages after Barton's section about the treaty, in a list intended to show that *"the strong religious convictions of so many Founding Fathers is evidenced through their leadership roles in establishing and guiding numerous religious societies or through serving in active ministry."* Barlow is included in this list as a *"Chaplain in the American Revolution for three years."* Barlow is also included in the appendix of biographical sketches at the end of the Barton's book.

> **The following is Barton's biographical sketch of Barlow (up until he became Consul to Algiers in 1795): "Joel Barlow (1754-1812; Connecticut) Minister, educator, attorney, poet, and diplomat; tutored by Rev. Nathaniel**

11. David Hunter Miller, ed., *Treaties and Other International Acts of the United States of America,* vol. 2, (Washington D.C.: Government Printing Office, 1931).

12. Richard Peters, ed., *The Public Statutes at Large of the United States of America,* vol. 8, (Boston: Little, Brown, and Company, 1867), 244.

> **Bartlett (1772-1773); attended Moore's School, Dartmouth, and entered Yale in 1774 in the same class as Oliver Wolcott (signer of the Declaration), Zephaniah Smith (author of America's first law text), and Noah Webster (considered the 'Schoolmaster of America'); graduated from Yale (1778); studied philosophy at Yale (1779-1787) but during those years he also taught school, managed a business, published a journal, wrote a version of the Psalms, served as a chaplain in the Continental Army (1780-1783), and was admitted to the bar (1786); travelled to France and London (1788); made citizen of France (1792); Consul to Algiers (1795-1797)..."**

To begin a sketch of Joel Barlow by saying he was a minister is beyond misleading. It is true that he was a chaplain in the army, but this was not because he had any genuine interest in being a minister. It is also true that he wrote a psalm book, but this was later banned by Congregationalist clergymen.

When the Revolutionary War began, Joel Barlow was a student at Yale College, and, although staying in school, he joined a militia unit and fought on vacations, distinguishing himself at the battle of White Plains. In 1778, he graduated from the college and began studying law. At this time, Timothy Dwight, a friend of Barlow's from Yale, was in the army serving as a chaplain. Dwight told Barlow that chaplains were performing a very useful service by keeping the morale of the troops up, but there weren't enough of them to go around. So, Barlow, being a patriot and wanting to help the cause in any way he could, decided to postpone his law studies and join the army – as a chaplain. He wasn't going to let the fact that he had no religious training stand in his way. He studied theology for all of six weeks, presented himself to an association of Congregationalist ministers, passed their test, got a license to preach, and became a chaplain. While serving in this capacity, Barlow put his talent as a poet to work and inspired the troops not with sermons, but by writing patriotic songs and poems. When the war ended, so did Barlow's career as a minister.

After the war, Barlow resumed his law studies, but after being admitted to the bar in 1786, discovered that he enjoyed studying law far more than actually practicing it. During this time, Barlow also co-founded a weekly newspaper, *The Hartford Mercury,* to which he regularly contributed both editorials and poems. But, he soon sold his interest in the paper to his partner to devote his time to completing his epic poem, *The Columbiad,* and preparing it for publication. In 1785, Barlow's talent as a poet had also landed him another job. He was hired by the General Association of Congregational Ministers of Connecticut to write an Americanized version of *Dr. Watts's Imitation of the Psalms of David.* Once his psalm book and *The Columbiad* were published, Barlow opened a bookstore in Hartford, specifically to promote these two works and maximize his income from them. As soon as sales of these two books slowed down, he sold the store.

Much of Barlow's other writing during this time was for *The Anarchiad,* a satirical political paper anonymously published from time to time by his literary club, the Hartford Wits. Among the original members of this club was David Humphreys, who, in 1797, as Commissioner Plenipotentiary in Lisbon, was the official who approved Barlow's translation of the Treaty of Tripoli and submitted it for ratification. Among those rejected for admission to the club were Oliver Wolcott and Noah Webster, two of the very religious founders that David Barton makes a point of associating Barlow with in his biographical sketch. Barlow may have started out together at Yale with Wolcott and Webster, but couldn't have ended up more different from these former classmates in both politics and religion. While Wolcott and Webster were die-hard New England Federalists and Congregationalists, Barlow became a Jeffersonian Republican and a deist.

By 1788, Barlow was running out of money. His law practice had never been very successful, the royalties from his psalm book and *The Columbiad* had slowed down, and *The Anarchiad,* although popular, didn't generate much income. Needing a job, Barlow went to work for the Scioto Company, a group of land speculators selling land claims in the Northwest Territory. Few Americans at this time had money to buy land, so Barlow was hired to be the company's agent in Europe. He first went to England, but, not having much luck there, moved on to France, where began to have some success. This didn't last long, however, because it was soon revealed that the Scioto Company's land sales were a scam. Barlow may have been a bit deceptive in his advertisements about the wonderful and easy life people would have in Ohio, claiming, for example, that it almost never snowed there, but he had no idea that the land claims themselves were not legitimate.

Barlow was left with no source of income other than what he could make from his writing. By this time, however, he was already caught up in the political affairs of France, and making a name for himself writing tracts supporting the views of the Girondists. For a while, he divided his time between England and France, but when his political writings began to get him in a bit of trouble in England, he decided to make France his permanent home. So, Barlow and his wife Ruth, who had been living in England, moved to France, where they lived for a number of years in what appears to have been a ménage à trois with Robert Fulton, the inventor of the steamboat.

One of Barlow's closest friends in France was Thomas Paine. In 1793, when Paine knew he was about to be arrested, he entrusted the manuscript of the first part of *Age of Reason* to Barlow, who got it published while Paine was imprisoned in Paris.

Eventually, the Congregationalists in Connecticut found out that the psalm book they were using in their churches had been written by a heathen, and clergymen started banning it. Although Barlow's version continued to be used by few other churches until the mid-1800s, Barlow's old friend, Timothy Dwight, by this time president of Yale, was hired to write a new one for the Congregationalists.

David Barton ends his story about the Treaty of Tripoli with a number of quotes from the letters and journal of William Eaton, Consul to Tunis under both Adams and Jefferson.

> **Barton introduces William Eaton with the following: "...the writings of General William Eaton, a major figure in the Barbary Powers conflict, provide even more irrefutable testimony of how the conflict was viewed at that time. Eaton was first appointed by President John Adams as 'Consul to Tunis,' and President Thomas Jefferson later advanced him to the position of 'U. S. Naval Agent to the Barbary States,' authorizing him to lead a military expedition against Tripoli. Eaton's official correspondence during his**

> **service confirms that the conflict was a Muslim war against a Christian America.**

First of all, William Eaton was not really a general. He had been in the army prior to his service as a consul, but the highest rank he achieved was captain. How he was given the rank of general – not by the United States, but by an exiled Bashaw of Tripoli – is explained later in this chapter. Second, Thomas Jefferson didn't exactly authorize Eaton to lead a military expedition against Tripoli. Eaton's appointment as a naval agent was not a promotion, as Barton implies, but merely a temporary change in his chain of command, described by Jefferson as an *"occasional employment."* As a consul, Eaton's instructions came from the Department of State, but, for reasons also explained later, Jefferson wanted him under the control of Commodore Barron, the naval commander in the Mediterranean. While Barron was authorized to use Eaton in a military expedition against Tripoli, Eaton himself was given no military authority.

> **According to Barton, "Eaton later complained that after Jefferson had approved his plan for military action, he sent him the obsolete warship 'Hero.' Eaton reported the impression of America made upon the Tunis Muslims when they saw the old warship and its few cannons:**
>
> > **[T]he weak, the crazy situation of the vessel and equipage [armaments] tended to confirm an opinion long since conceived and never fairly controverted among the Tunisians, that the Americans are a feeble *sect of Christians.*"**

Jefferson did not send Eaton the Hero for use in a military action. In fact, Jefferson didn't send Eaton the Hero at all. What Barton quotes was written by Eaton in June 1800, nine months before Jefferson took office as president, and nearly four years before he sent Eaton to Tripoli under Commodore Barron. The Hero is part of a completely different story. Apparently, Barton didn't want to pass up a perfectly good quote with the word *"Christians"* in it, and had to find a way to work it in to his story. Barton's anachronism aside, the fact that the Tunisians viewed the Americans as a *"sect of Christians"* says nothing more than that the Muslims in the Barbary states wrongly assumed that the United States was a Christian nation like the nations of Europe.

The Hero belongs to the story of a treaty made with Tunis in 1797. When this treaty was submitted to the Senate by John Adams in February 1798, it was not approved. The Senate would only go as far as passing a resolution of conditional approval, the condition being the removal or modification of three of the treaty's articles. In December 1798, Adams sent William Eaton and James Cathcart, the Consul to Tripoli, to renegotiate the three articles. Eaton and Cathcart set sail on the brig Sophia, which met up with a convoy of four other ships, including the Hero, which was carrying goods to Algiers for payment on a treaty with that state. Eaton and Cathcart stayed in Algiers long enough to make sure that the Dey was satisfied with the goods being delivered, then returned to the Sophia and sailed for Tunis.

After several weeks of negotiations with the Bey of Tunis, a modification of the three treaty articles was agreed upon. At this point, Cathcart sailed for Tripoli, leaving Eaton to deal with the Bey's demands for payment. In addition to the money and goods originally agreed to, the Bey now wanted extra presents for agreeing to modify the treaty, for the delay of the original payments, and, as was the custom, for receiving a new consul. He had heard that the United States gave Algiers a brand new frigate as compensation for late treaty payments, so he wanted one too.

The original cost of the treaty was to be $107,000 – $50,000 in cash, $22,000 in jewels and other presents for various officials, and $35,000 in naval stores and weapons. This included forty cannons, twelve thousand cannon balls, and about thirty thousand pounds of gunpowder. As of the spring of 1799, however, all the Bey had received was the $50,000 in cash and a few small presents. Eaton was stuck in Tunis this entire time making excuses for the delay of the jewels and other articles. Eventually, the Bey got tired of Eaton's excuses and threatened to declare war on the United States. But, just when it was beginning to look like the Bey was going to make good on his threats, the Hero arrived with the promised naval stores. The Bey was somewhat appeased because of the quality of these items, but there was still no sign of the jewels, which had been ordered from London, or the cannons, cannon balls, and gunpowder.

The opinion of the Tunisians that the Americans were a *"feeble sect of Christians"* was reinforced because the arrival of the tribute ship meant the United States was giving into their demands, not because Eaton was sent an obsolete warship, as David Barton claims. The *"crazy situation,"* which Eaton complained about in a number of letters, was that the high quality of the goods that were delivered gave the impression that America was a wealthy nation, but one that was afraid to fight – an impression that would lead to endless demands.

Barton follows the quote about the Hero with two more Eaton quotes from around the same time, which, like the Hero quote, prove nothing more than that the Muslims assumed America was a Christian nation.

> **"In a later letter to Pickering, Eaton reported how pleased one Barbary ruler had been when he received the extortion compensations from America which had been promised him in one of the treaties:**
>
> > **He said, 'To speak truly and candidly . . . . we must acknowledge to you that we have never received articles of the kind of so excellent a quality from any *Christian nation*.'**
>
> **When John Marshall became the new Secretary of State, Eaton informed him:**
>
> > **It is a maxim of the Barbary States, that 'The Christians who would be on good terms with them must fight well or pay well.'"**

As further *evidence* that the Barbary Wars were a *"conflict between Christian America and Muslim nations,"* Barton presents a few entries from William Eaton's journal. The journal Barton quotes is from 1805, when Eaton actually was on his military expedition, a march across the desert for which, in Barton's version of the story, Jefferson sent him a ship.

> **According to Barton: "...when General Eaton finally commenced his military action against Tripoli, his personal journal noted:**
>
> > **April 8th. We find it almost impossible to inspire these wild bigots with confidence in us or to persuade them that, being Christians, we can be otherwise than enemies to Musselmen. We have a difficult undertaking!"**

What Barton fails to mention about this journal entry is that the *"Musselmen"* Eaton was referring to weren't an enemy he was fighting. They were his own troops!

The plan that led to Eaton marching an army of Arabs across the desert in 1805 was hatched by Eaton four years earlier. In March 1801, when Jefferson took office as president, the Bashaw of Tripoli demanded that the United States pay $250,000 in tribute. This went directly against Article 10 of the 1797 treaty, which guaranteed that no further payment or annual tribute would ever be required.

It's interesting to note that Gary DeMar, while being very concerned with the differences between Barlow's translation of the 1797 treaty and the Arabic text, doesn't appear to have actually read the treaty. If he had, he would know that the United States wasn't paying tribute to Tripoli in 1801, yet he seems to think the demand for the $250,000 was an increase to existing tribute payments.

> **According to DeMar: "Piracy remained a problem despite the 1797 Treaty. In addition, Tripoli demanded increased tribute payments in 1801. When President Jefferson refused to increase the tribute, Tripoli declared war on the United States."**

Because the Bashaw of Tripoli's demand for a tribute payment violated the 1797 treaty, Jefferson ignored it. When the Bashaw's deadline for this payment came and went with no response at all from the United States, Tripoli declared war.

The Bashaw of Tripoli at this time, Jusuf Caramanli, was not the legitimate heir to the throne. Nine years earlier, Jusuf had driven the legitimate heir, his older brother Hamet, into exile and assumed power. When Tripoli declared war on the United States, William Eaton was still in Tunis. So was Hamet Caramanli.

Eaton approached Hamet and proposed a plan by which the United States would help restore him to his throne. Eaton thought his plan would accomplish two things. First, it would end the war because Hamet would negotiate a new peace treaty as soon as he regained power. Second, the use of military force to restore Hamet would send a message to the other Barbary States that the United States was not a country to mess with.

From the start, Eaton was at odds with the Jefferson administration. Eaton wanted to solve the problem with Tripoli militarily, and Jefferson wanted to solve it diplomatically. As of 1802, Eaton could get nothing more from Jefferson than very vague approval of his plan to restore Hamet. Secretary of State Madison wrote to Eaton in August of that year, informing him that the administration was not opposed to cooperating with an ally who shared a common goal if it was to the advantage of the United States to do so. However, Eaton was not given any means by which to carry out his plan, and Madison made it clear that, in the event that a treaty was negotiated with the reigning Bashaw, any plan to restore Hamet was to be abandoned. Jefferson and Madison were obviously under the impression at this point that Hamet had a sizeable army and much greater resources and support among his own people than he actually did. They had no intention of providing troops to Eaton, or paying for the army of Arabs that he would later assemble.

In May 1803, Eaton returned to the United States to try to settle his accounts with the government. Some of Eaton's expenses in Tunis were being questioned, such as a bill for the loss of income from his private ship, the Gloria, which he had taken upon himself to attach to the navy, although having no authority to do so. While in Washington on this business, Eaton went to see Jefferson in an attempt to talk him into providing a military force to restore Hamet.

Eaton wrote the following to his friend Timothy Pickering about his meeting with Jefferson. As was often the case in his letters to Pickering, Eaton was quite sarcastic about Jefferson and his policies.

> I waited on the President and the Attorney-General. One of them was civil, and the other grave....I endeavored to enforce

> conviction on the mind of Mr. Lincoln of the necessity of meeting the aggressions of Barbary by retaliation. He waived the subject, and amused me with predictions of a political millennium which was about to happen in the United States. The millennium was to usher in upon us as the irresistible consequence of the goodness of heart, integrity of mind, and correctness of disposition of Mr. Jefferson. All nations, even pirates and savages, were to be moved by the influence of his persuasive virtue and masterly skill in diplomacy.[13]

When Jefferson sent Eaton back to the Mediterranean, he gave him no specific authority or instructions. Eaton was far too eager to carry out his plan for Jefferson to give him the authority to do it. Instead, Jefferson sent Eaton back with Commodore Barron as a naval agent, leaving any plans involving Hamet to Barron's discretion, with instructions that if he thought Eaton's knowledge of the region would be useful, he could use him. But, at the same time, Barron was also instructed to assist the Consul General, Colonel Tobias Lear, in negotiating a peace treaty with Jusuf, the reigning Bashaw. As in 1802, it was made clear that if a treaty could be negotiated, any other plans were to be abandoned. Eaton was not happy with any of this, as he wrote to Timothy Pickering.

> The President becomes reserved; the Secretary of War "believes we had better pay tribute,"—he said this to me in his own office. Gallatin, like a cowardly Jew, shrinks behind the counter. Mr. Madison "leaves everything to the Secretary of the Navy Department." And I am ordered on the expedition by Secretary Smith,—who, by the by, is as much of a gentleman and a soldier as his relation with the Administration will suffer, —without any special instructions to regulate my conduct.[14]

When Eaton and Barron arrived in the Mediterranean in September 1804, all they knew of Hamet Caramanli's whereabouts was that he had gone into hiding somewhere in Egypt. A few weeks after their

13. Henry Adams, *History of the United States of America During the First Administration of Thomas Jefferson*, vol. 2, (New York: Charles Scribner's Sons, 1903), 431.
14. *ibid.*

arrival, Barron consented to a plan to let Eaton sail to Egypt with Captain Isaac Hull, find Hamet, and bring him and whatever military force he had back on Hull's ship, the Argus. Getting Hamet from Egypt to Derne, Tripoli's second largest city, and supporting Hamet's land operations from the sea, was all that Commodore Barron had in mind. When Hamet was first driven from the throne by his brother, he had been made governor of Derne. If Hamet, in a city he used to govern, couldn't muster the resources he needed to continue on to Tripoli on his own, Barron had no intention of helping him further. It would make no sense for the United States to spend any more money trying to restore Hamet to power if he wasn't going to have enough support among his people to remain in power.

Once he got to Egypt, Eaton, accompanied by marine lieutenant Presley O'Bannon, one navy lieutenant, and two midshipmen, posed as naval officers on a pleasure trip and headed for Cairo. After several setbacks, including being captured by a detachment of Turkish cavalry who mistook them for British spies, they managed to locate Hamet and his army of about seventy. Eaton was also able to obtain a letter of amnesty from the Viceroy, which would allow Hamet to move through Egypt without any trouble from the Turks. The Turkish governor of Alexandria, however, refused to permit Hamet's small army of Arabs to depart from his port, where Captain Hull and the Argus were waiting. This problem could have been taken care of by the Viceroy, but, by this time, Hamet was afraid to enter Alexandria.

The only alternative Eaton had was to march Hamet and his men five hundred miles across the desert. The following was Captain Hull's opinion of this plan.

> The plan you have formed of taking Derne, I think rather a Hazardous one, unless the Bashaw can bring into the field from Eight hundred to one Thousand Men, particularly as we are destitute of every article necessary for an expedition of the kind.[15]

Eaton's request for a detachment of a hundred marines was turned down. All Commodore Barron had only been authorized to do was pro-

15. Glenn Tucker, *Dawn Like Thunder, The Barbary Wars and the Birth of the U.S. Navy*, (Indianapolis: Bobbs-Merrill, 1963), 363.

vide Hamet's army with a small amount of arms, ammunition, and money, and to support Hamet's land operations from the sea. He had not been authorized to provide American troops for any land operation. All Eaton could get from Captain Hull were nine men – Lieutenant O'Bannon, one marine sergeant, six marine privates, and one navy midshipman – and $1,000. Hull left Alexandria with plans to sail to Syracuse, pick up provisions and try to get more money, and then meet up with Eaton and Hamet when they reached the Bay of Bomba, at which point they would be about sixty miles from Derne.

On February 23, 1805, two weeks before setting out on their march, Eaton and Hamet drew up and signed a convention, Eaton as agent of the United States, and Hamet as the legitimate Bashaw of Tripoli. The convention listed what the United States would provide to help Hamet regain his throne, and what Hamet would do for the United States once he was back in power. Everything promised by Hamet, of course, such as turning over future tribute payments from Denmark and Sweden to reimburse the United States for the help promised by Eaton, depended on their mission being successful, and, the help promised by Eaton depended on Commodore Barron agreeing to provide it. This convention also made Eaton commander-in-chief of Hamet's army, and any other troops they might recruit, which is how this man with no actual military authority became "General" Eaton.

By the time the march into the desert began on March 6, 1805, Eaton had assembled a strange little army of about four hundred men, consisting of three hundred Arabs, including Hamet's seventy; forty Greek mercenaries recruited in Alexandria; twenty-five Levanter cannoneers; a handful of other mercenaries and adventurers of various nationalities; and, of course, ten Americans, including himself.

During the two month, five hundred mile march to Derne, the army was usually starving, often couldn't find water, and had doubts from the start that Eaton would be able to pay them what he had promised. There were a number of disputes, usually over money, that led to parts of the army, and a few times even Hamet himself, threatening to mutiny. Most of these disputes were instigated by one particular Arab chief, El Tahib, who was constantly telling the Arab mercenaries, who were used to being paid up front, that they couldn't trust Eaton to pay them because he was a Christian. At one point early in the march, the only way to prevent a mutiny was for the marines to collect whatever money they had in their pockets and give it to the Arab chiefs. There were also disputes over food, one of which occurred on April 8, the date that Eaton wrote the journal entry quoted by David Barton.

On the morning of April 8, the army came upon a source of drinkable water and made what Eaton assumed would be a brief stop. At this point, they were only about ninety miles from the Bay of Bomba, so Eaton rode ahead to check out the route along the coast. When he returned, he found that, although it was still early in the day, Hamet had ordered the army to set up camp. Hamet had decided that he wouldn't go any further until a scout was sent to Bomba to make sure that Captain Hull had arrived with the promised provisions. With their only remaining food being a six day supply of rice rations, Eaton thought this was crazy.

Eaton ordered the rations cut off, but this didn't get the army to move. It just angered Hamet, who threatened to take his men and return to Egypt. It also made the Arab chiefs hatch a plan to seize the food supply. When Eaton got wind of this plan, he ordered the marines, the Greeks, and the Levanters form a line in front of the supply tent, where they stood for an hour facing two hundred mounted Arabs. Hamet, who had decided by this point not to leave, eventually got the Arabs to begin falling back. Just as things were calming down, however, Eaton made a big mistake. To show the Arabs how disciplined his little group of marines was, he ordered them to go through their manual of arms. The Arabs misunderstood this, and thought Eaton had ordered the marines to prepare to fire, so they remounted and charged. Someone did yell "fire," but apparently nobody wanted to fire the first shot, so nobody did. Hamet's officers and the more moderate Arab chiefs somehow managed to stop the Arabs before any blood was shed, after which Eaton agreed to issue one rice ration, and Hamet agreed that they would resume the march to Bomba the next morning.

When the army reached the Bay of Bomba on April 15, Captain Hull and the Argus were nowhere to be found. This caused another near revolt among the Arab mercenaries, who were then completely convinced that Eaton's promise that food and money would be waiting here had been a lie. But, the Argus and one of the navy's new ships, the Hornet, actually were nearby, and Captain Hull had seen the smoke from the army's fires. As soon as the sails of the approaching Argus were spotted, order was once again restored. The army camped at Bomba until April 23, then continued on to Derne, reaching a hilltop overlooking the city on April 25.

While camping outside of the city, Eaton and Hamet received information that two thirds of the inhabitants of Derne would support Hamet, but the governor, Hussein Bey, had eight hundred troops prepared to defend the city, and another fifteen hundred, sent from Tripoli by Jusuf, were only three days away. Commodore Barron had sent plenty of food, along with seven thousand Spanish dollars, but still refused to send any American troops. In fact, he wanted the officers who were with Eaton to return to their ships.

On the morning of April 27, the Argus, the Hornet, and the Nautilus bombarded Derne as Eaton and Hamet attacked by land. After a two and a half hour battle, they had complete possession of the city. Among the casualties were three of the marines, one killed in the battle, and two wounded, one of whom later died. Eaton was shot in the wrist.

When the fifteen hundred troops sent by Jusuf arrived, Hussein Bey, who had managed to escape, took command of them. On May 13, after several unsuccessful attempts by the Bey to buy over Hamet's mercenaries, Jusuf's army attacked, but was eventually driven back into the hills by Hamet's cavalry. After this, some of Jusuf's troops began to come over to Hamet's side.

Eaton was now ready to continue towards his ultimate goal – marching into Tripoli, still five hundred miles away, and restoring Hamet to the throne. Eaton wrote to Commodore Barron asking for more money and provisions, and again for a detachment of marines. Eaton was not happy with Barron's reply. Jusuf was willing to negotiate a peace treaty, so any further plans with Hamet were off. At the same time, Eaton received a letter from Consul General Lear, ordering him to leave Derne. Eaton disobeyed this order and remained in Derne until June 11, when the Constellation arrived with the news that the treaty with Jusuf had been concluded.

The new treaty cost the United States $60,000, but included no tribute. The payment was for the ransom of the crew of the Philadelphia, captured by Tripoli in 1803. Jusuf had agreed to a prisoner exchange, but he was holding three hundred prisoners, and the United States only had one hundred, so he demanded ransom for the other two hundred.

Eaton and the marines had to sneak on board the Constellation to get away from Derne. Hamet, who feared he would be killed if left behind, was also evacuated, along with the forty of his followers that Eaton called his "suite." The treaty negotiated by Lear included a provision that Jusuf release Hamet's family, who were being held captive, but a secret article gave Jusuf four years to do this. Hamet was taken to Syracuse and given an allowance of $200 a month, authorized by Commodore John Rodgers as a temporary arrangement until Congress decided what, if any, compensation he was entitled to.

When Madison wrote to Eaton in August 1802, he had said that if a plan to restore Hamet was begun, but abandoned by the United States because of a treaty with Jusuf, it might be fair to restore Hamet to a situation comparable to that which he was removed from. No guarantee of this was ever made, however, and Eaton had no authority to promise it. As things ended up, Hamet's situation in Syracuse was not comparable to the situation he had left in Egypt. Eaton thought Hamet deserved $30,000 to $40,000 in compensation. He ended up with only $6,800 – $4,400 from the monthly payments authorized by Rodgers, and an additional $2,400 appropriated by Congress. This amount was decided on after Jefferson, in response to an appeal from Hamet, laid the following message before Congress, explaining what his understanding of Eaton's plan had been, and what he had actually authorized.

> I lay before Congress the application of Hamet Caramalli [sic], elder brother of the reigning Bashaw of Tripoli, soliciting from the United States attention to his services and sufferings in the late war against that State; and, in order to possess them of the ground on which that application stands, the facts shall be stated according to the views and information of the Executive.
>
> During the war with Tripoli, it was suggested that Hamet Caramalli, elder brother of the reigning Bashaw, and driven by him from his throne, meditated the recovery of his inheritance, and that a concert in action with us was desirable to him. We considered that concerted operations by those

who have a common enemy, were entirely justifiable, and might produce effects favorable to both, without binding either to guarantee the objects of the other. But the distance of the scene, the difficulties of communication, and the uncertainty of information inducing the less confidence in the measure, it was committed to our agents as one which might be resorted to if it promised to promote our success.

Mr. Eaton, however, our late Consul, on his return from the Mediterranean, possessing personal knowledge of the scene, and having confidence in the effect of a joint operation, we authorized Commodore Barron, then proceeding with his squadron, to enter into an understanding with Hamet, if he should deem it useful; and as it was represented that he would need some aids of arms and ammunition, and even of money, he was authorized to furnish them to a moderate extent, according to the prospect of utility to be expected from it. In order to avail him of the advantages of Mr. Eaton's knowledge of circumstances, an occasional employment was provided for the latter as an agent for the Navy in that sea. Our expectation was, that an intercourse should be kept up between the ex-Bashaw, and the Commodore; that while the former moved on by land, our squadron should proceed with equal pace, so as to arrive at their destination together, and to attack the common enemy by land and sea at the same time. The instructions of June sixth, to Commodore Barron, show that a co-operation only was intended, and by no means an union of our object with the fortune of the ex-Bashaw; and the Commodore's letters of March twenty-second and May nineteenth, prove that he had the most correct idea of our intentions. His verbal instructions, indeed, to Mr. Eaton and Captain Hull, if the expressions are accurately committed to writing by those gentlemen, do not limit the extent of his co-operation as rigorously as he probably intended; but it is certain, from the ex-Bashaw's letter of January third, written when he was proceeding to join Mr. Eaton, and in which he says, "your operations should be carried on by sea, mine by land," that he left the position in which he was, with a proper idea of the nature of the co-operation. If Mr. Eaton's subsequent convention should appear to bring forward other objects, his letter of April twenty-ninth, and May first, views this convention but as provisional, the second article, as he expressly states, guarding it against any ill effect, and his letter of June thirtieth confirms this construction.

In the event it was found, that, after placing the ex-Bashaw in possession of Derne, one of the most important cities and provinces of the country, where he had resided himself as Governor, he was totally unable to command any resources, or to bear any part in co-operation with us. This hope was then at an end; and we certainly had never contemplated, nor were we prepared to land an army of our own, or to raise, pay, or subsist an army of Arabs, to march from Derne to Tripoli, and to carry on a land war at such a distance from our resources. Our means and our authority were merely naval; and that such were the expectations of Hamet, his letter of June twenty-ninth, is an unequivocal acknowledgment. While, therefore, an impression from the capture of Derne might still operate at Tripoli, and an attack on that place from our squadron was daily expected, Colonel Lear thought it the best moment to listen to overtures of peace then made by the Bashaw. He did so, and, while urging provisions for the United States, he paid attention also to the interests of Hamet; but was able to effect nothing more than to engage the restitution of his family, and even the persevering in this demand suspended for some time the conclusion of the treaty.

In operations at such a distance, it becomes necessary to leave much to the discretion of the agents employed: but events may still turn up beyond the limits of that discretion. Unable in such a case to consult his Government, a zealous citizen will act as he believes that would direct him were it apprised of the circumstances, and will take on himself the responsibility. In all these cases, the purity and patriotism of the motives should shield the agent from blame, and even secure a sanction where the error is not too injurious. Should it be thought by any that the verbal instructions said to have been given by Commodore Barron to Mr. Eaton, amount to a stipulation that the United States should place Hamet Caramalli on the throne of Tripoli; a stipulation so entirely unauthorized, so far beyond our views, and so onerous, could not be sanctioned by our Government; or should Hamet Caramalli, contrary to the evidence of his letters of January third, and June twenty-ninth, be thought to have left the position which he now seems to regret, under a mistaken expectation that we were, at all events, to place him on his throne, on an appeal to the liberality of the nation, something equivalent to the replacing him in his former situation, might be worthy its consideration.

A nation, by establishing a character of liberality and magnanimity, gains, in the friendship and respect of others, more than the worth of mere money. This appeal is now made by Hamet Caramalli to the United States. The ground he has taken being different, not only from our views, but from those expressed by himself on former occasions, Mr. Eaton was desired to state whether any verbal communications passed from him to Hamet which had varied what he saw in writing. His answer of December fifth is herewith transmitted, and has rendered it still more necessary that, in presenting to the Legislature the application of Hamet, I should present them, at the same time, an exact statement of the views and proceedings of the Executive, through this whole business, that they may clearly understand the ground on which we are placed. It is accompanied by all the papers which bear any relation to the principles of the co-operation, and which can inform their judgment in deciding on the application of Hamet Caramalli.[16]

16. *The Debates and Proceedings in the Congress of the United States,* vol. 15, 9th Cong., 1st Sess., (Washington D.C.: Gales and Seaton, 1852), 48-50.

> **David Barton wraps up his story about William Eaton with the following: "Shortly after the military excursion against Tripoli was successfully terminated, its account was written and published. Even the title of the book bears witness to the nature of the conflict:**
>
> > ***The Life of the Late Gen. William Eaton... commander of the Christian and Other Forces...which Led to the Treaty of Peace Between The United States and The Regency of Tripoli***
>
> **The numerous documents surrounding the Barbary Powers Conflict confirm that historically it was *always* viewed as a conflict between Christian America and Muslim nations...."**

The numerous documents surrounding the Barbary Powers Conflict, including both the writings of William Eaton and the Barbary treaties, actually confirm something a bit different – that there were always alliances and agreements between Americans and Muslims, whether their common, or individual, enemies were Christian or Muslim. During the time of the Barbary wars, the United States was just as likely to be at war with a Christian power as a Muslim power. Because of this, almost every Barbary treaty contained an article providing that, within gunshot of their respective ports, the Muslims would defend American ships that were under attack by Christian enemies, and the Americans would defend Muslim ships that were under attack by Christian enemies. The following articles appeared in both the 1786 treaty with Morocco, the first of the Barbary treaties, and the 1836 treaty with Morocco, the last. These are among the articles, which, because they contain the word "Christian," are listed by Barton in the footnote for his claim that the 1797 treaty with Tripoli was *"one of the many treaties in which each country officially recognized the religion of the other"*

> Article 10. If any Vessel of either of the parties shall have an engagement with a Vessel belonging to any of the Christian

> powers within gun shot of the forts of the other, the Vessel so engaged shall be defended and protected as much as possible until she is in safety; and if any American Vessel shall be cast on shore on the coast of Wadnoon or any Coast thereabout, the people belonging to her shall be protected and assisted until by the help of God they shall be sent to their Country.[17]
>
> Article 11. If we shall be at war with any christian power, and any of our Vessels sail from the ports of the United States, no Vessel belonging to the enemy shall follow, until twenty four hours after the departure of our Vessels, and the same regulation shall be observed towards the American Vessels sailing from our ports;—be their enemies Moors or Christians.[18]

The last argument used to dismiss the 1797 treaty with Tripoli actually has nothing to do with that treaty. This argument is based on the fact that the *not founded on the Christian religion* phrase does not appear in the later 1805 treaty with Tripoli.

> **According to Gary DeMar: "If the critics of a Christian America are going to be honest, then they must give an adequate reason why the 1805 treaty does not contain the words that seem to denounce the Christian religion in the 1797 treaty. They must also answer why the revised Treaty occurred during Thomas Jefferson's term as president, since Jefferson, when compared to Washington and Adams, was the most hostile to organized Christianity!"**

The *"adequate reason"* for the 1805 treaty not containing the same article regarding religion as the 1797 treaty is that the events that occurred between 1797 and 1805 made it necessary to rewrite it. The 1797 treaty had twelve articles. Only seven of these could be copied into the twenty article 1805 treaty without significant changes.

17. Richard Peters, ed., *The Public Statutes at Large of the United States of America,* vol. 8, (Boston: Little, Brown, and Company, 1867), 102.
18. *ibid,* 485.

Article 11 was not one of these seven. As of 1797, the United States had never *"entered into any voluntary war or act of hostility against any Mohametan nation,"* as was stated in Article 11. As of 1805, of course, this was no longer true, so it needed to be added that the only exception to this had been to defend the right to navigate the high seas. In rewriting the sentence, Tobias Lear left out the phrase *"is not in any sense founded on the Christian religion."* There is nothing significant about this. He probably left it out because it was unnecessary, and, with what was being added, made the sentence too long. By calling the new treaty a *"revised"* treaty, DeMar makes it sound as if Jefferson deliberately had the old treaty changed to remove the *not founded on the Christian religion* phrase. If Lear gave any thought at all to the new treaty reflecting the views of Thomas Jefferson, it was in what he added, not what he removed. The 1797 treaty only guaranteed that there would be no hostility between the two governments because of religious opinions. The new article also guaranteed the right of the individuals of both countries to practice their religions in either. The following is the sentence that appeared in Article 14 of the 1805 treaty.

> As the Government of the United States of America, has in itself no character of enmity against the Laws, Religion or Tranquility of Musselmen, and as the said States never have entered into any voluntary war or act of hostility against any Mahometan Nation, except in the defence of their just rights to freely navigate the High Seas: It is declared by the contracting parties that no pretext arising from Religious Opinions, shall ever produce an interruption of the Harmony existing between the two Nations; And the Consuls and Agents of both Nations respectively, shall have liberty to exercise his Religion in his own house; all slaves of the same Religion shall not be Impeded in going to said Consuls house at hours of Prayer.[19]

William Federer, in his book *America's God and Country,* and Mark Beliles and Stephen McDowell, in their book *America's Providential*

19. Richard Peters, ed., *The Public Statutes at Large of the United States of America*, vol. 8, (Boston: Little, Brown, and Company, 1867), 216.

History, not only point out that the phrase from the 1797 treaty doesn't appear in the 1805 treaty, but give Congress the power to negotiate and revise treaties.

> **According to William Federer: "Congress deleted from the previous June 7, 1797 treaty, an unauthorized phrase that the United States 'is not in any sense founded on the Christian religion...'."**

> **According to Mark Beliles and Stephen McDowell: "Congress renegotiated and ratified the 'Treaty of Tripoli' in 1805 after repudiating and deleting the phrase: 'The United States is not, in any sense, founded on the Christian religion.'"**

Thanks to the fact that Beliles's and McDowell's book is highly recommended as a history text among the Christian homeschooling community, countless homeschooled students are now being taught a version of the separation of powers in which Congress has the power to repudiate and delete a phrase from, renegotiate, and ratify a treaty.

— CHAPTER EIGHT —

Treaties with Christian Nations

According to the religious right version of American history, references to Christianity in treaties with European powers are to be interpreted as acknowledgements by the Americans who signed those treaties that America was a Christian nation.

> **D. James Kennedy, in his book *What If America Were A Christian Nation Again?*, states: "The Treaty of Paris of 1783, negotiated by Ben Franklin, John Adams, and John Jay, acknowledged the Trinity as it made official our separation with Britain."**
>
> **David Barton, in his book *Original Intent*, uses the same example: "...on September 8, 1783, the formal peace treaty with Great Britain was signed by John Adams, Benjamin Franklin, and John Jay. Like so many of the other official records of the Revolution, that document, too, openly acknowledged God. The opening line of the peace treaty declared:**
>
>> **In the name of the most holy and undivided Trinity."**

This reference to the trinity was not an acknowledgement by the government of the United States that America was a Christian nation. It was an acknowledgement by the government of England that *England* was a Christian nation. *"In the name of the Most Holy and Undivided Trinity"* was the customary way that England, like most of the Christian nations of Europe, began their treaties and other documents. The United States had nothing to do with this wording.

Unlike the Arabic and Turkish treaties in the previous chapter, in which the religious references of the other party were removed during the translation process, treaties with England were already in English, so they were just copied as is. Where the customary *"may God strengthen"* after the names of Barbary rulers was omitted, the customary *"by the grace of God"* between the name and title of Christian monarchs remained.

Most treaties began with a preamble that included the reason for the treaty, the names and titles of the parties involved, and the agents each had authorized to make the treaty. In these statements, the names of monarchs, and sometimes of agents, were followed by all of the titles they held. Some of these titles were religious and others were not, like those of George III.

> ...the most serene and most potent Prince George the Third, by the grace of God King of Great Britain, France, and Ireland, Duke of Brunswick and Lunenbourg, arch-treasurer and elector of the holy Roman Empire...[1]

In religious right history books, these strings of titles are sometimes edited to show only the religious titles, such as *Defender of the Faith.* This title, bestowed on Henry VIII by Pope Leo X in the 1520s for taking a stand against Martin Luther continued to be used by Henry, even after breaking with the Catholic Church. It was defiantly included in the Preface to the 39 Articles of the Church of England – *"being by God's Ordinance, according to Our just Title, Defender of the Faith..."* – and has been used by all monarchs of Great Britain since.

Although also containing religious references, what aren't included in the religious right history books are the silly sounding titles,

1. "Treaty of Paris, 1763," John Hamilton Gray, *Confederation; Or, The Political and Parliamentary History of Canada,* vol. 1, (Toronto: Copp, Clark & Co., 1872), 413.

such as that of the agent authorized to sign the Treaty of Paris for Spain.

> Don Jerome Grimaldi, Marquis de Grimaldi, Knight of the Order of the Holy Ghost, Gentleman of my Bed-chamber with employment, and my Ambassador Extraordinary to the Most Christian King.[2]

Lengthy strings of titles, like acknowledgements of the trinity, only appear in the treaties that were drafted by the agents of other governments, and then signed by the United States. When it was the other way around, and treaties with these same nations were written by the agents of the United States government, they did not contain unnecessary titles, religious or otherwise, and they did not acknowledge Christianity. The United States apparently just didn't care if an agent of Great Britain happened to be a *Knight of the Most Noble Order of the Garter,* or who was the most *Serene* or *Illustrious.* This simple opening statement from an 1818 convention with Great Britain is typical of the manner in which conventions and treaties written by the government of the United States began.

> The United States of America, and his Majesty the King of Great Britain and Ireland, desirous to cement the good understanding which happily subsists between them...[3]

This was followed by the names of the agents of both parties, followed by nothing more than their position in their government and who they were appointed by.

Further proof that the trinity opening was nothing more than a custom of the Christian powers like Great Britain, and not a declaration by the United States, is that it appears in all treaties made by Great Britain, whether the United States was a party to the treaty or not. The opening statement of the 1763 Treaty of Paris, which ended the Seven Years War in Europe and the French and Indian War in

2. Adam Shortt and Arthur G. Doughty, eds., *Documents Relating to the Constitutional History of Canada 1759-1791,* (Ottawa: S.E. Dawson, 1907), 93.
3. Richard Peters, ed., *The Public Statutes at Large of the United States of America,* vol. 8, (Boston: Little, Brown, and Company, 1867), 248.

America, contains language almost identical to the Peace Treaty of 1783. The Treaty of Paris was between Great Britain, France, and Spain.

> In the Name of the Most Holy and Undivided Trinity, Father, Son, and Holy Ghost. So be it.
>
> Be it known to all those whom it shall, or may, in any manner, belong, It has pleased the Most High to diffuse the spirit of union and concord among the Princes...[4]

The religious right American history books always use the same two examples of treaties with the trinity acknowledgement – the 1783 peace treaty with Great Britain, and the Convention of 1822, also with Great Britain. During this time period, the United States entered into twenty-five treaties or conventions with foreign nations. Out of these twenty-five, there were actually three that began with this acknowledgement. Apparently, when the Liars for Jesus were hunting through treaties looking for the trinity opening, they missed the 1816 treaty with Sweden and Norway.

Gary DeMar, in his book *America's Christian History: The Untold Story,* incorporates the trinity acknowledgement from the Convention of 1822 into his argument against the Treaty of Tripoli.

> **According to DeMar: "If the 1797 Treaty of Tripoli turns America into a secular state (which it does not), the treaty of 1822 reestablishes Trinitarian Christianity."**

William Federer, in his book *America's God and Country,* also uses the Convention of 1822, and, as in his story about the 1805 treaty with Tripoli, appears to be a little confused about how our government makes and ratifies treaties. In this case, he has the House of Representatives ratifying a convention. He also appears to think that Ireland had to ratify this treaty between Great Britain with the United States.

4. "Treaty of Paris, 1763," John Hamilton Gray, *Confederation; Or, The Political and Parliamentary History of Canada,* vol. 1, (Toronto: Copp, Clark & Co., 1872), 413.

> **According to Federer: "Congress of the United States of America 1822, ratified in both the House and the Senate of the United States, along with Great Britain and Ireland, the *Convention for Indemnity under Award of Emperor of Russia as to the True Construction of the First Article of the Treaty of December 24, 1814*. It begins with these words: 'In the name of the Most Holy and Indivisible Trinity.'"**

Since the goal of religious right American history books isn't actually to teach anything about history, not one Liar for Jesus who uses the Convention of 1822 as an example of the trinity acknowledgement explains the reason for this convention. They know their audience doesn't care what was being negotiated or why the Emperor of Russia was involved – as long as an official United States document mentions their religion.

The purpose of the convention of 1822 was to settle a dispute over one of the articles of the Treaty of Ghent, the treaty that ended the War of 1812. The dispute was over the amount of compensation owed to the United States by Great Britain for slaves captured by the British during the war. According to Article I of the treaty, the compensation owed for seized slaves depended on which country's territory the slaves happened to be captured in. The United States and Great Britain disagreed over the meaning of this article, so, according to another article of the treaty, they had to appoint a third party to arbitrate. The arbitrator they chose was the Emperor of Russia. Apparently, the fact that the dispute was over payment for the people stolen from the good Christian Americans who rightfully owned them is unimportant, as long as the dispute was settled *in the name of the Most Holy and Undivided Trinity*.

— CHAPTER NINE —

James Madison's Detached Memoranda

In 1946, a lost document written by James Madison was found among the family papers of one of his biographers. This small collection of essays, which Madison called *Detached Memoranda,* includes some anecdotes about Benjamin Franklin, explanations of some key events from the Washington administration, thoughts on banks and elections, and recollections of writing the *Federalist.* It also includes an essay entitled *Monopolies, Perpetuities, Corporations, Ecclesiastical Endowments,* much of which is about religion and the government. In this essay, Madison made clear his objections to mixing religion and government in even the smallest ways. A few of the practices he singled out as being unconstitutional or potentially dangerous were tax supported chaplains in Congress and in the military, and government proclamations of days of prayer and thanksgiving. Religious right American history authors hate this document, and usually attempt to discredit it in some way before even getting to its actual content.

Some begin by subtlety shedding a little doubt on the document's authenticity.

> **According to Daniel Dreisbach, in his book *Real Threat and Mere Shadow*: "The 'Detached Memoranda' is a problematic document thought to be in the hand of James Madison, discovered in 1946 in the family papers of Madison's biographer, William Cabell Rives."**

The *Detached Memoranda* are not *"thought to be"* in the hand of James Madison. They *are* in the hand of James Madison. There has never been any question about this.

> **According to David Barton, on his *WallBuilders* website: "Significantly, the 'Detached Memoranda' was 'discovered' in 1946 in the papers of Madison biographer William Cabell Rives and was first published more than a century after Madison's death by Elizabeth Fleet in the October 1946 William & Mary Quarterly."**

There is nothing at all *significant* about the fact that this document was discovered in 1946, and 1946 was not the first time that the document, at least the part regarding religion and government, was published. The entire essay *Monopolies, Perpetuities, Corporations, Ecclesiastical Endowments* was published in *Harper's Magazine* in 1914. This prior publication was mentioned by Elizabeth Fleet in her 1946 *William and Mary Quarterly* article – the same article that Barton refers to and cites as his source.

The interesting history of the *Detached Memoranda,* and how a copy of one of its essays came to be in the hands of Harper Brothers, was explained in part by Gaillard Hunt, who wrote an introduction to *Monopolies, Perpetuities, Corporations, Ecclesiastical Endowments* for *Harper's Magazine* in 1914. Hunt, of course, had no way of knowing that this essay was copied from a larger document that wouldn't be found until 1946, or that this document was used and quoted from by William Cabell Rives when he wrote his biography of Madison in the 1860s. This part of the document's history was filled in by Elizabeth Fleet in her 1946 article.

The following was Gaillard Hunt's introduction to the 1914 publication of *Monopolies, Perpetuities, Corporations, Ecclesiastical Endowments* in *Harper's Magazine.*

> James Madison retired from the Presidency in 1817 and died in 1836, nineteen years later. This was the growing period of American nationality, and it was during these years that an enduring attachment was formed for the frame of government under which the growth took place. So, as

Madison had been the master-builder of the government, he enjoyed extraordinary prestige, and whatever he said on public questions was regarded as oracular. He felt the weight of the responsibility and expressed his views carefully, realizing that he was addressing posterity. During the closing years of his life he prepared certain papers for posthumous publication, the chief one being the journal he had kept of the proceedings of the Federal Convention of 1787. This journal, with certain letters which he had grouped with it, was published by the United States Government in 1840 in three volumes under the title of *The Madison Papers.* Before this mode of publication was decided upon, however, the papers were offered by Mrs. Madison, who inherited them under the terms of her husband's will, to several publishers, and among others to Messrs. Harper & Brothers; but a satisfactory pecuniary arrangement could not be reached by private publication, and the papers were sold to the government.

It was not known that, at the same time with *The Madison Papers,* or perhaps a few months later, several essays which Madison had prepared for publication were place in the Messrs. Harpers' hands, but such, as it now appears, was the fact. All of these have since found their way into print, except the one which follows. It was written, or revised, by Madison sometime before 1832, and is in the penmanship of one of the amanuenses whom he employed at Montpelier. It is entitled "Monopolies, Perpetuities, Corporations, Ecclesiastical Endowments," and deals for the most part with the subject of religious freedom, of which he could justly claim to be one of the great champions. It was he who had caused the Virginia Bill of Rights to be amended so that it declared for free exercise of religion instead of toleration or permission to exercise religion; it was he who wrote the remonstrance against assessments for religious purposes in Virginia which broke down the bill for that purpose; it was he who carried through the Virginia legislature the bill for complete religious freedom which Jefferson had written. There

> are few historical characters whose views on this subject are as valuable as his.[1]

What was found in 1946, of course, was the document containing Madison's draft of this essay in his own handwriting. Elizabeth Fleet, with the newfound knowledge that *Monopolies, Perpetuities, Corporations, Ecclesiastical Endowments,* as well as parts of Rives's biography of Madison, came from this collection, told the rest of the document's story in her article. After mentioning the 1914 appearance of the essay in *Harper's Magazine,* and explaining that this was taken from a copy of this individual essay, prepared by Madison for publication, Fleet traced the history of Madison's original *Detached Memoranda* manuscript.

> Since leaving Madison's hands, the manuscript has had a curious history. Evidently it was one of the documents sold to the government in the second and final sale of her husband's papers by Mrs. Madison in 1848. By act of Congress in 1856 an appropriation was made for "printing and publishing" them and William Cabell Rives, a devoted young friend and admirer of Madison and one of Virginia's most distinguished antebellum statesmen was appointed to prepare the papers for publication. As was customary at a time when the government lacked the facilities for research now provided by the Library of Congress and the National Archives, the manuscripts were loaned to Rives and taken by him to Castle Hill, his Albemarle County estate. There in tranquil retirement from politics and diplomacy that Virginia gentleman pursued the studies of the Father of the Constitution—a labor of love that resulted in 1865 in the publication of four additional volumes of papers and eventually the three-volume biography of Madison. The manuscript titled by Madison "Detached Memoranda" was not included in the former, though quoted and used extensively for reference in the latter. Rives may have considered the memoranda too fragmentary and imperfect to be a part of the collected works of the great man. After

1. Gaillard Hunt, "Aspects of Monopoly One Hundred Years Ago," *Harper's Magazine,* Vol. 128, No. 766, March 1914, 489-490.

> the publication of these volumes the memoranda were lost sight of for a time. Over a period of many years Rives had accumulated his own collection of documents bearing on the formative period of our history, and he had secured for his immediate task loans of material from others. In the course of handling these hundreds of manuscripts it is not surprising that one was misplaced. The Madison Papers went back to Washington while Madison's "Detached Memoranda" remained with the Rives' family papers, where it was found in the spring of 1946, its yellowed pages folded and tied securely with a shoe string.[2]

Another tactic used by religious right authors to discredit the document is to misquote Elizabeth Fleet, making it appear as if she described the entire document as an unfinished, rough draft that Madison intended to correct later. This misquote is then used to support the notion that none of the opinions expressed by Madison in this document can be taken as definitive because he might have decided to change them in the final draft.

> **According to Daniel Dreisbach: "The fragmentary and tentative nature of the document suggests that it was 'hastily jotted down' subsequent to his retirement from the presidency, and it was intended 'to be corrected, expanded, and completed later."**
>
> **Dreisbach's source is James M. O'Neill's 1949 book *Religion and Education Under the Constitution*: "Madison's *Detached Memoranda* contains some interesting passages concerning the First Amendment. However, the weight to be accorded to these passages is a bit hard to determine. The Memoranda was apparently written some time between 1817 and 1832, and is said by Miss Fleet to have been 'hastily jotted down ...to be corrected, expanded, and completed later.' The tentative nature of this document is well-indicat-**

2. Elizabeth Fleet, "Madison's 'Detached Memoranda,'" *William and Mary Quarterly*, 3rd Series, Vol. 3, No. 4, October 1946, 535-536.

ed by the reference in it to the chaplains in Congress. Here Madison takes the position that the Congressional chaplains system violates the Constitution. He does this with no indication that it represents a complete change of mind on his part. He took the opposite position in 1789 when he served as a member of the joint committee to plan the chaplain system...."

What Elizabeth Fleet really said was that *Monopolies, Perpetuities, Corporations, Ecclesiastical Endowments,* as it appeared in both *Harper's* and her article, *was* Madison's final, corrected version. The corrections to this particular essay were made by Madison on the original manuscript, and the copy sold to *Harper's,* of course, contained these corrections. Fleet's point was exactly the opposite of what Dreisbach's and O'Neill's misquote implies. She concluded from the fact that Madison finished correcting this one essay and had a copy prepared for publication, and had made some corrections to other parts of the manuscript, that he had also intended to prepare the rest of the memoranda for publication. The following is the passage from which Dreisbach and O'Neill pluck the words for their misquote.

> All of the memoranda are written in the firm, flowing style of the vigorous Madison while some of the many corrections made in rounded, more studied letters and with different inks suggest revision by the cramped, rheumatic fingers of the aging statesman. Added to these is the fact that a part, copied by amanuensis, was sold to *Harper's Magazine* for publication. The conclusion to be drawn then, is that all the memoranda were hastily jotted down within a few years after Madison's retirement from the presidency to be corrected, expanded, and completed later that posterity might have a truer picture of that early and great period of American history through the eye of one who shaped so much of it.[3]

O'Neill's claim that Madison's opposition to tax-supported chaplains in the *Detached Memoranda* contradicted his position on this in

3. Elizabeth Fleet, "Madison's 'Detached Memoranda,'" *William and Mary Quarterly,* 3rd Series, Vol. 3, No. 4, October 1946, 534-535.

1789 is completely untrue, as will be explained later in this chapter. But, even if Madison had changed his opinion on this issue, and his position in the *Detached Memoranda* really did contradict his earlier position, it would still not support the claim that what Madison wrote in the *Detached Memoranda* was *"tentative"* and subject to change in a final draft. What appears in the manuscript, at least as far as this essay goes, was Madison's final word. This is what he had copied for publication.

Like J.M. O'Neill, most religious right American history authors, after implying that there is some question about the authenticity of the *Detached Memoranda*, go on to tell their readers to disregard the actual content of the document, claiming that the opinions of Madison later in his life don't matter because these opinions were inconsistent with his earlier actions or opinions. Their examples of these inconsistencies, however, are all either exaggerations, half-truths, or lies. The choice of examples varies from author to author. Those authors who give the date of the *Detached Memoranda* as sometime between 1817 and 1832, as most do, generally give examples from Madison's early life, but do not use anything later the 1789 committee referred to by O'Neill. Authors whose examples include anything from Madison's presidency, however, need to make it appear that he didn't write the *Detached Memoranda* until many, many years after he left that office. Obviously, in order for his actions while president to be earlier actions, the date of the *Detached Memoranda* would have to be long after 1817, the year he left the presidency, so these authors describe the time of its writing with vague phrases like *"later in life."* In reality, it was most likely written within five years of his leaving the presidency.

Madison did not date the *Detached Memoranda*. The rough time frame of sometime between between 1817 and 1832, which is used by most historians, was arrived at by combining William Cabell Rives's note that the manuscript was written after Madison left the presidency, and Gaillard Hunt's conclusion in 1914 that *Monopolies, Perpetuities, Corporations, Ecclesiastical Endowments* was written prior to 1832. Hunt based this 1832 date on nothing more than the fact that Madison wrote in the essay that a Catholic priest could never hope to become a chaplain to Congress, and the first Catholic chaplain to Congress was elected in 1832. What Elizabeth Fleet said in her article was that neither Rives or Hunt provided anything more regarding a date than *"subsequent to his retirement from the presidency in 1817"* and *"before 1832."* Although Fleet was merely noting what these other historians had said, the 1817 to 1832 time frame has been used ever since. It must be remembered, however, that Hunt did not see the essay in Madison's handwriting. Fleet herself ruled out a date as late as Hunt's 1832. As she pointed out, Madison's rheumatism caused a noticeable change in his handwriting towards the end of his life, and, with the exception of some of his later corrections, the *Detached Memoranda* is clearly in his earlier handwriting. If Gaillard Hunt, who had just finished editing a new edition of Madison's papers a few years before writing his introduction for *Harper's Magazine,* had seen the manuscript found in 1946, he would known, like Fleet, that it was written much earlier than 1832.

The early end of the 1817 to 1832 time frame can also be moved. This document could not have been written as early as 1817. Madison made a reference in *Monopolies, Perpetuities, Corporations, Ecclesiastical Endowments* to the investigation of charity mismanagement in England by the Brougham Commission. Parliament member Henry Brougham didn't publish his accusations against these charitable institutions until 1818, and his commission didn't get under way until 1819. The fact that Madison referred to this in the past tense, saying that the management of these charities had *"been lately scrutinized,"* indicates that he wrote it at some point after the Brougham Commission made its first report. Between this, the handwriting, and a few other clues,[4]

4. One interesting thing that indicates a date in the early part of the 1820s is that Madison wrote about, but did not acknowledge being the author of, his 1785 Memorial and Remonstrance against religious assessments in Virginia. Madison wrote this document anonymously, and, although it was widely suspected from the start that he was its author, he refused to publicly acknowledge the fact for over four decades. The year he began to acknowledge it as his was 1826. A July 1826 letter from George Mason (grandson of the Constitutional Convention delegate and Virginia constitution author) apparently convinced Madison that it was important that people know he was the author. Mason, who had come across a copy of the Memorial and Remonstrance, and was distributing it in an effort to combat the rise in religious fanaticism at that time, wrote to Madison that he was about to print a larger edition, and wanted to put his name on it. Mason, however, was not a hundred percent sure that Madison had written it, and wanted confirmation. Mason's words, such as "It is from such papers as this that posterity will draw their maxims of Religious, as from the early papers of our Revolution their axioms of political & civil, liberty," caused Madison to break his forty year silence and take credit for the document. Madison wrote back to Mason, confirming that he had been the author, and that the elder George Mason had been one of the two men who had asked him to write it. The fact that Madison did not acknowledge this in the Detached Memoranda seems to indicate not only that he wrote it before July 1826, but that he made his changes to it before that time.

the date of *Detached Memoranda* can be narrowed with a reasonable degree of certainty to the early part of the 1820s.

Most of Madison's corrections to *Monopolies, Perpetuities, Corporations, Ecclesiastical Endowments* were merely grammatical, and did not alter the meaning of the document. The few changes that did affect its meaning, however, rather than toning down or retracting anything, actually made Madison's statements stronger.

In a sentence referring to his reluctant compliance with Congress's requests that he proclaim fast days and thanksgiving days during the War of 1812, Madison made the following changes, obviously realizing upon rereading his words that in order to *weaken* a political right, that right had to exist in the first place. (The bold, underlined words in these quotes replaced the struck out words, or were inserted between words.)

> It was thought not proper to refuse a compliance altogether; but a form & language were employed, which were meant to ~~weaken~~ **deaden** as much as possible any **claim of** political right to enjoin religious observances...[5]

In a statement opposing chaplains in the military, he said that although it could be argued that they were necessary because those serving in the military, particularly sailors on ships, might have no other access to religious worship, the practice was still a dangerous mixture of religion and government. Madison apparently changed his original words, which referred to separating religion from government as a *"good principle,"* because they implied that this was merely a good idea, rather than a clear constitutional principle.

> But is it not safer to adhere to a ~~good~~ **right** principle, and trust to its consequences, than confide in the reasoning however specious in favor of a ~~bad~~ **wrong** one?[6]

To the beginning of a sentence referring to attempts by churches to incorporate, get land grants from the government, and be exempted from taxes, Madison added a clause to emphasize the fact that several

5. *The James Madison Papers at the Library of Congress, Series 2, Additional Correspondence and Related Items,* Library of Congress Manuscript Division.
6. *ibid.*

such things had somehow managed to get as far as making it through Congress, in spite of the fact that they were clearly unconstitutional. Madison noted among his examples of this to see his vetoes of the bills, which, although violating the First Amendment, had reached his desk while he was president.

> **Strongly guarded as is the separation between Religion & Govt in the Constitution of the United States**, ~~T~~**t**he danger of encroachment by Ecclesiastical Bodies, may be illustrated by precedents already furnished in their short history.[7]

Referring to the unsuccessful attempt in 1786 by a minority of delegates in the Virginia Assembly to insert the name Jesus Christ in the preamble to the *Bill for Establishing Religious Freedom,* Madison turned what was originally just a description of the effect of this would have had into an accusation that it was the deliberate object of these delegates to restrict the religious freedom intended by the bill.

> ...by proposing to insert the words "Jesus Christ" after the words "our lord" in the preamble, the ~~effect~~ **object** of which, ~~would have been~~ **was** to imply a restriction of the liberty defined in the Bill, to those professing his religion **only**.[8]

Madison covered many topics related to religion and government in the *Detached Memoranda.* Religious right American history authors, however, are only concerned about two of these – tax-supported chaplains and government proclamations of days of prayer and thanksgiving. This is because their biggest arguments in favor of school prayer, religious displays on public property, etc., are that Congress has chaplains and most of our early presidents proclaimed days of prayer and thanksgiving.

The following is what Madison wrote in the *Detached Memoranda*

7. *The James Madison Papers at the Library of Congress, Series 2, Additional Correspondence and Related Items,* Library of Congress Manuscript Division.

8. *ibid.* Madison obviously intended to replace the words "would have been" with the word "was." Although he very clearly wrote the word "was" above "would have been," he neglected to cross out the words "would have been." Because of this, the words "would have been" were left in by both Fleet and the transcriber of the copy that was sold to Harper Brothers. With Madison's other change of the word "effect" to the word "object," it was his clearly his intention to make the other change, and failing to cross out "would have been" was simply an oversight.

on the subject of chaplains.

On chaplains to Congress:

> Is the appointment of Chaplains to the two Houses of Congress consistent with the Constitution, and with the pure principle of religious freedom?
>
> In strictness the answer on both points must be in the negative. The Constitution of the U. S. forbids everything like an establishment of a national religion. The law appointing Chaplains establishes a religious worship for the national representatives, to be performed by Ministers of religion, elected by a majority of them; and these are to be paid out of the national taxes. Does not this involve the principle of a national establishment, applicable to a provision for a religious worship for the Constituent as well as of the representative Body, approved by the majority, and conducted by Ministers of religion paid by the entire nation.
>
> The establishment of the chaplainship to Congs is a palpable violation of equal rights, as well as of Constitutional principles: The tenets of the chaplains elected shut the door of worship agst the members whose creeds & consciences forbid a participation in that of the majority. To say nothing of other sects, this is the case with that of Roman Catholics & Quakers who have always had members in one or both of the Legislative branches. Could a Catholic clergyman ever hope to be appointed a Chaplain? To say that his religious principles are obnoxious or that his sect is small, is to lift the evil at once and exhibit in its naked deformity the doctrine that religious truth is to be tested by numbers, or that the major sects have a right to govern the minor.
>
> If Religion consist in voluntary acts of individuals, singly, or voluntarily associated, and it be proper that public functionaries, as well as their Constituents shd discharge their

> religious duties, let them like their Constituents, do so at their own expense. How small a contribution from each member of Congs wd suffice for the purpose? How just wd it be in its principle? How noble in its exemplary sacrifice to the genius of the Constitution; and the divine right of conscience? Why should the expence of a religious worship be allowed for the Legislature, be paid by the public, more than that for the Ex. or Judiciary branch of the Govt.
>
> Were the establishment to be tried by its fruits, are not the daily devotions conducted by these legal Ecclesiastics, already degenerating into a scanty attendance, and a tiresome formality?[9]

On chaplains in the military:

> Better also to disarm in the same way, the precedent of Chaplainships for the army and navy, than erect them into a political authority in matters of religion. The object of this establishment is seducing; the motive to it is laudable. But is it not safer to adhere to a right principle, and trust to its consequences, than confide in the reasoning however specious in favor of a wrong one. Look thro' the armies & navies of the world, and say whether in the appointment of their ministers of religion, the spiritual interest of the flocks or the temporal interest of the Shepherds, be most in view: whether here, as elsewhere the political care of religion is not a nominal more than a real aid. If the spirit of armies be devout, the spirit out of the armies will never be less so; and a failure of religious instruction &, exhortation from a voluntary source within or without, will rarely happen: and if such be not the spirit of armies, the official services of their Teachers are not likely to produce it. It is more likely to flow from the labours of a spontaneous zeal. The armies of the Puritans had their appointed Chaplains; but without these there would have been no lack of public devotion in that devout age.

9. Elizabeth Fleet, "Madison's 'Detached Memoranda,'" *William and Mary Quarterly,* 3rd Series, Vol. 3, No. 4, October 1946, 558-559.

> The case of navies with insulated crews may be less within the scope of these reflections. But it is not entirely so. The chance of a devout officer, might be of as much worth to religion, as the service of an ordinary chaplain. But we are always to keep in mind that it is safer to trust the consequences of a right principle, than reasonings in support of a bad one.[10]

The usual religious right response Madison's arguments against tax-supported chaplains in the *Detached Memoranda* is to point out that he was on the 1789 committee mentioned by J.M. O'Neill. This is one of the many lies about James Madison created by implying that he agreed with every decision of every legislative body or committee that he ever sat on – simply because he was there. In order to use this committee as evidence that Madison supported tax-supported chaplains in 1789, however, his presence alone isn't enough. The purpose of the committee also has to be misrepresented.

> **According to David Barton, in his book *Original Intent*: "...in 1789, Madison served on the Congressional committee which authorized, approved, and selected paid Congressional chaplains."**

This committee had nothing to do with deciding whether or not Congress would have chaplains. That precedent had been set by the Continental Congress and was not going to change. This committee had nothing to do with selecting the chaplains either.

At the request of the Senate in April 1789, a joint committee was appointed to write a set of rules for conferences between the two houses of Congress. One of the House members elected to this committee was, of course, James Madison. Because the Senate and the House were going to be sharing chaplains, this same joint committee was also charged with the task of coming up with rules regulating their appointment. This was the committee's only involvement with chaplains.

The following, from *Debates and Proceedings of Congress,* April 9, 1789, is Barton's source for his claim that the committee, and James

10. Elizabeth Fleet, "Madison's 'Detached Memoranda,'" *William and Mary Quarterly,* 3rd Series, Vol. 3, No. 4, October 1946, 559-560.

Madison, by virtue of being appointed to the committee, *"authorized, approved, and selected"* chaplains.

> The Speaker laid before the House a letter from Oliver Elsworth, Esq. a member of the Senate, stating the appointment of a committee of that House to confer with a committee to be appointed on the part of this House, in preparing a system of rules to govern the two Houses in cases of conference, and to regulate the appointment of Chaplains.
>
> Whereupon, Messrs. Boudinot, Sherman, Tucker, Madison, and Bland, were elected by ballot for that purpose.[11]

Madison never approved of tax-supported chaplains. His opinion in 1789, as well as when he wrote the *Detached Memoranda,* was that if members of Congress wanted to hire chaplains, they should do so with their own money. He also objected to the official election of chaplains by Congress, which he considered to be a government endorsement of the majority religion of that body.

In 1822, Madison wrote a letter to Edward Livingston, a member of the Louisiana legislature. Livingston was one of three legal scholars commissioned to revise the laws of the state of Louisiana, which, up until that time, had been a confusing mixture of the Napoleonic Code, civil law written by the legislature, and a smattering of common law that had made its way there from other states. Livingston sent Madison a copy of a pamphlet he had written on the plan for the revisal. After complimenting Livingston on the manner in which he proposed to keep religion out of Louisiana's new law code, Madison went on to express the same opinions on chaplains and thanksgiving proclamations found in the *Detached Memoranda.* In this same letter, he also explicitly stated that he had not approved of tax-supported chaplains in 1789.

> I observe with particular pleasure the view you have taken on the immunity of Religion from civil jurisdiction, in every case where it does not trespass on private rights or the public peace. This has always been a favorite principle with me;

11. *The Debates and Proceedings of the Congress of the United States of America*, vol. 1, 1st Cong., 1st Sess., (Washington D.C.: Gales & Seaton, 1834), 109.

> and it was not with my approbation, that the deviation from it took place in Congress, when they appointed chaplains, to be paid from the National Treasury. It would have been a much better proof to their constituents of their pious feeling if the members had contributed for the purpose, a pittance from their own pockets. As the precedent is not likely to be rescinded, the best that can now be done may be to apply to the Constitution the maxim of the law, *de minimis non curat.*[12]

In a statement similar to the last sentence of this paragraph from his letter to Livingston, Madison wrote the following in the *Detached Memoranda.* In that document, as in the letter, it appeared immediately after his opinion on tax-supported chaplains.

> Rather than let this step beyond the landmarks of power have the effect of a legitimate precedent, it will be better to apply to it the legal aphorism de minimis non curat lex [the law does not concern itself with trifles]: or to class it "cum maculis quas aut incuria fudit, aut humana parum cavit natura [faults proceeding either from negligence or from the imperfection of our nature]."[13]

Madison had good reason to be concerned about tax-supported chaplains being considered a legitimate precedent. The existence of these chaplains had already become a favorite argument among the religious right of his day. The arguments used by today's religious right to justify Ten Commandments monuments in courthouses and "under God" in the Pledge of Allegiance are not new. They began appearing during the 1810s and 1820s in the battles over issues such as Sunday mail delivery. What Madison undoubtedly found most alarming, however, was that things like chaplains in Congress were being claimed as precedents not only by religious organizations, but by members of Congress. One of the first instances of this occurred in 1811, when

12. James Madison to Edward Livingston, July 10, 1822, *Letters and Other Writings of James Madison,* vol. 3, (New York: R. Worthington, 1884), 274.

13. Elizabeth Fleet, "Madison's 'Detached Memoranda,'" *William and Mary Quarterly,* 3rd Series, Vol. 3, No. 4, October 1946, 559.

Madison vetoed *An act incorporating the Protestant Episcopal Church in the town of Alexandria, in the District of Columbia.*

Madison's reasons for this veto, which are found later in this chapter, were accepted by the majority of the House. Many of the representatives of 1811 had just never given much thought to the First Amendment's establishment clause before this, and hadn't realized that the bill violated it. One even made a comment often heard today – that he had always thought the amendment meant only that a national religion couldn't be established. The majority of the House, after reading Madison's veto message, decided that he understood the First Amendment better than they did, and wanted to drop the bill. Some, however, wanted to take another vote and try to override the veto. This minority included Laban Wheaton, a representative from Massachusetts, who presented an argument as melodramatic as any heard from today's religious right, warning that the failure of this bill would lead to religion being banned altogether in the entire District of Columbia. One thing Wheaton used to justify the bill, of course, was the appointment of tax-supported chaplains by the first Congress.

> Mr. W. said he did not consider the bill any infringement of the Constitution. If it was, both branches of the Legislature, since the commencement of the government, had been guilty of such infringement. It could not be said, indeed, that they had been guilty of doing much about religion; but they had at every session appointed Chaplains, to be of different denominations, to interchange weekly between the Houses. Now, if a bill for regulating the funds of a religious society could be an infringement of the Constitution, the two Houses had so far infringed it by electing, paying or contracting with their Chaplains. For so far it established two different denominations of religion. Mr. W. deemed this question of very great consequence. Were the people of this District never to have any religion? Was it to be entirely excluded from these ten miles square?[14]

Laban Wheaton was apparently unable to convince the majority of the House that religion was in danger, or that the existence of chap-

14. *The Debates and Proceedings of the Congress of the United States of America*, vol. 22, 11th Cong., 3rd Sess., (Washington D.C.: Gales & Seaton, 1853), 984.

lains justified further violations of the First Amendment. When another vote was taken on the bill, it failed 74-29.[15]

Remarkably, what Madison called a *"step beyond the landmarks of power"* that should not have *"the effect of a legitimate precedent"* has appeared in the opinions of a number of Supreme Court justices, one even invoking Madison's name and implying that he voted in favor of paying chaplains.

> **According to Justice Reed, in his dissenting opinion, McCollum v. Board of Education, 1948: "The practices of the federal government offer many examples of this kind of 'aid' by the state to religion. The Congress of the United States has a chaplain for each House who daily invokes divine blessings and guidance for the proceedings. The armed forces have commissioned chaplains from early days."**

> **According to Justice Burger, delivering the opinion of the court, Lynch v. Donnelly, 1984: "In the very week that Congress approved the Establishment Clause as part of the Bill of Rights for submission to the states, it enacted legislation providing for paid Chaplains for the House and Senate." and "It is clear that neither the 17 draftsmen of the Constitution who were Members of the First Congress, nor the Congress of 1789, saw any establishment problem in the employment of congressional Chaplains to offer daily prayers in the Congress, a practice that has continued for nearly two centuries. It would be difficult to identify a more striking example of the accommodation of religious belief intended by the Framers."**

> **Justice Burger, in his dissenting opinion, Wallace v. Jaffree, 1985: "Some who trouble to read the opinions in these cases will find it ironic - perhaps even bizarre - that on the very day we heard arguments in**

15. *The Debates and Proceedings of the Congress of the United States of America,* vol. 22, 11th Cong., 3rd Sess., (Washington D.C.: Gales & Seaton, 1853), 997.

> **the cases, the Court's session opened with an invocation for Divine protection. Across the park a few hundred yards away, the House of Representatives and the Senate regularly open each session with a prayer. These legislative prayers are not just one minute in duration, but are extended, thoughtful invocations and prayers for Divine guidance. They are given, as they have been since 1789, by clergy appointed as official chaplains and paid from the Treasury of the United States."**

Justice Burger, in his footnote to a misleading description of the 1789 committee in *Marsh v. Chambers,* 1983, not only implied that Madison's appointment to that committee somehow indicated his approval of chaplains, but that he approved of paying them with public money by voting for the bill authorizing their payment. In order to give this impression, Burger made it sound as if Madison voted for an individual bill whose sole purpose was authorizing the payment of chaplains. There was no such bill. Chaplains were just among the many employees listed in *An Act for allowing compensation to the members of the Senate and House of Representatives of the United States, and to the officers of both Houses,*[16] which, of course, Madison did vote for.

> **According to Justice Burger's footnote: "It bears note that James Madison, one of the principal advocates of religious freedom in the Colonies and a drafter of the Establishment Clause,...was one of those appointed to undertake this task by the House of Representatives...and voted for the bill authorizing payment of the chaplains."**
>
> **Justice Scalia, in his dissenting opinion, Lee v. Weisman, 1992, referred to Marsh v. Chambers: "As we detailed in Marsh, congressional sessions have opened with a chaplain's prayer ever since the First Congress."**

16. Richard Peters, ed., *The Public Statutes at Large of the United States of America*, vol. 1, (Boston: Charles C. Little and James Brown, 1845), 71.

The last of the many subjects addressed by Madison in *Monopolies, Perpetuities, Corporations, Ecclesiastical Endowments,* and one of the two mentioned by the religious right American history authors, was proclamations of national days of prayer.

> Religious proclamations by the Executive recommending thanksgivings & fasts are shoots from the same root with the legislative acts reviewed.
>
> Altho' recommendations only, they imply a religious agency, making no part of the trust delegated to political rulers.
>
> The objections to them are: 1. that Govts ought not to interpose in relation to those subject to their authority but in cases where they can do it with effect. An *advisory* Govt is a contradiction in terms. 2. The members of a Govt as such can in no sense, be regarded as possessing an advisory trust from their Constituents in their religious capacities. They cannot form an ecclesiastical Assembly, Convocation, Council, or Synod, and as such issue decrees or injunctions addressed to the faith or the Consciences of the people. In their individual capacities, as distinct from their official station, they might unite in recommendations of any sort whatever, in the same manner as any other individuals might do. But then their recommendations ought to express the true character from which they emanate. 3. They seem to imply and certainly nourish the erronious idea of a *national* religion. The idea just as it related to the Jewish nation under a theocracy, having been improperly adopted by so many nations which have embraced Xnity, is too apt to lurk in the bosoms even of Americans, who in general are aware of the distinction between religious & political societies. The idea also of a union of all to form one nation under one Govt in acts of devotion to the God of all is an imposing idea. But reason and the principles of the Xn religion require that all the individuals composing a nation even of the same precise creed & wished to unite in a universal act of religion at the same time, the union ought to be effected thro' the inter-

vention of their religious not of their political representatives. In a nation composed of various sects, some alienated widely from others, and where no agreement could take place thro' the former, the interposition of the latter is doubly wrong: 4. The tendency of the practice, to narrow the recommendation to the standard of the predominant sect. The 1st proclamation of Genl Washington dated Jany 1. 1795 (see if this was the 1st)[17] recommending a day of thanksgiving, embraced all who believed in a supreme ruler of the Universe. That of Mr. Adams called for a *Xn* worship. Many private letters reproached the Proclamations issued by J. M. for using general terms, used in that of Presidt W–n; and some of them for not inserting particulars according with the faith of certain Xn sects. The practice if not strictly guarded naturally terminates in a conformity to the creed of the majority and a single sect, if amounting to a majority. 5. The last & not the least objection is the liability of the practice to a subserviency to political views; to the scandal of religion, as well as the increase of party animosities. Candid or incautious politicians will not always disown such views. In truth it is difficult to frame such a religious Proclamation generally suggested by a political State of things, without referring to them in terms having some bearing on party questions. The Proclamation of Pres: W. which was issued just after the suppression of the Insurrection in Penna and at a time when the public mind was divided on several topics, was so construed by many. Of this the Secretary of State himself, E. Randolph seems to have had an anticipation.

The original draught of that Instrument filed in the Dept. of State (see copies of these papers on the files of J. M.)[18] in

17. Madison never did check to see if this was the first before having this copied for publication. It was actually the second. Washington, at the request of Congress, issued a proclamation for a day of thanksgiving in October 1789. Apparently, Madison, who was a member of Congress at the time, forgot about this. Madison's note, which appears in Fleet's 1946 transcription, does not appear in the 1914 Harper's Magazine publication of the essay. The January 1, 1795 is what appeared in 1914.

18. This note is also omitted in the 1914 publication.

> the hand writing of Mr Hamilton the Secretary of the Treasury. It appears that several slight alterations only had been made at the suggestion of the Secretary of State; and in a marginal note in his hand, it is remarked that "In short this proclamation ought to savour as much as possible of religion, & not too much of having a political object." In a subjoined note in the hand of Mr. Hamilton, this remark is answered by the counter-remark that "A proclamation of a Government which is a national act, naturally embraces objects which are political" so naturally, is the idea of policy associated with religion, whatever be the mode or the occasion, when a function of the latter is assumed by those in power.
>
> During the administration of Mr Jefferson no religious proclamation was issued. It being understood that his successor was disinclined to such interpositions of the Executive and by some supposed moreover that they might originate with more propriety with the Legislative Body, a resolution was passed requesting him to issue a proclamation.
>
> It was thought not proper to refuse a compliance altogether; but a form & language were employed, which were meant to deaden as much as possible any claim of political right to enjoin religious observances by resting these expressly on the voluntary compliance of individuals, and even by limiting the recommendation to such as wished simultaneous as well as voluntary performance of a religious act on the occasion.[19]

Religious right American history authors are quick to point out the fact that Madison, although denouncing the practice in the *Detached Memoranda,* did make a few prayer day proclamations while he was president. They completely ignore, however, that he indicated in the *Detached Memoranda* and elsewhere that, although reluctantly complying with the requests from Congress, he never liked this practice.

19. Elizabeth Fleet, "Madison's 'Detached Memoranda,'" *William and Mary Quarterly,* 3rd Series, Vol. 3, No. 4, October 1946, 560-562.

According to David Barton, in his book *Original Intent*: "...throughout his Presidency (1809-1816), Madison endorsed public and official religious expressions by issuing several proclamations for national days of prayer, fasting, and thanksgiving."

Madison's compliance with Congress's requests can hardly be considered an endorsement of official religious expression. He obviously wished this practice had never been started, but thought it *"not proper to refuse a compliance altogether"* when Congress asked him to do it during the War of 1812. Madison did not regularly make these proclamations *"throughout his presidency,"* as Barton claims. He issued none during the three years before the war, and none during the two years following it. Those that he did issue were so general and unauthoritative, or, as Madison put it, *"mere designations of a day,"* that they were objected to many religious leaders. In his 1813 proclamation, he even included the following statement about the separation between church and state.

> If the public homage of a people can ever be worthy the favorable regard of the Holy and Omniscient Being to whom it is addressed, it must be that in which those who join in it are guided only by their free choice, by the impulse of their hearts and the dictates of their consciences; and such a spectacle must be interesting to all Christian nations as proving that religion, that gift of Heaven for the good of man, freed from all coercive edicts, from that unhallowed connection with the powers of this world which corrupts religion into an instrument or an usurper of the policy of the state, and making no appeal but to reason, to the heart, and to the conscience, can spread its benign influence everywhere and can attract to the divine altar those freewill offerings of humble supplication, thanksgiving, and praise which alone can be acceptable to Him whom no hypocrisy can deceive and no forced sacrifices propitiate.[20]

20. Proclamation of July 23, 1813, *The Debates and Proceedings of the Congress of the United States of America*, vol. 27, 13th Cong., Appendix, (Washington D.C.: Gales & Seaton, 1854), 2674.

Madison made it very clear that he was addressing these proclamations only to people who were already religious and would want to use such a day for religious purposes. In one, he addressed "*the several religious denominations and societies so disposed*;" in another, "*all who shall be piously disposed.*" In effect, he was merely making an announcement to those who wanted to take part, rather than a recommendation to those who didn't.

Obviously, Madison considered himself to be capable of honoring the requests of Congress without crossing any constitutional line. He was very aware, however, that not all presidents had been, or would be, as careful in their wording as he was. This had already been proven by John Adams, whose proclamations were not only objected to for violating the First Amendment, but were seen as politically motivated. One of Adams's proclamations actually caused a riot in Philadelphia on the day appointed for the fast. The difficulty of separating these proclamations from political issues was, of course, Madison's fifth objection to them in the *Detached Memoranda.*

It was undoubtedly Adams that Madison was referring to when he noted in his 1822 letter to Edward Livingston that there had already been a "*deviation*" from the Constitution in these executive proclamations.

> There has been another deviation from the strict principle in the Executive proclamations of fasts and festivals, so far, at least, as they have spoken the language of *injunction,* or have lost sight of the equality of *all* religious sects in the eye of the Constitution. Whilst I was honored with the executive trust, I found it necessary on more than one occasion to follow the example of predecessors. But I was always careful to make the Proclamations absolutely indiscriminate, and merely recommendatory; or rather mere *designations* of a day on which all who thought proper might *unite* in consecrating it to religious purposes, according to their own faith and forms.[21]

In the *Detached Memoranda,* Madison wrote that it was understood

21. James Madison to Edward Livingston, July 10, 1822, *Letters and Other Writings of James Madison,* vol. 3, (New York: R. Worthington, 1884), 274-275.

that he *"was disinclined to such interpositions of the Executive."* After not issuing a single fast or thanksgiving day proclamation during the first three years of his presidency, Madison knew that it was generally assumed by the clergy that he was following the example of Jefferson, and would refuse if asked. Madison was apparently correct about this. As Benjamin Rush explained to John Adams, the General Assembly of the Presbyterian Church did not think Madison would agree to issue a proclamation when the War of 1812 began, so they didn't even bother to request one.

> The General Assembly of the Presbyterian Church have just finished a long and interesting session. Among other things done by them, they have addressed a petition to Congress praying that the post offices may not be opened on the Sabbath day. A vote was lost in the Assembly for petitioning the President to appoint a national fast. It was objected to only because a majority believed it would not be attended with success.[22]

The Presbyterians were probably right. It's a pretty safe bet that Madison, like Jefferson, would have refused the request if it had come from a religious organization.

James H. Hutson, in the companion book to his 1998 *Religion and the Founding of the American Republic* exhibit at the Library of Congress, does a little speculating about the reasons for Madison's alleged inconsistencies on chaplains and prayer days – citing unnamed critics who accused Madison of sacrificing his constitutional principles for political popularity, and conjuring up a tension between Madison's religious and constitutional views.

> **According to Hutson: "In his Detached Memoranda Madison criticized the religious policies he approved as a member of Congress and followed as president—the appointment of chaplains and the proclamations of days of fasting and thanksgiving—suggesting there may**

22. Benjamin Rush to John Adams, June 4, 1812, John A Shultz and Douglass Adair, eds., *The Spur of Fame: Dialogues of John Adams and Benjamin Rush, 1805-1813,* (Indianapolis: Liberty Fund, 1999), 242.

> **have been some substance to the charges of critics that he was an opportunist, ever willing to sacrifice his constitutional convictions for political popularity. On the other hand, there seems to have been a tension between Madison's religious and constitutional views that may account for the statements in the Detached Memoranda."**

Hutson goes on to claim that Madison *"approved the results of"* the religious revivals that were going on in the early part of the 1800s. In reality, however, the fanaticism produced by these revivals, and the resulting efforts of religious organizations and legislators to push religion into the government, was probably what prompted Madison to write such an extensive essay about the dangers of mixing religion and government at this time. To support his claim, Hutson quotes a few phrases out of context from a letter written by Madison in 1819, not long, of course, before he wrote *Detached Memoranda.*

> **According to Hutson: "Madison approved the results of the revivals that rolled through Virginia during the early years of the nineteenth century. In a letter written in 1819 he seemed to relish the troubles of the Anglican—now Episcopal—church, whose places of worship, 'built under the establishment at the public expense, have in many instances gone to ruin, or are in a very dilapidated state, owing chiefly to a desertion of the flocks to other worships.' That the defecting evangelical flocks gathered in 'Meeting Houses...of the plainest and cheapest sort' was, for Madison, a recommendation, not a reproach. He believed that 'on a general comparison of the present and former times the balance is clearly and vastly on the side of the present, as to the number of religious teachers, the zeal which actuates them, the purity of their lives, and the attendance of the people on their instructions.' Although there is no evidence that Madison was a closet evangelical, it seems apparent that, late in life, he retained substantial sympathy for the doctrine of the new birth**

and for its social consequences that he had learned long ago at Princeton.

The 1819 letter quoted by Hutson was not about the religious revivals of the time. Madison was comparing the condition of Virginia's churches during the establishment of the Anglican Church to their condition since being free of established religion. These were the *"present and former times"* he was referring to. Madison's letter was to Robert Walsh, a journalist and publisher, founder of the magazine *American Review of History and Politics* and the Philadelphia newspaper the *National Gazette,* and later, Consul General of the United States in Paris. In 1819, Walsh, in an effort to correct the misconceptions that the people of England had of the United States, was writing a book entitled *Appeal from the Judgment of Great Britain Respecting the United States.* In February of that year, Walsh sent James Madison a request for information about Virginia for his book. One of Walsh's questions was about the state of religion in Virginia since the disestablishment of the Anglican Church during the Revolution. The following was Madison's entire answer to that question, a completely objective description of the condition of churches in Virginia, from which James Hutson plucks a few phrases to create his story about Madison's *"substantial sympathy for the doctrine of the new birth."*

> That there has been an increase of religious instruction since the Revolution, can admit of no question. The English church was originally the established religion; the character of the clergy, that above described.[23] Of other sects there were but few adherents, except the Presbyterians, who predominated on the West side of the Blue Mountains. A little time previous to the Revolutionary struggle the Baptists sprang up, and made a very rapid progress. Among the

23. Earlier in the letter, Madison gave the following description of the Virginia clergy prior to disestablishment of the Anglican Church: "The indolence of most, and the irregular lives of many, of the established clergy, consisting, in a very large proportion, of foreigners, and these, in no inconsiderable proportion, of men willing to leave their homes in the parent country, where their demerit was an obstacle to a provision for them, and whose degeneracy here was promoted by their distance from the controuling eyes of their kindred and friends; by the want of Ecclesiastical superiors in the Colony, or efficient ones in G. Britain, who might maintain a salutary discipline among them; and finally, by their independence both of their congregations and of the civil authority for their stipends."

early acts of the Republican Legislature were those abolishing the Religious establishment, and putting all sects at full liberty and on a perfect level. At present, the population is divided, with small exceptions, among the Protestant Episcopalians, the Presbyterians, the Baptists, and the Methodists. Of their comparative numbers I can command no sources of information. I conjecture the Presbyterians and Baptists to form each about a third, and the two other sects together, of which the Methodists are much the smallest, to make up the remaining third. The old churches, built under the establishment at the public expence, have in many instances gone to ruin, or are in a very dilapidated state, owing chiefly to a transition of the flocks to other worships. A few new ones have latterly been built, particularly in the towns. Among the other sects, Meeting Houses, have multiplied and continue to multiply; though in general they are of the plainest and cheapest sort. But neither the number nor the style of the religious edifices is a true measure of the state of religion. Religious instruction is now diffused throughout the community by preachers of every sect, with almost equal zeal, though with very unequal acquirements; and at private houses, and open stations, and occasionally in such as are appropriated to civil use, as well as buildings appropriated to that use. The qualifications of the preachers, too, among the new sects where there was the greatest deficiency, are understood to be improving. On a general comparison of the present and former times, the balance is certainly vastly on the side of the present, as to the number of religious teachers, the zeal which actuates them, the purity of their lives, and the attendance of the people on their instructions. It was the universal opinion of the century preceding the last, that civil Government could not stand without the prop of a religious establishment, and that the Christian religion itself would perish if not supported by a legal provision for its Clergy. The experience of Virginia conspicuously corroborates the disproof of both opinions. The civil Government, though bereft of everything like an associated hierarchy; possesses the requisite stability, and per-

> forms its functions with complete success; whilst the number, the industry, and the morality of the Priesthood, and the devotion of the people have been manifestly increased by the total separation of the church from the State.[24]

While Madison went along with Congress's prayer day requests, he did not go along with the three bills they passed during his presidency that violated the First Amendment. Madison, as mentioned earlier, noted in the *Detached Memoranda* to see these three bills as examples of the *"danger of encroachment by Ecclesiastical Bodies."*

> Strongly guarded as is the separation between Religion & Govt in the Constitution of the United States the danger of encroachment by Ecclesiastical Bodies, may be illustrated by precedents already furnished in their short history. (See the cases in which negatives were put by J.M. on two bills passed by Congs and his signature withheld from another. See also attempt in Kentucky for example, where it was proposed to exempt houses of worship from taxes.)[25]

The first veto, dated February 21, 1811, was of *An act incorporating the Protestant Episcopal Church in the town of Alexandria, in the District of Columbia.*

This was actually the second time Madison prevented this same church from incorporating. In 1784, the Virginia House of Delegates had voted in favor of a bill to incorporate the church, but then decided to postpone its passage until their next session. The reason for the postponement was the uncertain future of Patrick Henry's bill to assess a tax for the support of Christian ministers. The House of Delegates decided to distribute copies of Henry's bill throughout the commonwealth first, and wait for the reaction of the people before taking further action on either bill. At the same time, Madison's *Memorial and Remonstrance* against Henry's bill was also

24. James Madison to Robert Walsh, March 2, 1819, *Letters and Other Writings of James Madison*, vol. 3, (New York: R. Worthington, 1884), 124-125.

25. Elizabeth Fleet, "Madison's 'Detached Memoranda,'" *William and Mary Quarterly*, 3rd Series, Vol. 3, No. 4, October 1946, 555.

Madison's note to see his veto messages, etc., was apparently included in the final version of the essay, and did appear as a footnote in the 1914 *Harper's Magazine* publication.

circulated. The response of the people, after reading both the bill and Madison's objections to it, was an overwhelming three to one against the assessment. After Henry's bill was defeated, Madison reintroduced Thomas Jefferson's *Bill for Establishing Religious Freedom,* which had been written in 1777, but never passed. This time it passed, becoming law in 1786, and making the incorporation of any church in Virginia out of the question. Madison had also written a petition on behalf of the members of the church, the majority of whom opposed their clergy on the incorporation. This petition, however, became unnecessary once the religious freedom bill was passed. In 1811, of course, Alexandria was part of the District of Columbia, so when this same *Protestant Episcopal Church* once again tried to incorporate, the matter ended up before Congress, and Madison, this time with his veto, once again prevented it from doing so.

One of Madison's many problems with church incorporations was that they require laws to be made regarding the rules, procedures, and even the mode of worship of a church. The bill to incorporate this church dictated things such as the election and removal of ministers and vestrymen, and the requirements to be eligible to vote in church elections. It also prohibited this individual church from doing anything that was inconsistent with *"any rule or canon of the Protestant Episcopal Church of the State of Virginia."*

Madison's other big objection to this particular bill was that it included a provision which would give the church a legal agency in carrying out charitable works, which he feared might set a precedent for giving religious organizations *"a legal agency in carrying into effect a public and civil duty."* If Madison thought this was unconstitutional when it didn't even involve government money, faith-based initiatives must have him rolling in his grave.

The following was Madison's February 21, 1811 veto message to the House of Representatives.

> To the House of Representatives of the United States:
>
> Having examined and considered the bill entitled "An Act incorporating the Protestant Episcopal Church in the town of Alexandria, in the District of Columbia," I now return the bill

to the House of Representatives, in which it originated, with the following objections:

Because the bill exceeds the rightful authority to which governments are limited by the essential distinction between civil and religious functions, and violates, in particular, the article of the Constitution of the United States, which declares, that "Congress shall make no law respecting a religious establishment." The bill enacts into, and establishes by law, sundry rules and proceedings relative purely to the organization and polity of the church incorporated, and comprehending even the election and removal of the Minister of the same; so that no change could be made therein by the particular society, or by the general church of which it is a member, and whose authority it recognizes. This particular church, therefore, would so far be a religious establishment by law; a legal force and sanction being given to certain articles in its constitution and administration. Nor can it be considered, that the articles thus established are to be taken as the descriptive criteria only of the corporate identity of the society, inasmuch as this identity must depend on other characteristics; as the regulations established are generally unessential, and alterable according to the principles and canons, by which churches of that denomination govern themselves; and as the injunctions and prohibitions contained in the regulations would be enforced by the penal consequences applicable to a violation of them according to the local law;

Because the bill vests in the said incorporated church an authority to provide for the support of the poor, and the education of poor children of the same; an authority which being altogether superfluous if the provision is to be the result of pious charity, would be a precedent for giving to religious societies, as such, a legal agency in carrying into effect a public and civil duty.[26]

26. *The Debates and Proceedings of the Congress of the United States of America,* vol. 22, 11th Cong., 3rd Sess., (Washington D.C.: Gales & Seaton, 1853), 982-983.

Madison's second veto, dated February 28, 1811, was of *An act for the relief of Richard Tervin, William Coleman, Edwin Lewis, Samuel Mims, Joseph Wilson, and the Baptist Church at Salem Meeting House, in the Mississippi Territory.* Madison's objection to this bill was that it contained a land grant to a church.

> Because the bill, in reserving a certain parcel of land of the United States for the use of said Baptist Church, comprises a principle and precedent, for the appropriation of funds of the United States, for the use and support of religious societies; contrary to the article of the Constitution which declares that Congress shall make no law respecting a religious establishment.[27]

Since the land grant for the church was only one of six land grants listed in this bill, the House amended it to remove the grant to the church, after which Madison signed it. Madison was congratulated by other Baptist churches for his veto of this bill.

Madison's third example, which he referred to as a bill from which he withheld his signature, was what is known as a *pocket veto.* According to Article 1, Section 7 of the Constitution, if the president doesn't return a bill to Congress within ten days, it automatically becomes a law. The exception to this is when the president can't return a bill because Congress is adjourned. If a president is presented with a bill that they don't want to sign, and there are less than ten days left in that session of Congress, they can simply hang on to it until Congress adjourns. This is what Madison did with a bill that would have exempted Bible societies from import duties.

This bill, presented to Madison in April 1816, was to exempt all Bible societies in the United States from import duties on printing plates. As mentioned in Chapter One, there were two separate petitions submitted by the Philadelphia Bible Society at the same time, one to the Senate, which was rejected, and another to the House. The one rejected by the Senate contained a request for an exemption for all Bible Societies from import duties on already printed Bibles, including those to be sold by the societies. The other, simultaneously

27. *The Debates and Proceedings of the Congress of the United States of America,* vol. 22, 11th Cong., 3rd Sess., (Washington D.C.: Gales & Seaton, 1853), 1097-1098.

presented to the House, requested an exemption only on the plates to print Bibles, which were primarily to be distributed to the poor for free. This was the one that managed to make it through Congress as *An act for the free importation of stereotype plates, and to encourage the printing and gratuitous distribution of the Scriptures, by the bible societies within the United States*, but, of course, did not make it past Madison.

Most religious right American history authors stick to the issues of chaplains and prayer day proclamations in their discussions of the *Detached Memoranda,* and confine their assertions of Madison's inconsistency to those issues. A few, however, come up with other examples to support this claim. These are all addressed in other chapters of this book, or in chapters that will appear in Volume II. The reason for this is that these same lies are more often used by other authors for other purposes, and are more closely related to the subjects of other chapters. David Barton, for example, includes in his list of six inconsistencies the lie that Madison *"economically aided a Bible Society in its goal of the mass distribution of the Bible,"* which is found in the first chapter of this book. He also wrongly attributes a sentence from the 1776 Virginia Declaration of Rights to Madison. This same sentence, correctly attributed to its real author, appears for other reasons in Volume II, so Barton's misattribution will be explained there. Barton and James H. Hutson both point out Madison's use of the phrase *"national religion"* in the *Detached Memoranda,* construing this to mean that he considered the First Amendment to prohibit nothing more than the establishment of a national religion. Similar assertions are made using Madison's comments in the debates on the Bill of rights, so both are addressed in the Volume II chapter about the Bill of Rights. Barton also quotes letters written by a very young James Madison to a college friend who was struggling with the decision to leave his theological studies to pursue a career politics. This correspondence, which also comes up in an unrelated lie from another author, appears in Volume II as well.

— CHAPTER TEN —

The Election of 1800

Most religious right American history books contain at least a few quotes from various founders warning of the danger of atheists and infidels in the government. While the majority of these quotes, and misquotes, come from debates and letters about the Constitution's *no religious test* clause, there are some that come from another source – the anti-Jefferson pamphlets distributed by religious leaders during the presidential campaign of 1800. Quoting these pamphlets, however, is a bit tricky for those authors who, elsewhere in their books, attempt to prove that Thomas Jefferson was a devout Christian. The problem is that the religious leaders who wrote these pamphlets weren't trying to prove that Jefferson *was* a Christian. They were trying to prove that he *wasn't.* Today's religious right authors, not wanting to pass up a goldmine of quotes about the importance of electing only Christians to the government, have found a few ways to get around the fact that their predecessors considered Jefferson not only irreligious, but a danger to religion. Some claim that the pamphleteers of 1800 were wrong about Jefferson but right about everything else. Others quote the statements about the dangers of electing infidels, and simply omit that Jefferson was the infidel these statements were aimed at.

One of Jefferson's biggest adversaries was a Dutch Reformed minister from New York, Rev. William Linn. During the campaign of 1800, Rev. Linn published *Serious Considerations on the Election of a President: Addressed to the Citizens of the United States*, a pamphlet in which he argued that Jefferson was unfit to be elected president because he was at best a deist, and at worst an atheist. Much of the evidence presented by Linn to support his assertions came from Jefferson's own book, *Notes on the State of Virginia.*

Although a number of other ministers wrote similar pamphlets, Rev. Linn's *Serious Considerations* is the one most often quoted in the religious right American history books. The reason for this is that, eleven years earlier, Linn had been elected by the House of Representatives as their first chaplain. By coupling quotes from his 1800 pamphlet with his election by the House of Representatives in 1789, the authors of these books are able to imply that the same Congress that wrote the Bill of Rights also endorsed Linn's opinion that allowing atheists and infidels to hold public office was a danger to America.

> **In his book *America's God and Country,* William Federer describes Rev. Linn, and uses what is probably the most popular quote from *Serious Considerations:* "William Linn on May 1, 1789, was elected by the United States House of Representatives as its chaplain, and a salary of $500 was appropriated from the Federal treasury. Being a respected minister in New York City, and the father of the famous poet John Blair Linn (1777-1804), William Linn alleged:**
>
>> **Let my neighbor once persuade himself that there is no God, and he will soon pick my pocket, and break not only my leg but my neck. If there is no God, there is no law; no future account; government then is the ordinance of man only, and we cannot be subject for conscience sake."**

What William Federer neglects to mention is that this quote was Rev. Linn's response to the following statement from Jefferson's *Notes on Virginia.*

> The legitimate powers of government extend to such acts only as are injurious to others. But it does me no injury for

> my neighbour to say there are twenty gods, or no god. It neither picks my pocket nor breaks my leg.[1]

David Barton, in his book *The Myth of Separation,* does mention that *Serious Considerations* was an attack on Jefferson. He even quotes Jefferson's statement from *Notes on Virginia,* and acknowledges that this is what Rev. Linn was responding to. Barton just fails to attribute Jefferson's statement to Jefferson, attributing it only to an anonymous *prominent man* of the founding era. Then, to eliminate any possible connection to Jefferson, he places these statements about two hundred pages after the part of his book on the election of 1800, and omits the fact that Linn's statement came from *Serious Considerations.*

> **According to Barton: "The argument of whether religion is necessary to society and government is not new. The same dispute occurred between two prominent men in the founding era. The first asserted:**
>
> > **The legitimate powers of government extend to such acts only as are injurious to others. But it does me no injury for my neighbour to say there are twenty gods, or no god. It neither picks my pocket nor breaks my leg.**
>
> **William Linn, an outspoken critic of this philosophy, responded with a statement that summarized the convictions of the majority of the Founders and that has since been confirmed by experience in this country:**
>
> > **Let my neighbor once persuade himself that there is no God, and he will soon pick my pocket, and break not only my leg but my neck. If there is no God, there is no law; no future account; government then is the ordinance of man only, and we cannot be subject for conscience sake."**

1. Andrew A. Lipscomb and Albert Ellery Bergh, eds., *The Writings of Thomas Jefferson,* vol. 2, (Washington, DC: Thomas Jefferson Memorial Association, 1904), 221.

The following is the section of Linn's *Serious Considerations* in which the quote used by Barton and Federer appears.

> THERE is another passage in Mr. Jefferson's Notes which requires the most serious attention. In showing that civil rulers ought not to interfere with the rights of conscience, and that the legitimate powers of government extend to such acts only as they are injurious to others, he says, "The legitimate powers of government extend to such acts only as are injurious to others. But it does me no injury for my neighbour to say there are twenty gods, or no god. It neither picks my pocket nor breaks my leg." The whole passage is written with a great degree of spirit, it is remarkable for that conciseness, perspicuity and force which characterize the style of Mr. Jefferson.
>
> Some have ventured from the words I have quoted, to bring even the charge of atheism against him. This is a high charge, and it becomes carefully to examine the ground upon which it rests. Though the words themselves, their connection, and the design for which they are introduced may be insufficient to support it, yet there are concurrent circumstances to be taken into consideration, and which will fix at least a suspicion. These circumstances are, a general disregard of religious things, the associates at home and abroad, and the principles maintained in conversation. with these things I am not so well acquainted as many. I shall only mention what passed in conversation between Mr. Jefferson and a gentleman of distinguished talents and services, on the necessity of religion to government. The gentleman insisted that some religious faith and institutions of worship, claiming a divine origin, were necessary to the order and peace of society. Mr. Jefferson said that he differed widely from him, and that "he wished to see a government in which no religious opinions were held, and where the security for property and social order rested entirely upon the force of the law." Would not this be a nation of Atheists? Is it not natural, after the free declaration of such a sentiment, to suspect the man himself of Atheism? Could one who is impressed with the existence of a God, the Creator,

> Preserver, and Governor of all things, to whom we are under a law and accountable; and the inseparable connection of this truth with the social order and the external happiness of mankind, express himself in this manner?
>
> PUTTING the most favorable construction upon the words in the Notes, they are extremely reprehensible. Does not the belief influence the practice? How then can it be a matter of indifference what a man believes? The doctrine that a man's life may be good, let his faith be what it may, is contradictory to reason and the experience of mankind. It is true that a mere opinion of my neighbour will do me no injury. Government cannot regulate or punish it. The right of private opinion is inalienable. But let my neighbour once persuade himself that there is no God, and he will soon pick my pocket, and break not only my leg but my neck. If there is no God, there is no law; no future account; government then is the ordinance of man only, and we cannot be subject for conscience sake. No colours can paint the horrid effects of such a principle, and the deluge of miseries with which it would overwhelm the human race.
>
> How strongly soever Mr. Jefferson may reason against the punishments of law of erroneous opinion, even of atheism; they are not the less frightful and dangerous in their consequences....[2]

Rev. Linn went on to point out a number of blasphemous statements found in *Notes on Virginia,* a book that questioned *facts* like the great flood, and contradicted the story of Adam and Eve. He warned his readers that Jefferson even wanted to keep the Bible out of schools and, instead of teaching children from *"the most ancient and only authentic history in the world,"* teach them only *"the facts contained in profane history."*[3] After presenting all his evidence, Linn went on to assert that even if Jefferson didn't overtly try to rid the country of reli-

2. William Linn, *Serious Considerations on the Election of a President: Addressed to the Citizens of the United States*, (New York, 1800), 17-20.
3. *ibid.*, 15.

gion, he would undermine it simply by setting a bad example.

> To do Mr. Jefferson, however more than justice, let us suppose that he will make no attempts either by word or act to unsettle the religious belief; that he will no try his favorite project of a government without religion; and that he will not think it "high time for this country to get rid of religion and the clergy;" will not the station of President alone have a most baneful influence: Does not every person acquainted with human nature, and who is attentive to the state of manners in society, know that the principles and manners if those called the higher ranks, and especially of those in the administration of government, soon pervade all classes? Let the first magistrate be a professed infidel and infidels will surround him. Let him spend the sabbath in feasting, in visiting or receiving visits, in riding abroad, but never in going to church; and to frequent public worship will become unfashionable. Infidelity will become the prattle from the highest to the lowest condition in life, and universal desoluteness will follow. "The wicked walk on every side, when the vilest men are exalted."[4]

Using this reasoning, Rev. Linn concluded that it was better to elect an immoral and dishonest man who hypocritically professed Christianity than an honest infidel who wouldn't lie and say he was a Christian.

> ...Though a man professing christianity may be as immoral in his conduct as a man professing infidelity, yet who of these two is the best man to put into a place of high trust and extensive influence, is a totally different question. I contend that the man professing christianity is infinitely safer; and that christians cannot consistently with the dictates of their confidence, and the obligations which they owe to their Divine Redeemer, voluntarily choose any other. The profession will have great weight with the community; it will more

4. William Linn, *Serious Considerations on the Election of a President: Addressed to the Citizens of the United States*, (New York, 1800), 25-26.

> or less restrain the man himself, and may operate in time to the entire reformation of his life. But on the infidel we have no hold. In what way will you bind him who has broken the bands of religion and cast away its cords from him?[5]

Rev. Linn's idea of attacking Jefferson with his own *Notes on Virginia* quickly caught on. A typical letter to the editor, appearing in the *Gazette of the United States* on May 3, 1800, attacked Jefferson with *"the proof from his own book,"* and then asked, *"who will now dare to give his vote for this audacious howling Atheist?"*[6]

Jefferson's supporters responded to Linn's attack with their own publications, which, in turn, were answered by other pamphlets reiterating and defending Linn's assertions. One of these, *The Voice of Warning to Christians on the Ensuing Election of a President of the United States,* was written by John Mitchell Mason, who had also assisted Linn in writing *Serious Considerations*.

> Fellow Christians,
>
> A crisis of no common magnitude awaits our country. The approaching election of a president is to decide a question not merely of preference to an eminent individual, or particular views of policy, but, what is infinitely more, of national regard or disregard to the religion of Jesus Christ. Had the choice been between two infidels or two professed Christians, the point of politics would be untouched by me. Nor, though opposed to Mr. Jefferson, am I to be regarded as a partizan; since the principles which I am about to develope, will be equally unacceptable to many on both sides of the question. I dread the election of Mr. Jefferson, because I believe him to be a confirmed infidel: you desire it, because, while he is politically acceptable, you either doubt this fact, or do not consider it essential. Let us, like brethren, reason this matter.

5. William Linn, *Serious Considerations on the Election of a President: Addressed to the Citizens of the United States*, (New York, 1800), 33.

6. Richard N. Rosenfeld, *American Aurora: A Democratic-Republican Returns*, (New York, St. Martin's Press, 1997), 782.

> The general opinion rarely, if ever, mistakes a character which private pursuits and public functions have placed in different attitudes; yet it is frequently formed upon circumstances which elude the grasp of argument even while they make a powerful and just impression. Notwithstanding, therefore, the belief of Mr. Jefferson's infidelity, which has for years been uniform and strong, wherever his character has been a subject of speculation—although that infidelity has been boasted by some, lamented by many, and undisputed by all, yet as it is now denied by his friends, the charge, unsupported by other proof, could hardly be pursued to conviction. Happily for truth and for us, Mr. Jefferson has written; he has printed. While I shall not decline auxiliary testimony, I appeal to what he never retracted, and will not deny, his *Notes on Virginia.*[7]

Mimicking Linn, Mason wrote at length about how Jefferson's scientific theories and speculations contradicted certain Bible stories, then continued with the following.

> ...I intreat Christians to consider the sweeping extent of this infidel doctrine of "different races." If it be true, the history of the bible, which knows of but one, is a string of falsehoods from the book of Genesis to that of the Revelation; and the whole system of redemption, predicated on the unity of the human race, is a cruel fiction. I ask Christians again, whether they would dare to speak and write on this subject in the stile of Mr. Jefferson? Whether any believer in the word of the Lord Jesus, who is their hope, could entertain such doubts? Whether a writer, acute, cautious, and profound, like Mr. Jefferson, could, as he had before done in the case of the deluge, pursue a train of argument, which he knew infidels before him had used to discredit revelation, and on which they still have great reliance—Whether, instead of vindicating the honor of the scripture, he could, in such circumstances,

7. John Mitchell Mason, *The Voice of Warning to Christians,* reprinted in Ellis Sandoz, ed., *Political Sermons of the American Founding Era: 1730-1805,* vol. 2, (Indianapolis: Liberty Fund, 1998).

> be as mute as death on this point; countenancing infidels by inforcing their sentiments; and yet be a Christian? The thing is impossible! And were any other than Mr. Jefferson to be guilty of the same disrespect to God's word, you would not hesitate one moment in pronouncing him an infidel.
>
> It is not only with his philosophical disquisitions that Mr. Jefferson mingles opinions irreconcileable with the scriptures. He even goes out of his way for the sake of a fling at them. "Those," says he, "who labor in the earth, are the chosen people of God, if ever he had a chosen people, whose breasts he has made his peculiar deposit for substantial and genuine virtue."
>
> How does a Christian ear relish this "profane babbling?" In the first place, Mr. Jefferson doubts if ever God had a chosen people. In the second place, if he had, he insists they are no other than those who labor in the earth. At any rate, he denies this privilege to the seed of Abraham; and equally denies your being his people, unless you follow the scythe and the plow. Now, whether this be not the lie direct to the whole testimony of the bible from the beginning to the end, judge ye.[8]

Mason, referring to Jefferson's statement that those who labor in the earth are the chosen people of God, asked the question, *"How does a Christian ear relish this profane babbling?"* Well, William Federer seems to relish it enough to quote it as evidence of how religious Jefferson was. Apparently, today's religious right just can't spot blasphemy like the religious right of Jefferson's day could.

> **In his book *America's God and Country,* Federer states: "In Query XIX of his Notes on the State of Virginia, Thomas Jefferson wrote:**
>
> > **Those who labor in the earth, are the chosen**

8. John Mitchell Mason, *The Voice of Warning to Christians,* reprinted in Ellis Sandoz, ed., *Political Sermons of the American Founding Era: 1730-1805,* vol. 2, (Indianapolis: Liberty Fund, 1998).

> **people of God...whose breasts he has made his peculiar deposit for substantial and genuine virtue."**

In his book *The Myth of Separation,* David Barton quotes a lengthy excerpt about Rev. Linn's attack from John Eidsmoe's book *Christianity and the Constitution.* This section of Barton's book, as already mentioned, appears over two hundred pages before the attribution of Jefferson's *twenty gods or no god* statement to an anonymous prominent man. Eidsmoe is among those religious right authors who don't attempt to prove that Jefferson was a lifelong Christian, but merely assert that his association with the Unitarian Joseph Priestley led him to become sort of a Christian in the 1790s. Because of this, Eidsmoe, unlike Barton, can properly attribute the *twenty gods or no god* statement to Jefferson without obviously contradicting himself. Like Barton, however, Eidsmoe does not connect this statement to *Serious Considerations* or the election of 1800. Eidsmoe presents Jefferson's statement and Linn's response to it twenty-three pages after his description of *Serious Considerations*, then follows these quotes with an opinion that, by the 1790s, Jefferson had probably *"modified his earlier 1781 viewpoint."*

In order to place the *twenty gods or no god* statement at as early a date as possible, Eisdmoe gives it a date of 1781. This was the year that Jefferson, in response to a request for information about the various states from the Marquis de Barbé-Marbois, began compiling what would later be expanded on and published as *Notes on the State of Virginia.* What Eidsmoe fails to mention, however, is that the first printing of this book in English wasn't until 1787, when an edition was printed in London, and that Jefferson never retracted *"his earlier 1781 viewpoint"* in that edition, or the several subsequent American editions published through the 1790s, or later. In fact, Jefferson's failure to revise his book and retract his blasphemy, although having the opportunity to do so with each new printing, was what Linn and the other pamphleteers used as their evidence that he *hadn't* changed these opinions as of 1800.

The reason that Eidsmoe, while able to attribute the *twenty gods or no god* statement to Jefferson, does not connect it to Linn's 1800 attack is that he wants to give the impression that *Serious Consider-*

ations merely questioned things like Jefferson's church attendance and denominational affiliation. All Eidsmoe quotes from the pamphlet are questions such as *"Does Jefferson ever go to church? How does he spend the Lord's day? Is he known to worship with any denomination of Christians?,"* and a short excerpt showing Linn's opinion that an infidel like Jefferson shouldn't be elected – nothing, however, that would indicate that this opinion was based on anything more damning than Jefferson's disregard of the Sabbath or lack of regular church attendance. Eidsmoe immediately follows this with a comment that *"John Adams, Jefferson's opponent, was much more orthodox in his Christian faith...,"* implying that Linn supported Adams, and that he did so because Adams was a *more orthodox* Christian than Jefferson. But, Linn didn't support Adams either. He actually supported the other Federalist candidate, Charles Cotesworth Pinckney, and, as will be explained later in this chapter, this was for reasons that had nothing to do with religion.

Before the passage of the Twelfth Amendment in 1804, it was not specified which candidate was running for president, and which for vice president. The electors simply chose two names from among the candidates. Whoever got the most electoral votes was president, and whoever came in second was vice president. If Pinckney, although presumably the candidate for vice president, happened to get the most votes, and the incumbent Adams came in second, Pinckney would be president and Adams vice president. This is what Rev. Linn's faction wanted. Arranging for Pinckney to get more votes than Adams was a simple matter of having enough Pinckney electors throw away their second vote on some other candidate who had no chance of winning. This plan to switch the positions of Adams and Pinckney, however, did not change the fact that they both had to beat Jefferson.

John Eidsmoe could be given the benefit of the doubt that he just wrongly assumed that Linn supported Adams, and even that this was for religious reasons, if it wasn't for the fact that he goes on to selectively quote from two of the pamphlets rebutting *Serious Considerations,* both of which clearly indicate that this was not the case. One of these is *A Vindication of Thomas Jefferson; Against the Charges Contained in a Pamphlet Entitled, "Serious Considerations,"&c.,* written by DeWitt Clinton under the name Grotius. From Clinton's pamphlet, Eidsmoe quotes a few statements rebutting Linn's charges of deism, such as: *"And let me add...that he has for a long time supported out of his own private revenues, a worthy minister of the Christian church—an instance of liberality not to be met with in any of his rancorous enemies, whose love of religion seems principally to consist in their unremitted endeavors to degrade it into a handmaid of faction."* Eidsmoe completely disregards, however, the parts of this pamphlet that, like the following, clearly indicate that Linn supported Pinckney, and not Adams.

> You know, sir, that the people of the United States are divided into two great parties; that the most numerous is decidedly in favor of Mr. Jefferson for President; that the real candidate of the other is Mr. Pinckney, and the nominal one Mr. Adams; that the minority despair of carrying their point unless they create a division among the friends of Mr. Jefferson; that it is one of their first and leading wishes to secure the election of Mr. Pinckney; that no other candidate besides Mr. Jefferson can be fixed upon on the republican side with the same chance of success, and without producing a schism; and that the public opinion and public sensibility are now warmly in his favor. The tendency of your pamphlet is, by rendering him odious, to defeat his election, and this is also your avowed design.[9]

The other pamphlet quoted by Eidsmoe is *A Solemn Address to Christians & Patriots Upon the Approaching Election of a President of the United States, in Answer to a Pamphlet, Entitled, "Serious Considerations," &c.*, written by Tunis Wortman under the name Timoleon. In his pamphlet, Wortman presented a list of eight propositions, and then explained why it was the duty of both Christians and patriots to base their vote on these propositions. Eidsmoe quotes only the fifth of Wortman's eight propositions: *"That the charge of deism...is false, scandalous and malicious – that there is not a single passage in the Notes on Virginia, or any of Mr. Jefferson's writings, repugnant to Christianity; but on the contrary, in every respect, favourable to it."*

9. DeWitt Clinton, *A Vindication of Thomas Jefferson; Against the Charges Contained in a Pamphlet Entitled, "Serious Considerations," &c.*, (New York: Printed by David Denniston, 1800), 40-41.

He completely ignores Wortman's seventh proposition, however, which asserted that the election of Pinckney was Linn's ultimate goal.

> 7th. That a party has long existed, and still exists, hostile to the constitution, and with reason, suspected of favouring the interests of a foreign power—that Mr. Pinckney is the candidate of that party, and therefore cannot be a republican.[10]

Eidsmoe also ignores Wortman's dedication of the pamphlet to Rev. Linn, in which he called Linn a *"a partizan of Mr. Pinckney."* Wortman did not spell out Linn's name because *Serious Considerations* had been published anonymously, and had not been attributed to Rev. Linn in the Federalist newspapers that reprinted it. Wortman, however, like many of Jefferson's supporters, knew that Linn was the author.

DEDICATION

To the Reverend Dr. L——

"Thou shalt not bear false-witness against thy neighbour."
—The ninth commandment.

> I am not an admirer of dedications, nor will you, sir, be flatterd by the following. Your present situation, and the nature of the subject upon which I am about to remark, have rendered it proper that the ensuing observations should be particularly inscribed to yourself.
>
> You are not only a divine, but also a party politician. For my own part, I think these two characters absolutely incompatible. From the minister of religion, we have a right [to] expect exemplary purity and sincerity. In the statesman, we constantly discover cunning, intrigue and duplicity: It remains for you to reconcile these opposite characters to each other.

10. Tunis Wortman, *A Solemn Address to Christians & Patriots Upon the Approaching Election of a President of the United States, in Answer to a Pamphlet, Entitled, "Serious Considerations," &c.*, reprinted in Ellis Sandoz, ed., *Political Sermons of the American Founding Era: 1730-1805*, vol. 2, (Indianapolis: Liberty Fund, 1998).

> You are a partizan of Mr. Pinckney; in the presence of your maker, I would tell you so. I allow you the rights of opinion as a man, but I cannot permit you, with impunity, to abuse the influence you possess with your congregation.
>
> I am an advocate for religion, in its purity and truth; if I am an unworthy, yet I am, nevertheless, a sincere son of the church: I cannot tamely see that church and its heavenly doctrines prophaned to party purposes; my bosom burns with indignation at the attempts to render christianity the instrument of tyrants.
>
> A pamphlet has lately made its appearance, entitled, *"Serious Considerations."* I hesitate not, in the language of lawyers, to call it false, scandalous and malicious; it has the clerical mark upon it: Yet, I say not that you are the author, but I firmly declare that, by adopting its sentiments and declarations, you have rendered it your own.[11]

While DeWitt Clinton's pamphlet was basically just a point by point rebuttal of Linn's charges against Jefferson, Wortman, before addressing these specific charges, wrote about the political principles of all the candidates and explained his eight propositions. Wortman's first proposition was that it was the duty of Christians to keep religion separate from politics.

> 1st. That it is your duty, as christians, to maintain the purity and independence of the church, to keep religion separate from politics, to prevent an union between the church and the state, and to preserve your clergy from temptation, corruption and reproach.[12]
>
> Religion and government are equally necessary, but their

11. Tunis Wortman, *A Solemn Address to Christians & Patriots Upon the Approaching Election of a President of the United States, in Answer to a Pamphlet, Entitled, "Serious Considerations,"* &c., reprinted in Ellis Sandoz, ed., *Political Sermons of the American Founding Era: 1730-1805*, vol. 2, (Indianapolis: Liberty Fund, 1998).

12. *ibid.*

> interests should be kept separate and distinct. No legitimate connection can ever subsist between them. Upon no plan, no system, can they become united, without endangering the purity and usefulness of both—the church will corrupt the state, and the state pollute the church....
>
> ...The inevitable consequence of an union of the church with the state, will be the mutual destruction of both. Religion, instead of remaining an active and efficient director of faith and conduct, will be converted into an engine to promote the ruin of the constitution....[13]

By disregarding much of the content of the pamphlets published during the campaign of 1800, John Eidsmoe is able to draw the following conclusions.

> **According to Eidsmoe: "First, no one questioned the propriety of inquiry into a presidential candidate's religious beliefs" and "Second, should a deist be president was not the issue. No one argued that. The question was whether Jefferson was a deist or Christian."**

But, Tunis Wortman, in several places in the very same pamphlet that Eidsmoe quotes from, did, in fact, argue that even if Jefferson was a deist, he would still be the best choice for president.

> ...Suppose, for a moment, that there are three candidates for the presidency—Mr. Jefferson, Mr. Adams, and Mr. Pinckney —that Mr. Jefferson was in reality a deist, but a decided friend to the republican constitution of his country—that the two others were very pious & sincere christians, but secretly friends to aristocracy or monarchy, & hostile to the spirit of the present constitution, which of the three would be the most dangerous man? Mr. Jefferson, in such case, even if he

13. Tunis Wortman, *A Solemn Address to Christians & Patriots Upon the Approaching Election of a President of the United States, in Answer to a Pamphlet, Entitled, "Serious Considerations,"* &c., reprinted in Ellis Sandoz, ed., *Political Sermons of the American Founding Era: 1730-1805*, vol. 2, (Indianapolis: Liberty Fund, 1998).

> had the intentions, could not be of the smallest disservice to religion: thanks to heaven, christianity has taken too deep a root to be capable of being shaken by the opinions, or even the enmity of any president. I know of no other method by which religion can be injured by any government in this country, except by its setting one powerful church above the heads of the rest. But this Mr. Jefferson is incapable of doing; for according to such position; he would be equally indifferent to all; in this sense, strange as it may appear, christianity would have much more to apprehend from a bigot than an infidel....[14]

David Barton, in *The Myth of Separation,* introduces the excerpt he borrows from Eidsmoe's book with an assertion similar to Eidsmoe's conclusions.

> **Referring to the practice of electing only Christians, Barton claims: "That this was the practice of the nation under the Constitution is underscored in the events surrounding the nation's second Presidential race between John Adams and Thomas Jefferson. The entire focus of the race was on whether or not Jefferson was actually a Christian. If he was not, he would not hold office."**

Interestingly, a number of the men on David Barton's list of founders who belonged to religious societies, found in his other book, *Original Intent,* clearly disagreed that a candidate's religious beliefs should be considered as a qualification for office. One of these Bible society members, New Jersey Governor Joseph Bloomfield, publicly condemned the Federalists' use of religion as a campaign issue and urged voters to base their decision on Jefferson's actions. The following is from Governor Bloomfield's September 1800 *Address to the People of New Jersey.*

14. Tunis Wortman, *A Solemn Address to Christians & Patriots Upon the Approaching Election of a President of the United States, in Answer to a Pamphlet, Entitled, "Serious Considerations," &c.*, reprinted in Ellis Sandoz, ed., *Political Sermons of the American Founding Era: 1730-1805*, vol. 2, (Indianapolis: Liberty Fund, 1998).

> Look up to that man, whose whole life, from the day on which he immortalised himself, by drawing up the Declaration of Independence to the present, has not given to his enemies a single cause of reproach; who cannot be impeached of immorality nor of vice: whose hands and whose coffers have never been soiled by speculation or gambling: whose domestic character is uncontaminated by the reproaches of any one debauchery: whose talents as a governor in his native state, as an ambassador abroad, as legislator and secretary of state, and whose pursuits have been from first to last, to promote toleration in religion and freedom in politics: to cultivate the arts and the virtues at home, and to shun the vices and depravities of corrupt foreign governments—in a word, a man against whom falsehood has raised its voice, under the garb of religion, only because he has banished tythes and an established church from his native state, and who would brand him with the name of Infidel because he is not a fanatic....[15]

Benjamin Rush, included in Barton's list as founder and manager of the Philadelphia Bible Society, also thought the clergy should stay out of politics. Rush was one of the few people to whom Jefferson wrote anything at all about the clergy's campaign against him. The following was Rush's response to Jefferson's letter about the attacks.

> I agree with you likewise in your wishes to keep religion and government independant of each other. Were it possible for St. Paul to rise from his grave at the present juncture, he would say to the Clergy who are now so active in settling the political Affairs of the World: "Cease from your political labors, your kingdom is not of *this* World. Read my Epistles. In no part of them will you perceive me aiming to depose a pagan Emperor, or to place a Christian upon a throne. Christianity disdains to receive Support from human Governments. From this, it derives its preeminence over all the religions that ever have, or ever shall exist in the World.

15. Arthur M. Schlesinger, ed., *History of American Presidential Elections, 1789-1968,* Vol. 1, (New York: Chelsea House Publishers, 1985), 137-138.

> Human Governments may receive Support from Christianity but it must be only from the love of justice, and peace which it is calculated to produce in the minds of men. By promoting these, and all the other Christian virtues by your precepts, and example, you will much sooner overthrow errors of all kind, and establish our pure and holy religion in the World, than by aiming to produce by your preaching, or pamphlets any change in the political State of mankind."[16]

A number of significant issues and events led to the formation of parties in the 1790s, and the eventual split of the Federalist Party[17] into the factions that existed by the election of 1800. Even before the end of the first Congress, two distinct parties had emerged – the Democratic-Republicans, led by Thomas Jefferson, and the Federalists, led by Alexander Hamilton.

The first big rift in the new government was over Hamilton's economic plan – specifically the assumption by the federal government of the Revolutionary War debts of the states. In January 1790, four months after his appointment as the first Secretary of the Treasury, Hamilton presented his *Report on Public Credit* to the House of Representatives. At this time, the federal government's debts amounted to about $54 million, about twenty percent of which was foreign, and eighty percent domestic. The combined Revolutionary War debts of the state governments were estimated by Hamilton, at that time, to be about $25 million. Hamilton's plan was that the federal government assume the state debts, consolidating the state and federal debts into one big $79 million federal debt. The federal government would not pay this debt, but would fund it by issuing new government bonds, and instituting new taxes to pay the interest. One of the goals of this plan, of course, was to shift the loyalty of the wealthiest Americans from the states to the federal government. Once the wealthy creditors and speculators exchanged their old state debt certificates for the new fed-

16. Benjamin Rush to Thomas Jefferson, October 6, 1800, *The Thomas Jefferson Papers, Series 1, General Correspondence, 1651-1827*, Library of Congress Manuscript Division, #18402

17. The Federalist Party that emerged in the new government should not be confused with what a "federalist" was during the time of the writing and ratifying of the Constitution. A federalist at that time was simply someone who supported the new Constitution. The Federalist Party that formed in the early 1790s wanted a far more powerful federal government than the Republicans who had identified themselves as federalists only a few years earlier..

eral bonds, their financial interests would be tied to the success of the federal government rather than the success of their individual states.

The opposition to Hamilton's plan was led in the House of Representatives by James Madison. The first objection was that the assumption of the state debts favored the states that had done the least to reduce their own debts, particularly Massachusetts and South Carolina. States that had already paid much of their debt would be taxed to pay the debts of the states that hadn't. There was also the problem of determining which state debts were legitimately the result of the common war effort, and which were the result of state projects that benefited only an individual state.

Another objection was that Hamilton's plan would not only reward those who had speculated in debt certificates after the Revolutionary War, but would do so at the expense of the original certificate holders, who had not only sold their certificates at a fraction of their face value, but would now be taxed to raise the money that the government needed to pay face value to the speculators. This was the speculation referred to by Governor Bloomfield in his 1800 address, when he noted the fact that Jefferson had taken no part in it as evidence of his highly moral character.

During the war, merchants and farmers who supplied the army, as well as most of the soldiers, had been paid in debt certificates, issued by both Congress and the state governments. In the years following the war, these certificates were essentially worthless because neither Congress nor the states had the money to redeem them. By 1789, the majority of the farmers, merchants, and soldiers, few of whom could afford to wait for the government to get on its feet, had been forced to sell their certificates to speculators for a fraction of their face value.

Several different kinds of debt certificates had been issued by the Confederation Congress. As of 1790, the only type that were still in the hands of the original holders in any large degree were loan certificates. These were the certificates issued for actual loans of money, so the original holders were generally those who were well off enough to hold on to them. What the speculators bought up were the certificates issued to soldiers, small merchants, farmers, and other civilian workers at the end of the war. These "final settlement certificates," as they were called, were issued by Congress to settle the accounts of civilians beginning in 1872, and soldiers in 1784. Virtually all enlisted men, and even many officers, sold their certificates as soon as they got them, flooding the market and depressing the value of all types of certificates. For the next few years, final settlement certificates sold for about ten or fifteen cents on the dollar.

Prices began to climb when the Constitutional Convention was called in 1787, and rose with each major step towards the formation of the new government. The Convention caused a jump from fifteen to nineteen cents on the dollar, and ratification of the Constitution by enough states to ensure its adoption caused another jump from nineteen to twenty-five cents. At this point, many smaller investors, satisfied with making an average forty percent profit, sold. This caused a temporary dip of a few cents until the first Congress convened in the spring of 1789 and George Washington was inaugurated.

In September 1789, George Washington signed the bill creating the Treasury Department, and appointed Alexander Hamilton as Secretary of the Treasury. Once this happened, nobody holding Confederation Congress certificates wanted to sell them. This caused a serious problem for securities brokers who had an increasing number of orders to fill, particularly from European investors. What were still very available, however, were the certificates issued by the individual states. These, of course, were much riskier. While the Constitution guaranteed that the new federal government would pay the debts incurred by Congress under the Articles of Confederation, the payment of most state certificates depended entirely on the federal government assuming the debts of the states. Hamilton's circle of friends in New York, knowing that he was going to propose the debt assumption in January 1790, took a gamble and began buying up state certificates in the fall of 1789. By December 1789, Confederation certificates were up to fifty cents on the dollar, and state certificates were going for anywhere from nine to thirty-three cents, depending on what measures, if any, each state government had taken to back their own certificates.

As soon as Hamilton's report was read in the House, another wave of speculation hit. Speculators who hadn't already begun buying state certificates quickly dispatched agents to outlying rural areas to search out and buy up as many as possible before their current holders heard the news that they might soon be worth face value. James Jackson, a representative from Georgia, who, up until this point, had considered speculation immoral but tended to agree with the speculators' argument no actual fraud had been committed, drew the line at this.

> Since this report has been read in this House, a spirit of havoc, speculation, and ruin, has arisen, and has been cherished by people who had an access to the information the report contained, that would have made a *Hastings* blush to have been connected with, though long inured to preying on the vitals of his fellow men. Three vessels, sir, have sailed within a fortnight from this port, freighted for speculation; they are intended to purchase up the state and other securities in the hands of the uninformed, though honest citizens of North Carolina, South Carolina, and Georgia. My soul rises indignant at the avaricious and immoral turpitude which so vile a conduct displays.[18]

It's interesting to note that many of the founders most heavily involved in speculating are also some of the most often quoted and mentioned founders in the religious right American history books. In fact, a number of them, most notably American Bible Society founder Elias Boudinot, appear on David Barton's list of Bible society members. Among the other speculators frequently mentioned in the religious right history books are Fisher Ames, who wrote that the Bible should be used as a schoolbook; Abraham Baldwin, a chaplain in the Revolutionary War; Caleb Strong, a Vice President of the American Bible Society; and Charles Cotesworth Pinckney, President of the Charleston Bible Society, and, of course, the candidate supported by Rev. Linn's faction in the election of 1800. The biggest speculator of all, however, was Jonathan Dayton, the man who made up the story about prayers at the Constitutional Convention. It was generally the not so religious founders, like Thomas Jefferson and James Madison, who considered profiting from the financial problems of veterans and patriots to be immoral.

On February 11, 1790, Madison made a motion that only original certificate holders be paid face value, and all others be paid the highest market value, with the balance going to the original holders. According to Madison's plan, all of the speculators would still make a

18. *The Debates and Proceedings of the Congress of the United States of America*, vol. 1, 1st Cong., 2nd Sess., (Washington D.C.: Gales & Seaton, 1834), 1132.

profit, many of them an enormous profit, but the soldiers and other original holders would at least get something. Bible society founder and speculator Elias Boudinot was the first to object to this.

> Mr. Boudinot said, he had long been in the habit of paying great respect to the sentiments of the gentleman from Virginia; but he feared, on this occasion, he had not viewed the subject with his usual accuracy. He was not surprised that the gentleman was led away by the dictates of his heart, for he believed he really felt for the misfortunes of his fellow-citizens, who had been prey to avaricious men....[19]

Apparently, Elias Boudinot did not count himself among the avaricious men he pretended to denounce. Like the other speculators in the House, he argued that the purchases of certificates were perfectly legal, and that the soldiers had known exactly what they were doing when they sold them. It was common knowledge, however, that most speculators had obtained the certificates by convincing the soldiers that they would never be worth much, and might end up being worth nothing at all. The most outrageous argument from the speculators' side was that any soldier who believed the certificates would go down in value had committed fraud when they sold them to the speculators. Another representative from this side argued that there might be soldiers who were better off for having sold their certificates because they could have invested what they got for them in something else and made a profit. Yet another argued that it would be an insult to the honor of the soldiers to offer them any further compensation for their service, and that they would not accept it. It was claimed that this was the opinion of the New York branch of the Society of the Cincinnati, an organization of former army officers. This claim, however, was found to be completely untrue. Madison's motion was debated in the House for a solid week, but was ultimately defeated.

Hamilton's overall plan did not pass when the House first voted on it on April 12, 1790. It failed by a vote of 31 to 29. William Maclay, a senator from Pennsylvania who often went to listen to the debates in the House when the Senate wasn't doing anything, described in his

19. *The Debates and Proceedings of the Congress of the United States of America*, vol. 1, 1st Cong., 2nd Sess., (Washington D.C.: Gales & Seaton, 1834), 1238.

journal the reaction of the speculators to this initial defeat.

> Sedgwick, from Boston, pronounced a funeral oration over it. He was called to order; some confusion ensued; he took his hat and went out. When he returned, his visage, to me, bore the visible marks of weeping. Fitzsimons reddened like scarlet; his eyes were brimful. Clymer's color, always pale, now verged to a deadly white; his lips quivered, and his nether jaw shook with convulsive motions; his head, neck, and breast contracted with gesticulations resembling those of a turkey or goose nearly strangled in the act of deglutition. Benson bungled like a shoemaker who had lost his end. Ames's aspect was truly hippocratic—a total change of face and features; he sat torpid, as if his faculties had been benumbed. Gerry exhibited the advantages of a cadaverous appearance, at all times placid and far from pleasing; he ran no risk of deterioration. Through an interruption of hectic lines and consumptive coughs he delivered himself of a declaration that the delegates of Massachusetts would proceed no further, but send to their State for instructions.
>
> Happy impudence sat enthroned on Lawrence's [Laurance] brow. He rose in puffing pump and moved that the committee should rise, and assigned the agitation of the House as a reason. Wadsworth hid his grief under the rim of a round hat. Boudinot's wrinkles rose in ridges and the angles of his month were depressed and assumed a curve resembling a horse's shoe. Fitzsimons first recovered recollection, and endeavored to rally the discomfited and disheartened heroes. He hoped the good sense of the House would still predominate and lead them to reconsider the vote which had been now taken; and he doubted not but what it would yet be adopted under proper modifications. The Secretary's [Hamilton] group pricked up their ears, and Speculation wiped the tear from either eye. Goddess of description, paint the gallery; here's the paper, find fancy quills or crayons yourself.[20]

20. Edgar S. Maclay, ed., *Journal of William Maclay,* (New York: D. Appleton and Company, 1890), 237-238.

Although strongly objecting to the assumption, Jefferson, who had arrived in New York at the end of March to take his position as Secretary of State, was convinced by Hamilton that there was a very real danger of the union breaking up if it wasn't passed. This, of course, is what led to the famous dinner at which Jefferson and Madison cut a deal with Hamilton, supplying two Virginia votes for the assumption in exchange for enough northern votes to locate the nation's capital on the Potomac. The following was Jefferson's description of the situation he walked into when he arrived in New York, and his account of the compromise.

> It is well known that, during the war the greatest difficulty we encountered was the want of money or means to pay our soldiers who fought, or our farmers, manufacturers and merchants, who furnished the necessary supplies of food and clothing for them. After the expedient of paper money had exhausted itself, certificates of debt were given to the individual creditors, with assurance of payment, so soon as the United States should be able. But the distresses of these people often obliged them to part with these for the half, the fifth, and even a tenth of their value; and speculators had made a trade of cozening them from the holders, by the most fraudulent practices, and persuasions that they would never be paid. In the bill for funding and paying these, Hamilton made no difference between the original holders and the fraudulent purchasers of this paper. Great and just repugnance arose at putting these two classes of creditors on the same footing, and great exertions were used to pay to the former the full value, and to the latter, the price only which he had paid, with interest. But this would have prevented the game which was to be played, and for which the minds of greedy members were already tutored and prepared. When the trial of strength on these several efforts had indicated the form in which the bill would finally pass, this being known within doors sooner than without, and especially, than to those who were in distant parts of the Union, the base scramble began. Couriers and relay horses by land, and swift sailing pilot boats by sea, were flying in all directions. Active partners and agents were asso-

ciated and employed in every State, town, and country neighborhood, and this paper was bought up at five schillings and even as low as two schillings in the pound, before the holder knew that Congress had already provided for its redemption at par. Immense sums were thus filched from the poor and ignorant, and fortunes accumulated by those who had themselves been poor enough before. Men thus enriched by the dexterity of a leader, would follow of course the chief who was leading them to fortune, and become the zealous instruments of all his enterprises.

This game was over, and another was on the carpet at the moment of my arrival; and to this I was most ignorantly and innocently made to hold the candle. This fiscal maneuvre is well known by the name of the Assumption. Independently of the debts of Congress, the states had, during the war, contracted separate and heavy debts; and Massachusetts particularly, in an absurd attempt, absurdly conducted, on the British post of Penobscott: and the more debt Hamilton could rake up, the more plunder for his mercenaries. This money, whether wisely or foolishly spent, was pretended to have been spent for general purposes, and ought therefore to be paid from the general purse. But it was objected that nobody knew what these debts were, what their amount, or what their proofs. No matter; we will guess them to be twenty millions. But of these twenty millions, we do not know how much should be reimbursed to one State, nor how much to another. No matter; we will guess. And so another scramble was set on foot among the several states, and some got much, some little, some nothing. But the main object was obtained, the phalanx of the Treasury was reinforced by additional recruits. This measure produced the most bitter and angry contest ever known in Congress, before or since the Union of the States. I arrived in the midst of it. But a stranger to the ground, a stranger to the actors on it, so long absent as to have lost all familiarity with the subject, and as yet unaware of it's object, I took no concern in it. The great and trying question however was lost in the House of Representatives. So high were the feuds excited by this subject, that on its rejection, business was suspended. Congress met and adjourned from day to day without doing any thing, the parties being too much out of temper to do business together. The Eastern members particularly, who, with Smith from South Carolina, were the principal gamblers in these scenes, threatened a secession and dissolution. Hamilton was in despair. As I was going to the President's one day, I met him in the street. He walked me backwards and forwards before the President's door for half an hour. He painted pathetically the temper into which the legislature had been wrought, the disgust of those who were called the creditor states, the danger of the *secession* of their members, and the separation of the states. He observed that the members of the administration ought to act in concert; that though this question was not of my department, yet a common duty should make it a common concern; that the President was the centre on which all administrative questions ultimately rested, and that all of us should rally around him, and support with joint efforts, measures approved by him; and that the question having been lost by a small majority only, it was probable that an appeal from me to the judgment and discretion of some of my friends, might effect a change in the vote, and the machine of government, now suspended, might be again set into motion. I told him that I was really a stranger to the whole subject; not having yet informed myself of the system of finances adopted, I knew not how far this was a necessary sequence; that undoubtedly, if it's rejection endangered a dissolution of our Union at this incipient stage, I should deem that the most unfortunate of all consequences, to avert which all partial and temporary evils should be yielded. I proposed to him, however, to dine with me the next day, and I would invite another friend or two, bring them into conference together, and I thought it impossible that reasonable men, consulting together coolly, could fail, by some mutual sacrifices of opinion, to form a compromise which was to save the Union. The discussion took place. I could take no part in it but an exhortatory one, because I was a stranger to the circumstances which should govern it. But it was finally agreed, that whatever importance had been attached to the rejection of this proposition, the preservation of the Union and of concord among the States was more important, and that therefore it would be better that the vote of rejection should be rescinded, to effect which, some members should change their votes. But it was observed that this pill would be peculiarly bitter to the southern States, and that some concomitant measure should be adopted, to sweeten it a little to them. There had before been propositions to fix the seat of government either at Philadelphia, or at Georgetown on the Potomac; and it was thought that by giving it to Philadelphia for ten years, and to Georgetown permanently afterwards, this might, as an anodyne, calm in some degree the ferment which might be excited by the other measure alone. So two of the Potomac members (White and Lee, but White with a revulsion of stomach almost convulsive), agreed to change their votes, and Hamilton undertook to carry the other point. In doing this the influence he had established over the eastern members, with the agency of Robert Morris with those of the middle States, effected his side of the engagement; and so the Assumption was passed, and twenty millions of stock divided among favored States, and thrown in as pabulum to the stock-jobbing herd. This added to the number of votaries to the Treasury and made its chief the master of every vote in the legislature, which might give to the government the direction suited to his political views.

I know well, and so must be understood, that nothing like a majority in Congress had yielded to this corruption. Far from it. But a division, not very unequal, had already taken place in the honest part of that body, between the parties styled republican and federal. The latter being monarchists in principle, adhered to Hamilton of course, as their leader in that principle, and this mercenary phalanx added to them insured him always a majority in both Houses: so that the whole action of the legislature was now under the direction of the Treasury. Still the machine was not complete. The effect of the funding system, and of the Assumption, would be temporary; it would be lost with the loss of the individual members whom it had

> enriched, and some engine of influence more permanent must be contrived, while these myrmidons were yet in place to carry it through all opposition. This engine was the Bank of the United States....[21]

Two years later, in a letter to George Washington, Jefferson said that he regretted the 1790 deal with Hamilton more than any other mistake he had ever made. Jefferson, after being abroad for such a long time, was admittedly out of touch with what was going on in America. He was also completely unfamiliar with Hamilton. The two had never even met before Jefferson's arrival in New York. Jefferson just didn't realize until it was too late that the assumption was only the first phase of Hamilton's plan.

The next battle was over the establishment of the Bank of the United States. Jefferson's argument against this was that nothing in the Constitution gave the federal government the authority to establish a bank. Locating the bank in Philadelphia was also seen by many southerners as the beginnings of a scheme to keep the capital from being moved to the Potomac. Before signing the Bank Bill, which passed the Senate on January 20, 1791, and the House on February 8, Washington asked Jefferson for a formal statement of his objections to it. After receiving Jefferson's objections, as well as those of Attorney General Edmund Randolph, Washington asked Hamilton to respond to them.

The arguments on both sides hinged on the meaning of clause of the Constitution that says *"To make all Laws which shall be necessary and proper for carrying into Execution"* the powers vested in the government by the Constitution. Jefferson argued that there were no laws that could not be executed without establishing a bank, so a bank was not necessary, but merely a convenience. Hamilton's response to this was that *"necessary often means no more than needful, requisite, incidental, useful, or conducive to"*[22] and that *"the degree in which a measure is, or is not, necessary cannot be a test of constitutional right, but of expediency only."*[23] He also added that a bank was the *"proper"* means by which to carry out the power to regulate currency. In the end,

21. Saul K. Padover, ed., *The Complete Jefferson,* (New York: Duell, Sloan & Pearce, Inc., 1943), 1208-1210.
22. Joanne B. Freeman, ed., *Alexander Hamilton, Writings,* (New York: Literary Classics of the United States, 2001), 618.
23. *ibid.,* 631.

Hamilton got his way and Washington signed the Bank Bill. The immediate effect on the legislative process was exactly what Jefferson had feared it would be.

> ...While the government remained at Philadelphia, a selection of members of both Houses were constantly kept as directors who, on every question interesting to that institution, or to the views of the federal head, voted at the will of that head; and, together with the stockholding members, could always make the federal vote that of the majority. By this combination, legislative expositions were given to the constitution, and all the administrative laws were shaped on the model of England, and so passed. And from this influence we were not relieved, until the removal from the precincts of the bank, to Washington.
>
> Here then was the real ground of the opposition which was made to the course of administration. Its object was to preserve the legislature pure and independent of the executive, to restrain the administration to republican forms and principles, and not permit the constitution to be construed into a monarchy, and to be warped, in practice, into all the principles and pollutions of their favorite English model. Nor was this an opposition to General Washington. He was true to the republican charge confided to him; and has solemnly and repeatedly protested to me, in our private conversations, that he would lose the last drop of his blood in support of it; and he did this the oftener and with the more earnestness, because he knew my suspicions of Hamilton's designs against it, and wished to quiet them. For he was not aware of the drift, or of the effect of Hamilton's schemes. Unversed in financial projects and calculations and budgets, his approbation of them was bottomed on his confidence in the man.[24]

The next big issue was the war between France and Great Britain. Almost all Americans had supported the French Revolution when it

24. Saul K. Padover, ed., *The Complete Jefferson,* (New York: Duell, Sloan & Pearce, Inc., 1943), 1210-1211.

first began, and even most Federalists, while not particularly liking the French, still supported it as of the end of 1792. In December of that year, when Americans heard about the French victory over the armies of Austrian and Prussian at Valmy, celebrations were held all over the country. This all changed, however, in April 1793, when news reached the United States that France had declared war on Great Britain.

In addition to the general attachment of the Federalists to the British, Hamilton's economic program depended on British trade. Without the revenue raised by import duties on British goods, which accounted for about three quarters of all imports, the program would collapse. The problem was that, according to one of the treaties negotiated with France by Benjamin Franklin in 1778, the United States was obligated to defend the French West Indies against the British.

As usual, Washington asked both Jefferson and Hamilton for their advice. Hamilton's opinion was that the treaty with France should be suspended because it was made with a government that no longer existed, and that it shouldn't be restored unless a permanent new government was instituted, and, even then, only if America approved of that government. Jefferson considered the treaty to be with the people of France, not their late monarchy, and thought it should remain in force. He also pointed out that the French hadn't suspended the treaty when America changed its own form of government by adopting a new Constitution. On April 22, 1793, Washington, taking Hamilton's advice, declared America's neutrality in the conflict, but, at Jefferson's suggestion, did so without actually using the word neutrality. Washington's proclamation was essentially a warning to American citizens that if they got involved, they were on their own, and would not only receive no protection from the United States government, but would be prosecuted for any violations of the law of nations committed within the jurisdiction of the United States.

Around this same time, the first of the democratic societies, which would soon spring up all over the country, were being established. The democratic societies were political clubs, formed by Republicans to organize their party against the policies of the Federalist administration by corresponding with each other to circulate information. The Federalists blamed the formation of these societies on the influence of the French, and on one Frenchman in particular, *Citizen Genet.* Edmond Charles Genet had come to America in 1793 as a minister of the revolutionary French government. Arriving in South Carolina a few weeks before Washington's proclamation of neutrality, Genet began to enlist volunteers to attack Spanish Florida and Louisiana, and to fit out ships as privateers to disrupt British trade. He then went to Philadelphia and, not getting the reception he expected from Washington, threatened to instigate a revolt of the American people against the government.

In August 1793, Hamilton tried to convince George Washington that Genet was behind the formation of the democratic society in Philadelphia, and urged him to make a public statement censuring these societies. Jefferson quickly assured Washington that there was no truth to Hamilton's accusation. Washington, apparently not sure who to believe, did not make any statement at this time. The Federalists, however, continued to accuse the democratic societies of trying to instigate rebellions against the government. What they needed was a real rebellion to pin on them. A year later, they got their wish – the Whiskey Rebellion. The only problem was that this rebellion had actually begun before the democratic societies were formed. Nevertheless, Hamilton, by August 1794, had Washington thoroughly convinced that the democratic societies were to blame.

The excise tax on whiskey was one of the new taxes passed in 1791 to pay the interest on the large national debt created by Hamilton's economic plan. For a number of reasons, this tax put western farmers, many of whom made a significant part of their living selling whiskey, at a disadvantage to distilleries located in cities and towns. With almost all of the country's money concentrated in the east, whiskey was also depended on as a medium of exchange for frontier farmers, who used it to barter with merchants for necessities. Because the excise tax was a tax paid by the producers of whiskey rather than its consumers, it was the farmers who had to come up with the money to pay it. The problem was that, more often than not, the farmers did not receive cash payment for their whiskey, so there was no exchange of money out of which to take the tax.

Beginning in the summer of 1791, large public meetings were held in Pennsylvania's western counties, at which various resolutions were passed. One of the earliest resolutions, passed at a meeting in Washington County on August 23, 1791, called on the citizens to treat the excise officers *"with contempt, and absolutely to refuse all kind of communication or intercourse with the officers, and to withhold from them all aid, support, or comfort.*"[25]

Public meetings, armed protests, harassment of excise officers and farmers who complied with the law, and incidents such as the tarring and feathering of an official sent to open a tax office in Washington County, were happening long before the formation of the democratic societies. In fact, Alexander Hamilton began urging George Washington to use military force to enforce the tax in 1792, the year before any of these societies were formed, and two years before the events of 1794 that became known as the Whiskey Rebellion.

The escalation of the rebellion in the summer of 1794 was not caused by the excise tax itself, but by a particular action taken by the federal court in Philadelphia in May 1794. The farmers of western Pennsylvania had a number of other grievances against the government, most unrelated to the tax. One that was related, however, was the unfairness of a law requiring all excise cases arising in Pennsylvania to be heard in Philadelphia. The inconvenience and expense of having to attend a court three hundred miles away was seen as deliberately discriminatory. In May 1794, Congress finally responded to the complaints about this, passing an act that allowed state courts to hear excise cases if the nearest federal court was more than fifty miles from the site of the alleged violation. This act was signed by George Washington on June 5, 1794. On May 31, 1794, the very same day the act was passed by Congress, the federal court in Philadelphia, knowing that the new law would be enacted within a few days, issued legal processes against seventy-five western distillers under the old law. The July 1794 events known as the Whiskey Rebellion occurred when United States Marshal David Lenox, accompanied by the local excise inspector, John Neville, attempted to serve these processes.

The first shot of the Whiskey Rebellion was fired on July 15, 1794 at the home of William Miller, a farmer accused of having an unregistered still. Miller, who was about to sell his farm and move his family to Kentucky, refused to accept the process, which would have delayed his move by requiring him to appear in Philadelphia in August, and ordered Neville and Lenox off his property. A group of thirty or forty farmers, armed with pitchforks and muskets, had followed Neville and Lenox to

25. Leland D. Baldwin, *Whiskey Rebels: The Story of a Frontier Uprising,* (Pittsburgh, PA: University of Pittsburgh Press, 1939), 78.

Williams's farm, and one fired a warning shot at the officers as they were riding away.

At the same time that this was going on, the Mingo Creek Militia happened to be gathering in response to a request from George Washington for militiamen to deal with Indian attacks on the frontier. The next day, having heard about the incident at Williams's farm, about forty of the Mingo Creek militiamen, led by John Holcroft, marched on Neville's estate, demanding that he surrender his commission. A shot fired by Neville from inside his house hit, and according to most accounts killed, William Miller's nephew, Oliver Miller. Neville then ordered his slaves to fire on the militiamen. The militia retreated, but Neville, knowing they would be back, applied to Fort Pitt for protection. Eleven soldiers, along with Major Abraham Kirkpatrick, were sent to Neville's estate, and Neville himself was evacuated. The next day, July 17, a much larger force of rebels, led by James McFarlane, a captain in the Revolutionary War and at this time a major in the militia, showed up demanding to see Neville. Major Kirkpatrick informed the militiamen that Neville was no longer there. McFarlane then demanded that the soldiers leave, but Kirkpatrick refused. After allowing Neville's family to be evacuated, the militiamen opened fire on the soldiers. During the hour long battle, Neville's house and barn were set on fire. The soldiers eventually surrendered, but not before killing Major McFarlane.

A series of meetings, held over the next few weeks at the Mingo Creek meeting house and the home of David Bradford, resulted in the assembly of an estimated five to seven thousand rebels at Braddock's Field on August 1. From Braddock's field, the rebel army marched through Pittsburgh, then crossed the Monongahela River, proceeded to Major Kirkpatrick's property, and burned down his barn.

On August 7, George Washington issued a proclamation in which he ordered the rebels to disperse by September 1, quoting the law that gave him the authority to call forth the militia of Pennsylvania and other states if they didn't. On the same day that he issued the proclamation, Washington also directed his Secretary of War, Henry Knox, to send a circular letter to the governors of Pennsylvania, Virginia, Maryland, and New Jersey, requesting a total of nearly thirteen thousand militiamen, a number that was later increased to fifteen thousand.

Washington made one more attempt to settle the dispute without the use of military force, dispatching three commissioners to the area to offer the rebels amnesty in exchange for their signatures on a statement of submission to the laws of the federal government. The commissioners had two meetings with a delegation of rebel leaders, the first from August 21 to 23, and the second on September 1 and 2. On September 24, after returning to Philadelphia, the commissioners submitted a report in which they concluded that military action would be necessary to enforce the laws.

On October 2, the rebel leaders resolved unanimously to agree to the terms offered by the commissioners, and appointed two representatives, David Redick and William Findley, to present the resolution to George Washington. By this time, however, the militia requested by Washington on August 7 were already on their way to Western Pennsylvania. Some of the troops had started moving as early as September 19, and Washington, on September 25, had issued a proclamation stating that military force would be used.

A somewhat popular myth about the Whiskey Rebellion is that Washington personally led the troops into western Pennsylvania and squashed the rebellion. In reality, Washington was already on his way back to Philadelphia by the time the troops moved into the area where the rebellion had taken place. He did spend about about a week at Carlisle, Pennsylvania, a rendezvous point for the various militia units, and did review the troops at Bedford, where he also had a visit from his family and checked on some property he was trying to sell. By the time the troops got to western Pennsylvania, however, there was no rebellion to squash. Washington had known this by the time he left Carlisle on October 12. David Redick and William Findley met with Washington at Carlisle on October 9 and 10, and assured him that the rebels would put up no resistance, and would be unarmed as they voluntarily showed up at meetings to submit to the government's terms. In other words, fifteen thousand troops were on their way to fight nobody.

As expected, there was no battle when the troops marched into the western counties in late October. The government, however, needed to put on a show. The real leaders of the rebellion were nowhere to be found, so twenty less significant participants were *captured* and hauled off to Philadelphia for interrogation. Eighteen were eventually released. The other two were charged with and convicted of treason, and then pardoned by Washington. One of these two was described by his neighbors as being mentally impaired.

While many historians have theorized that Hamilton himself somehow instigated the Whiskey Rebellion to provide an excuse to demonstrate the authority of the federal government to enforce its laws, the evidence of this is purely circumstantial. What is certain, however, is that Hamilton couldn't have been happier that the rebellion occurred, and that he made the most of it. Washington, as already mentioned, was easily convinced that the democratic societies were to blame. Of course, the fact that Jefferson, who by this time had resigned as Secretary of State, was no longer around to refute these accusations made this even easier.

The following is from a letter written by Washington to Governor Henry Lee of Virginia on August 26, 1794. This is one of several letters showing that Washington, by this time, not only believed that the democratic societies were responsible for the Whiskey Rebellion, but that Citizen Genet was responsible for the democratic societies.

> I consider this insurrection as the first *formidable* fruit of the Democratic Societies; brought forth I believe too prematurely for their own views, which may contribute to the annihilation of them.
>
> That these societies were instituted by the *artful* and *designing* members (many of their body I have no doubt mean well, but know little of the real plan,) primarily to sow the seeds of jealousy and distrust among the people, of the government, by destroying all confidence in the Administration of it; and that these doctrines have been budding and blowing ever since, is not new to any one, who is acquainted with the characters of their leaders, and has been attentive to their manœuvres. I early gave it as my opinion to the confidential characters around me, that, if these Societies were not counteracted (not by prosecutions, the ready way to make them grow stronger) or did not fall into disesteem from the knowledge of their origin, and the views with which they had been instituted by their father, Genet, for purposes well known to the Government; that they would shake the government to its foundation. Time and circumstances have confirmed me in this opinion, and I deeply regret the probable consequences, not as they will

> affect me personally, (for I have not long to act on this theatre, and sure I am that not a man amongst them can be more anxious to put me aside, than I am to sink into the profoundest retirement) but because I see, under a display of popular and fascinating guises, the most diabolical attempts to destroy the best fabric of human government and happiness, that has ever been presented for the acceptance of mankind.[26]

The Federalist newspapers were also busy connecting Genet to the democratic societies, and the societies to the Whiskey Rebellion. For example, on Oct. 15, 1794, *Wood's Newark Gazette* presented the following step by step progression of the formation of the societies, and a prediction of their downfall.

> "A New Chapter—Political
>
> "1. This is the book of the generation and downfall of Jacobinism.
> "2. Brissot begat the Jacobin clubs of Paris. The Jacobin clubs of Paris begat Genet, and his French brethren:
> "3. Genet begat the Democratic Societies in America; the Democratic Societies begat the Pittsburgh Rebellion and its consequences:
> "4. The Pittsburgh Rebellion begat an armament of 15,000 men:
> "5. The armament of 15,000 men will beget an expense of near two million dollars, of which all the people of the United States must bear a proportion:
> "6. The expense will beget an attention of the people to the rise and origin; and
> "7. That attention will beget the detestation and downfall of Jacobinism are eight generations.
>
> "Thus endeth the first political chapter."[27]

26. George Washington to Governor Henry Lee, August 26, 1794, John C. Fitzpatrick, ed., *The Writings of George Washington from the Original Manuscript Sources, 1745-1799,* vol. 33, (Washington D.C.: Government Printing Office, 1931), 475-476.

27. Eugene Perry Link, *Democratic-Republican Societies, 1790-1800,* (Morningside Heights, NY: Columbia University Press, 1942), 19-20.

There was just one little problem with blaming the formation of the democratic societies on Genet – the first democratic society was formed before Genet arrived in America. The man behind the first society was Revolutionary War General Peter Muhlenberg. This society, called The German Republican Society, was formed in Philadelphia sometime near the end of March 1793. Genet didn't arrive in America until April 8. He then stayed in South Carolina for a several weeks before heading north. The first circular of The German Republican Society was printed in Philadelphia's German newspaper, the *Philadelphische Correspondenz,* on April 9. A reader of this paper wrote to Philip Freneau, requesting that he print an English translation in his paper, the *National Gazette,*[28] which he did on April 13. The following was the last paragraph of the request to Freneau.

> It would be to the advantage of Pennsylvania and the union if political societies were established throughout the United States, as they would prove powerful instruments in support of the present system of equality, and formidable enemies to aristocracy in whatever shape it might present itself. May the example of the German Republican Society prove a spur to the friends of equality throughout the United States.[29]

Two days later, on April 15, the *National Gazette's* story about the German Republicans was reprinted by Benjamin Franklin Bache, grandson of Benjamin Franklin, in his paper, the *Aurora and General Advertiser.* All of these articles in the Philadelphia newspapers predated Genet's May 16 arrival in Philadelphia by at least a month.

The man behind Philadelphia's second democratic society was Dr. David Rittenhouse – a noted scientist and inventor; President of the American Philosophical Society, succeeding founder Benjamin Franklin after his death in 1790; and Director of the United States Mint from

28. Freneau's National Gazette was established in 1791 to combat John Fenno's Gazette of the United States, the Federalist newspaper in which Hamilton, under various psuedonyms, promoted his and the administrations views. Jefferson facilitated the establishment of the National Gazette by bringing New York newspaper editor, and college friend of James Madison, Philip Freneau to Philadelphia as a translator for the State Department, a part time job that would give him a salary while he established a Republican newspaper to publish anti-administration articles written by James Madison, also under psuedonyms.

29. Eugene Perry Link, *Democratic-Republican Societies, 1790-1800,* (Morningside Heights, NY: Columbia University Press, 1942), 8.

1792 to 1795. The formation of The Democratic Society of Pennsylvania was announced to the public on July 4, 1793. By the time Rittenhouse formed this society, another democratic society, The Norfolk and Portsmouth Republican Society, had already been formed in Virginia.

The reason for a second society being formed in Philadelphia was that the first one was comprised of only German-Americans, and some parts of their mission and constitution were specific to the rights and concerns of German-Americans. The Democratic Society of Pennsylvania was more universal, and its constitution, written by Alexander J. Dallas, became the model for most of the nearly forty other societies that were formed in other parts of the country over the next few years. The declarations and constitutions of all of these societies contained statements like the following, from the first circular of The Democratic Society of Pennsylvania.

> ...The seeds of luxury appear to have taken root in our domestic soil; and the jealous eye of patriotism already regards the spirit of freedom and equality, as eclipsed by the pride of wealth and the arrogance of power. This general view of our situation has led to the institution of the Democratic Society. A constant circulation of useful information, and a liberal communication of republican sentiments, were thought to be the best antidotes to any political poison, with which the vital principles of civil liberty might be attacked; for by such means, a fraternal confidence will be studiously marked; and a standard will be erected, to which, in danger and distress, the friends of liberty may successfully resort. To obtain these objects, then, and to cultivate on all occasions the love of peace, order, and harmony; an attachment to the constitution and a respect to the laws of our country will be the aim of the Democratic Society.[30]

The Federalists, of course, immediately started looking for a way to stop this network of communication and its influence on public opinion. The Whiskey Rebellion was their opportunity, but the only societies that could be connected to it in any way at all were the two

30. Eugene Perry Link, *Democratic-Republican Societies, 1790-1800,* (Morningside Heights, NY: Columbia University Press, 1942), 11.

in the counties where the rebellion occurred – The Society of United Freemen in Mingo Creek, and The Democratic Society in Washington County, both of which were formed in the spring of 1794. Naturally, there were participants in the rebellion who were also members of these local societies. Seven members of the Washington County society were among the five hundred rebels who took part in one or both of the attacks on Neville's home. The Mingo Creek society, which was comprised almost entirely of farmers, did take one action as a society, passing a resolution in support of the opposition to the excise tax. The rest of the nearly forty societies in other parts of the country, however, were not even remotely involved. In fact, members of some of these societies were among the volunteers who went to suppress the rebellion, and several societies passed resolutions approving of the federal government's use of military force. Nevertheless, George Washington, based on the misinformation he was given, denounced *"certain self-created societies"* in his November 19, 1794 message to Congress.

> ...The arts of delusion were no longer confined to the efforts of designing individuals. The very forbearance to press prosecutions was misinterpreted into a fear of urging the execution of the laws; and associations of men began to denounce threats against the officers employed. From a belief that, by a more formal concert, their operation might be defeated, certain self-created societies assumed the tone of condemnation....[31]

The Senate, which was still controlled by the Federalists, quickly approved a reply to the president that included a response to this statement, complete with the words *"self-created societies."* The Federalists in the House wanted to do the same thing. The Republicans, however, knowing that Washington had been misinformed about these societies, thought they should just leave the subject out of their reply entirely. They had no intention of agreeing with the accusation, and in this house they now had a slim majority.

The committee appointed on November 20 to draft the House's

31. *Journal of the House of Representatives of the United States,* vol. 2, 3rd Cong. 2nd Sess., (Washington D.C.: Gales and Seaton, 1826), 233-234.

reply to Washington's message consisted of one Federalist – Theodore Sedgwick, one Republican – James Madison, and Thomas Scott, a representative from Pennsylvania who wasn't clearly attached to either party. The committee came back with a list of proposed resolutions addressing various points made by Washington. What was conspicuously absent from this list, however, was a resolution addressing the accusation made against the democratic societies.

On November 24, Thomas Fitzsimons, one of Hamilton's mouthpieces in the House, moved that the following be added.

> As part of this subject, we cannot withhold our reprobation of the self created societies, which have risen up in some parts of the union, misrepresenting the conduct of the Government, and disturbing the operation of the laws, and which, by deceiving and inflaming the ignorant and the weak, may naturally be supposed to have stimulated and urged the insurrection.[32]

Fitzsimons's motion sparked a heated five day debate. The Republicans repeatedly pointed out two things. First, the Federalists had not been able to produce any evidence to support their accusation, and second, the rebellion had obviously started before the democratic societies existed. Ironically, the evidence they used to support this second point was a letter written by Hamilton. Thomas Scott, who was obviously the deciding vote on the committee that drafted the resolutions to be included in the reply, happened to be from Washington County, where the rebellion had occurred. In the debate, he said he knew for a fact that certain leaders of the local democratic societies were also leaders of the rebellion, but added that these were the only societies that could be connected to the rebellion in any way. On November 26, the third day of the debate, it was suggested that a committee be appointed to fully investigate the causes of the rebellion, and if any of the societies or members of societies were found to have been involved, accuse them by name rather than censuring all the societies.

Alexander Hamilton had been watching the debate, and knew the Federalists were losing. On November 27, he made one last ditch

32. *The Debates and Proceedings of the Congress of the United States of America,* vol. 4, 3rd Cong., 2nd Sess., (Washington D.C.: Gales & Seaton, 1855), 899.

effort to provide evidence to support his accusation, supplying the following *"recently received"* information to Thomas Fitzsimons.

> Seeing the debates on the subject of Democratic Societies, I called at your house to state some facts.
>
> It is true that the opposition to the excise laws began from causes foreign to Democratic Societies, but it is well ascertained by proof in the course of judiciary investigations that the insurrection immediately is to be essentially attributed to one of those societies sometimes called the Mingo-Creek Society, sometimes the Democratic Society. An early and active member of it commanded the first attack at Neville's House; another active member of that Society, McFarlane, the second attack. Benjamin Parkinson, the president, and several other members of it seemed to have directed the second attack as a committee. This may be asserted as founded upon good proof and information recently received, though it would not be consistent with decorum to name me. Make what use you please of this, and communicate it to other friends.[33]

Fitzsimons didn't bother using Hamilton's information. Nobody was disputing that members of the societies in western Pennsylvania were among the rebels, so having their names or asserting that they *"seemed to have"* acted as a committee wasn't going to make any difference. Besides this, Hamilton didn't even get the facts that were already known right, such as the fact that the Mingo Creek Society and the Washington County Democratic Society were two separate societies.

The Republicans won this round, and, in the end, the words *"self-created societies"* in Fitzsimons's proposed amendment were replaced by *"individuals or combinations of men."* Having to get in the last word, however, Uriah Tracy, a Federalist representative from Connecticut, wanted to go on record as declaring *"to the Whole House that, by 'combinations of men,' he understood the Democratic societies."*[34]

33. Alexander Hamilton to Thomas Fitzsimons, November 27, 1794, Henry Cabot Lodge, ed., *The Works of Alexander Hamilton,* vol. 10, (New York: G.P. Putnam's Sons, 1904), 78-79.

34. *The Debates and Proceedings of the Congress of the United States of America,* vol. 4, 3rd Cong., 2nd Sess., (Washington D.C.: Gales & Seaton, 1855), 947.

One thing that was pointed out a number of times in the debate over the self-created societies was that many of the same Federalists who wanted to suppress the democratic societies belonged to their own self-created society, the Society of the Cincinnati. Apparently, this society didn't count because its members supported the policies of the administration. Thomas Jefferson noted the hypocrisy of this when he wrote to James Madison about Washington's message.

> The denunciation of the democratic societies is one of the extraordinary acts of boldness of which we have seen so many from the faction of monocrats. It is wonderful indeed, that the President should have permitted himself to be the organ of such an attack on the freedom of discussion, the freedom of writing, printing and publishing. It must be a matter of rare curiosity to get at the modifications of these rights proposed by them, and to see what line their ingenuity would draw between democratical societies, whose avowed object is the nourishment of the republican principles of our Constitution, and the society of the Cincinnati, a *self-created* one, carving out for itself hereditary distinctions, lowering over our Constitution eternally, meeting together in all parts of the Union, periodically, with closed doors, accumulating a capital in their separate treasury, corresponding secretly and regularly, and of which society the very persons denouncing the democrats are themselves the fathers, founders and high officers. Their sight must be perfectly dazzled by the glittering of crowns and coronets, not to see the extravagance of the proposition to suppress the friends of general freedom, while those who wish to confine that freedom to the few, are permitted to go on in their principles and practices. I here put out of sight the persons whose misbehavior has been taken advantage of to slander the friends of popular rights; and I am happy to observe, that as far as the circle of my observation and information extends, everybody has lost sight of them, and views the abstract attempt on their natural and constitutional rights in all its nakedness. I have never heard, or heard of, a expression or opinion which did not condemn it as an inexcusable aggression. And with respect to the transactions against the excise law, it

appears to me that you are all swept away in the torrent of governmental opinions, or that we do not know what these transactions have been. We know of none which, according to the definitions of the law, have been anything more than riotous. There was indeed a meeting to consult about a separation. But to consult on a question does not amount to a determination of that question in the affirmative, still less to the acting on such a determination; but we shall see, I suppose, what the court lawyers, and courtly judges, and would-be ambassadors will make of it. The excise law is an infernal one. The first error was to admit it by the Constitution; the second, to act on that admission; the third and last will be, to make it the instrument of dismembering the Union, and setting us all afloat to choose what part of it we will adhere to. The information of our militia, returned from the westward, is uniform, that though the people there let them pass quietly, they were objects of their laughter, not of their fear; that one thousand men could have cut off their whole force in a thousand places of the Alleghany; that their detestation of the excise law is universal, and has now associated to it a detestation of the government; and that a separation which perhaps was a very distant and problematical event, is now near, and certain, and determined in the mind of every man. I expected to have seen some justification of arming one part of the society against another; of declaring a civil war the moment before the meeting of that body which has the sole right of declaring war; of being so patient of the kicks and scoffs of our enemies, and rising at a feather against our friends; of adding a million to the public debt and deriding us with recommendations to pay it if we can etc., etc. But the part of the speech which was to be taken as a justification of the armament, reminded me of parson Saunders' demonstration why *minus* into *minus* make plus. After a parcel of shreds of stuff from Æsop's fables and Tom Thumb, he jumps all at once into his *ergo, minus* multiplied into minus make *plus.* Just so the fifteen thousand men enter after the fables, in the speech.[35]

35. Thomas Jefferson to James Madison, December 28, 1794, Andrew A. Lipscomb and Albert Ellery Bergh, eds., *The Writings of Thomas Jefferson,* vol. 9, (Washington D.C.: Thomas Jefferson Memorial Association, 1904), 293-296.

One of the questions that came up during the debate in the House of Representatives over Washington's 1794 message was just how far Congress should go in responding that they agreed with the president, particularly when they weren't informed of all the specifics of a situation. What prompted this question was the vagueness of Washington's statement about the goals of his foreign policy. The House couldn't very well disagree with Washington's objectives, such as *"to cultivate peace with all the world,"* but agreeing with his statement could be taken as agreeing with how he was obtaining his objectives. The problem with this was that they had no idea how Washington was obtaining his objectives, and many of the representatives suspected that they might not approve when they found out. The reason for this suspicion was that they knew John Jay had been sent to England.

After Washington proclaimed the neutrality of the United States in the war between Great Britian and France, Great Britain issued two orders-in-council. The first, issued in June 1793, expanded the definition of what was considered contraband. The second, issued in November 1793, prohibited neutral countries from trading with the French West Indies. These were ports had been closed to neutral trade before the war, but were opened by France when the war began. American merchants ignored these orders, and the British began confiscating American ships and impressing American seamen, claiming they were deserters from the British navy. By March 1794, nearly four hundred ships had been taken. This, however, was only one of several major problems the United States had with the British. Another was that British troops, in defiance of the 1783 treaty that ended the Revolutionary War, were still holding their forts in the Northwest Territory.

While Hamilton was talking Washington into sending John Jay to England to negotiate a treaty, a handful of Federalists who were in on the real plan kept Congress busy debating and approving defensive measures, believing they were preparing for a war with England.

The choice of John Jay for the mission to England met with immediate disapproval from Republicans. Jay, who at the time was also Chief Justice of the Supreme Court, was decidedly pro-British, and, although of French descent himself, despised the French. He was also extremely unpopular and distrusted in the western part of the country because he would have given up American navigation rights on the Mississippi if his negotiations with the Spanish in 1786 had resulted in a treaty.

Washington obviously anticipated that Jay's mission was going to cause trouble with France. Within a month of Jay's departure, Washington appointed a Republican, James Monroe, as foreign minister to France, replacing Federalist Gouverneur Morris, whose recall had already been requested by the French. As will be explained in Volume II, even the Federalist controlled Senate had questioned Washington's appointment of Morris. In fact, some senators opposed this appointment so strongly that they were ready to stop the practice of appointing regular foreign ministers altogether rather than confirm Morris's appointment.

As expected, Jay's treaty favored Great Britain tremendously. With the exception of the British agreeing to remove their troops from the Northwest Territory, and a provision for a commission to examine claims for American shipping losses, the treaty was a total surrender. When the Federalist controlled Senate passed it on June 24, 1795, it did so without a single vote to spare. Even after approving it, the Senate, knowing how unpopular it was going to be with the American people, took an oath of secrecy to keep its terms from being made public for as long as possible. Because the Senate had amended one article, the treaty had to go back to England for approval before Washington signed it. One of the ten senators who voted against it, however, Stevens Thomson Mason of Virginia, disregarded the oath of secrecy and leaked the treaty to both the French ambassador and the press. Benjamin Franklin Bache published a summary of it in his newspaper on June 29, 1795, then printed and distributed copies of the entire thing. By the time Washington proclaimed the treaty in February 1796, people all over the country were already protesting in the streets, many burning effigies of Jay and Washington. Hamilton was stoned by an angry mob in New York, and Jay, who resigned from the Supreme Court, later said he could have ridden the entire length of the country at night by the light of all the burning effigies of himself. One state legislature even demanded a constitutional amendment allowing for the recall of senators when they found out that one of their senators had voted in favor of the treaty. Some of the democratic societies, unsure of whether or not Washington would try to run for a third term, called for an amendment limiting the president to two terms. Washington, however, had no intention of seeking another term.

In the election of 1796, most Federalists supported Vice President Adams to succeed George Washington, which, of course, he did. Adams, however, already had a few enemies, most notably Alexander Hamilton. Hamilton attempted to tamper with the 1796 election by persuading southern electors to vote for South Carolinian Thomas Pinckney (brother of the 1800 candidate Charles Cotesworth Pinckney). This was basically the same plan as in 1800, but with a different Pinckney. When the New England states got wind of Hamilton's scheme, however, their electors neutralized it by not giving their second vote to Pinckney. The unexpected result was that, although Adams came in first, Jefferson, the Republican candidate for president, came in a second. Pinckney, the presumed Federalist vice presidential candidate came in third. Republican Thomas Jefferson was vice president to John Adams, a Federalist president. Jefferson, however, didn't think this would present a problem. According to the Constitution, unless something happened to the president, his only job as vice president was to be president of the Senate. This made him part of the legislative branch of the government, not the executive.

By the time Adams took office in 1797, a faction of his party already wanted to declare war on France. A not unexpected result of the Jay Treaty was that the French started seizing American ships headed for British ports. One of the last things George Washington had done as president was to send Charles Cotesworth Pinckney to Paris to try to negotiate with the revolutionary government. French foreign minister Talleyrand, however, had refused to see him. Adams did not want to give up on diplomacy and tried again, ordering Pinckney, then in Holland, to return to Paris and make another attempt at opening negotiations. He also appointed two other commissioners, Elbridge Gerry and John Marshall, to join Pinckney.

Talleyrand sent three agents to meet with the commissioners. The French agents, referred to in the commissioners' dispatches as X, Y, and Z, informed the commissioners that there would be no negotiations until three demands were met – a large loan from the United States, a bribe for Talleyrand, and a formal apology from John Adams for some anti-French remarks he had made. The commissioners refused to submit to these demands and returned to America. The X.Y. Z. correspondence was made public and used by the Federalists to renew pro-war sentiments, which had begun to wane, even in the Federalist strongholds in the north. Adams, however, although taking measures to prepare for war, still hoped a diplomatic solution.

In June 1798, the United States entered an undeclared naval war with France, with an act of Congress giving American merchant vessels permission to arm and defend themselves against French ships. That same year, the Federalists passed the *Alien and Sedition Acts,* their version of the Patriot Act. Creating and then preying on fears that the French were somehow going to take over the United States, the Federalists had many Americans willing to give up their rights in the name of national security. It became illegal to *"write, print, utter, or publish"* anything criticizing the government, which, of course, had been the ultimate goal of the Federalists when they went after the democratic societies in 1793. The president was given the authority to *"apprehend, restrain, secure, or remove"* any resident alien on a mere suspicion of being a threat to America, and the length of time it took for an immigrant to become an American citizen was dramatically increased. To become a citizen under the old law, an immigrant had to be a resident of the United States for five years, and of their state for one year. These requirements were increased to fourteen years and five years respectively.

As the election of 1800 got closer, the pro-war faction of the Federalist Party, which included religious leaders like Rev. William Linn, had had enough of Adams, who had sent another set of commissioners to France in 1799. On September 30, 1800, Oliver Ellsworth, William Richardson Davie, and William Vans Murray concluded a treaty with France, but word of this did not reach the United States until after the election. Adams had kept the United States out of a war it was not prepared to fight, but had destroyed whatever chance he had of being elected to a second term in the process.

On January 26, 1799, Thomas Jefferson wrote his famous letter to Elbridge Gerry in which he laid out what was to become his party's platform. Gerry was a bit of a political anomaly. He was a wealthy Massachusetts merchant, a speculator, and a stockholder in the Bank of the United States – all the makings of a Federalist. He was, however, an almost fanatical Republican. He was one of only three delegates who stayed to the end of the Constitutional Convention but did not sign the Constitution. Gerry considered the Constitution to form a government that was far more national than republican. Later, as Governor of Massachusetts, he even redistricted his state to favor Republican candidates. One of the new districts was said to resemble the shape of a salamander, which is where the term "gerrymander" comes from. In this same 1799 letter to Gerry, Jefferson wrote at length about the X.Y.Z. affair, and its effect on the country. Jefferson was sure that the other two commissioners, both Federalists, had actually wanted their mission to France to fail, and that Gerry, who had been a last minute replacement for a third Federalist, Francis Dana, was the only one of the three who had sincerely wanted to avoid a war.

> ...when Pinckney, Marshal, and Dana were nominated to settle our differences with France, it was suspected by many, from what was understood of their dispositions, that their mission would not result in a settlement of differences; but would produce circumstances tending to widen the breach, and to provoke our citizens to consent to a war with that nation, & union with England. Dana's resignation, & your appointment gave the first gleam of hope of a peaceable issue to the mission. for it was believed that you were sincerely disposed to accommodation: & it was not long after your arrival there before symptoms were observed of that difference of views which had been suspected to exist.—In the meantime however the aspect of our government towards the French republic had become so ardent that the people of America generally took the alarm. to the Southward their apprehensions were early excited. in the Eastern States also they at length began to break out. meetings were held in many of your towns, & addresses to the government agreed on in opposition to war. the example was spreading like a wildfire. other meetings were called in other places, & a general concurrence of sentiment against the apparent inclinations of the government was imminent; when, most critically for the government, the despatches of Oct. 22. prepared by your collegue Marshall with a view to their being made public, dropped into their laps. it was truly a God-send to them, & they made the most of it. many thousands of copies were printed & dispersed gratis, at the public expense; & the zealots for war co-operated so heartily, that there were instances of single individuals who

> printed & dispersed 10, or 12,000 copies at their own expense. the odiousness of the corruption supposed in those papers excited a general & high indignation among the people. unexperienced in such maneuvres, they did not permit themselves even to suspect that the turpitude of private swindlers might mingle itself unobserved, & give its own hue to the communications of the French government, of whose participation there was neither proof nor probability. it served, however, for a time, the purpose intended. the people in many places gave a loose to the expressions of their warm indignation, & of their honest preference of war to dishonour. the fever was long & successfully kept up, and in the meantime war measures as ardently crowded....[36]

Jefferson, who, even as vice president, was not immune to the Sedition Act, did not sign this letter, in which he made quite a few *seditious* statements. He also asked Gerry, a fellow signer of the Declaration of Independence, to burn certain pages of it after reading them, and ended with the following statement.

> ...and did we ever expect to see the day when, breathing nothing but sentiments of love to our country & it's freedom & happiness, our correspondence must be as secret as if we were hatching it's destruction![37]

In spite of the temporary success of the Federalists' propaganda, Jefferson was confident that the people of the United States were coming to their senses, as he wrote to Thomas Lomax in March 1799.

> The spirit of 1776 is not dead. It has only been slumbering. The body of the American people is substantially republican. But their virtuous feelings have been played on by some fact with more fiction; they have been the dupes of artful manœuvres, and made for a moment to be willing instruments in forging chains for themselves. But time and truth

36. Thomas Jefferson to Elbridge Gerry, January 26, 1799, Barbara B. Oberg, ed., *The Papers of Thomas Jefferson,* vol. 30, (Princeton, NJ: Princeton University Press, 2003), 647-648.
37. *ibid.,* 650.

> have dissipated the delusion, and opened their eyes. They see now that France has sincerely wished peace, and their seducers have wished war, as well for the loaves and fishes which arise out of war expenses, as for the chance of changing the Constitution, while the people should have time to contemplate nothing but the levies of men and money....[38]

Not all of the rumors spread about Thomas Jefferson during the campaign of 1800 had to do with his religious beliefs. One particular rumor circulated in Jefferson's home state of Virginia was that he had changed and become an advocate of an aristocratic government while part of the Adams administration. It was claimed that Jefferson had aristocratic tendencies long before this, having stood by and done nothing while property ownership was made a requirement to be eligible to vote or hold office in Virginia's constitution. In July 1800, Jefferson received a letter from Jeremiah Moore, a Baptist minister in Virginia. While the Virginia Baptists had no doubt that Jefferson's commitment to religious freedom was as strong as ever, they wanted his reassurance that his political principles hadn't changed before supporting him in the election.

> ...it would gratify a number of your friends to hear you say you were in heart an enemy to the doctrine of aristocracy in Virginia and Every where Else. the part you took against the Religious Establishment when I had the honour with others of putting a petition into your hands Signed by 10000 Subscribers praying the disolution of those Tyrannical Chains Still lives in my memory and has sometimes afforded me pleasure in being able to say without doubt that you were a friend to religious liberty and it would add to my happiness to be able to say with Equal Certainty that you remain a friend to a general mode of suffrage in opposition to that partial one which now prevails in this Commonwealth.[39]

38. Thomas Jefferson to Thomas Lomax, March 12, 1799, H.A. Washington, ed., *The Writings of Thomas Jefferson: Being His Autobiography, Correspondence, Reports, Messages, Addresses, and Other Writings, Official and Private,* vol. 4, (New York: Derby & Jackson, 1859), 300.

39. Jeremiah Moore to Thomas Jefferson, July 12, 1800, *The Thomas Jefferson Papers, Series 1, General Correspondence, 1651-1827,* Library of Congress Manuscript Division, #18319.

Jefferson assured Rev. Moore that his opinion in favor of a general suffrage had never changed, and explained that he had not been in Virginia in 1776 when the state's constitution was written and adopted.

> The times are certainly such as to justify anxiety on the subject of political principles, & particularly those of the public servants. I have been so long on the public theatres that I supposed mine to be generally known. I make no secret of them: on the contrary I wish them known to avoid the imputation of those which are not mine. You may remember perhaps that in the year 1783. after the close of the war there was a general idea that a convention would be called in this state to form a constitution. In that expectation I then prepared a scheme of constitution which I meant to have proposed. This is bound up at the end of the *Notes on Virginia,* which being in many hands, I may venture to refer to it as giving a general view of my principles of government. It particularly shews what I think on the question of the right of electing & being elected, which is principally the subject of your letter. I found it there on a year's residence in the country; or the possession of property in it, or a year's enrollment in it's militia. When the constitution of Virginia was formed I was in attendance at Congress. Had I been here I should probably have proposed a general suffrage: because my opinion has always been in favor of it. Still I find very honest men who, thinking the possession of some property necessary to give due independence of mind, are for restraining the elective franchise to property. I believe we may lessen the danger of buying and selling votes, by making the number of voters too great for any means of purchase: I may further say that I have not observed men's honesty to increase with their riches.[40]

Because he had told Rev. Moore that his 1783 draft of a new constitution for Virginia could still be relied on as an accurate assessment

40. Thomas Jefferson to Jeremiah Moore, August 14, 1800, Paul Leicester Ford, ed., *The Works of Thomas Jefferson, Federal Edition,* vol. 9, (New York and London: G.P. Putnam's Sons, 1905), 142-143.

of his political principles, Jefferson needed to point out the one thing in that draft that he had changed his mind about. When Jefferson wrote this in 1783, he had opposed allowing members of the clergy to hold public office in that state. With the Anglican Church only recently disestablished, there was too great a risk that its clergymen would attempt to use public offices as a way to regain some power. In 1800, however, nearly fifteen years after the complete and permanent disestablishment of religion in Virginia, Jefferson thought that it was safe to remove the restriction.

> The clergy, by getting themselves established by law, & ingrafted into the machine of government, have been a very formidable engine against the civil and religious rights of man. They are still so in many countries & even in some of these United States. Even in 1783, we doubted the stability of our recent measures for reducing them to the footing of other useful callings. It now appears that our means were effectual. The clergy here seem to have relinquished all pretension to privilege and to stand on a footing with lawyers, physicians &c. They ought therefore to possess the same rights.[41]

Jefferson's letter to Rev. Moore is used by a handful of religious right American history authors because, in it, Jefferson wrote that he had changed his mind about allowing clergymen to hold public office in Virginia. Mark Beliles, for example, cites it as his source for one of the claims on the list his version of the *Jefferson Bible* of things that Jefferson *"supported government being involved in."* Beliles, however, citing no other source, adds school teachers to this claim.

According to Beliles, Jefferson supported: "allowing clergymen to hold public office or be school teachers."

Jefferson said absolutely nothing in this letter indicating that he supported clergymen being school teachers. The only mention of

41. Thomas Jefferson to Jeremiah Moore, August 14, 1800, Paul Leicester Ford, ed., *The Works of Thomas Jefferson, Federal Edition,* vol. 9, (New York and London: G.P. Putnam's Sons, 1905), 143.

education in his letter to Rev. Moore was the following comment about the political principles being taught in some schools.

> I have with you wondered at the change of political principles which has taken place in many in this state however much less than in others. I am still more alarmed to see, in the other states, the general political dispositions of those to whom is confided the education of the rising generation. Nor are all the academies of this state free from grounds of uneasiness. I have great confidence in the common sense of mankind in general: but it requires a great deal to get the better of notions which our tutors have instilled into our minds while incapable of questioning them, & to rise superior to antipathies strongly rooted.[42]

Contrary to dire predictions of Rev. William Linn and the other religious alarmists, both America and religion managed to survive the eight years of Thomas Jefferson's presidency. But even many years later, rumors of Jefferson's irreligious tendencies were still a source of concern for some. One of these was Massachusetts Congressman Cyrus King.

Jefferson had provided that Congress would have the first opportunity to buy his extensive library upon his death, but when the library in Washington D.C. was destroyed by the British in 1814, he offered to sell it to them immediately. Cyrus King was a bit worried about what the infidel Jefferson's library might contain.

> **In his book *America's God and Country,* William Federer writes: "In response to Thomas Jefferson's announcing his plans to donate his personal library of 6,487 books to the Library of Congress, Cyrus King, before the committee moved:**
>
> > **To report a new section authorizing the Library Committee, as soon as said library shall be received at Washington, to select there from all**

42. Thomas Jefferson to Jeremiah Moore, August 14, 1800, Paul Leicester Ford, ed., *The Works of Thomas Jefferson, Federal Edition,* vol. 9, (New York and London: G.P. Putnam's Sons, 1905), 143-144.

books of an atheistical, irreligious, and immoral tendency, if any such there be, and send the same back to Mr. Jefferson without any expense to him."

Federer, apparently not wanting to pass up the opportunity to show how religious another early politician was, quotes Cyrus King, in spite of the fact that King obviously wouldn't have agreed with his own assertion that Jefferson was a devout Christian. According to the records of the House, the other representatives had quite a bit of fun with King's motion, and he ended up withdrawing it.

> Mr. King afterwards moved to recommit the bill to a select committee, with instructions to report a new section authorizing the Library Committee, as soon as said library shall be received at Washington, to select therefrom all books of an atheistical, irreligious, and immoral tendency, if any such there be, and send the same back to Mr. Jefferson without any expense to him. This motion Mr. K. thought proper afterwards to withdraw.
>
> This subject, and the various motions relative thereto, gave rise to a debate which lasted to the hour of adjournment; which, though it afforded much amusement to the auditors, would not interest the feelings or judgement of any reader.[43]

43. *The Debates and Proceedings in the Congress of the United States,* vol. 28, 13th Cong., 3rd Sess., (Washington D.C.: Gales and Seaton, 1854), 1105.

— CHAPTER ELEVEN —

More Lies About Benjamin Franklin

While his famous motion for prayers at the Constitutional Convention is by far the most popular, and often the only, Benjamin Franklin story in religious right American history books, some books contain a number of other Franklin lies. Many of these are simply out of context quotes, such as the following from David Barton's book *Original Intent,* which has become a favorite on websites that support censorship.

> **According to Barton: "Concerning the balance between the freedom of the press and the responsibility of the press, printer and publisher Benjamin Franklin explained:**
>
> > **If by the liberty of the press were understood merely the liberty of discussing the propriety of public measures and political opinions, let us have as much of it as you please; But if it means the liberty of affronting, calumniating [falsely accusing], and defaming one another, I, for my part...[am] willing to part with my share of it when our legislators shall please so to alter the law, and shall cheerfully consent to exchange my liberty of abusing others for the privilege of not being abused myself."**

What Barton quotes is from a satire written by Franklin in 1789 entitled *An Account of the Supremest Court of Judicature in Pennsylvania, viz., The Court of the Press.* Franklin was condemning abuses of the press, as well as people who supported these abuses by creating a market for them, but he wasn't seriously proposing limiting the freedom of the press. By the end of this article, Franklin had arrived at what he thought was a very practical solution to the problem – leave the freedom of the press alone, but change the battery laws to make it perfectly legal for a victim of libel to give their libeller *"a good drubbing."*

> ...since so much has been written and published on the federal constitution, and the necessity of checks in all other parts of good government has been so clearly and learnedly explained, I find myself so far enlightened as to suspect some check may be proper in this part also; but I have been at a loss to imagine any that may not be construed an infringement of the sacred *liberty of the Press.* At length, however, I think I have found one that, instead of diminishing general liberty, shall augment it; which is, by restoring to the people a species of liberty, of which they have been deprived by our laws, I mean the *liberty of the Cudgel.*—In the rude state of society prior to the existence of laws, if one man gave another ill language, the affronted person would return it by a box on the ear, and, if repeated, by a good drubbing; and this without offending against any law. But now the right of making such returns is denied, and they are punished as breaches of the peace; while the right of abusing seems to remain in full force, the laws made against it being rendered ineffectual by the *liberty of the Press.*
>
> My proposal then is, to leave the liberty of the Press untouched, to be exercised in its full extent, force, and vigour, but to permit the *liberty of the Cudgel* to go with it *pari passu.* Thus, my fellow-citizens, if an impudent writer attacks your reputation, dearer to you perhaps than your life, and puts his name to the charge, you may go to him as openly and break his head. If he conceals himself behind the print-

> er, and you can nevertheless discover who he is, you may in like manner way-lay him in the night, attack him behind, and give him a good drubbing. If your adversary hire better writers than himself to abuse you the more effectually, you may hire brawny porters, stronger than yourself, to assist you in giving him a more effectual drubbing.—Thus far goes my project as to *private* resentment and retribution. But if the public should ever happen to be affronted, *as it ought to be,* with the conduct of such writers, I would not advise proceeding immediately to these extremities; but that we should in moderation content ourselves with tarring and feathering, and tossing them in a blanket.[1]

Another popular misquote comes from Benjamin Franklin's 1784 pamphlet, *Information To Those Who Would Remove To America.* As Minister to France, Franklin was constantly getting inquiries from people considering a move to America, and became aware that there were certain misconceptions among the French about what they could expect. Rather than continuing to answer these inquiries individually, he published a pamphlet correcting the common misconceptions, and explaining why certain types of people would find great opportunities in America, while others would be disappointed.

> **In his book *The Myth of Separation,* David Barton writes: "Franklin was in France—the home of the 'enlightenment,' land of the rejection of religion, bastion of atheism and marital infidelity; notice his description of America for the French:**
>
> > **Bad examples to youth are more rare in America, which must be a comfortable consideration to parents. To this may be truly added, that serious religion, under its various denominations, is not only tolerated, but respected and practised. Atheism is unknown there; infidelity rare and secret; so that persons may live**

1. J.A. Leo Lemay, ed., *Benjamin Franklin, Writings,* (New York: Literary Classics of the United States, 1987), 1153-1154.

> **to a great age in that country, without having their piety shocked by meeting with either an Atheist or an Infidel."**

By omitting the beginning of this paragraph, Barton makes it look like atheists and infidels were the bad examples that Franklin was referring to. Barton begins his quote with the last sentence of a statement about the rarity of unemployment in America, which, without the rest of the paragraph, makes it appear to be the first sentence of a statement about religion. This was the final paragraph of a fairly long pamphlet, the main point of which was that America was a country where there were very few people lived in poverty, very few would be considered wealthy by European standards, and virtually everyone worked. Idleness, not atheism, was the bad example to youth that Franklin was talking about.

At this time in Europe, unemployment among young men was high because there were too many tradesmen competing for a limited amount of work. There weren't any uninhabited areas left where the settlement of new farmers would create a demand for other businesses. European tradesmen were reluctant to take on apprentices because their apprentices would become their future competition. America, on the other hand, was expanding, and had a growing demand for tradesmen of all descriptions, making unemployment low and apprenticeships easy to come by. The following is the beginning of Franklin's statement about bad examples, ending with the sentence that Barton begins with.

> The almost general Mediocrity of Fortune that prevails in America obliging its People to follow some Business for subsistence, those Vices, that arise usually from Idleness, are in a great measure prevented. Industry and constant Employment are great preservatives of the Morals and Virtue of a Nation. Hence bad Examples to Youth are more rare in America, which must be a comfortable Consideration to Parents....[2]

Franklin's description of religion in America was aimed at the

2. J.A. Leo Lemay, ed., *Benjamin Franklin, Writings,* (New York: Literary Classics of the United States, 1987), 982.

French Protestants. This was written in 1784, five years before the French Revolution began, when France was still a Catholic country in which Protestants were persecuted. They were barred from most professions and trade guilds, couldn't hold public office, couldn't enroll their children in schools, etc. Children of Protestant marriages were considered illegitimate and not legally entitled to inheritances, and Protestant girls were sometimes kidnapped and placed in convents. Even in areas where Protestants were permitted to practice their religion, their churches could not be built near Catholic churches, and had to be disguised as houses or shops. In areas where Protestants were completely prohibited from practicing their religion, they resorted to giving their ministers code names, and changed their places of worship frequently to avoid detection. The only places where Protestants had anything like religious freedom were the cities, where wealthy Protestants owned banking and shipping businesses that were necessary to the economy.

The only way Protestants could enter most trades or professions was to obtain a *Certificate of Catholicity,* which stated that they had converted to Catholicism. If a Protestant needed a certificate to get a job, they would attend a Catholic church for a few months, pretend they had converted, and get one. Everyone knew that the process of obtaining these certificates was just a game. The Protestants weren't really converting, and many of the clergymen issuing the certificates were actually atheists and infidels who only became clergymen for political power. This is why Franklin made the unusual comment that "*serious*" religion was practiced in America. As Foreign Minister to France, he couldn't very well come right out and say the state religion was a joke, so he just snuck in a little dig at it, while letting the Protestants know that, in America, they would be welcomed in all of the trades and professions described in his pamphlet without having to hide their religion.

A number of religious right American history authors do actually agree with mainstream historians that Benjamin Franklin was no more than a deist. There are some, however, who are determined to prove that every single one of our founders was a devout Christian. As evidence of Franklin's devotion to Christianity, these authors often bring up his friendship with Rev. George Whitefield, disregarding or misquoting Franklin's own words describing this friendship.

In his book *America's God and Country,* William Federer presents his own interpretation of the events involving Rev. Whitefield found in Franklin's autobiography.

> **According to Federer: "Benjamin Franklin became very appreciative of the preaching of George Whitefield, even to the extent of printing many of his sermons and journals."**

Nowhere in his autobiography did Franklin write anything indicating whether or not he appreciated Whitefield's preaching. In fact, in the same paragraph on which Federer bases his lie, Franklin made a point of stating that he was *not* one of Whitefield's followers. Whitefield simply hired Franklin as a printer, and they became friends.

> Some of Mr. Whitefield's enemies affected to suppose that he would apply these Collections to his own private Emolument; but I who was intimately acquainted with him (being employed in printing his Sermons and Journals, &c.), never had the least Suspicion of his Integrity, but am to this day decidedly of Opinion that he was in all his Conduct a perfectly *honest Man.* And methinks my Testimony in his Favour ought to have the more Weight, as we had no religious Connection. He us'd indeed sometimes to pray for my Conversion, but never had the Satisfaction of believing that his Prayers were heard. Ours was a mere civil Friendship, sincere on both Sides, and lasted to his Death.[3]

Federer continues, putting his own spin on what was actually Franklin's description of a little acoustic experiment.

> **According to Federer: "In his *Autobiography,* Franklin wrote about attending Whitefield's crusades at the Philadelphia Courthouse steps. He noted over 30,000 people were present, and that Whitefield's voice could be heard nearly a mile away."**

3. J.A. Leo Lemay, ed., *Benjamin Franklin, Writings,* (New York: Literary Classics of the United States, 1987), 1408.

One thing that impressed Franklin about Whitefield was how remarkably loud and clear his voice was. But, Franklin doubted that anyone, even Whitefield, could speak loudly enough to be heard by crowds as large as the newspapers claimed he had preached to. One evening, when Whitefield was preaching in Philadelphia, Franklin decided to do some calculations to see if the stories could be true. Franklin was obviously far more interested in how loud Whitefield could talk than what he was saying.

> ...He preach'd one Evening from the Top of the Court House steps, which are in the Middle of Market Street, and on the West Side of Second Street which crosses it at right angles. Both Streets were fill'd with his Hearers to a considerable Distance. Being among the hindmost in Market Street, I had the Curiosity to learn how far he could be heard, by retiring backwards down the Street towards the River; and I found his Voice distinct till I came near Front Street, when some Noise in that Street obscur'd it. Imagining then a Semi-Circle, of which my Distance should be the Radius, and that it were fill'd with Auditors, to each of whom I allow'd two square feet, I computed that he might well be heard by more than Thirty-Thousand. This reconcil'd me to the Newspaper Accounts of his having preach'd to 25000 People in the Fields, and to the antient Histories of Generals haranguing whole Armies, of which I had sometimes doubted.[4]

Federer continues: "Benjamin Franklin built a grand auditorium for the sole purpose of having his friend George Whitefield preach in it when he came to Pennsylvania."

First of all, Franklin did not build this building. A collection was taken up by the people of Philadelphia to build it. The clergy of Philadelphia wouldn't allow Whitefield to preach in their churches, so he had to preach outdoors. This made the people realize that the city needed an auditorium. Franklin later became one of the trustees of

4. J.A. Leo Lemay, ed., *Benjamin Franklin, Writings,* (New York: Literary Classics of the United States, 1987), 1409.

the building. Second, the building was not built for the sole purpose of providing a place for Whitefield to preach. It was built for any preacher of any religion, Christian or not, who needed a venue in the city. The following are Franklin's accounts of how the auditorium was paid for, what its purpose was, and how he became a trustee of the building. It is also in this account that Franklin himself said he didn't belong to any religious denomination.

> ...And it being found inconvenient to assemble in the open Air, subject to its Inclemencies, the Building of a House to meet in was no sooner propos'd, and Persons appointed to receive Contributions, but sufficient Sums were soon receiv'd to procure the Ground and erect the Building, which was 100 long & 70 broad, about the Size of Westminster hall; and the Work was carried on with such Spirit as to be finished in a much shorter time than could have been expected. Both House and Ground were vested in Trustees, expressly for the Use of any Preacher of any religious Persuasion who might desire to say something to the People at Philadelphia; the Design in building not being to accommodate any particular Sect, but the Inhabitants in general; so that even if the Mufti of Constantinople were to send a Missionary to preach Mohammedanism to us, he would find a Pulpit at his Service.[5]
>
> It is to be noted that the Contributions to this Building being made by People of different Sects, Care was taken in the Nomination of Trustees, in whom the Building & Ground was to be vested, that a Predominancy should not be given to any Sect, lest in time that Predominancy might be a means of appropriating the whole to the Use of such Sect, contrary to the original Intention; it was therefore that one of each sect was appointed, viz. one Church-of-England-man, one Presbyterian, one Baptist, one Moravian, &c. Those in case of Vacancy by Death were to fill it by Election from among the Contributors. The Moravian happen'd not to please his

5. J.A. Leo Lemay, ed., *Benjamin Franklin, Writings*, (New York: Literary Classics of the United States, 1987), 1406-1407.

> Colleagues, and on his Death, they resolved to have no other of that Sect. The Difficulty then was, how to avoid having two of some other Sect, by means of the new Choice. Several Persons were named, and for that Reason not agreed to. At length one mention'd me, with the Observation that I was merely an honest Man, & of no sect at all; which prevail'd with them to chuse me....[6]

Federer continues: "After the crusades, Franklin donated the auditorium to be the first building of the University of Pennsylvania."

Obviously, since Franklin didn't own the building to begin with, he couldn't have donated it to the University of Pennsylvania. Because Franklin was a trustee of both the auditorium and what at the time was called the Philadelphia Academy, he helped negotiate the deal transferring ownership of the building, which was already being used by the school. The religious fervor of the Great Awakening had been short-lived, and by the time the Philadelphia Academy was outgrowing its original building around 1750, the auditorium was rarely being used.

> ...The Enthusiasm which existed when the House was built had long since abated, and its Trustees had not been able to procure fresh Contributions for paying the Ground Rent, and discharging some other Debts the Building had occasion'd, which embarrass'd them greatly. Being now a Member of both Sets of Trustees, that for the Building & that for the Academy, I had good Opportunity of negociating with both, & brought them finally to an Agreement, by which the Trustees for the Building were to cede it to those of the Academy, the latter undertaking to discharge the Debt, to keep for ever open in the Building a large Hall for occasional Preachers, according to the original Intention, and maintain a Free School for the instruction of poor Children....[7]

6. J.A. Leo Lemay, ed., *Benjamin Franklin, Writings,* (New York: Literary Classics of the United States, 1987), 1419.

7. *ibid.*, 1419.

Religious right authors who argue against the idea that Benjamin Franklin was a deist also dismiss the fact that Franklin used this word to describe himself. Because the only time Franklin came right out and called himself a deist was in the part of his autobiography about his teenage years, they claim that his deism was nothing more than a phase he went through. Their indisputable evidence that Franklin got over his teenage deism phase is, of course, his famous speech calling for prayers at the Constitutional Convention.

> **According to John Eidsmoe, in his book *Christianity and the Constitution:* "But the speech reveals that eighty-one year-old Franklin had drastically changed his beliefs since he had been a teenage deist. For his central, italicized statement that 'God governs in the affairs of men' violates the cardinal tenet of deism, that God does not intervene in human affairs."**

Well, Franklin was no teenager when he wrote the following to his friend Rev. Whitefield. This was written in 1769, when Franklin heard the news that British soldiers had been sent to Boston. Franklin was sixty-three at the time.

> ...I *see* with you that our affairs are not well managed by our rulers here below; I wish I could *believe* with you, that they are well attended to by those above: I rather suspect, from certain circumstances, that though the general government of the universe is well administered, our particular little affairs are perhaps below notice, and left to take the chance of human prudence or imprudence, as either may happen to be uppermost....[8]

Another popular Franklin misquote comes from his plan for education in Pennsylvania.

> **In an article on his *WallBuilders* website, David Barton claims: "In Benjamin Franklin's 1749 plan of edu-**

8. Benjamin Franklin to George Whitefield, before September 2, 1769, J.A. Leo Lemay, ed., *Benjamin Franklin, Writings,* (New York: Literary Classics of the United States, 1987), 845.

cation for public schools in Pennsylvania, he insisted that schools teach 'the necessity of a public religion ...and the excellency of the Christian religion above all others, ancient or modern'."

In his book *Original Intent,* Barton uses this same quote, edited in the same way, in a list prefaced by the following statement: "Representative quotes of many Founders demonstrate their preference for Christianity and provide no evidence of any alleged 'mandate to promote a visible, pluralistic society.'"

First of all, Franklin didn't *insist* that schools teach anything. His 1749 education plan was a compilation of ideas drawn from various existing education plans, which he listed at the beginning of the pamphlet. He called this a *"Paper of Hints towards forming a Plan,"* and requested that readers submit their suggestions to him.

Barton's misquote comes from Franklin's description of the many things that students would learn about by using history books as reading texts. This included the historical role and effects of religion.

> *History* will also afford frequent Opportunities of showing the Necessity of a *Publick Religion,* from its Usefulness to the Publick; the Advantage of a Religious Character among private Persons; the Mischiefs of Superstition, etc. and the Excellency of the Christian Religion above all others antient or modern.[9]

Something that needs to be taken into consideration when reading this is that the definitions of certain words have changed a bit since 1749. David Barton, who lists *"Failure to Account For Etymology"* as one of nine ways that secularists are revising history, apparently doesn't find it necessary for himself to account for etymology.

According to Barton: "'Etymology' (the study of word derivations) deals with the manner in which the

9. J.A. Leo Lemay, ed., *Benjamin Franklin, Writings,* (New York: Literary Classics of the United States, 1987), 336-337.

> **meanings of words change over the years. Even though word definitions and usage may change dramatically in only a few years, revisionists regularly ignore these changes, thus making completely inaccurate portrayals and assertions."**

There are two words in Franklin's course description that were used differently in 1749. The first is the word *necessity,* which at that time was commonly used as a synonym for *inevitability.* Noah Webster, in his 1828 Dictionary, provided this sample phrase: *"the necessity of a consequence from certain premises."* All Franklin was saying was that, as history would show, it was inevitable that a common (public) set of religious beliefs would develop in a society because this was useful.

The next part of Franklin's sentence, *"the Advantage of a Religious Character among private Persons; the Mischiefs of Superstition, etc.,"* is deleted by Barton to make this quote fit a list in his book of quotes that he uses to demonstrate the founders' *"preference for Christianity."* Obviously, what Franklin was talking about was examining both the good and bad consequences of the religious beliefs and superstitions of historical characters.

The second word that had another common meaning in Franklin's day is *excellency.* While an excellency could mean a good quality, it was also used to mean something *excelling* or surpassing something else. By the *"excellency of the Christian religion above all others, ancient or modern"* he was referring to the fact that Christianity had replaced ancient religions, and become more popular and widespread than other modern religions. The books suggested by Franklin to demonstrate this were not religious books, but histories of Greece and Rome, which, of course, would teach about the downfall of the ancient Greek and Roman religions and the rise of Christianity.

Like Jefferson's plan for public schools in Virginia, Franklin's plan for Pennsylvania included no actual religious instruction, but instead proposed that moral lessons be taught by *"making continual Observations of the Rise or Fall of any Man's character, Fortune, Power, etc., mention'd in History...."*[10]

A very common accusation made by religious right American his-

10. J.A. Leo Lemay, ed., *Benjamin Franklin, Writings,* (New York: Literary Classics of the United States, 1987), 336.

tory authors is that secularists are revising history by degrading the character of the founders. Among the typical examples used to support these accusations are excerpts from various history books in which certain founders are portrayed as womanizers or adulterers. Although there will be an entire chapter in Volume II about the religious right's claims that this is revisionism, and their attempts to portray all of the founders as unrealistically perfect, the subject is mentioned here because the founder most often used as an example of this is, of course, Benjamin Franklin.

While religious right authors scour the writings of the founders for references to the Bible, and quote or misquote these references in every way possible to fit their stories, there is one letter by Franklin, in which he explicitly mentioned the Ten Commandments, that they don't use. The following was written by a seventy-two year old Franklin to Madame Brillon, a married woman in her mid-thirties, and one of two women he pursued more than casually during his time in France.

> People commonly speak of Ten Commandments.—I have been taught that there are twelve. The first was increase & multiply & replenish the earth. The twelfth is, A new Commandment I give unto you, *that you love one another.* It seems to me that they are a little misplaced, And that the last should have been the first. However I never made any difficulty about that, but was always willing to obey them both whenever I had an opportunity. Pray tell me my dear Casuist, whether my keeping religiously these two commandments tho' not in the Decalogue, may not be accepted in Compensation for my breaking so often one of the ten I mean that which forbids Coveting my neighbour's wife, and which I confess I break constantly God forgive me, as often as I see or think of my lovely Confessor, and I am afraid I should never be able to repent of the Sin even if I had the full Possession of her.
>
> And now I am Consulting you upon a Case of Conscience I will mention the Opinion of a certain Father of the church which I find myself willing to adopt though I am not sure it is orthodox. It is this, that the most effectual way to get rid of a

> certain Temptation is, as often as it returns, to comply with and satisfy it.
>
> Pray instruct me how far I may venture to practice upon this Principle?[11]

11. Benjamin Franklin to Madame Brillon, March 10, 1778, J.A. Leo Lemay, ed., *Benjamin Franklin, Writings*, (New York: Literary Classics of the United States, 1987), 919.

— CHAPTER TWELVE —

More Lies About Thomas Jefferson

While different types of lies about Thomas Jefferson are created for different purposes, most of those regarding the years of his presidency are designed primarily to make it appear that he approved of government financial support for religion. One such lie, found in religious right American history books for years, has recently become very popular among the supporters of faith-based initiatives.

> **According to David Barton's *WallBuilders* website: "Jefferson assured a Christian religious school that it would receive 'the patronage of the government.'"**

> **According to Mark Beliles, in the introduction to his version of the *Jefferson Bible*: "...in an 1804 letter to the Ursuline nuns in New Orleans, he personally promised his government would help their Catholic school."**

Because it contains the word *"patronage,"* the letter referred to by Beliles and quoted by Barton is used to imply that Jefferson promised government funding to this school. He did nothing of the kind.

When the United States purchased Louisiana from France in 1803, the nuns at the Ursuline convent in New Orleans, like many of the territory's inhabitants, were concerned about the status of their property. The Ursulines' convent and school had been built on land granted by government of France in 1734, and much of the income that supported these institutions came from two other properties, granted by the later Spanish government. Following the purchase of the territory, a wide variety of rumors were spread by anti-American natives of New Orleans. Among these were two about the convent. One was that the United States government planned to confiscate the convent's property and immediately expel the nuns from the country. The other was that no new novices would be allowed to enter the convent, but that the government would let the nuns who were already there stay, and then take the property after they all died off.

The nuns' uncertainty about their future in New Orleans actually began before the United States' purchase, when the French prefect, Pierre-Clemént Laussat, arrived to take possession of Louisiana from Spain in March 1803. On June 10, 1803, the territory's twenty-six priests were given permission by their superiors to return to Spain if they wanted to, and all but four did. Although the Ursulines were assured by Laussat that they had nothing to fear from the French government, most of them, including the convent's mother superior, also left New Orleans, requesting to be sent to Havana. Only nine of the twenty-five decided to stay, electing Sr. Therese de St. Xavier Farjon to be their new mother superior.

Within a week of the official proclamation of the treaty ceding Louisiana to the United States, William C.C. Claiborne, the territorial governor, attended a ceremony at the convent and personally assured the remaining nuns that both their property and religious liberty would be protected by their new government. On December 27, 1803, Claiborne wrote to Secretary of State James Madison that he had visited the convent, and that the nuns who had fled to Havana would soon be returning.

As far as Claiborne could tell, he had successfully convinced the nuns that their property and other rights were protected by the treaty of cession and the Constitution. In June 1804, however, he was asked by Mother Farjon to forward a letter from the convent to Thomas Jefferson. Claiborne sent this to Jefferson, accompanied by the following cover letter.

> At the particular request of the Superior of the Convent in this city, I have the honor to enclose you a communication from the Ursuline Nuns.

> These respectable ladies merit and possess a great share of the public esteem; their conduct is exemplary, and their time is usefully employed in the education of female youth. During my short residence in this city, I have paid the Nuns very great respect and given them assurances of the protection and friendly regard of the Government of the United States. I believe I have succeeded in conciliating their affections, and rendering their minds tranquil: it seems however that, they of late entertain some fears that their property cannot be secured to them and their successors without an act of Congress, and I understand that it is on this subject they have addressed you.[1]

Mother Farjon's letter, as Claiborne had expected, was a request from the nuns to have their property officially confirmed to them by Congress.

> Emboldened by the favorable mention you have been pleased to make of their order, the Nuns of St. Ursula at New Orleans take the liberty of addressing you on a subject highly interesting to their institution! They believe that without any direct application, the treaty of Cession, and the sence of Justice which marks the character of the United States, would have secured to them the property they now possess, but considering a sacred deposit, they would fail in a duty they deem essential were they to ommit requesting, that it may be formally confirmed to them & their successors, & that you may be pleased to communicate this request to the Congress of the United States in such a manner as you may deem proper....[2]

Jefferson's reply to this letter is the source of the lie that he promised financial support to a Catholic school. The sentence this is based on, however, had nothing to do with money. Jefferson obviously suspected from the timing of the nuns' request that this sudden

1. William C.C. Claiborne to Thomas Jefferson, June 15, 1804, *The Thomas Jefferson Papers Series 1, General Correspondence, 1651-1827,* Library of Congress Manuscript Division, #24464.
2. Sr. Therese de St. Xavier Farjon to Thomas Jefferson, June 13, 1804, *ibid.,* #24447.

renewal of concern about their property might have been caused by a recent incident in which another Catholic church in New Orleans was shut down by United States officials. Claiborne had been promising the nuns for months that there was no truth to the rumors that their property might be confiscated, and that the government of the United States would never interfere with a religious institution, so the closing of this church, and the fact that Claiborne had apparently done nothing to stop it, would naturally have given them cause to doubt his promises.

The situation that caused the closing of the church had to do with a dispute between two rival priests. Laussat had replaced the priest at this church, but the head of the Catholic church in Louisiana objected to the appointment and reinstated the old priest. When both priests, along with their supporters, showed up for mass on the same Sunday, the district commandant closed the church to prevent a riot from breaking out. Jefferson did not approve of this preemptive action, as he wrote to Madison on July 5, 1804.

> I think it was an error in our officer to shut the doors of the church, and in the Governor to refer it to the Roman catholic head. The priests must settle their differences in their own way, provided they commit no breach of the peace. If they break the peace they should be arrested. On our principles all church-discipline is voluntary; and never to be enforced by the public authority; but on the contrary to be punished when it extends to acts of force. The Govr. should restore the keys of the church to the priest who was in possession.[3]

About a week after writing this to Madison, Jefferson received the letter from the Ursuline convent. Jefferson knew that there was no point in laying the convent's request before Congress because they were not yet making determinations about land claims in the territory, so he began his reply by assuring the nuns that their property was secure even without an official confirmation. The rest of his letter, based on his assumption that the nuns' concern was caused by the clos-

3. Thomas Jefferson to James Madison, July 5, 1804, James Morton Smith, ed., *The Republic of Letters: The Correspondence Between Thomas Jefferson and James Madison 1776-1826*, vol. 2, (New York and London: W.W. Norton & Company, 1995), 1328.

ing of the church, was a reassurance that the local government would never interfere with their convent or school. What needs to be understood here is that most of the government in New Orleans at this time was made up of officials from the former government who were retained by the United States until a permanent government could be formed. These officials were anything but objective when it came to local religious and political disputes, and in many cases, such as the fight over this church, these disputes were both political and religious.

The following, written on July 13 or 14, 1804,[4] was Jefferson's reply to the convent.

> I have received, holy sisters, the letter you have written me wherein you express anxiety for the property vested in your institution by the former governments of Louisiana. The principles of the constitution and government of the United States are a sure guaranty to you that it will be preserved to you sacred and inviolate, and that your institution will be permitted to govern itself according to it's own voluntary rules, without interference from the civil authority. Whatever diversity of shade may appear in the religious opinions of our fellow citizens, the charitable objects of your institution cannot be indifferent to any; and it's furtherance of the wholesome

4. It should be noted that the dates usually given for both the Ursuline's letter to Jefferson (March 21, 1804) and his reply (May 15, 1804) are wrong, not just in religious right history books, but from other sources as well, including the Ursuline convent itself. The correct date of the convent's letter is June 13, 1804. There apparently exists a very similar letter dated March 21, but this letter was never sent to Jefferson. The most likely explanation for this is that the March 21 letter was written in reaction to the rumors that the government was planning to confiscate the convent's property, but never sent to Jefferson because Governor Claiborne was able convince the nuns that the rumors weren't true. Three months later, when the nuns began to doubt Claiborne's promises and decided to send the letter after all, it was rewritten with a number of insignificant wording changes. This second version, very clearly dated June 13, 1804, was the letter that was sent to Jefferson, enclosed by Claiborne with his letter of June 15. Both the convent's and Claiborne's letters are in the Jefferson Papers at the Library of Congress.

Two copies of Jefferson's reply exist – the original, in the possession of the Ursuline convent in New Orleans, and Jefferson's copy, in the Jefferson Papers at the Library of Congress. These copies are identical, written by Jefferson with his "polygraph," a machine that had two connected pens, the second pen making an exact duplicate of a letter as it was written. Jefferson did not date this letter when he wrote it. On his copy, however, there is a note in his handwriting that it was written on July 13 or 14, 1804. The copy sent to the convent had no date on it. At some later time, an incorrect date of May 15 was written on the convent's copy. This date, although clearly not in Jefferson's handwriting, has apparently never been questioned, most likely because the nuns' unsent letter of March 21 was believed to be a copy of the letter that was actually sent to Jefferson, which would make a reply dated May 15 possible.

> purposes of society, by training up it's younger members in the way they should go, cannot fail to ensure it the patronage of the government it is under. Be assured it will meet all the protection which my office can give it.
>
> I salute you, Holy Sisters, with friendship and respect.[5]

All Jefferson meant by the last few sentences of this letter was that, due to the universal nature of their work, he didn't think the nuns would have any problems with local officials, but, if they did, they would have the protection of his office, which had authority over these local officials.

A year later, the nuns actually did end up being on one side of the dispute between the rival priests, when the priest who lost the fight over the other church declared the convent to be the only place in New Orleans where sacraments could be administered. This priest began holding his services at the convent, but no trouble appears to have resulted from this. A new dispute was soon brewing over another priest who was replaced when New Orleans was placed under the authority of the Bishop of Baltimore, John Carroll.

Another lie, which often accompanies the one about the Ursulines' school, involves the same Bishop Carroll.

> **According to Mark Beliles, in the introduction to his version of the Jefferson Bible: "He used his influence while President to get the Commissioners of the District of Columbia to allow land to be purchased by the Catholic Church."**

First of all, this wasn't about *allowing* the church to buy land. Churches could buy land just like anyone else. This was about the church trying to negotiate a better price for a lot in Washington, something that many purchasers tried to do. The district's commissioners were known to come down on the price if the purchaser offered something advantageous in exchange. Usually, this was pay-

5. Thomas Jefferson to Sr. Therese de St. Xavier Farjon, July 13 or 14, 1804, *The Thomas Jefferson Papers Series 1, General Correspondence, 1651-1827,* Library of Congress Manuscript Division, #24602.

ment in full at the time of purchase, or short term rather than long term credit. At this time, the commissioners could barely keep up the interest payments on the debts to Maryland and Virginia for the land they had ceded for the district, let alone finance the construction of federal buildings, so deals were sometimes made to generate quick money. Lower prices were also given to purchasers who promised to make improvements to the property that fit the commissioners' plans for the city's development. Their main concern at this time was housing, which was in such short supply that almost everyone who worked in or visited Washington had to stay in Georgetown.

Bishop Carroll probably thought that sending his application to Jefferson rather than the Board of Commissioners might get him some preferential treatment, not because he wanted to build a church, but because Jefferson would remember his patriotism and services to the country during the Revolutionary War. Jefferson had known Carroll since 1776, when he volunteered to accompany Benjamin Franklin, Samuel Chase, and his cousin, Charles Carroll, on their diplomatic mission to Canada. The Continental Congress accepted Carroll's offer, thinking that having a Catholic priest along might help the delegation convince the mostly Catholic Canadians to side with the Americans. The seventy year old Franklin became very ill on this trip, and it was Bishop Carroll who took care of him and got him safely back to Philadelphia.

The story that Jefferson used his influence to get the commissioners to approve the church's application comes from his reply to Carroll. Reading only this letter, it would appear that Jefferson did try to influence the commissioners. Jefferson's letter to the commissioners, however, shows that he did not. He just let Bishop Carroll think he did. The following was Jefferson's reply to Carroll, written on September 3, 1801.

> I have received at this place the application signed by yourself and several respectable inhabitants of Washington on the purchase of a site for a Roman Catholic Church from the Commissioners. as the regulation of price rests very much with them, I have referred the paper to them, recommending to them all the favor which the object of the purchase would wage, the advantages of every kind which it would promise,

> and their duties permit. I shall be happy on this and every other occasion of showing my respect & concern for the religious society over which you preside in these states and in tendering to yourself assurances of my high esteem and consideration.[6]

This was Jefferson's letter to the Board of Commissioners, written on the same day.

> I take the liberty of referring to you the inclosed application from Bishop Carrol & others for respecting the purchase of a site for a church. it is not for me to interpose in the price of the lots for sale. at the same time none can better than yourselves estimate the considerations of propriety & even of advantage which would urge a just attention to the application, nor better judge of the degree of favor to it which your duties would admit. with yourselves therefore I leave the subject, with assurances of my high consideration & respect.[7]

Jefferson was obviously exaggerating a bit when he told Bishop Carroll that he had recommended to the commissioners *"all the favor which the object of the purchase would wage"* and *"the advantages of every kind which it would promise."* In reality, he barely gave an opinion on the subject, leaving it entirely up to the commissioners to decide if there was any advantage to accepting the application, and putting absolutely no pressure on them to do so. No new Catholic church was built in Washington until two decades later, and that was built on privately donated land, so it appears that the commissioners must have turned down Bishop Carroll's application.

According to an article on David Barton's *WallBuilders* website: "Jefferson urged local governments to make land available specifically for Christian purposes."

6. Thomas Jefferson to Bishop John Carroll, September 3, 1801, *The Thomas Jefferson Papers, Series 1, General Correspondence, 1651-1827,* Library of Congress Manuscript Division, #19966.

7. Thomas Jefferson to William Thornton, Alexander White, and Tristam Dalton, Commissioners, September 3, 1801, *Thomas Jefferson Papers, Series 3, District of Columbia Miscellany, 1790-1808,* Library of Congress Manuscript Division, #586.

Barton cites only one source for this extremely vague claim – Jefferson's letter to Bishop Carroll.

Most lies about property in the District of Columbia have to do tax exemptions for churches. These lies are based on federal laws that indirectly led to the exemption of church property from taxation. For example, the May 3, 1802 act of Congress incorporating the City of Washington stated that the corporation *could* tax property, the only restriction being a limit on the amount of the tax. This, of course, also meant that the corporation could decide *not to* tax a property. The act of Congress did not contain anything specifically about church property. It was the trustees of the city who decided to exempt it. But, because it was the act of Congress, by saying nothing on the subject, that had given the trustees of the city the power to *not* tax church property, the act of Congress is cited as a source for claims that *federal* laws exempted church property from taxes. The most popular tax exemption story, however, comes from another 1802 act of Congress, passed on the same day as the act incorporating of the City of Washington.

> **According to Robert Cord, in his book *Separation of Church and State:* "Subsidy to religious organizations, which may work for the common good, through tax exemption is not uncommon in the United States and was legislated by Congress in 1802 and even signed into law by President Thomas Jefferson."**
>
> **Gary DeMar, in his book *America's Christian History,* quotes another book by Cord, claiming: "...if Jefferson 'construed the establishment clause absolutely, he violated his oath of office, his principles, and the Constitution when, in 1802, he signed into federal law tax exemption for the churches in Alexandria County Virginia.'"**

The act referred to in this lie did not grant a tax exemption to the churches in Alexandria County. It merely gave the authority to assess and apply the existing county taxes to different officials, solving a problem created by another act passed a year earlier.

The lie is based on the fact that Alexandria County, while it was part of the District of Columbia, remained under the laws of Virginia, just as Washington County, the part of the district ceded by Maryland, remained under Maryland law. In Virginia, church property was exempt from taxes, so church property in Alexandria County remained exempt from taxes. The act of 1802 had nothing to do with what could or couldn't be taxed. This had never been changed. What had been changed, however, by an act passed in 1801, was who had the authority to assess the taxes previously assessed by the county courts of Maryland and Virginia, which had lost their jurisdiction over the territory ceded by their states. As of the same date, residents of the ceded territory were no longer subject to state taxes, but they were still subject to county taxes, which paid for things such as county roads and the support of the poor within the counties. Since the county courts of Maryland and Virginia could no longer assess these taxes, Congress had to give someone else the authority to do this. The following section of *An Act supplementary to the act intituled 'An act concerning the District of Columbia,'* signed by John Adams on March 3, 1801, created and gave this authority to boards of commissioners.

> SEC. 4. *And be it further enacted,* That the magistrates, to be appointed for the said district, shall be and they are hereby constituted a board of commissioners within their respective counties, and shall possess and exercise the same powers, perform the same duties, receive the same fees and emoluments, as the levy courts or commissioners of county for the state of Maryland possess, perform and receive; and the clerks and collectors, to be by them appointed, shall be subject to the same laws, perform the same duties, possess the same powers, and receive the same fees and emoluments as the clerks and collectors of the county tax of the state of Maryland are entitled to receive.[8]

Giving these commissioners the same powers as the levy courts of Maryland worked out fine for Washington County, which had been

8. Richard Peters, ed., *The Public Statutes at Large of the United States of America,* vol. 2, (Boston: Charles C. Little and James Brown, 1845), 115.

part of Maryland. It did not, however, work well in Alexandria County, which had been part of Virginia. The act of 1802 amended this section of the act of 1801, giving Alexandria County's justices of the peace the power to assess and apply the taxes in that county in the same manner as the Virginia county courts. The following section of *An Act additional to, and amendatory of, an act, intituled 'An act concerning the District of Columbia,'* passed on May 3, 1802, is the basis of the claim that Thomas Jefferson exempted churches in Alexandria County from taxes.

> SEC. 6. *And be it further enacted,* That the taxes to be levied in the county of Alexandria, shall hereafter be assessed by the justices of the peace of the said county, and the poor of the town and country parts of the said county of Alexandria shall be provided for respectively, in like manner as the county and corporation courts were authorized to do by the laws of Virginia, as they stood in force within the said county, on the first Monday in December, in the year one thousand eight hundred.[9]

The reason for specifying that the justices of the peace would have the powers that the courts had on the first Monday in December 1800 was that this was the date that the courts and legislatures of Virginia and Maryland lost their authority over the territory ceded by their states. Laws passed by the Virginia legislature after this date did not apply in the ceded territory unless also enacted by Congress.[10] The reason for giving the justices of the peace the same powers as the county and *corporation* courts was that the town of Alexandria, which was also part of Virginia's cession, was incorporated under Virginia law.

The misconception that, by this act of 1802, Congress adopted the Virginia tax code, thereby exempting church property *at that time,*

9. Richard Peters, ed., *The Public Statutes at Large of the United States of America,* vol. 2, (Boston: Charles C. Little and James Brown, 1845), 194.

10. Congress began working on *An act concerning the District of Columbia* in December 1800, and, although this act, which stated that the laws of Virginia and Maryland "as they now exist" wasn't signed until February 27, 1801, Congress continued in future legislation to use the date of the first Monday in December 1800, the date of the formal cession, as the date on which state legislation ceased to have an effect in the District of Columbia.

began in 1970, when Chief Justice Warren Burger, in Walz v. Tax Commission of New York, misinterpreted the act's sixth section.

> **According to Chief Justice Burger: "It is significant that Congress, from its earliest days, has viewed the Religion Clauses of the Constitution as authorizing statutory real estate tax exemption to religious bodies. In 1802 the 7th Congress enacted a taxing statute for the County of Alexandria, adopting the 1800 Virginia statutory pattern which provided tax exemptions for churches."**

Chief Justice Burger's erroneous statement works out very well for the Liars for Jesus, because the date of 1802 makes this a story about their favorite target, Thomas Jefferson.

> **Robert Cord, in another part of his book *Separation of Church and State*, quotes Chief Justice Burger's statement, then comments: "The Chief Justice could also have noted, but did not, that Thomas Jefferson, then President of the United States, did not veto this federal law on the assumption that it was or created 'an establishment of religion' forbidden by the First Amendment. In fact, Jefferson signed it."**

As already explained, the Virginia tax statutes, along with all the other laws of Virginia, were never at any time not in force in Alexandria County. An act signed by George Washington in March 1791 kept them in force for the decade between the selection of the territory to be part of the District of Columbia and the formal cession of the territory to the federal government in December 1800, and the decision to leave them in force after the territory was ceded was made while John Adams was president.

The first act regarding the District of Columbia was *An Act for establishing the temporary and permanent seat of the Government of the United States.* This act, signed by George Washington in 1790, set the first Monday in December 1800 as the date that the government was to move from Philadelphia to the District of Columbia. The first section of this act accepted the site for the federal district, which was, as of 1790, to be entirely on the Maryland side of the Potomac. This section also provided that the laws of Maryland were to remain in force in the district until the December 1800 moving date, and, after this date, would continue in force unless Congress passed laws that changed them.

> ...*Provided nevertheless,* That the operation of the laws of the state within such district shall not be affected by this acceptance, until the time fixed for the removal of the government thereto, and until Congress shall otherwise by law provide.[11]

In 1791, this act was amended, allowing the location of the district to include territory from Virginia, but restricting the construction of any public buildings to the Maryland side of the Potomac. With the exception of prohibiting public buildings on the Virginia side, everything in the act of 1790 applied to the territory being ceded by Virginia *"as if the same had been within the purview of"* that act.[12] This meant that the laws of Virginia were to remain in force on the Virginia side of the district.

When the government moved to Washington in 1800, the House of Representatives was at a complete loss as to what they were supposed to do about the laws in the district. All the Constitution said was that a district not exceeding ten miles square was to be established as the seat of government, and all the act of 1790 said was that the state laws were in force in the district until Congress changed them. After a heated debate on New Year's Eve 1800, the House concluded that there was no practical way to establish a uniform code of laws for the district at that time. Since nothing in the Constitution or the act of 1790 actually required them to change the laws, they decided to leave the Maryland side of the district under Maryland law, and the Virginia side under Virginia law, at least until they could think of a better solution.

While there was no pressing need to change the laws themselves, Congress did have to provide for the enforcement of the existing laws,

11. Richard Peters, ed., *The Public Statutes at Large of the United States of America,* vol. 1, (Boston: Charles C. Little and James Brown, 1845), 130.
12. *ibid.,* 215.

establish courts, and appoint federal officials to perform any duties previously performed in the ceded territory by state or county officials. This was all done in the two acts signed by John Adams on February 27 and March 3, 1801. The first section of the act of February 27 stated that the laws of Maryland and Virginia would remain in force. This section wasn't really necessary because, without Congress passing any laws to the contrary, these laws would have remained in force anyway.

> SECTION 1. *Be it enacted by the Senate and House of Representatives of the United States in Congress assembled,* That the laws of the state of Virginia, as they now exist, shall be and continue in force in that part of the District of Columbia, which was ceded by the said state to the United States, and by them accepted for the permanent seat of government; and that the laws of the state of Maryland, as they now exist, shall be and continue in force in that part of the said district, which was ceded by that state to the United States, and by them accepted as aforesaid.[13]

This act also established courts, and provided for a marshal, a district attorney, justices of the peace, and other necessary officials. The act of March 3, 1801 was a supplement to the act of February 27, that, among other things, specified the powers and jurisdiction of the newly created district courts. This was the act quoted earlier that provided for commissioners to assess county taxes, and gave these commissioners the powers of the levy courts of Maryland. The sixth section of the act of 1802, the one used by Robert Cord and others to create the lie that Jefferson exempted churches from taxation, actually did nothing more than transfer the power to assess taxes in Alexandria County, according to the already existing tax statutes, from the commissioners appointed under the act of 1801 to the justices of the peace in that county.

The majority of lies about Jefferson during his presidency have to do with laws that he signed rather than his personal religious beliefs. The goal of these lies, when they come from authors who admit that

13. Richard Peters, ed., *The Public Statutes at Large of the United States of America*, vol. 2, (Boston: Charles C. Little and James Brown, 1845), 103-104.

Jefferson wasn't a Christian, is to make it appear that he approved of or encouraged government support of religion, in spite of the fact that he wasn't very religious himself. Those authors who attempt to portray Jefferson as a lifelong Christian, however, need to invent some evidence of this to cover this eight year period of his life.

> **According to William Federer, in his book *America's God and Country Encyclopedia of Quotations*: "President Thomas Jefferson, March 4, 1805, offered *A National Prayer for Peace:***
>
> > **Almighty God, Who has given us this good land for our heritage; We humbly beseech Thee that we may always prove ourselves a people mindful of Thy favor and glad to do Thy will. Bless our land with honorable ministry, sound learning, and pure manners.**
> >
> > **Save us from violence, discord, and confusion, from pride and arrogance, and from every evil way. Defend our liberties, and fashion into one united people the multitude brought hither out of many kindreds and tongues.**
> >
> > **Endow with Thy spirit of wisdom those whom in Thy Name we entrust the authority of government, that there may be justice and peace at home, and that through obedience to Thy law, we may show forth Thy praise among the nations of earth.**
> >
> > **In time of prosperity fill our hearts with thankfulness, and in the day of trouble, suffer not our trust in Thee to fail; all of which we ask through Jesus Christ our Lord, Amen."**

Federer gives two sources for this prayer. The first is the 1944 book *The Life and Selected Writings of Thomas Jefferson.* All that appears on the page of this book cited by Federer, however, is Jefferson's second Inaugural Address, given on March 4, 1805, the same date used by Federer for the prayer. Federer's second source is a newsletter published by the *Plymouth Rock Foundation,* one of many Christian reconstructionist organizations that masquerade as historical societies.

The real source of the prayer is the 1928 edition of the United States version of the Episcopal Church's *Book of Common Prayer,* published over a century after Jefferson's death. This prayer, titled *For Our Country,* was a new addition in the 1928 edition. It does not appear in the 1789 edition, which was the edition in use in 1804, or the next edition, published in 1892. Since appearing in Federer's book, however, the prayer has been attributed to Thomas Jefferson on hundreds of Christian American history websites. On a few websites, this same prayer is attributed to George Washington.

> **According to an article on David Barton's *WallBuilders* website: "While President, Jefferson closed his presidential documents with the phrase, 'In the year of our Lord Christ; by the President; Thomas Jefferson.'" Barton's footnote contains nothing but the following to support this claim: "For example, his presidential act of October 18, 1804, from an original document in our possession."**

> **D. James Kennedy, in his book *What If America Were a Christian Nation Again?*, claims to have a copy of what is presumably David Barton's mysterious document: "I have a photocopy of the conclusion of one of the many documents that he signed as president, and it says, 'In the year of our Lord Christ 1804.' He was the first president, and to my knowledge, the only president who did that. Jefferson, the anti-Christian, the irreligious infidel, said that it is Christ who is our Lord, and no one else."**

Thomas Jefferson did not date any documents *"In the year of our Lord Christ."* He did, however, sign a handful of documents, such as pardons, written and dated by others, and it is possible that one of these may have been dated in this manner. The words *"by the President,"* which Barton claims are part of the phrase on his document, would, of course, only appear on a document drawn up by someone else and given to the president for his signature. Barton's *WallBuilders* website contains images of numerous other documents, but, oddly, no image of this one that they claim to have in their possession, probably because an image of their document would show that it was not actually written by Jefferson.

The *WallBuilders* document is most likely something ending with a paragraph similar to the following, which is from a pardon signed by Jefferson in 1803 for Samuel Miller. To the left of this paragraph was a space for the seal of the United States, and below it, in the same handwriting as the rest of the document, are the words *"By the President"* where Jefferson's signature was to be filled in.

> In testimony whereof, I have hereunto set my hand and caused the seal of the United States to be affixed the Twenty fifth day of July, in the year of our Lord one thousand Eight hundred and three, and in the Twenty eighth year of the Independence of the said United States.
>
> By the President[14]

Jefferson, of course, didn't actually write this pardon. In fact, he didn't even sign it on the date that it says he did. Jefferson was at Monticello on July 25, 1803. James Madison, who was in Washington, had the pardon written, and mailed it to him on July 26. Jefferson received it on July 29, and mailed it back signed on July 31.[15] Jefferson obviously didn't even care if the date on a pardon was accurate, let alone how it was worded.

The date given by *WallBuilders* for their document, October 18,

14. *The Thomas Jefferson Papers, Series 10, Addenda to the Thomas Jefferson Papers, 1781-1829,* Library of Congress Manuscript Division.

15. James Madison to Thomas Jefferson, July 26, 1803, James Morton Smith, ed., *The Republic of Letters: The Correspondence Between Thomas Jefferson and James Madison 1776-1826,* vol. 2, (New York and London: W.W. Norton & Company, 1995), 1273. Thomas Jefferson to James Madison, July 31, 1803, *ibid.,* 1274. Madison's letter of July 26, in the Thomas Jefferson Papers at the Library of Congress, is marked received July 29.

1804, makes it pretty likely that what they have is the pardon signed by Jefferson for a George McFarland. Based on Jefferson's papers and correspondence from October 1804, and the fact that Congress was not in session at this time, the only official documents he would have signed on October 18 were appointments and this pardon. Out of these possibilities, the one most likely to have been written by someone who would have dated it *"In the year of our Lord Christ"* is the pardon. On October 4, 1804, Jefferson listed this pardon on a "to do list"[16] he was making for James Madison, who was at home in Virginia in the early part of the month. By the time Madison returned to Washington and got someone to write the pardon, it would probably have been around October 18.

Whatever the *WallBuilders* document is, it does not support the claim that Jefferson *"closed his presidential documents"* in the manner that this particular document was closed. Not one presidential document actually written by Jefferson was even dated *"in the year of our Lord,"* let alone *"In the year of our Lord Christ."*

An interesting thing about the Liars for Jesus is that even in cases where a story is basically true, they manage to turn it into a lie by adding lies to it. More often than not, the lies are added to make Thomas Jefferson the center of the story. Church services being held in the Capitol building is a good example of this. Church services actually were held in the Capitol building, and Jefferson really was known to attend them. This true story, however, isn't good enough, so lies are added to it to make Jefferson more involved.

> **The following is from the version that appears on David Barton's *WallBuilders* website: "According to the congressional records for late November of 1800, Congress spent the first few weeks organizing the Capitol rooms, committees, locations, etc. Then, on December 4, 1800, Congress approved the use of the Capitol building as a church building.**

16. Thomas Jefferson to James Madison, October 4 and 5, 1804, James Morton Smith, ed., *The Republic of Letters: The Correspondence Between Thomas Jefferson and James Madison 1776-1826,* vol. 2, (New York and London: W.W. Norton & Company, 1995), 1347.

Jefferson obviously did not intend to mail these "letters" to Madison's home in Virginia knowing that Madison would be leaving any day to return to Washington. They were clearly a list of things to do after he returned.

> **The approval of the Capitol for church was given by both the House and the Senate, with House approval being given by Speaker of the House, Frederick Augustus Muhlenberg, and Senate approval being given by the President of the Senate, Thomas Jefferson. Interestingly, Jefferson's approval came while he was still officially the Vice-President but after he had just been elected President."**

Neither the Senate nor Thomas Jefferson had anything whatsoever to do with this. The House of Representatives didn't need or ask for the approval of the Senate when the chaplains requested the use of the House chamber for Sunday services. The House itself didn't even vote on it. The Speaker simply announced that the chaplains had proposed to hold services in their chamber on Sundays, and the House got on with the more important business of the day – deciding where the stenographers should sit.[17]

Typical of religious right American history authors, David Barton has no problem twisting a few other things to make them fit his lies. To involve Jefferson in this story, and make it appear that he had some sort of power to prevent these religious services, Barton not only claims that this use of the House chamber needed the Senate's approval, but implies that Jefferson, as president of the Senate, had the authority to approve this on behalf of the Senate. Barton also has Jefferson already elected president on December 4, 1800. The election of 1800, held on December 3, was, of course, a tie between Jefferson and Aaron Burr. Jefferson was not elected until the House of Representatives elected him in February 1801. And, obviously, even if Jefferson had been the clear winner on December 3, he would not have known this on December 4.

> **According to James H. Hutson, in the *Religion and the Founding of the American Republic* companion book: "As president, Jefferson put his rejuvenated faith into practice in the most conspicuous form of public witness possible, regularly attending worship services**

17. *The Debates and Proceedings of the Congress of the United States of America,* vol. 10, 6th Cong., 2nd Sess., (Washington D.C.: Gales & Seaton, 1851), 797-799.

> **where the delegates of the entire nation could see him—in the 'hall' of the House of Representatives. According to the recollections of an early Washington insider, 'Jefferson during his whole administration, was a most regular attendant. The seat he chose the first sabbath day, and the adjoining one, which his private secretary occupied, were ever afterwords [sic] by the courtesy of the congregation, left for him.'"**

> **Also according to Hutson: "How did attending church services in Congress, which was, after all, public property, square with the constitutional scruples generally imputed to Jefferson about mixing religious and public spheres? Perhaps he reasoned that, since the House of Representatives, a member of a separate and independent branch of the government, was organizing and sponsoring the services, his principles would not be unduly compromised. This would not explain, however, why Jefferson permitted executive branch employees under his direct control, members of the Marine Band, to participate in House church services. Splendidly attired in their scarlet uniforms, the Marine musicians made a 'dazzling appearance' in the House on Sundays, as they tried to help the congregation by providing instrumental accompaniment to its psalm singing."**

D. James Kennedy, in his book *What If America Were A Christian Nation Again?,* goes even further, claiming that Jefferson not only permitted, but ordered the Marine band to play at these services.

> **According to Kennedy: "He wasn't pleased with the music, so he ordered the marine band to come to church on Sunday. They were paid out of the federal treasury to support the singing of hymns and psalms in the church."**

The *"early Washington insider"* referred to and quoted by Hutson was Margaret Bayard Smith, wife of Samuel Harrison Smith, a Philadelphia newspaper editor who moved to Washington in 1800 to establish a national newspaper, *The National Intelligencer*. By selectively quoting Mrs. Smith's description of Sundays at the Capitol, authors like Hutson give the impression that what took place there were solemn religious services, which, most importantly, were attended by Thomas Jefferson. Judging by Mrs. Smith's entire description of these services, however, it's not surprising that Jefferson, who complained about the lack of any social life in Washington, was such a *"regular attendant."*

> ...I have called these Sunday assemblies in the capitol, a *congregation,* but the almost exclusive appropriation of that word to religious assemblies, prevents its being a descriptive term as applied in the present case, since the gay company who thronged the H. R. looked very little like a religious assembly. The occasion presented for display was not only a novel, but a favourable one for the youth, beauty and fashion of the city, Georgetown and environs. The members of Congress, gladly gave up their seats for such fair auditors, and either lounged in the lobbies, or round the fire places, or stood beside the ladies of their acquaintance. This sabbath-day-resort became so fashionable, that the floor of the house offered insufficient space, the platform behind the Speaker's chair, and every spot where a chair could be wedged in was crowded with ladies in their gayest costume and their attendant beaux and who led them to their seats with the same gallantry as is exhibited in a ball room. Smiles, nods, whispers, nay sometimes tittering marked their recognition of each other, and beguiled the tedium of the service. Often, when cold, a lady would leave her seat and led by her attending beau would make her way through the crowd to one of the fire-places where she could laugh and talk at her ease. One of the officers of the house, followed by his attendant with a great bag over his shoulder, precisely at 12 o'clock, would make his way through the hall to the depository of letters to put them in the mail-bag, which sometimes had a most ludicrous effect, and always diverted attention from the

> preacher. The musick was as little in union with devotional feelings, as the place. The marine-band, were the performers. Their scarlet uniform, their various instruments, made quite a dazzling appearance in the gallery. The marches they played were good and inspiring, but in their attempts to accompany the psalm-singing of the congregation, they completely failed and after a while, the practice was discontinued,—it was *too* ridiculous.[18]

More serious, and much more sparsely attended, religious services were held in other public buildings. These solemn, four hour long communion services, as Hutson points out, were held in buildings under the control of the executive branch. This is pointed out, of course, to make Jefferson responsible for these services, although there isn't one shred of evidence that the organizers of the services asked Jefferson for permission to hold them. Hutson, ignoring Mrs. Smith's description of the services at the Capitol, also makes the following understatement about the difference between those services and the far more serious services in the other buildings.

> **According to Hutson: "Church services in the executive branch buildings were more 'religious' than those in the Capitol, because the sacraments were celebrated in the former, but not, apparently, in the latter."**

The obvious reason that church services were held in the public buildings of Washington during the Jefferson administration was that the city did not yet have churches, or any other buildings, that could accommodate them. When the government moved to Washington in 1800, the only churches that existed were a tobacco shed being used by the Episcopalians, and a small Catholic chapel built in 1794 for the Irish stonemasons who had moved to the city to work on the federal buildings. The practice of holding services at the Capitol, once started, continued much longer than was necessary, and services were still being held there decades after churches were built. According to Mrs.

18. Gaillard Hunt, ed., *The First Forty Years of Washington Society, Portrayed by the Family Letters of Mrs. Samuel Harrison Smith (Margaret Bayard) from the Collection of Her Grandson, J. Henley Smith,* (New York, C. Scribner's Sons, 1906), 13-14.

Smith's account, however, these gatherings were more social than religious until many years after the days of Jefferson.

Authors who insist that Jefferson was a devout, lifelong Christian need to cover every period of his life, from his childhood to his retirement, and usually include a number of lies and half-truths about his actions as a member of the Virginia legislature and Governor of Virginia. These lies will be addressed in Volume II, in chapters about the specific subjects they relate to. Two of the most popular stories from this period of time, however, have to do with Jefferson's involvement, as a private citizen, with his local church in Virginia. The first is about Jefferson's service as a church vestryman.

> **D. James Kennedy, in his book *What If America Were A Christian Nation Again?*, claims that Jefferson "followed the Anglican faith in its orthodoxy all his life. He went to a Christian school and was taught by Christian pastors. As a grown man, he served on the vestry of the Anglican Church, which was the equivalent of being an elder in the Presbyterian Church."**

Serving on the vestry of an Anglican Church is often claimed by religious right authors to be evidence of Thomas Jefferson's, as well as George Washington's, devotion to religion. Both Jefferson and Washington, did, in fact, serve as vestrymen. So did most other wealthy landowners in colonial Virginia. For many of them, however, this had little or nothing to do with religion. Prior to the disestablishment of the Anglican Church, these vestries were also the local governments. This was as much the equivalent of being on the town council as being an elder in the Presbyterian Church. In addition to managing the affairs of the church, the vestrymen were the local officials who levied and collected taxes, appropriated money for welfare and public works, and fixed and confirmed land boundaries.

William Meade, Bishop of the Protestant Episcopal Church in Virginia, gave the following reason for Jefferson's, as well as Jefferson's mentor George Wythe's, service as vestrymen.

> Even Mr. Jefferson and [George] Wythe, who did not conceal their disbelief in Christianity, took their parts in the

> duties of vestrymen, the one at Williamsburg, the other at Albemarle; for they wished to be men of influence.[19]

The second uses Jefferson's response as a private citizen to the passage of one of his own bills in the Virginia legislature.

> **According to Mark Beliles, in the introduction to his version of the *Jefferson Bible:* "When his Anglican church lost its financial and popular support during the Revolutionary War, he personally led in an effort to start a new church called the Calvinist Reformed Church. He put forth his own money to secure as its pastor a man named Charles Clay who, significantly, was a notable evangelical."**

What Beliles neglects to mention is that it was Jefferson himself who played the biggest role in causing the Anglican Church to lose its financial support during the Revolutionary War. Jefferson's support of Charles Clay's new church was his answer as a private citizen to the passage of his *Bill Exempting Dissenters from Contributing to the Support of the Church* by the Virginia Assembly in 1777.

With this bill, Jefferson put an end, at least for the time being, to tax-supported religion in Virginia. The last thing he wanted, however, was for the passage of this bill to result in the failure of Virginia's churches. Jefferson's *Bill Exempting Dissenters* was only the first step in the disestablishment of religion in his state. This bill exempted dissenters from taxes for the support of the Anglican Church, making all contributions voluntary, but did not preclude the legislature from instituting a general assessment for the support of all religious sects at a later date. At this stage in the game, it needed to be demonstrated that Virginia's churches could survive on voluntary contributions. If it looked as if the churches would not survive on voluntary contributions, support for a general assessment would grow. For this reason, as well as his friendship with Charles Clay, Jefferson did everything he could to support the church in his own county. He not only contributed to Clay's church himself, but drafted a subscription petition

19. William Meade, *Old Churches, Ministers and Families of Virginia,* vol. 1, (Philadelphia: J.B. Lippincott, 1857), 191.

to get others in his county to pledge yearly contributions. He even paid the subscriptions of others when they failed to pay them themselves. The following was the preamble to the petition.

> Whereas by a late act of General assembly freedom of Religious opinion and worship is restored to all, and it is left to the members of each religious society to employ such teachers as they think fit for their own spiritual comfort and instruction, and to maintain the same by their free and voluntary contributions: We the subscribers...[20]

The friendship between Jefferson and Charles Clay spanned more than four decades, from the beginning of the Revolutionary War until Clay's death in 1820. Clay, unlike many Anglican ministers in Virginia, was a patriot, immediately denouncing Britain upon the passage of the Intolerable Acts.

When the Intolerable Acts were passed in 1774, the Virginia Assembly needed to make the people of Virginia understand that the actions of the British against the distant colony of Massachusetts, such as closing of the Port of Boston, affected all the colonies, not just Massachusetts. A committee, which included Thomas Jefferson, decided that proclaiming a fast day would be the best way to make people pay attention. While proclamations of fast days and thanksgiving days were common in New England, they were a rare occurrence in the south. Jefferson and his committee knew that if the Virginia Assembly called a fast day, something it hadn't done in over twenty years, the people would take the situation seriously. Many Anglican ministers refused to comply with the Assembly's request, and some even had their congregations pray for the British. Rev. Clay, however, delivered exactly the kind of *"sermon suited to the occasion"* that Jefferson was hoping for. In 1777, when Jefferson drafted the subscription petition for Clay's church, he listed Clay's patriotism as one of the reasons that the citizens of Albemarle County should support him.

> ...and moreover approving highly the political conduct of the Revd. Charles Clay, who, early rejecting the tyrant and tyran-

20. Julian P. Boyd, ed., *The Papers of Thomas Jefferson,* vol. 2, (Princeton, NJ: Princeton University Press, 1950), 6.

> ny of Britain, proved his religion genuine by it's harmony with the liberties of mankind, and, conforming his public prayers to the spirit and the injured rights of his country, ever addressed the God of battles for victory to our arms, while others impiously prayed that our enemies might vanquish and overcome us...[21]

Anglican ministers in America, all of whom had sworn an oath to the King of England, handled the Revolution in a variety of ways. Among those who were loyalists, some left for England, some remained in America but stopped preaching, and some, as already mentioned, had their congregations pray for America to lose the war. Those who were patriots replaced their prayers for the royal family with prayers for the Continental Congress, and most began calling their churches Protestant Episcopal rather than Anglican. This, however, wasn't enough of a break from the Church of England for Rev. Clay. Although ordained as an Anglican minister, as was required of all clergymen in colonial Virginia regardless of their denomination, Clay had not attended an Anglican seminary, but had studied theology with a Presbyterian minister. In his draft of the subscription petition for Clay's church, Jefferson, wrongly assuming that Clay would just rename his church like the other patriotic Anglicans were doing, called the new church Protestant Episcopal.[22] This was changed to *"Calvinistical Reformed"* on the final copy. Mark Beliles's claim that Jefferson personally led an effort to start a Calvinist church is a little ridiculous, considering that Jefferson seems to have had no idea what kind of church Clay was starting.

Charles Clay was a minister for only fifteen years, from 1769 to 1784, apparently becoming more interested in politics than religion. He was a member of Virginia's convention to ratify the Constitution in 1788, and a few years later ran for Congress. After leaving the ministry, Clay returned to his family home in Bedford, where Jefferson later built his second home, Poplar Forest. Jefferson spent several months a year in Bedford, where Clay and his sons – Odin, Cyrus,

21. Julian P. Boyd, ed., *The Papers of Thomas Jefferson,* vol. 2, (Princeton, NJ: Princeton University Press, 1950), 6.

22. *The Thomas Jefferson Papers, Series 1, General Correspondence, 1651-1827,* Library of Congress Manuscript Division, #406.

Junius, and Paulus – were frequent visitors. It appears from Jefferson's correspondence with Clay that whatever conversations they did have about religious subjects occurred at Poplar Forest, which means they didn't take place until at least thirty years after Clay started his Calvinistical church.

Charles Clay is also mentioned by Mark Beliles in another of his lies. In an effort to back up a claim that only a few clergymen disliked Jefferson, and that the clergy's attacks on him during the election of 1800 were *"isolated cases,"* Beliles makes up a list of clergymen who ran for office as *"overt Jeffersonians."*

> **According to Mark Beliles: "Eight clergymen ran for public office as overt Jeffersonians (All lived in central Virginia), and some did so as a result of his overt support and urging (Charles Clay, Charles Wingfield, William Woods, John Waller, Henry Fry, John Goss, Peter Muhlenberg, and John Leland)."**

There are a number of things wrong with Beliles's claim, one or more of which applies to seven out of the eight clergymen listed. First of all, only four of the eight even ran for public office. Second, out of the four who did run for office, only two could have run as *"overt Jeffersonians."* The other two ran before Jefferson himself could be called an overt Jeffersonian – one of them before Jefferson even entered politics. And, third, although all eight *"lived in central Virginia"* at some time, only six were Virginians.

Of the four who actually did run for office, only one did so at the urging of Jefferson. This was William Woods, also known as "Baptist Billy." What Beliles fails to mention is that Virginia's 1776 constitution prohibited clergymen from running for the state Assembly. In other words, what Jefferson suggested to Woods was that he make himself eligible to run by surrendering his credentials as a minister. Woods did leave the ministry, and was elected to the Virginia Assembly.

Charles Clay unsuccessfully ran for Congress in both 1790 and 1792, but, as already mentioned, had already left the ministry by this time. It is very clear from their correspondence that Jefferson, although friends with Clay, had nothing to do with his decision to run.

In fact, Jefferson wasn't even aware that Clay was a candidate in 1790 until he heard about it in New York, as he wrote on January 27 of that year.

> ...I understand you are a candidate for the representation of your district in Congress. I cannot be with you to give you my vote; nor do I know who are to be the Competitors: but I am sure I shall be contented with such a representative as you will make, because I know you are too honest a patriot not to wish to see our country prosper by any means, tho' they be not exactly those you would have preferred; and that you are too well informed a politician, too good a judge of men, not to know, that the ground of liberty is to be gained by inches, that we must be contented to secure what we can get from time to time, and eternally press forward for what is yet to get. It takes time to persuade men to do even what is for their own good. Wishing you every prosperity in this & in all your other undertakings (for I am sure, from my knowlege of you they will always be just).[23]

When Clay ran again in 1792, he asked Jefferson to write to certain influential men in his district, which he listed by name. Clay had indiscriminately shown Jefferson's letter of January 27 to people in his district during the campaign of 1790, but this had backfired. Patrick Henry, who had supported Clay at first, began to fight against him as soon as he found out that he was friends with Jefferson.[24] Jefferson, who had a policy of not endorsing candidates, denied Clay's 1792 request. The following are excerpts from Jefferson's September 11, 1792 letter to Clay.

> Your favor of Aug. 8, came duly to hand, and I should with pleasure have done what you therein desired, as I ever should what would serve or oblige you; but from a very early period of my life I determined never to intermeddle with elections of the people, and have invariably adhered

23. Thomas Jefferson to Charles Clay, January 27, 1790, *The Thomas Jefferson Papers, Series 1, General Correspondence, 1651-1827,* Library of Congress Manuscript Division, #9078.

24. Charles Clay to Thomas Jefferson, August 8, 1792, *ibid.,* #13301.

> to this determination....
>
> ...In writing the letter to you on the former occasion, I went further than I had ever before done, but that was addressed to yourself to whom I had a right to write, and not to persons either unknown to me or very capable of judging for themselves.[25]

The other four Virginians listed by Beliles – Charles Wingfield, John Waller, Henry Fry, John Goss – were just ministers that Jefferson happened to know, or know of. Only one of these four, Henry Fry, ever ran for public office.

Henry Fry was a Methodist minister in Charlottesville, and a member of the Virginia House of Burgesses. Jefferson, however, had nothing to do with Fry's political career. Fry, who was five years older than Jefferson, was a member of the House of Burgesses from 1761 to 1765. Jefferson was an eighteen year old college student when Fry was elected, and wasn't elected to the House of Burgesses himself until 1769.

Charles Wingfield, a Presbyterian minister in Charlottesville, never ran for any public office. He was a justice of the peace in Albemarle County for a number of years, but this was an appointed, not an elected, position.

John Waller was a Baptist minister from Virginia who moved to South Carolina in 1793, and died there in 1802. Waller never ran for any public office. His only connection to anything political was his selection by the Baptist General Assembly to petition the Virginia legislature during the fight for religious liberty in the 1780s. If Jefferson knew, or even knew of, Waller, it would most likely have been through James Madison.

John Goss was a Baptist minister who spent at least part of his time in Charlottesville. He was one of two Baptist ministers who took turns holding the monthly Baptist services during the period when the Charlottesville courthouse was shared by four different sects. Goss wasn't born until 1775, so he would obviously have been too young to run for office in Virginia when ministers were still eligible,

25. Thomas Jefferson to Charles Clay, September 11, 1792, *The Thomas Jefferson Papers, Series 1, General Correspondence, 1651-1827*, Library of Congress Manuscript Division, #13371.

and there is no evidence that he ran for any public office later.

The other two ministers listed by Beliles – John Leland and Peter Muhlenberg – were not Virginians, although both spent time in Virginia.

John Leland was a Baptist minister from Massachusetts who lived in Virginia from 1776 to 1791. Leland's big connection to Jefferson is that he delivered the famous "mammoth cheese," a gift to the president from the people of Cheshire, Massachusetts. Leland never ran for any public office.

Peter Muhlenberg was a Lutheran minister from Pennsylvania who was sent to Virginia in 1771 to serve a German speaking congregation. Prior to this, Muhlenberg had been sent to Germany to study for the ministry, but had left school and joined the Royal Dragoons. When he returned to Philadelphia in 1766, his father, also a Lutheran minister, had a friend pull some strings to get him released from the army. Muhlenberg continued his theological studies with his father and became an ordained minister in 1768.

When the Revolutionary War began, Muhlenberg, who had already led protests against the British, served on the Committee of Safety and Correspondence, represented his county at Williamsburg, and formed a German regiment in Virginia. After the war, Muhlenberg, who had risen from the rank of Colonel to Major General, did not return to the ministry. He moved back to Pennsylvania, and, throughout the 1780s, held various offices in that state. He was elected to the first Congress as a Representative from Pennsylvania, and served a total three terms. He was also elected to the Senate in 1801, but resigned after a only few months. After leaving the Senate, he was appointed supervisor of revenue and then customs collector for the state of Pennsylvania by Thomas Jefferson.

Muhlenberg is also the subject of a very popular myth that appears not only in religious right American history books, but a number of other books about the Revolutionary War. The story is that, on January 21, 1776, Muhlenberg preached his last sermon, at the end of which he dramatically ripped off his clerical robes, revealing an army uniform underneath, and issued a call to arms. Not a single contemporary source supports this story. It was created by Muhlenberg's grandnephew, Henry Augustus Muhlenberg, in his 1849 book *The Life of Major-General Peter Muhlenberg of the Revolutionary Army,* and is based on nothing more than a figurative statement in Samuel

Kercheval's 1833 book *A History of the Valley of Virginia,* which said that Muhlenberg *"laid off his gown and took up the sword."* In spite of the fact that the story isn't true, there is a statue of Muhlenberg in the United States Capitol building, donated by the State of Pennsylvania in 1889, that depicts him taking off his clerical robes to reveal his uniform.

D. James Kennedy, in his book *What If America Were A Christian Nation Again?,* copies Beliles's claim about ministers running for office as Jeffersonians, but miscounts the number of names, making it nine.

> **According to Kennedy: "Now someone may point out to you that several ministers wrote letters highly critical of Jefferson. Yes, there were five of them. But on the other hand, Jefferson had 110 personal friends who were clergymen. In fact he encouraged nine of them to run for public office...."**

Kennedy apparently arrives at his claim that *"Jefferson had 110 personal friends who were clergymen"* from Beliles's claim that Jefferson *"admired, supported, commended, and worked in partnership with well over 100 different Christian clergymen."* Where he gets the number five for the number of ministers who wrote letters highly critical of Jefferson is a complete mystery.

Kennedy, screwing up another of Beliles's lies, blames Jefferson's lack of orthodox Christian beliefs on France.

> **According to Kennedy: "While Jefferson was in France, his wife, whom he adored, died, leaving him with his two-year-old daughter. Then both his mother and his best friend also died. Ordinarily, he would have gone to the congregation of the church where he served and found solace and consolation from them, and his pastor would have helped him work through his grief. There was no such church in Paris."**

Jefferson was not in France when these people died. His wife died in 1782. She didn't leave him with a two year old daughter, but died a few months after giving birth to a daughter who died two years later. His mother died in 1776, six years before his wife, and his best friend,

Dabney Carr, three years before that, in 1773. Jefferson did not leave for Europe until 1784, when he succeeded Benjamin Franklin as Minister to France. Jefferson was at Monticello when his wife died in 1782. According to his autobiography, when Congress proposed that he go to France a few months later, he gladly accepted the appointment because he needed a *"change of scene."*[26] He did not end up going to France at this time, however. While he was waiting to sail from Baltimore, word was received from France that a provisional peace treaty with Great Britain had been signed, making his trip unnecessary.

Beliles, while blaming Jefferson's *"questioning and analysis of orthodox Christianity"* on the French, at least gets the dates of the deaths of his wife, daughter, mother, and best friend right.

> **The following, from Beliles's book, is what D. James Kennedy was attempting to copy: "Jefferson's religious life underwent a critical change following the deaths of his wife, in 1782, and of his two year old daughter, in 1784. He also lost his best friend in 1773 and his mother in 1776, but his wife and daughter's death left him completely devastated and emotionally despondent. This personal tragedy, coupled with the lack of congregational support and close pastoral advice that he was used to back home in America, begins a watershed period that perhaps determines the remainder of his religious life. There are very few references to attendance at church while in France."**

Another popular Jefferson story has to do with his proposal while on a committee to design a seal for the United States. This is another story that has some truth to it. Most religious right authors, however, turn it into a half-truth by including only part of Jefferson's proposal, and leaving the proposal of John Adams, also on the committee, out of the story entirely.

> **According to William Federer, in his book *America's God and Country*: "Shortly after the signing of the**

26. Andrew A. Lipscomb and Albert Ellery Bergh, eds., *The Writings of Thomas Jefferson*, vol. 1, (Washington D.C.: Thomas Jefferson Memorial Association, 1904), 76.

Declaration of Independence, a committee was appointed to draft a seal for the newly united states which would express the spirit of the nation. Thomas Jefferson proposed:

> The children of Israel in the wilderness, led by a cloud by day, and a pillar of fire by night."

According to David Barton, in his book *Original Intent:* "On the same day that Congress approved the Declaration, it appointed John Adams, Thomas Jefferson, and Ben Franklin to draft a seal to characterize the spirit of the new nation. Franklin proposed:

> Moses lifting up his wand, and dividing the Red Sea, and Pharaoh in his chariot overwhelmed with the waters. This motto: 'Rebellion to tyrants is obedience to God.'

Jefferson proposed:

> The children of Israel in the wilderness, led by a cloud by day, and a pillar of fire by night."

According to James H. Hutson, Chief of the Manuscript Division at the Library of Congress, in the companion book to his *Religion and the Founding of the American Republic* Exhibit: "That a deeply religious society should produce deeply religious leaders is no surprise, but the power of religion in revolutionary America was also displayed in the legislative activities of those described as theological liberals. Consider the actions of Franklin and Jefferson when they were appointed in July 1776 to a committee to devise a seal for the United States. Both men suggested a familiar Old Testament episode that was a transparent allegory for America's ordeal, the account in the book of Exodus of God's intervening to save the people of Israel by drowning

> **Pharaoh (George III) and his pursuing armies in the Red Sea. In the opinion of these two torchbearers of the Enlightenment, nothing less than the story of a biblical miracle would be an appropriate emblem for their confessing countrymen."**

All of the religious right American history authors leave the same two things out of this story. The first is that, while Jefferson did propose the children of Israel for the front of the seal, he proposed Hengist and Horsa for the back. Hengist and Horsa, according to Anglo-Saxon legend, were Germanic heathens hired as mercenaries to protect Britain after the fall of the Roman Empire in the fifth century. These two brothers tricked and defeated the King who had hired them, stopping the spread of Christianity and keeping most of Britain pagan for the next few hundred years. Regardless of whether or not Hengist and Horsa were actual historical figures, it was during this period of time, as Jefferson pointed out on numerous occasions, that the common law was introduced in Britain, making it impossible for the common law to have been based on the Bible. The second omission is that John Adams, the most religious of the three committee members, did not propose a Bible story, but proposed Hercules surrounded by a few pagan goddesses. The following is from a letter from John to Abigail Adams. This letter from Adams is what David Barton, while leaving Adams out of his story completely, cites as his source.

> I am put upon a committee to prepare a Device for a Golden Medal to commemorate the Surrender of Boston to the American Arms, and upon another to prepare Devices for a Great Seal for the confederated States. There is a Gentleman here of French Extraction, whose Name is Du simitiere, a Painter by Profession whose Designs are very ingenious, and his Drawings well executed. He has been applied to for his Advice. I waited on him yesterday, and saw his Sketches. For the Medal he proposes Liberty with her Spear and Pileus, leaning on General Washington. The British Fleet in Boston Harbour, with all their Sterns towards the Town, the American Troops, marching in. For the Seal he proposes. The Arms of the several Nations from whence America has been peopled, as Eng-

> lish, Scotch, Irish, Dutch, German &c. each in a Shield. On one side of them Liberty, with her Pileus, on the other a Rifler, in his Uniform, with his Rifled Gun in one Hand, and his Tomahauk, in the other. This Dress and these Troops with this Kind of Armour, being peculiar to America—unless the Dress was known to the Romans. Dr. F[ranklin] shewed me, yesterday, a Book, containing an Account of the Dresses of all the Roman Soldiers, one of which, appeared exactly like it....
>
> ...Dr. F. proposes a Device for a Seal. Moses lifting up his Wand, and dividing the Red Sea, and Pharaoh, in his Chariot overwhelmed with the Waters. This Motto. Rebellion to Tyrants is Obedience to God.
>
> Mr. Jefferson proposed. The Children of Israel in the Wilderness, led by a Cloud by day, and a Pillar of Fire by night, and on the other Side Hengist and Horsa, the Saxon Chiefs, from whom We claim the Honour of being descended and whose Political Principles and Form of Government We have assumed.
>
> I proposed the Choice of Hercules, as engraved by Gribeline in some Editions of Lord Shaftsburys Works. The Hero resting on his Clubb. Virtue pointing to her rugged Mountain, on one Hand, and perswading him to ascend. Sloth, glancing at her flowery Paths of Pleasure, wantonly reclining on the Ground, displaying the Charms both of her Eloquence and Person, to seduce him into Vice. But this is too complicated a Group for a Seal or Medal, and it is not original.[27]

Jefferson's 1776 proposal for the seal of the United States is also cited as a source for other claims, such the following.

According to Mark Beliles, in the introduction to his version of the *Jefferson Bible*: Jefferson "established religious mottos on coins, etc."

27. John Adams to Abigail Adams, August 14, 1776, Paul H. Smith, ed., *Letters of Delegates to Congress, 1774-1789,* vol. 4, (Washington D.C.: Library of Congress, 1979), 678-679.

According to D. James Kennedy, getting Beliles's lie about mottos on coins wrong, claims that Jefferson: "included God in our national motto."

Beliles actually cites two sources for his claim that Jefferson established religious mottos on coins. In addition to Jefferson's proposal for the great seal, he cites a circular letter sent by the Continental Congress to the governors of the states in November 1780.[28] This letter contains nothing whatsoever about either coins or mottos. It was a letter informing the governors that the Continental Congress had stopped issuing currency and would need additional aid from the states to supply the Army. The copy of this letter sent to Jefferson, then Governor of Virginia, included a requisition for food.

D. James Kennedy's claim that it was Jefferson who *"included God in our national motto"* is completely ridiculous. As John Adams mentioned in his letter, Benjamin Franklin's suggestion for a motto was *"Rebellion to Tyrants is Obedience to God."* Although Jefferson would later use this motto on a personal seal, the motto chosen by the Continental Congress for the United States was, of course, *E Pluribus Unum.* This remained our national motto until 1956, when it was changed to *In God We Trust.*

28. Gaillard Hunt, ed., *Journals of the Continental Congress, 1774-1789,* vol. 18, (Washington D.C.: Government Printing Office, 1910), 1038-1040.

— CHAPTER THIRTEEN —

Jefferson, Madison, and Blackstone?

One name almost always found in arguments that our laws are based on the Bible is Sir William Blackstone, an English jurist and law professor, whose lectures were published in the 1760s as a four volume work entitled *Commentaries on the Laws of England.* Blackstone's *Commentaries* contains many references to Christianity, most found in a chapter entitled *"Of Offences Against God and Religion."* The first step of these Blackstone arguments is to present a few passages from this chapter. The following are two of the most popular.

> [T]he preservation of Christianity, as a national religion, is, abstracted from its own intrinsic truth, of the utmost consequence to the civil state, which a single instance will sufficiently demonstrate....[1]

> To deny the possibility, nay, actual existence of witchcraft and sorcery, is at once to contradict the revealed word of God in various passages both of the Old and New Testaments...[2]

Once they've established that Blackstone considered Christianity to be an integral part of English common law, and pointing out the

1. Blackstone, William, *Commentaries on the Laws of England,* vol. 4, (Oxford: Clarendon Press, 1765-1769), 43.
2. *ibid,* 60.

widespread use of his *Commentaries* in America, the Liars for Jesus single out Thomas Jefferson and James Madison, claiming that they were two of Blackstone's biggest fans. But, the truth is that Jefferson and Madison were among those who most strongly disapproved of the use of Blackstone's *Commentaries* in America.

> **According to David Barton, in his book *Original Intent*: Blackstone's "influence in America was so great that Edmund Burke told the British Parliament:**
>
> > **I hear that they have sold nearly as many of *Blackstone's Commentaries* in America as in England."**

The reason for pointing out the popularity of Blackstone's in America is, of course, to imply that all of our founders considered Christianity to be an integral part of American law. The real reason that so many copies of Blackstone's were sold in America, however, had nothing to do with religion, or even American law. When Blackstone's first became available in America, it wasn't only lawyers who were running out to buy it. It was average colonists who wanted to educate themselves on the laws of England in order to understand their rights as British subjects and to be able to recognize when these rights were being violated. For this reason, sales of all law books had increased to some degree in the years leading up to the Revolution. When Blackstone's was printed in America in 1771, it was an instant best-seller. This was the first law book written in language and arranged in a way that non-lawyers could easily understand. It was *The Laws of England for Dummies,* and every American who could read was reading it.

The sentence that David Barton takes out of context from Edmund Burke's March 1775 speech comes from a part of that speech in which Burke attributed the *"disobedient spirit in the colonies"* in part to the large number of colonists reading law books.

> ...The colonists have now fallen into the way of printing them for their own use. I hear that they have sold nearly as many of Blackstone's Commentaries in America as in England.

> General Gage marks out this disposition very particularly in a letter on your table. He states, that all the people in his government are lawyers, or smatterers in law; and that in Boston they have been enabled, by successful chicane, wholly to evade many parts of one of your capital penal constitutions. The smartness of debate will say, that this knowledge ought to teach them more clearly the rights of legislature, their obligations to obedience, and the penalties of rebellion. All this is mighty well. But my honourable and learned friend on the floor, who condescends to mark what I say for animadversion, will disdain that ground. He has heard, as well as I, that when great honours and great emoluments do not win over this knowledge to the service of the state, it is a formidable adversary to government. If the spirit be not tamed and broken by these happy methods, it is stubborn and litigious. *Abeunt studia in mores.* This study renders men acute, inquisitive, dexterous, prompt in attack, ready in defence, full of resources. In other countries, the people, more simple, and of a less mercurial cast, judge of an ill principle in government only by an actual grievance; here they anticipate the evil, and judge of the pressure of the grievance by the badness of the principle. They augur misgovernment at a distance; and snuff the approach of tyranny in every tainted breeze.[3]

After establishing that Blackstone's *Commentaries* was very religious, and that it sold well in America, the next step is to connect its use to some prominent founders. The two founders whose opinions of Blackstone's are most often lied about are, of course, Thomas Jefferson and James Madison.

> **According to David Barton, in his book *Original Intent*: "Blackstone's *Commentaries on the Laws,* introduced in 1766, became *the* law book of the Founding Fathers. (In fact, so strong was its influence in America that Thomas Jefferson once quipped that American lawyers used *Blackstone's* with the same**

3. Philip B. Kurland and Ralph Lerner, eds., *The Founders' Constitution,* vol. 5, (Indianapolis: Liberty Fund, 1987), 68.

> **dedication and reverence that Muslims used the Koran.)"**

The *quip* referred to by Barton is found in an 1810 letter from Jefferson to John Tyler, a Virginia judge, Governor of Virginia, and father of the future president.

> I have long lamented with you the depreciation of law science. The opinion seems to be that Blackstone is to us what the Alcoran is to the Mahometans, that everything which is necessary is in him, and what is not in him is not necessary. I still lend my counsel and books to such young students as will fix themselves in the neighborhood. Coke's institutes and reports are their first, and Blackstone their last book, after an intermediate course of two or three years. It is nothing more than an elegant digest of what they will then have acquired from the real fountains of the law.[4]

Because the sole purpose of the authors of the religious right version of American history is to promote the notion that America is a Christian nation, they present everything only in reference to religion. Most of these books are little more than lists of isolated quotes and events, completely separated from any other factors that led to these quotes or events. The Blackstone lies are a good example of this. Of course Thomas Jefferson didn't think the religious laws in Blackstone's were part of American law. That goes without saying. His two biggest reasons for disliking Blackstone's, however, had nothing to do with its religious content.

The first is that Jefferson just didn't consider Blackstone's to be very instructive for law students. He often described it as nothing more than a summary of what was found in earlier books, and told the students that he advised to read it only after studying everything else. Jefferson's opinion was that reading Blackstone's led students to think they knew a lot more than they actually did, as he wrote in 1812 in another letter to John Tyler.

4. Thomas Jefferson to John Tyler, May 26, 1810, Andrew A. Lipscomb and Albert Ellery Bergh, eds., *The Writings of Thomas Jefferson*, vol. 12, (Washington D.C.: Thomas Jefferson Memorial Association, 1907), 392-393.

> A student finds there a smattering of everything, and his indolence easily persuades him that if he understands that book, he is master of the whole body of the law. The distinction between these, and those who have drawn their stores from the deep and rich mines of Coke on Littleton, seems well understood even by the unlettered common people, who apply the appellation of Blackstone lawyers to these ephemeral insects of the law.[5]

The second, and most important, reason that Jefferson disapproved of Blackstone's was that it contained British principles that were incompatible with, and even dangerous to, the republican principles of American government. It wasn't the founding generation that was heavily influenced by Blackstone, as the religious right authors claim. Most lawyers among the founders had studied law before Blackstone's *Commentaries* was even published. It was Blackstone's influence on the next generation of lawyers that Jefferson was worried about. The use of Blackstone's as a primary textbook was part of Jefferson's overall concern about what was being taught in America's colleges in the early 1800s, particularly in the Northern states, where lawyers who had been among the "British" Federalists in the 1790s were teaching the next generation. This was the faction that had always favored hanging on to the aristocratic and monarchical customs of England, ideas that were glorified by Blackstone.

Jefferson wrote about this in an 1814 letter to Horatio Spafford, who had just published *A Gazetteer of the State of New York* and sent him a copy. Spafford noted in this book that, in his state, the British principles that had never ceased to exist among merchants and the clergy had also crept into the law profession. One of the influences Jefferson blamed this on was Blackstone's *Commentaries.*

> They [lawyers] have, in the Mother country, been generally the firmest supporters of the free principles of their constitution. But there too they have changed. I ascribe much of this to the substitution of Blackstone for my Lord Coke, as an ele-

5. Thomas Jefferson to John Tyler, June 17, 1812, Andrew A. Lipscomb and Albert Ellery Bergh, eds., *The Writings of Thomas Jefferson,* vol. 13, (Washington D.C.: Thomas Jefferson Memorial Association, 1907), 166-167.

> mentary work. In truth, Blackstone and Hume have made tories of all England, and are making tories of those young Americans whose native feelings of independence do not place them above the wily sophistries of a Hume or a Blackstone. These two books, but especially the former, have done more towards the suppression of the liberties of man, than all the million of men in arms of Bonaparte and the millions of human lives with the sacrifice of which he will stand loaded before the judgment seat of his Maker. I fear nothing for our liberty from the assaults of force; but I have seen and felt much, and fear more from English books, English prejudices, English manners, and the apes, the dupes, and designs among our professional crafts.[6]

Jefferson attributed the popularity of Blackstone's *Commentaries* over *"the real fountains of the law"* primarily to its arrangement and readability – not its content. Coke's *Institutes of the Lawes of England,* always preferred by Jefferson, and always first on every list of books he prepared for law students, was much more tedious and difficult to read. This problem was solved in 1818, when the first volume of J. H. Thomas' *Systematic Arrangement of Lord Coke's First Institute of the Laws of England* was published. Jefferson highly approved of Thomas's edition, and Francis Gilmer's decision to use it in the law school at the University of Virginia.

> I am very glad to find from a conversation with Mr. Gilmer, that he considers Coke Littleton, as methodized by Thomas, as unquestionably the best elementary work, and the one which will be the text-book of his school. It is now as agreeable reading as Blackstone, and much more profound.[7]

There is no question that Jefferson did not want Blackstone's *Commentaries,* or any law professor who was influenced by it, at the

6. Thomas Jefferson to Horatio G. Spafford, March 17, 1814, Andrew A. Lipscomb and Albert Ellery Bergh, eds., *The Writings of Thomas Jefferson,* vol. 14, (Washington D.C.: Thomas Jefferson Memorial Association, 1907), 119-120.

7. Thomas Jefferson to unknown recipient, October 25, 1825, *ibid.,* vol. 16, 128-129.

University of Virginia, writing the following to James Madison in 1826.

> In the selection of our Law professor, we must be rigorously attentive to his political principles. You will recollect that before the Revolution, Coke Littleton was the universal elementary book of law students, and a sounder Whig never wrote, nor of profounder learning in the orthodox doctrines of the British constitution, or in what were called English liberties. You remember also that our lawyers were then all Whigs. But when his black-letter text, and uncouth, but cunning learning got out of fashion, and the honeyed Mansfieldism of Blackstone became the students' hornbook, from that moment, that profession (the nursery of our Congress) began to slide into toryism, and nearly all the young brood of lawyers now are of that hue. They suppose themselves, indeed, to be Whigs, because they no longer know what Whigism or republicanism means. It is in our seminary that that vestal flame is to be kept alive; it is thence it is to spread anew over our own and the sister States. If we are true and vigilant in our trust, within a dozen or twenty years a majority of our own legislature will be from one school, and many disciples will have carried its doctrines home with them to their several States, and will have leavened thus the whole mass....[8]

Jefferson commented on the negative influence of Blackstone's *Commentaries* in many other letters, including one written in 1811 to William Cabell Rives on the subject of his education.

> Nothing can be sounder than your view of the importance of laying a broad foundation in other branches of knolege whereon to raise the superstructure of any particular science which one would chuse to profess with credit & usefulness. The lamentable disregard of this since the revolution has filled our country with Blackstone lawyers, Sangrado physi-

8. Thomas Jefferson to James Madison, February 17, 1826, James Morton Smith, ed., *The Republic of Letters: The Correspondence Between Thomas Jefferson and James Madison 1776-1826,* vol. 3, (New York and London: W.W. Norton & Company, 1995), 1965.

> cians, a ranting clergy, & a lounging gentry, who render neither honor nor service to mankind...[9]

Although Coke's *Institutes* always remained first on his list of recommended law books, there was one edition of Blackstone's *Commentaries* that Jefferson did approve of, and, for the short time that it was available, specified it when advising students. This was an annotated American edition published by St. George Tucker. Tucker, who was later appointed United States district judge for Virginia by President James Madison, had, like Jefferson, studied law under George Wythe. In 1803, Tucker was asked to succeed Wythe as professor of law at the College of William and Mary. Having only a few months to prepare a curriculum, Tucker decided to take the latest edition of Blackstone's *Commentaries* and note where the United States and Virginia Constitutions and laws differed from the laws of England. He also added numerous essays on subjects such as the extent to which English common law applied in America. Tucker's five volume work was published as *Blackstone's Commentaries: With Notes of Reference to the Constitution and Laws of the Federal Government of the United States; And of the Commonwealth of Virginia.*

Tucker's opinions about the negative influence of the use of Blackstone's as a textbook in America were the same as Jefferson's. The following is an excerpt from *On the Study of Law,* from Tucker's edition.

> ...On the appearance of the Commentaries, the laws of England, from a rude chaos, instantly assumed the semblance of a regular system. The *viginti annorum lucubrationes* it was thought might thereafter be dispensed with, and the student who had read the Commentaries three or four times over, was lead to believe that he was a thorough proficient in the law, without further labour, or assistance; the crude and immethodical labours of Sir Edward Coke were laid aside, and that rich mine of learning, his Commentary upon Littleton, was thought to be no longer worthy of the

9. Thomas Jefferson to William Cabell Rives, September 18, 1811, *The Thomas Jefferson Papers Series 1, General Correspondence, 1651-1827,* Library of Congress Manuscript Division, #34460.

labour requisite for extracting its precious ore. This sudden revolution in the course of study may be considered as having produced effects almost as pernicious as the want of a regular and systematic guide, since it cannot be doubted that it has contributed to usher into the profession a great number, whose superficial knowledge of the law has been almost as soon forgotten, as acquired. And this evil we may venture to pronounce has been much greater in the Colonies dependent upon Great-Britain, than in England itself, for the laws of the Colonies not being at all interwoven with the Commentaries, the colonial student was wholly without a guide in some of the most important points, of which he should have been informed; admitting that he were acquainted with the law of England upon any particular subject, it was an equal chance that he was ignorant of the changes introduced into the colonial codes; which either from inexperience, inattention, or other accidental circumstances have undergone a variety of modifications, provisions, suspensions, and repeals, in almost all the colonies dependent upon great Britain. The Commentaries, therefore though universally resorted to as a guide to the colonial student, were very inadequate to the formation of a lawyer, without other assistance; that assistance from the partial editions of colonial laws (at least in Virginia) was extremely difficult to be obtained. Few gentlemen, even of the profession, in this country, have ever been able to boast of possessing a *complete* collection of its laws; the Editor confesses that his own endeavours to procure one have hitherto been ineffectual.

Not many years after the reception of the Commentaries into the libraries of gentlemen of the profession, and the adoption of them as a guide to those who wished to acquire it, the revolution which separated the present United States of America from Great Britain took effect; this event produced a corresponding revolution not only in the principles of our government, but in the laws which relate to property, and in a variety of other cases, equally contradictory to the law, and irreconcileable to the principles contained in the

> Commentaries. From this period, that celebrated work could only be safely relied on as a methodical guide, in delineating the general outlines of law in the United States, or at most, in apprizing the student of what the *law had been;* to know *what it now is,* he must resort to very different sources of information; these, although the period which has elapsed since their first introduction is scarcely more than twenty years, are now so numerous, (at least in this state) and so difficult to be procured, that not one in fifty students of law has at this day any chance of perusing them.
>
> Notwithstanding these circumstances, the Commentaries have continued to be regarded as the *student's guide,* in the United States; and many there are, who without any other aid have been successful candidates for admission to the bar in this state, and perhaps in others: it cannot, therefore, be surprising that so many who have obtained licences to practice, discover upon their entrance into the profession a total want of information respecting the laws of *their own* country....[10]

Tucker also had quite a bit to say on the subject of religion and government.

> ...The pretext of religion, and the pretences of sanctity and humility, have been employed throughout the world, as the most direct means of gaining influence and power. Hence the numberless martyrdoms and massacres which have drenched the whole earth with blood, from the first moment that civil and religious institutions were blended together. To separate them by mounds which can never be overleaped, is the only means by which our duty to God, the peace of mankind, and the genuine fruits of charity and fraternal love, can be preserved or properly discharged. This prohibition, therefore, may be regarded as the most powerful cement of the federal government, or rather, the violation of it will prove

10. St. George Tucker; Clyde N. Wilson, ed., *View of the Constitution of the United States with Selected Writings,* (Indianapolis: Liberty Fund, 1999), 2-4.

> the most powerful engine of separation. Those who prize the union of the states will never think of touching this article with unhallowed hands....[11]

> Civil establishments of formularies of faith and worship, are inconsistent with the rights of private judgement. They engender strife . . . they turn religion into a trade . . . they shore up error . . . they produce hypocrisy and prevarication . . . they lay an undue bias on the human mind in its inquiries, and obstruct the progress of truth . . . genuine religion is a concern that lies entirely between God and our own souls. It is incapable of receiving any aid from human laws. It is contaminated as soon as worldly motives and sanctions mix their influence with it. Statesmen should countenance it only by exhibiting, in their own example, a conscientious regard to it in those forms which are most agreeable to their own judgments, and by encouraging their fellow citizens in doing the same. They cannot, as public men, give it any other assistance. All, besides, that has been called a public leading in religion, has done it an essential injury, and produced some of the worst consequences.[12]

Tucker, although in no way condoning atheism, argued that it was less dangerous to government than superstitions and religious fanaticism.

> It has been long a subject of dispute, which is worse in it's effects on society, such a religion or speculative atheism. For my own part, I could almost give the preference to the latter . . . Atheism is so repugnant to every principle of common sense, that it is not possible it should ever gain much ground, or become very prevalent. On the contrary, there is a particular proneness in the human mind to superstition, and nothing is more likely to become prevalent . . . Atheism leaves us to the full influence of most of our natural feelings

11. St. George Tucker; Clyde N. Wilson, ed., *View of the Constitution of the United States with Selected Writings,* (Indianapolis: Liberty Fund, 1999), 235-236.
12. *ibid.,* 373.

> and social principles; and these are so strong in their operation, that, in general, they are a sufficient guard to the order of society. But superstition counteracts these principles, by holding forth men to one another as objects of divine hatred; and by putting them on harrassing, silenceing, imprissoning and burning one another, in order to do God service . . . Atheism is a sanctuary for vice, by taking away the motives to virtue arising from the will of God, and the fear of future judgment. But superstition is more a sanctuary for vice, by teaching men ways of pleasing God, without moral virtue; and by leading them even to compound for wickedness, by ritual services, by bodily penances and mortifications; by adoring shrines, going pilgrimages, saying many prayers, receiving absolution from the priests, exterminating heretics, &c....[13]

One of the most popular lies about an endorsement of Blackstone's *Commentaries* is a misquote from a letter written in 1821 by James Madison to publishers Littell and Henry. This misquote first appeared in the 1966 book *The Christian History of the Constitution of the United States of America* by the late Liar for Jesus Verna Hall. It has since appeared in books by David Barton, William Federer, John Eidsmoe, and other religious right American history authors.

> **John Eidsmoe, citing Verna Hall's book as his source, includes this misquote in his book *Christianity and the Constitution*: "James Madison wrote in 1821, 'I very cheerfully express my approbation of the proposed edition of Blackstone's Commentaries'."**

Eidsmoe, copying Hall, cuts off the end of Madison's sentence and completely disregards the rest of the letter. Like Jefferson's approval of Tucker's edition of Blackstone's, Madison's approval was of a proposed Americanized edition. Littell and Henry were planning to publish an edition similar to Tucker's, but include the laws of all the

13. St. George Tucker; Clyde N. Wilson, ed., *View of the Constitution of the United States with Selected Writings*, (Indianapolis: Liberty Fund, 1999), 374-375.

states. Tucker had briefly mentioned some differences between the states regarding the degree to which they had adopted English common law, but, like other law professors and jurists who had published commentaries on Blackstone's *Commentaries*, had only written in depth on the laws of his own state. As Madison's letter clearly shows, the reason he cheerfully approved of this proposed edition was the publisher's plan to include a comparison of all the state codes.

> I very cheerfully express my approbation of the proposed edition of Blackstone's Commentaries, accompanied by a comparative view of the law of the United States and of the several States.
>
> Such a work, executed with the ability to be presumed in its authors, must be very useful in several respects. It will be so not only to the Bench and the Bar, but to the citizens generally, by facilitating to those of each State a knowledge of the laws of the others, in which the intercourses of business give them an interest. Nor will a comparison of the different Codes be without value to the legislator, also, who will be able to extract whatever improvements may be found in the examples before him. And it may well be supposed that there are few of the different codes which do not contain something worthy of adoption, as well as something requiring amendment. Finally, such a work will have a tendency to assimilate gradually the codes of all the States on subjects not merely local; to assimilate them, too, according to a model formed by a selection of the best parts and features of each.
>
> The people of the United States federal association have now the same Constitution, and the same code of laws. A uniformity among the State codes would extend the advantage, without violating the Constitutional separation, jurisdiction, and independence of the States themselves.
>
> Should it be an object with the compilers to include in their review of the State laws observations on the practical advan-

> tages on inconveniences of such as differ in different States, it will not a little enrich the instruction they are about to give to their Country; and, indeed, to all who make the science of legislation their study.[14]

David Barton, in his book *Original Intent,* includes the same Madison misquote, introducing it with the following statement: "Blackstone's Commentaries were purchased as the law book for the U.S. Senate, and James Madison heartily endorsed Blackstone..."

Blackstone's *Commentaries* was not purchased as *"the"* law book for the U.S. Senate. It was one law book they purchased. In the years before Congress had a real library, they bought books as they needed them. In 1794, because of the *Citizen Genet* affair, the Senate was working on a bill for punishing illegal privateers. Two books they wanted to refer to for this were Emmerich de Vattel's *The Law of Nations* and Blackstone's *Commentaries,* and both were purchased at this time. The Senate's purchase of Blackstone's had nothing to do with its religious content. The part of Blackstone's that the Senate was interested in was a chapter entitled *"Of Offences Against the Law of Nations,"* which dealt with things such as piracy and ambassadors. They purchased Blackstone's in 1794 to look up piracy laws and cases, which are cited in the footnotes of the act for punishing illegal privateers in the *Public Statutes at Large.*

What needs to be understood here is that the wide range of subjects covered in the four volumes of Blackstone's *Commentaries* include criminal offenses, civil offenses, maritime offenses, etc. The religious right American history books, however, mention nothing but the section on offenses against God and religion. They then construe any use or mention by any founder or early American jurist of anything whatsoever from Blackstone's into a complete agreement by that founder or jurist with everything found in Blackstone's, especially, of course, the section on offenses against religion. Instances can be found of even the most ardent Blackstone critics quoting something from his *Commentaries* at some point in their lives, so just about

14. James Madison to Littell and Henry, October 18, 1821, *Letters and Other Writings of James Madison,* vol. 3, (New York: R. Worthington, 1884), 233.

any of the founders can be made to look like a Blackstone fan.

What also needs to be understood is that the courts of the United States derive their authority from only two places – the Constitution and acts of Congress. Even if a particular federal crime is exactly the same as a common law offense found in Blackstone's, it is only recognized as a crime by the courts of the United States because a federal statute made that particular offense a crime. For example, in one early case involving the attempted bribery of a commissioner of the revenue, the circuit court in Philadelphia ruled that it had no jurisdiction over the case. The problem was that, although Congress had passed a law making the bribery of judges and certain other officials a federal crime, commissioners of the revenue were not among the specific officials listed in that act of Congress. There was no federal statute that made it a crime to bribe the particular type of official involved in this case. It didn't matter that it was a crime at the common law to bribe *any* public official because, as already stated, the courts of the United States derive their authority from only two places – the Constitution and acts of Congress.

Common law offenses against God and religion are different from offenses such as bribery because Congress, of course, does have a constitutional authority to make laws respecting bribery of federal officials, but does not have a constitutional authority to make laws respecting religion. So, although Blackstone classified both bribery and offenses against God and religion as crimes against the public, nothing from his chapter on offenses against God and religion, so diligently quoted by all the religious right American history authors, can ever become part of the laws of the United States by an act Congress. And, no use of Blackstone's *Commentaries* by the early Congresses for reasons that had nothing to do with this chapter can be construed to mean that they thought otherwise.

That the common law was not, and could not be, applicable to the government of the United States was explained very clearly by James Madison in a report presented to the General Assembly of Virginia in January 1800. The reason for Madison's report was to explain the resolutions of Virginia and Kentucky against the Alien and Sedition Acts of 1798, and to address arguments that had been used to oppose these resolutions. One argument that Madison thought was almost too ridiculous to address was that Congress had the authority to pass the Sedition Act because the common law was part of the laws of the United States. The following are some excerpts from the part of Madison's report in which he responded to this argument. In this report, Madison presented a series of questions to show that the sheer impracticality of applying common law to the federal government should be reason enough to dismiss the notion that the framers of the Constitution would ever have intended it to apply.

> Several attempts have been made to answer this question, which will be examined in their order. The committee will begin with one, which has filled them with equal astonishment and apprehension; and which, they cannot but persuade themselves, must have the same effect on all, who will consider it with coolness and impartiality, and with a reverence for our Constitution, in the true character in which it issued from the sovereign authority of the people. The committee refer to the doctrine lately advanced as a sanction to the Sedition Act: "that the common or unwritten law," a law of vast extent and complexity, and embracing almost every possible subject of legislation, both civil and criminal, "makes a part of the law of these States; in their united and national capacity."
>
> The novelty, and in the judgment of the committee, the extravagance of this pretension, would have consigned it to the silence, in which they have passed by other arguments, which an extraordinary zeal for the act has drawn into the discussion. But the auspices, under which this innovation presents itself, have constrained the committee to bestow on it an attention, which other considerations might have forbidden....
>
> ...There are two passages in the Constitution, in which a description of the law of the United States, is found - The first is contained in article III. sect. 2, in the words following. "This Constitution, the laws of the United States, and treaties made, or which shall be made under their authority." The second is contained in the 2d paragraph of art. VI. as fol-

lows: "This Constitution and the laws of the United States which shall be made in pursuance thereof and all treaties made, or which shall be made under the authority of the United States, shall be the supreme law of the land." The first of these descriptions was meant as a guide to the judges of the United States; the second as a guide to the judges in the several States. Both of them consist of an enumeration, which was evidently meant to be precise and compleat. If the common law had been understood to be a law of the United States, it is not possible to assign a satisfactory reason why it was not expressed in the enumeration.

In aid of these objections, the difficulties and confusion inseparable from a constructive introduction of the common law, would afford powerful reasons against it.

Is it to be the common law with, or without the British statutes?

If without the statutory amendments, the vices of the code would be insupportable?

If with these amendments, what period is to be fixed for limiting the British authority over our laws?

Is it to be the date of the eldest or the youngest of the colonies?

Or are the dates to be thrown together, and a medium deduced?

Or is our independence to be taken for the date?

Is, again, regard to be had to the various changes in the common law made by the local codes of America?

Is regard to be had to such changes, subsequent, as well as prior, to the establishment of the Constitution?

Is regard to be had to future, as well as past changes?

Is the law to be different in every State, as differently modified by its code; or are the modifications of any particular State, to be applied to all?

And on the latter supposition, which among the States codes would form the standard?

Questions of this sort might be multiplied with as much ease, as there would be difficulty in answering them.

The consequences flowing from the proposed construction, furnish other objections equally conclusive; unless the text were peremptory in its meaning, and consistent with other parts of the instrument.

These consequences may be in relation; to the legislative authority of the United States; to the executive authority; to the judicial authority, and to the governments of the several States.

If it be understood that the common law is established by the Constitution, it follows that no part of the law can be altered by the legislature; each of the statutes already passed as may be repugnant thereto would be nullified, particularly the "Sedition Act" itself which boasts of being a melioration of the common law; and the whole code with all its incongruities, barbarisms, and bloody maxims would be inviolably saddled on the good people of the United States.

Should this consequence be rejected, and the common law be held, like other laws, liable to revision and alteration, by the authority of Congress; it then follows, that the authority of Congress is co-extensive with the objects of common law; that is to say, with every object of legislation: For to every such object, does some branch or other of the common law extend. The authority of Congress would therefore be no longer under the limitations, marked out in the Constitution. They would be authorized to legislate in all cases whatsoever.

In the next place, as the President possesses the executive powers of the Constitution, and is to see that the laws be faithfully executed, his authority also must be co-extensive with every branch of the common law. The additions which this would make to his power, though not readily to be estimated claims the most serious attention.

This is not all; it will merit the most profound consideration, how far an indefinite admission of the common law, with a latitude in construing it, equal to the construction by which it is deduced from the Constitution, might draw after it the various prerogatives making part of the unwritten law of England. The English constitution itself is nothing more than a composition of unwritten laws and maxims.

In the third place, whether the common law be admitted as of legal or of constitutional obligation, it would confer on the judicial department a discretion little short of a legislative power.

On the supposition of its having a constitution obligation, this power in the judges would be permanent and irremediable by the legislative. On the other supposition, the power would not expire, until the legislature should have introduced a full system of statutory provisions. Let it be observed too, that besides all the uncertainties above enumerated, and which present an immense field for judicial discretion, it would remain with the same department to decide what parts of the common law would, and what would not, be properly applicable to the circumstances of the United States.

A discretion of this sort, has always been lamented as incongruous and dangerous, even in the colonial and State courts; although so much narrowed by positive provisions in the local codes on all the principal subjects embraced by the common law. Under the United States, where so few laws exist on those subjects, and where so great a lapse of time must happen before the vast chasm could be supplied, it is manifest that the power of the judges over the law would, in fact, erect them into legislators; and that for a long time, it would be impossible for the citizens to conjecture, either what was, or would be law.

In the last place, the consequence of admitting the common law as the law of the United States, on the authority of the individual States, is as obvious as it would be fatal. As this law relates to every subject of legislation, and would be paramount to the constitutions and laws of the States, the admission of it would overwhelm the residuary sovereignty of the States, and by one constructive operation new model the whole political fabric of the country.

From the review thus taken of the situation of the American colonies prior to their independence; of the effect of this event on their situation; of the nature and import of the Articles of Confederation; of the true meaning of the passage in the existing Constitution from which the common law has been deduced; of the difficulties and uncertainties incident to the doctrine; and of its vast consequences in extending the powers of the federal government, and in superseding the authorities of the State governments; the committee feel the utmost confidence in concluding that the common law never was, nor by any fair construction, ever can be, deemed a law for the American people as one community, and they indulge the strongest expectation that the same conclusion will finally be drawn, by all candid and accurate enquirers into the subject. It is indeed distressing to reflect, that it ever should have been made a question, whether the Constitution, on the whole face of which is seen so much labour to enumerate and define the several objects of federal power, could intend to introduce in the lump, in an indirect manner, and by a forced construction of a few phrases, the vast and multifarious jurisdiction involved in the common law; a law filling so many ample volumes; a

> law overspreading the entire field of legislation; and a law that would sap the foundation of the Constitution as a system of limited and specified powers. A severer reproach could not in the opinion of the committee be thrown on the Constitution, on those who framed, or on those who established it, than such a supposition would throw on them.[15]

One argument occasionally used by those who insist that the laws of the United States are based on the common law is that the common law is mentioned in the Seventh Amendment.

> **Tim LaHaye, in his book *Faith of Our Founding Fathers,* quotes the following from John W. Whitehead's book *The Second American Revolution*: "The common law was important in the constitutional sense that it was incorporated into the Constitution by direct reference in the Seventh Amendment. This amendment reads: 'In suits at common law, where the value in controversy shall exceed twenty dollars, the right of trial by jury shall be preserved; and no fact tried by a jury, shall be otherwise re-examined in any court of the United States, than according to the rules of the common law.' By implication, this means that the framers intended to be governed in practice as well as in principle by the higher law...."**

The Seventh Amendment doesn't imply anything of the kind. It doesn't imply anything at all. The reason that the founders wrote virtually nothing about this amendment was that there was really nothing to say about it. It simply defines what kinds of civil cases a jury trial is guaranteed in, and what the roles of the judge and jury are in these cases. The reason the framers chose to use the common law of England as the standard for this was that the practices for civil trials in the state courts varied from state to state, depending on how much of the common law each state had adopted, repealed, or replaced by statute law.

There actually was an attempt a few days before the end of the

15. Jack N. Rakove, ed., *James Madison, Writings,* (New York: Literary Classics of the United States, 1999), 632-641.

Constitutional Convention to add the right to a jury trial in civil cases into the body of the Constitution. The subject was first brought up on September 12, 1787, and on September 15, it was proposed that the words *"a trial by jury shall be preserved as usual in civil cases"*[16] be inserted into Article III. The problem, of course, was defining what *"as usual"* meant. Nathaniel Gorham, a delegate from Massachusetts, immediately raised the following objection: *"The constitution of Juries is different in different States and the trial itself is usual in different cases in different States."*[17] Several other delegates voiced similar objections, and the motion failed. Many of the state ratifying conventions, however, listed the trial by jury in civil cases among their proposed amendments, so it was included in the Bill of Rights, with *"as usual"* defined as *"according to the rules of the common law."*

> **According to John Eidsmoe, in his book *Christianity and the Constitution*: "One of Blackstone's former students, Jeremy Bentham, charged that Blackstone was an arch-conservative and an 'enemy of reformation.' But, fortunately, Bentham never gained the following in America that he had in England."**

Eidsmoe's claim that Bentham never gained the following in America that he had in England is extremely misleading. Bentham may not have been as widely read in America as he was in Europe, but among his followers were some of the country's most influential lawmakers. Most notable among these was Edward Livingston, who credited Bentham's 1802 book *Legislation Civil and Criminal* as his inspiration to draft the first laws for Louisiana in 1804, and also attributed most of the complete Louisiana code, written in the 1820s, to him. The following are excerpts from two letters written by Livingston to Bentham in 1829, the first regarding his decision in 1804 to begin his work on the laws of Louisiana, and the second regarding the complete Louisiana code.

> Although strongly impressed with the defects of our actual system of penal law, yet the perusal of your works first gave

16. Max Farrand, ed., *The Records of the Federal Convention of 1787,* vol. 2, (New Haven, CT: Yale University Press, 1911), 628.
17. *ibid.*

> method to my ideas, and taught me to consider legislation as a science governed by certain principles applicable to all its different branches, instead of an occasional exercise of its powers, called forth only on particular occasions, without relation to or connection with each other.[18]

> In laying before you this work, I offer you little that you have not a legitimate title to: for, hereafter, no one can in criminal jurisprudence, propose any favourable change that you have not recommended, or make any wise improvement that your superior sagacity has not suggested.[19]

Livingston's work was praised by many prominent jurists of the day, including James Kent, who, although doubtful that he would approve of much of Livingston's code, changed his mind after reading it. He didn't like all of it, but admitted that his own ideas were becoming outdated. Kent and Livingston disagreed about a few major things, such as the death penalty, which Kent was for and Livingston against. Kent did apparently try, however, to read Livingston's work with as an open a mind as he could.

The following is what Kent wrote to Livingston when he was first asked to read and comment on his Louisiana code.

> ...It is very likely I shall have some old-fashioned notions and prejudices hoary with age and inflexible from habit; but I am determined to give you what I think, on the reading of all the work, and to deal out my praise and censure just as my judgment dictates.[20]

And, this is what Kent wrote to Livingston after reading it.

> Though I shall always be dissatisfied with any code that

18. Charles Havens Hunt, *Life of Edward Livingston,* (New York: D. Appleton & Company, 1864), 96-97.

19. Edward Livingston to Jeremy Bentham, August 10, 1829, Jonathan Harris, Philip Schofield, eds., *Legislator of the World: Writings on Codification, Law, and Education (The Collected Works of Jeremy Bentham),* (Oxford: Clarendon Press, 1998), 384.

20. James Kent to Edward Livingston, February 1826, Charles Havens Hunt, *Life of Edward Livingston,* (New York: D. Appleton & Company, 1864), 280.

> strips the courts of their common-law powers over contempts, and ceases to be a wholesome terror to evilminded dispositions by the total banishment of the axe, musket, or halter from its punishments, yet I admit the spirit of the age is against me, and I contentedly acquiesce.
>
> You have done more in giving precision, specification, accuracy, and moderation to the system of crimes and punishments than any other legislator of the age, and your name will go down to posterity with distinguished honor.[21]

Blackstone had quite a few critics, yet John Eidsmoe mentions only Jeremy Bentham by name, knowing that his influence on the founders isn't as obvious as that of the others. Eidsmoe doesn't mention Joseph Priestley, for example, who was not only a critic of Blackstone, but also a big influence on Bentham. Priestley is too well known to the readers of religious right American history books, many of which present him as the man who caused Jefferson to become sort of a Christian. John Adams, however, in an 1812 letter to Benjamin Rush, listed Priestley as one of the Blackstone critics who, many years earlier, had influenced both Jefferson and Madison.

> At the same time how will we vindicate our friends Jefferson and Madison? You and I know that they very early read and studied Furneaux' controversy with Blackstone and Priestley's controversy with Blackstone, on the subject of ecclesiastical establishments. They also read Blackburne's *Confessional.* From these and Locke and Price, &c., they adopted a system which they had influence enough to introduce in Virginia. They abolished the whole establishment. This was enough to procure them the characters of atheists all over the world. ...[22]

Furneaux's and Priestley's controversies with Blackstone were pub-

21. James Kent to Edward Livingston, 1826, Charles Havens Hunt, *Life of Edward Livingston,* (New York: D. Appleton & Company, 1864), 280-281.

22. John Adams to Benjamin Rush, September 4, 1812, John A Shultz and Douglass Adair, eds., *The Spur of Fame: Dialogues of John Adams and Benjamin Rush, 1805-1813,* (Indianapolis: Liberty Fund, 1999), 267.

lished in 1773 by Philadelphia publisher Robert Bell, the publisher of Blackstone's *Commentaries* in America. As a companion to his 1773 edition of Blackstone's *Commentaries*, Bell printed a volume containing the letters and pamphlets written against Blackstone by his critics. The entire title of this volume was *"The Palladium of Conscience; Or, the Foundation of Religious Liberty Displayed, Asserted, and Established, Agreeable To Its True and Genuine Principles Above the Reach of the All Petty Tyrants, Who Attempt to Lord It Over the Human Mind. Containing Furneaux's Letters to Blackstone. Priestley's Remarks on Blackstone. Blackstone's Reply to Priestley. And Blackstone's Case of the Middlesex-Election; with Some Other Curious Tracts, Worthy of High Rank in Every Gentleman's Literary Repository, Being a Necessary Companion for Every Lover of Religious Liberty. And an Interesting Appendix to Blackstone's Commentaries on the Laws of England."*

While Jefferson and Madison might have been influenced by other Blackstone critics, whose criticisms of Blackstone came out a few years before Bentham's, they were certainly not unfamiliar with Bentham's work. During Madison's presidency, Bentham offered his services to America to digest the laws of he United States and the laws, both written and unwritten, of all the individual states. Madison, however, didn't think that Bentham realized what this would actually entail, and had doubts that, beginning such an overwhelming project at sixty-five years of age, he could possibly complete it, let alone with the same quality of his earlier work. Bentham first proposed the project to Madison shortly after the War of 1812 began. After the war, Madison sent John Quincy Adams, the new foreign minister to Great Britain, to meet with Bentham. Madison later wrote the following to Adams about Bentham. This letter was written in December 1817, so Adams must not have written to Madison about his meeting with Bentham until after returning to the United States in 1817 to take his position as James Monroe's Secretary of State.

> I am glad to find that your personal interviews with Mr. Bentham afforded an entertainment which may have been some recompense for the trouble which I contributed to give you in relation to him. The celebrity which this philosophic politician has acquired abroad, as well as in his own Country, does not permit one to doubt the extent of his capacity or of

> his researches; and there is still less room to question the philanthropy which adorns his character. It is unfortunate that he has not added to his merits a style and manner of conveying his ideas which would do more justice to their profoundness and importance. With all his qualifications, however, I greatly overrate, or he greatly underrates, the task which he has been so anxious to employ his intellectual labours and treasures, for the reformation of our Code of laws, especially in the advanced age at which the work was to be commenced. And I own that I find some difficulty in reconciling the confidence he feels in the adequacy of his powers, not only for a digest of our statutes into a concise and clear system, but a reduction of our unwritten to a text law, with that penetrating and accurate judgement for which he has the reputation. The disinterestedness and friendly zeal, nevertheless, which dictated the offer of his services to our Country, are entitled to its acknowledgements, and no one can join in them with more cordiality than myself.[23]

In his book *The Myth of Separation,* David Barton tells a story about *Updegraph v. Commonwealth,* an 1824 blasphemy case in Pennsylvania. In his story, Barton not only misquotes Blackstone, but makes it appear that this misquote came from Pennsylvania Supreme Court Justice Thomas Duncan. He also attempts to mask the fact that this case was being heard in a state court in order to imply that the federal courts did, in fact, recognize common law offenses against religion, which, as already explained, did not and could not ever happen.

> **According to Barton, "Since the indictment was for blasphemy, the court needed to establish a legal definition of the word. It turned to the writings of Sir William Blackstone:**
>
> > **Blasphemy against the Almighty is denying His being or Providence or uttering contumelious reproaches on our Savior Christ. It is punished**

23. James Madison to John Quincy Adams, December 23, 1817, *Letters and Other Writings of James Madison,* vol. 3, (New York: R. Worthington, 1884), 52-53.

at common law by fine and imprisonment, for Christianity is part of the laws of the land."

Barton's quote is not found in Blackstone's *Commentaries,* nor is it found in *Updegraph v. Commonwealth.* It is a combination of words and phrases, some from Blackstone's and some from the case, altered and assembled by Barton to fit his story. Barton follows this misquote with several pages of excerpts from the case, systematically omitting from these excerpts anything showing that Justice Duncan was referring to the laws of Pennsylvania, not the laws of the United States, and anything indicating exactly what it was that made Mr. Updegraph's offense a crime under Pennsylvania law.

The following is the definition of blasphemy and its punishments as they appear in Blackstone's *Commentaries.*

> The fourth species of offenses therefore, more immediately against God and religion, is that of blasphemy against the Almighty, by denying his being or providence; or by contumelious reproaches of our Saviour Christ. Whither also may be referred all profane scoffing at the holy scripture, or exposing it to contempt and ridicule. These are offenses punishable at common law by fine and imprisonment, or other infamous corporal punishment: Christianity is part of the laws of England.[24]

The first thing done by Barton to create his misquote is, of course, Americanizing Blackstone's *"Christianity is part of the laws of England,"* by getting rid of England and making it *"Christianity is part of the laws of the land."* Justice Duncan, however, not only didn't use Barton's misquote of the sentence, he didn't quote Blackstone's version either. What Duncan actually quoted was a third version, written by James Wilson.

Wilson, a framer of both the United States and Pennsylvania Constitutions, and an associate justice of the United States Supreme Court, was among the jurists in various states who took on the job of digesting the laws of their states in the late 1700s and early 1800s, either at the request of their state legislatures or unofficially for the pur-

24. Blackstone, William, *Commentaries on the Laws of England,* vol. 4, (Oxford: Clarendon Press, 1765-1769), 59.

pose of teaching. Wilson was initially appointed in 1791 by Pennsylvania's House of Representatives to digest the laws of the commonwealth, but this was never sanctioned by the Senate. Wilson, nevertheless, because of the importance of the project, continued working on it privately until his death in 1798. After Wilson's death, his son, Bird Wilson, organized what his father had completed, and included it in *The Works of the Honourable James Wilson, L.L.D., Late One of the Associate Judges of the Supreme Court of the United States, and Professor of Law in the College of Philadelphia,* published in 1804.

The reason works like Wilson's were desperately needed was that, contrary to what the religious right American history books say, the common law of England was not universally applied in America. Each state adopted whatever was useful for their state, and, over the years, written statutes and state constitutions superceded much of this. By the late 1700s, there was a lot of confusion as to what the laws actually were. In the preface to his father's *Works,* Bird Wilson included the following, which stated the object of the resolution passed by Pennsylvania's House of Representatives.

> In March, 1791, the house of representatives in the general assembly of Pennsylvania, resolved to appoint a person to revise and digest the laws of the commonwealth; to ascertain and determine how far any British statutes extended to it; and to prepare bills, containing such alterations, additions, and improvements as the code of laws, and the principles and forms of the constitution then lately adopted might require.[25]

Wilson was the authority referred to by later Pennsylvania justices like Thomas Duncan when they needed to determine what parts of English common law had been applied to begin with, and what out of this was still recognized as the common law of the state. What James Wilson determined to be the common law of Pennsylvania was, of course, somewhat different from what appeared in Blackstone's *Commentaries.* There was no chapter titled *"Of Offences Against God and Religion."* Wilson classified blasphemy as a *"common nui-*

25. Bird Wilson, ed., *The Works of the Honourable James Wilson, L.L.D., Late One of the Associate Judges of the Supreme Court of the United States, and Professor of Law in the College of Philadelphia,* vol. 1, (Philadelphia: Bronson and Chauncey, 1804), iv.

sance," and placed it last on the list of this type of offense, after such things as eavesdropping, having a disorderly house, and keeping hogs in the city. The following was Wilson's definition of common nuisances.

> Common nuisances are a collection of personal injuries, which annoy the citizens generally and indiscriminately—so generally and indiscriminately, that it would be difficult to assign to each citizen his just proportion of redress; and yet, on the whole, so "noisome," that publick peace, and order, and tranquillity, and safety require them to be punished or abated.[26]

Wilson reduced the offense of blasphemy and its punishments from what appeared in Blackstone's to the following, which is what Justice Duncan actually quoted in *Updegraph v. Commonwealth.*

> Profaneness and blasphemy are offences, punishable by fine and by imprisonment. Christianity is a part of the common law.[27]

The reason Justice Duncan quoted this was that the main argument presented by Mr. Updegraph's attorney was that the law his client was convicted of violating, a state blasphemy statute passed in 1700, was virtually repealed by the United States Constitution and the constitution of Pennsylvania, because it was a religious law. Justice Duncan disagreed, pointing out that if this were true, James Wilson, a framer of both constitutions, would have completely removed blasphemy as a common law offense. But, as Justice Duncan emphasized repeatedly, and David Barton omits repeatedly, the blasphemy law of 1700 was not retained for a religious purpose, but only to preserve the peace. Blasphemy was not considered in Pennsylvania to be an offense against God or religion. Publicly expressing a religious opinion that disputed Christianity was not a crime. It was only

26. Bird Wilson, ed., *The Works of the Honourable James Wilson, L.L.D., Late One of the Associate Judges of the Supreme Court of the United States, and Professor of Law in the College of Philadelphia,* vol. 3, (Philadelphia: Bronson and Chauncey, 1804), 109-110.
27. *ibid.,* 112.

a crime to attack religion with the intent of provoking people and disturbing the peace.

> **According to Barton, in the version of the story in his other book, *Original Intent*: "Updegraph, indicted under the State law against blasphemy, was found guilty by the jury; that verdict was appealed.**
>
> **Since the central question revolved around the issue of blasphemy, the court needed to establish a legal definition of the word."**

Barton follows this by claiming that the court turned to Blackstone for a legal definition of blasphemy, and then uses the same misquote he created for *The Myth of Separation.* But, the court did not turn to Blackstone for a definition of blasphemy. There was no need to turn anywhere for a definition. The state law of 1700 that Updegraph was indicted under contained Pennsylvania's definition of blasphemy, and this was never anything but a state case. The appeal was heard by the Supreme Court of Pennsylvania, not the Supreme Court of the United States, a detail blurred by Barton, which, along with omitting references to Pennsylvania, gives the impression that this was a Supreme Court case. After he gets to the point in the story where he says the verdict was appealed, Barton begins to generically refer to *"the court."*

Pennsylvania's definition of blasphemy from 1700, quoted by Justice Duncan in the very first sentence of his opinion, stated that a person had to *"wilfully, premeditatedly, and despitefully blaspheme, and speak loosely and profanely of Almighty God."*[28] This is obviously quite different from simply denying the being of God, as in Blackstone's definition. Barton not only ignores Pennsylvania's definition, but, of course, claims that the court turned to Blackstone for his definition. He also ignores Justice Duncan's comment that the state law contained *"a precision of definition, and a discrimination so perfect between prosecutions for opinions seriously, temperately, and argumentatively expressed, and despiteful railings,"*[29] and that this precision of definition was what ultimately led Justice Duncan to

28. *Updegraph v. Commonwealth,* 11 Serg. & Rawle 394 Pa. (1824).
29. *ibid.*

reverse the judgement against Mr. Updegraph.

> **In *Original Intent,* after substituting his misquoted version of Blackstone's definition for the definition in the Pennsylvania law used by Justice Duncan, Barton continues: "By the legal definition, Updegraph had clearly violated the law. His attorney, however, argued that his conviction should be overturned for two reasons: (1) Updegraph was a member of a debating association which convened weekly, and what he said had been uttered in the course of an argument on a religious question; (2) that both the State and federal Constitution protected freedom of speech, and that if any State law against blasphemy did exist, the federal Constitution had done away with it; Christianity was no longer part of the law."**

What Barton neglects to mention here is that there were three, not two, arguments presented by Updegraph's attorney. Barton omits the third argument because it was this argument that caused Justice Duncan to reverse the ruling of the lower court. In *The Myth of Separation,* David Barton mentions only the same two arguments, and then claims that the court *"sustained the jury's verdict and the legality of laws on blasphemy,"* making it appear that the lower court's ruling was upheld.

Whether or not Mr. Updegraph said what he did as a member of a debating association was not the question before Justice Duncan. The jury had found that Updegraph broke the law, and it was not up to Justice Duncan to reexamine the facts of the case and decide if this verdict was right or wrong. As Duncan put it, *"this court cannot look beyond the record, nor take any notice of the allegation."*[30] The question before Pennsylvania's Supreme Court was not whether or not Mr. Updegraph was guilty of breaking the blasphemy law, but whether or not the law he had broken was still in force. Justice Duncan, as already explained, decided that it was.

The third argument – the one omitted by Barton – was that the

30. *Updegraph v. Commonwealth,* 11 Serg. & Rawle 394 Pa. (1824).

indictment wasn't written properly. This was the argument that worked. In spite of his obvious personal opinions about the merits of Christianity, Justice Duncan agreed and reversed the judgement. It was the *"precision of definition"* in the state law that made the indictment no good. The word *"profanely"* had been left out, and according to Justice Duncan, *"the legislature has adopted this word as a description or definition of the crime, the omission is fatal."*[31] Duncan then, as he had throughout the case, made a clear distinction between the laws of the state and the state's common law.

> As for blasphemy at the common law, the indictment cannot be sustained, for the sentence is founded on the act of assembly, and distribution of the fine to the poor, is not a part of a common law punishment. The general rule is, that all indictments on statutes, must state all the circumstances which constitute the definition of the offence, so as to bring the defendant precisely within it; and not even the fullest description of the offence, even the terms of a legal definition, would be sufficient, without keeping to the expressions of the act. A case directly in point is the indictment for perjury, on the statute; the word wilfully must be inserted, because it is part of the description the act gives of the crime; though in indictments for some offences at common law, that precise term is not essential, but may be supplied by others conveying the same idea; and in indictments on the black act, the term wilfully is essential, as being used by the legislature, and maliciously, will not suffice.[32]

Justice Duncan also made a clear distinction that, while Christianity was recognized as part of the common law, it was not part of the laws of the land. Responding to a somewhat melodramatic argument in which Updegraph's lawyer brought up the barbaric blasphemy punishments throughout history, Duncan made the following statement.

> There is no reason for the counsel's exclamation, are these things to be revived in this country, where Christianity does

31. *Updegraph v. Commonwealth*, 11 Serg. & Rawle 394 Pa. (1824).
32. *ibid.*

> not form part of the law of the land! — it does form, as we have seen, a necessary part of our common law...[33]

One thing the authors of the religious right version of American history don't have to lie about is the fact that most of the founders did think that common law had its roots in the Bible. John Eidsmoe, in his book *Christianity and the Constitution,* presents a typical history of the common law of England, which most of the founders probably would have agreed with.

> **According to Eidsmoe: "The common law of England is generally founded on biblical principals. The Anglo-Saxon Alfred the Great, for example, started his legal code with a recitation of the Ten Commandments and excerpts from the Mosaic law. There were additions to the Anglo-Saxon law. In the eleventh century Henricus Bracton systemized the common law according to Roman law as revised by the Justinian Code. The result was a Christianized version of Roman law."**

Thomas Jefferson also traced the history of the common law, but came to a different conclusion. Following a few questions about the credibility of the history of the Bible itself, Jefferson proceeded to explain, in an 1814 letter to John Adams, how the notion that the Bible was the source of English common law was based on a fallacy that had been around so long that nobody bothered to question it.

> It is not only the sacred volumes they have thus interpolated, gutted, and falsified, but the works of others relating to them, and even the laws of the land. We have a curious instance of one of these pious frauds in the laws of Alfred. He composed, you know, from the laws of the Heptarchy, a digest for the government of the United Kingdom, and in his preface to that work he tells us expressly the sources from which he drew it, to wit, the laws of Ina, of Offa and Aethelbert (not naming the Pentateuch). But his pious inter-

33. *Updegraph v. Commonwealth,* 11 Serg. & Rawle 394 Pa. (1824).

polator, very awkwardly, premises to his work four chapters of Exodus (from the 20th to the 23d) as a part of the laws of the land; so that Alfred's preface is made to stand in the body of the work. Our judges, too, have lent a ready hand to further these frauds, and have been willing to lay the yoke of their own opinions on the necks of others; to extend the coercions of municipal law to the dogmas of their religion, by declaring that these make a part of the law of the land. In the Year-Book 34, H. 6, p. 38, in Quare impedit, where the question was how far the common law takes notice of the ecclesiastical law, Prisot, Chief Justice, in the course of his argument, says, "A tiels leis que ils de seint eglise ont, en ancien scripture, covient a nous a donner credence; car ces common luy sur quels touts manners leis sont fondes; et auxy, sin, nous sumus obliges de canustre lour esy de saint eglise," etc. Finch begins the business of falsification by mistranslating and misstating the words of Prisot thus: "to such laws of the church as have warrant in Holy Scripture our law giveth credence." Citing the above case and the words of Prisot in the mar in Finch s law, B. I, c. 3, here then we find ancien scripture, ancient writing, translated "holy scripture." This, Wingate, in 1658, erects into a maxim of law in the very words of Finch, but citing Prisot and not Finch. And, Sheppard, tit. Religion, in 1675 laying it down in the same words of Finch, quotes the Year-Book, Finch and Wingate. Then comes Sir Matthew Hale, in the case of the King v. Taylor, I Ventr. 293, 3 Keb. 607, and declares that "Christianity is part and parcel of the laws of England." Citing nobody, and resting it, with his judgment against the witches, on his own authority, which indeed was sound and good in all cases into which no superstition or bigotry could enter. Thus strengthened, the court in 1728, in the King v. Woolston, would not suffer it to be questioned whether to write against Christianity was punishable at common law, saying it had been so settled by Hale in Taylor's case, 2 Stra. 834. Wood, therefore, 409, without scruple, lays down as a principle, that all blaspheming and profaneness are offenses at the common law, and cites Strange. Blackstone, in 1763, repeats, in the words of Sir

> Matthew Hale, that "Christianity is part of the laws of England", citing Ventris and Strange, ubi supra. And Lord Mansfield, in the case of the Chamberlain of London v. Evans, in 1767, qualifying somewhat the position, says that "the essential principles of revealed religion are part of the common law. "Thus we find this string of authorities all hanging by one another on a single hook, a mistranslation by Finch of the words of Prisot, or on nothing. For all quote Prisot, or one another, or nobody. Thus Finch misquotes Prisot; Wingate also, but using Finch's words; Sheppard quotes Prisot, Finch and Wingate; Hale cites nobody; the court in Woolston's case cite Hale; Wood cites Woolston's case; Blackstone that and Hale, and Lord Mansfield volunteers his own ipse dixit. And who now can question but that the whole Bible and Testament are a part of the common law?[34]

In *Updegraph v. Commonwealth,* Justice Duncan did exactly what Jefferson was talking about. To establish that Christianity had always been a part of the common law, Duncan began with the following statement, then proceeded to cite the same cases that appear in Jefferson's letter to Adams.

> From the time of Bracton, Christianity has been received as part of the common law of England. I will not go back to remote periods, but state a series of prominent decisions, in which the doctrine is to be found.[35]

Jefferson clearly did not agree that Christianity had been received as part of the common law from the time of Bracton. Unlike Justice Duncan, Jefferson did *"go back to remote periods."* What he found was that Christianity was not received as part of the common law until 1613, three and a half centuries after Bracton, and even that was the result of a mistranslation.

In an 1814 letter to Thomas Cooper, Jefferson included a copy of

34. Thomas Jefferson to John Adams, January 24, 1814, Lester J. Cappon, ed., *The Adams-Jefferson Letters: The Complete Correspondence Between Thomas Jefferson and Abigail and John Adams,* (Chapel Hill and London: The University of North Carolina Press, 1988), 422-423.

35. *Updegraph v. Commonwealth,* 11 Serg. & Rawle 394 Pa. (1824).

the research he had done on the subject many years earlier as a law student, which was just a more detailed version of what he later wrote to John Adams. Jefferson's earlier version included more evidence, such as a list of all the laws of Alfred that contradicted the Bible passages he was supposed to have prefaced his work with, and the following about Bracton.

> Bracton gives us a very complete and scientific treatise of the whole body of the common law. He wrote this about the close of the reign of Henry III., a very few years after the date of the Magna Charta. We consider this book as the more valuable, as it was written about the time which divides the common and statute law, and therefore gives us the former in its ultimate state. Bracton, too, was an ecclesiastic, and would certainly not have failed to inform us of the adoption of Christianity as a part of the common law, had any such adoption ever taken place. But no word of his, which intimates anything like it, has ever been cited.[36]

36. Thomas Jefferson to Thomas Cooper, February 10, 1814, Andrew A. Lipscomb and Albert Ellery Bergh, eds., *The Writings of Thomas Jefferson,* vol. 14, (Washington, DC: Thomas Jefferson Memorial Association, 1907), 91-92.

Index

Made in the USA
Lexington, KY
18 July 2010